EDINBURG

EDINBURGH

The Making of a Capital City

Edited by
BRIAN EDWARDS and PAUL JENKINS

EDINBURGH UNIVERSITY PRESS

Edinburgh University Press Ltd
22 George Square, Edinburgh

Typeset in Palatino by
Servis Filmsetting Ltd, Manchester and
printed and bound in Spain by
GraphyCems

A CIP record for this book is available from the British Library

ISBN 0 7486 1868 6 (paperback)

Contents

List of illustrations   vii

Notes on the contributors   xi

Acknowledgements   xii

Foreword by Sarah Boyack MSP   xiii

Introduction   1
Brian Edwards and Paul Jenkins

Part I: The Athens of the North

Introduction   19

1. The evolution of the medieval and Renaissance city   21
Ian Campbell and Margaret Stewart

2. Twinning cities: modernisation versus improvement in the two towns of Edinburgh   42
Charles McKean

3. Landscape, topography and hydrology   64
John Stuart-Murray

Part II: The City in the Industrial Age

Introduction   83

4. Landscapes of capital: industry and the built environment in Edinburgh, 1750–1920   85
Richard Rodger

5. Edinburgh – a tenement city?   103
Peter Robinson

Part III: Urban Management in the Early 20th Century

Introduction   129

6. 'Conservative surgery' in Old Edinburgh, 1880–1940   131
Lou Rosenburg and Jim Johnson

7. Housing and suburbanisation in the early and mid-20th century   150
Miles Glendinning

8. The changing role of the planner before and after the Second World War and the effect on urban form   168
Cliff Hague

Part IV: The City in the Post-industrial and Post-modern Age

Introduction   183

9.   Creation and conservation of the built environment in the later 20th century   185
      Paul Jenkins and Julian Holder

10.   Preparing for the 21st century: the city in a global environment   204
      Derek Kerr

11.   The changing image and identity of the city in the 21st century: 'Athens of the North'
      or 'North of Athens'   217
      Cliff Hague and Paul Jenkins

      Conclusion: learning from history   231
      Brian Edwards and Paul Jenkins

Appendices   243
Select bibliography   249
Index   253

Illustrations

FIGURES

Introduction

INT.1   View of Edinburgh showing the importance of topography   2
INT.2   Two key institutions: (a) Edinburgh University; (b) Edinburgh College of Art   3
INT.3   Lizars' view of Waterloo Place   4
INT.4   The Castle   7
INT.5   Housing in the High Street from the 17th century and the 18th   11
INT.6   Housing in the High Street from the 20th century and the 21st   12
INT.7   The new Scottish Parliament   14
INT.8   The façade of the Scottish Parliament building   15

Chapter 1

1.1   The Netherbow Port   23
1.2   The Earl of Hertford's sack of Edinburgh   24
1.3   The Old Tolbooth of Edinburgh   25
1.4   James Gordon of Rothiemay's 1647 map of Edinburgh   26
1.5   Provost of Kirk o' Field's Lodging   28
1.6   New Parliament House   29
1.7   The John Knox House   31
1.8   Crockett's Land and Johnston's Land in the West Bow   33
1.9   Large-scale development built around an internal courtyard   34
1.10   The bridging of the canyons of the Cowgate and the Nor' Loch: north–south sections   36

Chapter 2

2.1   John Elphinstone's drawing of the High Street, c. 1760   43
2.2   The 'Union Jack' plan from John Laurie's *Plan of Edinburgh and Places Adjacent*   47
2.3   The formidable parade of George Street in the mid-19th century   49
2.4   Robert Adam's 1791 proposals for the north side of Charlotte Square   51
2.5   St George's West Church (now West Register House)   52
2.6   Great King Street   53
2.7   St Colme Street, 1825   53
2.8   Lisbon: the Arco da Rua Augusta   54
2.9   Scotland's Acropolis: Thomas Hamilton's proposal of 1825 for Calton Hill   55
2.10   Thomas Hamilton's elevation of the east side of the West and Upper Bows prior to
        demolition   56
2.11   View today of Victoria Street   57
2.12   The Mound, c. 1870   58
2.13   Waterloo Place, c. 1910   58

2.14   The Mound, showing planned contrast between the classical and medieval worlds   59
2.15   View of Edinburgh, c. 1880   60

Chapter 3

3.1   Section through crag and tail of Edinburgh   66
3.2   James Craig's competition plan for the New Town of Edinburgh, 1767   67
3.3   Plan of the Earl of Moray's estate   68
3.4   The site of Edinburgh and the adjoining landscape   70
3.5   The Water of Leith: 19th-century mills   72
3.6   Estimated extent of April 2000 flooding   73
3.7   Richard Meier's perspective sketch of proposals for Edinburgh Park   75
3.8   Artist's impression of the Waverley Valley, Princes Street Gardens and the Playfair
        Galleries   77
3.9   Schemata of the medieval and Enlightenment   78
3.10   Plan of the Scottish Parliament   79

Chapter 4

4.1   Growth in selected Edinburgh industries, 1840–1910   88
4.2   Industrial and residential building fluctuations, 1880–1914   89
4.3   The Water of Leith from the Dean Bridge   91
4.4   The deconcentration of manufacturing in Edinburgh, 1861–1911   93
4.5   The growth of Edinburgh and the Municipal Extension Act, 1856   93
4.6   Late 19th-century industrial estates, Edinburgh: (a) Fountainbridge; (b) Craigmillar   95
4.7   Industrial expansion, 1860–1900: (a) North British Rubber ; (b) Grove Biscuit Factory;
        (c) D. Bruce Peebles & Co.; (d) John Ford & Co.; (e) Royal Blind Asylum; (f) A. B. Fleming
        & Co.; (g) Bertrams Ltd   96

Chapter 5

5.1   Detail of Gordon of Rothiemay's Map of 1647   107
5.2   North side of the Lawnmarket, Edinburgh, c. 1880   109
5.3   Fragment of the Kirkwood Map of 1819   110
5.4   Nos 39–43 Castle Street   111
5.5   Plans of 39–43 Castle Street   111
5.6   Exterior and interior view of the corner of Drummond Place and London Street   112
5.7   Nos 1–17 Shaw's Place   115
5.8   Model tenement plan from the Report of a Committee of the Working Classes etc.,
        1860   116
5.9   Upper-floor plan submitted in 1887 for two working-class tenements in Dalry   117
5.10   Tenements with shops hard against the pavement in Dalry   118
5.11   Heriot's Trust Feu Plan for East Montgomery Street, Cross Street and London Road
        of 1887   119
5.12   Heriot's Trust elevations relating to the feuing of East Elgin Street and Montgomery
        Street   120
5.13   Nos 1–21 Wellington Street   121
5.14   Tenements at 111–114 Marchmont Road   122
5.15   Front and back of Warrender Park Terrace   123

Chapter 6

6.1   Chambers Street, the most prestigious example of street improvement carried out under the 1867 Improvement Scheme   133
6.2   The top of St Mary's Street, looking south   134
6.3   No. 6 James Court   135
6.4   Official publicity photo of the 1886 International Exhibition, showing The Old Edinburgh Street   136
6.5   Early photo of deck-access housing within the Tron Square development, 1900   138
6.6   Infill housing fronting onto the Lawnmarket   140
6.7   Lady Stair's House in Wardrop's Court   141
6.8   View of the forecourt of Riddle's Court, after the treatment known as 'opening out'   141
6.9   Huntly House in the 1880s   143
6.10 Nos 74–84 Grassmarket *after* reconstruction by City Architect E. J. Macrae 145
6.11 The south-facing frontage of Macrae's Richmond Place development   145
6.12 The northern side of the cul-de-sac development in Gifford Park   146

Chapter 7

7.1   Advertisement for Hillpark, Mactaggart and Mickel's most ambitious speculative housing development of the late 1930s   153
7.2   Tenement housing designed by City architect Ebenezer Macrae   154
7.3   'AIROH' aluminium prefab house, built in 1949 at Moredun   156
7.4   Chessel's Court redevelopment   159
7.5   Aerial view in 1989 of Leith Fort housing scheme   161
7.6   Aerial view of the Muirhouse housing scheme   162
7.7   Aerial view in 1991 of Wester Hailes   164

Chapter 9

9.1   Map showing key master-planned areas   188
9.2   Map showing notable buildings of the 1960s   189
9.3   Map showing notable buildings of the 1970s   190
9.4   Map showing notable buildings of the 1980s   191
9.5   Map showing notable buildings of the 1990s   192
9.6   Map showing notable buildings of the new millennium   193
9.7   George Square (south side), prior to demolition to make way for the new University Library   194
9.8   Chessel's Court prior to its restoration   195
9.9   Maps used by Sir Robert Matthew at 'The Conservation of Georgian Edinburgh' conference in May 1970   195
9.10 Design by John L. Paterson for the exhibition 'Two hundred summers in a city: Edinburgh 1767–1967'   196
9.11 The New Club, 85 Princes Street, prior to demolition   196
9.12 'Hermits and Termits', St Leonard's   197
9.13 Leith Fort redevelopment – the so-called 'terror towers'   198

Chapter 10

10.1 A view of the Exchange looking north from Lothian Road   208
10.2 A view of inside the Exchange   209

10.3   A view of the approach to the Exchange from Rutland Square   210
10.4   A view of Edinburgh Park, looking north   212
10.5   Looking north towards Alexander Graham Bell House, situated at the entrance to
        Edinburgh Park   212
10.6   An example of gentrified warehouses at Leith Docks   214
10.7   An example of a new housing development at Leith Docks   214

Conclusion

C.1   Edinburgh is both a festive city and, for three weeks of the year, a festival city   233
C.2   The design of Edinburgh Park to the west of the city   234
C.3   Terry Farrell and Partners' design of the Edinburgh International Conference Centre   235
C.4   The Grassmarket, where a former university computer building was converted to the
       Apex Hotel   237
C.5   Compaction and building height give Edinburgh the qualities of a European city rather
       than a British one   237
C.6   Edinburgh provides an example of sustainable development for other cities in the UK   238
C.7   View of Edinburgh Castle from the east end of King's Stables Road   241

PLATES

Between pages 130 and 131

1   Artist's impression of the Arthur's Seat volcano in Carboniferous times
2   Robert Barker's view of Edinburgh, 1792
3   The sixth Earl of Mar's plan for the reconstruction of Edinburgh, 1728
4   The Old Town has inspired many, from Robert Louis Stevenson to Patrick Geddes
5   New housing in Fishmarket Close
6   The Scottish Parliament Building

Notes on the contributors

DR IAN CAMPBELL is Reader in Architectural History and Theory in the School of Architecture at the Edinburgh College of Art.

BRIAN EDWARDS is Professor of Architecture in the School of Architecture at the Edinburgh College of Art.

DR MILES GLENDINNING is Head of Architectural Survey at the Royal Commission on the Ancient and Historical Monuments of Scotland.

CLIFF HAGUE is Professor of Town Planning in the School of the Built Environment at Heriot-Watt University.

DR JULIAN HOLDER is Director of the Centre for Conservation Studies in the School of Architecture at the Edinburgh College of Art.

DR PAUL JENKINS is Director of the Centre for Environment and Human Settlements in the School of the Built Environment at Heriot-Watt University.

JIM JOHNSON is an architect based in Edinburgh.

DEREK KERR is a Lecturer in the School of the Built Environment at Heriot-Watt University.

CHARLES MCKEAN is Professor of Scottish Architecture in the Department of History at the University of Dundee.

DR PETER ROBINSON is an architect and planner in Edinburgh.

RICHARD RODGER is Professor of Urban History and Director of the Centre for Urban History at the University of Leicester.

DR LOU ROSENBURG is Senior Research Fellow in the School of Architecture at the Edinburgh College of Art.

MARGARET STEWART is a Lecturer in Architectural History in the School of Architecture at the Edinburgh College of Art.

JOHN STUART-MURRAY is Head of the School of Landscape Architecture at the Edinburgh College of Art.

Acknowledgements

Thanks go to Jack Gillon at Edinburgh City Council and Helena Butler at the School of the Built Environment for help with providing Figure 1.10 and the GIS-based maps in Chapter 9 respectively.

Acknowledgement is made to Simon Littlewood for facts about the Edinburgh printing industry incorporated into Chapter 4. The author also dedicates the chapter to Simon Littlewood.

The editors wish to thank Edinburgh College of Art Research Board for a Small Research Grant essential to help bring this book to fruition. The editors also wish to thank Anne Boyle for her thorough and efficient editorial services, especially the generosity with which she dispensed her time.

Foreword

BY SARAH BOYACK MSP

Edinburgh is a city in transition. It was the birth-place of the Scottish Enlightenment, hosts the world's longest-running international arts festival, is Scotland's capital city, and is home to our new Scottish Parliament.

But as a compact city it faces some difficult challenges. How to expand and house its citizens while not destroying the compact nature of the city which makes it so distinctive without the unending urban sprawl that characterises so many cities?

One of Edinburgh's unique features is that it has managed to transform itself from a sleepy provincial city to a globally recognised city, without losing the identity that makes it attractive. Edinburgh has retained its historic core and landscape setting while accommodating a restructured economy and expanding business, financial and service sectors.

Our visionary new Parliament complex occupies a site in the heart of the Old Town and blends into Holyrood Park. Its escalating cost created a shadow over the first term of the Parliament. But in the first few months since it opened, over 200,000 visitors have seen the Parliament for themselves and opinion is increasingly favourable.

As a local MSP I can see the conflicts which characterise our planning system. How to ensure that people have a quality of life while living in the city centre. How to control the expansion of pubs and clubs. How to find room for affordable housing in a city where land values have escalated and property values have doubled in the last five years. How to create long-term jobs that pay well. How to address the pressure of rapidly increasing traffic and develop much-needed new transport infrastructure.

Edinburgh's past civic leaders have tried to deliver high-quality design with a new emphasis on planning and architecture that respects our environment and conserves our natural resources.

Our 21st-century challenge is how we incorporate sustainable development principles in the future development of the city. The authors of this book will help those of us involved in that process reflect on the importance of design and quality. That must be a good thing.

Introduction

Brian Edwards and Paul Jenkins

Cities are complex phenomena and are both fascinating and challenging. In today's world, cities are now home to more than half the global population and destined to continue to grow in importance worldwide – with more salience in the parts of the world that are still developing economically. In the developed world, cities have for several centuries largely dominated cultural, social, economic and political life. However, this does not mean they are static phenomena. On the contrary, they are the dynamic generators in most walks of life, constantly changing and evolving into new patterns of development. Increasingly these changes are self-conscious and deliberate – and Edinburgh has a long tradition of remaking itself in this way. This book thus seeks to examine some of the aspects of change in the city as a contribution to the understanding of both its making and remaking, and also how this might have a wider relevance for urban change elsewhere.

There are many important aspects affecting the making and remaking of cities, and it is our intention in this book to examine a range of these and how they have affected Edinburgh, as an example of a successful city over the past 800 years or so. Since we believe that contemporary urban change requires an understanding of historical context, chronology is the underlying structure of the book. Edinburgh has existed as a recognised urban area since at least the early 12th century, with a major expansion starting in the mid-18th century, and more recently the city has emerged as the capital of a revitalised Scottish nation in the 21st century. As such, many of the key aspects of city-making and remaking that have characterised urban development have taken place, and are documented in, the built environment of the city.

Edinburgh, unlike many northern cities, contin-ues to grow, and in this it is significantly affected by:

- political change – as the capital of Scotland in particular, but also within a changing local-government context;
- economic change – adapting to the effects of globalisation of capital and regionalisation within Europe;
- social and cultural change – with increasing diversity and a growing role as a national and international focal point; and
- environmental change – adapting to the agenda of sustainable development.

Edinburgh is an excellent example of urban innovation, and yet it remains conservative in many ways. The city has been studied by architects, planners, urban historians and geographers, as well as other specialists in the built environment over the years. Its unique physical character is recognised through the designation of the Old Town and New Town as a UNESCO World Heritage Site. It is also a major international cultural and tourism destination, with hundreds of thousands of visitors every year, not to mention the increasing number of people who come to work, and where possible live, in the city. What underlies this dynamism, and what are the successful characteristics of the city's making and remaking?

Key themes

As with many cities, location is a factor: Edinburgh is located partly due to the nature of key topographical and physical features – such as the defensive position of the castle and proximity to the North Sea via the port of Leith – and partly as a result of its territorial role in Scotland's political economy as national capital and major service centre (legal, financial and educational services predominantly). Its traditionally diverse economic base – which has also included a wide range of manufacturing – has been a significant factor in continued growth. The city has also been, and remains, socially proactive in many of its urban policies, and is particularly well established as a cultural centre. While constantly reaffirmed, these attributes are not new, and the tensions and opportunities that they foster – and that have been deliberately considered through at least the past three centuries – arguably can teach us much about urban development and the management of change. Thus, as well as furthering the general understanding of how Edinburgh as a complex urban entity has developed, one of the objectives of this book is to highlight the relative roles of public, private and voluntary intervention in city-making and remaking.

Why approach this from the point of view of the physical fabric, one might ask? As architects, the editors believe that the built environment (buildings, streets and urban spaces) is unique in that it reflects the wider political, economic, social and cultural values of the period which produce it, and those of subsequent periods which adapt it (or adapt to it). The long-term existence of much of the built environment in Edinburgh thus acts as evidence of history as well as conditioning current activity in ways quite different to other arts and sciences. This produces tension of course, especially in times of relatively rapid change. This in itself is expressed physically in the stresses between expansion, conservation and re-creation – a major theme running through this book. Other cities, such as London, have not survived these conflicting forces so well, thus losing the sense of place identity except in isolated pockets.

The physical character of Edinburgh has remarkable clarity and richness. Many of the initiatives discussed in this book have sought to preserve this character but also to bring it up to date, and on occasion to extend it into new territory. The identity of Edinburgh is based upon a play of contrasts – between the planned and organic city, between order and the picturesque,

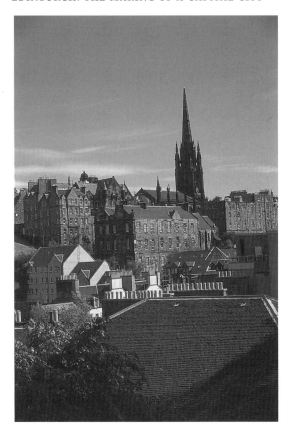

FIGURE INT.1   View of Edinburgh showing the importance of topography to the image of the city. *Brian Edwards*

between landscape and cityscape, and between hilltop and valley. The making and remaking of Edinburgh has over the centuries engaged with these contrasts, often reinforcing them by deliberate public, private and voluntary intervention. Edinburgh, like Rome and Paris, has planned its growth in pursuit of the public interest. In this sense, 'design' is a theme running through the book, at times suppressed by economic forces, at others used to promote the cultural realm.

In the general modern economic context of rapid global movement, the importance of place identity for urban economies has been well documented. The resultant 'place-marketing' of cities – whether for inward investment or provision of services such as tourism – has been a factor underpinning a shift of emphasis from nation-states to urban

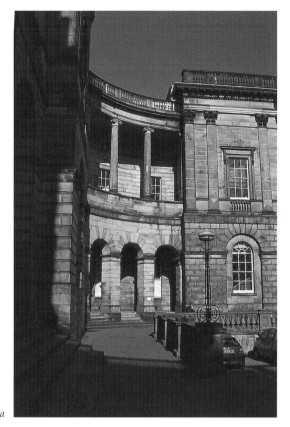

a   *b*

FIGURE INT.2   Two key institutions which helped shape the intellectual and artistic culture of the city: (a) Edinburgh University; (b) Edinburgh College of Art.   *Brian Edwards*

regions as major actors, particularly in Europe. In parallel, the sustainability of urban areas *vis-à-vis* their ecological footprint, as well as their socio-political regional insertion, has become an important factor in urban governance. This has focused even more attention on the attributes of place, including the built environment – whether through international 'signature' architecture, carefully crafted urban spatial and cultural images, or new forms of environmental action (e.g. Local Agenda 21). Here again there is much to learn from Edinburgh's successes and the occasional failure.

Edinburgh is what it is today not only because of diverse forms of quasi-biological 'structural adaptation' to external forces of urban change, but also because of the unique individuals and institutions ('agency') which have managed to interpret and guide the evolution of the city. A deeper understanding of the built environment requires the study of both the contextual structure and the individual agents which interact intimately in its production and adaptation – especially the architects, planners, urban managers, financiers and politicians who have played key roles. The chapters of this book therefore often highlight the role of key individuals as well as the contextual influences within which they worked, including their professional peer groups.

Edinburgh arguably has excelled in these various manifestations of urban innovation; and yet, as noted above, this has been in a generally 'conservative' context. The chapters of this book thus aim to understand how the resulting tensions of innovation and conservation, highlighted by Patrick Geddes over a century ago, have interacted

FIGURE INT.3   Lizars' view of Waterloo Place, Edinburgh from a drawing of 1851 by W. Banks showing the gateway to Calton Hill.   *Charles McKean*

to produce the unique built form of the city today. The chapters deliberately draw on the wide sweep of urban research and analysis concerning the transformation of Edinburgh, thereby representing both an overview and individual insight. The editors believe that this produces a richer intellectual offering than one based on limited authorship, and in itself demonstrates the seeking of balanced understanding between individual 'agency' and contextual 'structure'. In its basic overarching narrative, there is a clear debt to the synoptic approach of Geddes, especially the integration of social and economic themes with ecological and cultural ones.

However, other key themes are investigated in the book, and these provide the strands which link the different lines of research which are drawn on.

Each of the chapter authors is engaged in varying aspects of urban research, and each has examined Edinburgh from a different perspective. They have come together to contribute to this book in a collaborative way, drawing on their studies but also permitting a wider focus on certain key themes. This chapter introduces the themes and will be the basis for drawing conclusions at the end of the book from the intervening chapters. The key themes on which the authors focus include:

1. the importance of *space and topography* in the making and remaking of the city;
2. the *tension between innovation and conservation* in urban planning and design in Edinburgh throughout its history, and particularly since the 18th century;

3. the *relationship between political, economic and social change* and the expression of this in physical form;
4. the *role of agency* – that is, key individuals and institutions – in relation to the more structural influences in 3;
5. the relationship between the *broader ecology* of the city and *voluntary action*; and
6. the *sense of place* and the role of art and design in creating city *identity*.

Space and topography are fundamental elements in the formation of human settlements everywhere – space in the sense of geographical location in relation to both territory and physical elements, such as rivers, which have economic significance. Human settlements of long duration tend to have been formed where topography has permitted defence, and where rivers have provided water and later power, as well as proximity to the sea for transport. Some of these settlements have, over time, had territorial significance as centres of political power. In turn, these topographical and spatial factors have had significant influence on how such settlements have developed and become cities. They have influenced the economic base, the source of services such as water supply, the infrastructure development and the overall environmental quality. These themes are embedded in Edinburgh's past and present, and in this book are of specific relevance to Chapter 3 but also of importance in the city's early period (Chapter 1) and initial major expansion (Chapter 2). However, they also have an important role to play in the more recent expansion of the city from the post-Second World War period, and thus are aspects of relevance in Chapters 8 and 10.

The critical urban innovation of the 18th century in Edinburgh was the massive northerly expansion of the planned New Town. Although conservation possibly had a role to play in earlier attempts to develop parts of the Old Town, it was at this time – at the heels of the Enlightenment in Scotland – that the *tension between innovation and conservation* in urban planning and design first clearly manifested itself. The significant architectural and urban design heritage created by this

first large-scale expansion has continued to be a focus for this debate, although this later emphasised also the Old Town heritage. Both the medieval Old Town and the Georgian New Town are incorporated in a UNESCO World Heritage Site largely due to these conservation efforts. However, conservation affects more than these historic areas, and is a strong component of the city's planning – such as the role of the green belt and the support for heritage-led tourism and the annual Edinburgh International Festival. This tension informs much of the various strands of research in the book, but perhaps more so Chapters 6, 8 and 11.

While focusing on the unique physical aspects of Edinburgh, the authors are aware that physical form is a product of the *relationship between political, economic, social and cultural factors*. The role of the Union with England, with the dissolution of the Scottish parliament and its reconstitution nearly 300 years later, has had great significance for the city, as has its continued role as national capital throughout, with its unique legal and educational establishments. The early development of financial services and a diversified economic base continue to be the foundation of a strong economy today. How this economic success has been distributed socially, however, has varied enormously, and this is still an issue in the modern city. The city has provided a focal point for national culture, but in the last half-century this has taken on international significance through the International Festivals. How these two roles co-exist – as a city of national and international cultural focus – remains unresolved. However, in general, the intellectual innovation and political conservatism of the city have produced a wonderfully dynamic balance which is the envy of other cities. These underlying themes are examined in most of the chapters.

As explained above, the foundation of the book, in balancing the examination of the city's physical form with the forces which have conditioned this, does not mean that the authors take an exclusively 'structuralist' viewpoint, with the city as the mere product of macro-level forces. We believe that 'agency' in the form of specific individuals and institutions has as important a role to play in making and remaking the city. In other words, Edinburgh has its heroes (and villains) as well as its unique context. As such, the book focuses on the roles of some key people – and not only the more famous such as Patrick Geddes, but also the less famous – as well as the institutions which have permitted Edinburgh to innovate and conserve. The role of hitherto unknown figures emerges as important material which gives shape to the argument in Chapters 2, 4, 6, 8 and Chapter 9 in particular.

The city's ecological basis has continued to play an important role throughout the centuries. While dominating the city's location and early development, the emergence of wider collective action (public and private) from the mid-18th century led to a tendency for man to dominate the natural environment, with the creation of the New Town and its vast bridges spanning valleys, and investment in urban infrastructure such as water supply and drainage (Chapter 3). In this, the broader public has had varying roles of engagement, from the voluntary action organised in the Victorian period by Geddes and his like (Chapter 6) to the resistance to 'modernisation' of the Old and New Towns in the second half of the 20th century (Chapter 9). There is thus a long tradition of voluntary engagement of the public in the built environment which can be the basis for re-engagement with urban management, including the more pressing issues of the environment today (Chapter 11).

A further theme which is touched on in a number of chapters is the *sense of place* and the importance of *identity* in city life and development which permit (or constrain) it. While it is the specific focus of Chapter 11, this concept is present in the analysis of other chapters, such as Chapters 3, 5 and 8. Edinburgh is indeed a unique place, and its success in maintaining this through changing political, economic and socio-cultural contexts has also contributed to its success in the present day, when place identity is an important part of 'marketing' the city in the global economy, as Chapter 10 examines. How this will develop in the future is a key issue, as urban areas in Europe go through more structural change and Scotland as a whole is becoming arguably more peripheral. That, however, is the theme of another book, as our

intention here is to look to history as a guide to understanding the present, albeit with a view to approaching the future better.

Analytical foundation

Being a capital city, Edinburgh has long enjoyed a privileged position within Scottish urbanism. The economy of the city has been buoyed by its role as the political, cultural and administrative centre of the northern region of Britain, and more recently as the capital of a separate nation within the umbrella of the United Kingdom. The particular history of Edinburgh, as the authors confirm, is one of clear connection between artistic aspirations and political action. The actors within governance in the city, including its social and economic institutions, have continually put aesthetic concerns to the fore. Whether it has been the preservation of Edinburgh's distinctive skyline or the creation of handsome new streets and crescents, Edinburgh is a city which not only contains works of art but also is itself a 'work of art'. In this sense, Edinburgh confirms Jacob Burckhardt's thesis that we can regard certain cities as legible documents relaying in their built fabric the artistic values of their civilisation.[1] This is a theme explored largely in the latter part of the book.

This argument, subsequently tested in the context of London, Paris and Vienna by Donald Olsen,[2] rings equally true of Edinburgh. The politicians, architects, builders and inhabitants of Edinburgh have not only enjoyed a precious example of urban civilisation for over half a millennium but have also, generally speaking, contributed to its sensitive protection and growth. The city has been free of the critical upheavals which damaged Glasgow in the 19th century and Dundee in the 20th, although recent development pressure has left its mark in both the centre and suburbs (see Chapters 9 and 11).

Generally speaking, the physical structure and urban traditions of Edinburgh have been the starting point for future change. The 18th-century New Town recognised the importance of the 'street' as both a channel for public promenade and a corridor to exploit views of monuments (such as Edinburgh Castle) and the surrounding landscape (such as Calton Hill). It also continued with the Old Town pattern of tenement-building, disguising tenements as town houses in the smarter areas of the New Town. As the authors of Chapters 1 and 2 suggest, many of the urban ideas which are central to the character of the city are European rather than British in origin. However, the kind of radical surgery which, under Haussmann, transformed Paris, and earlier under the hand of John Nash had reordered central London, had no equivalent in Edinburgh. Here, the historic Old Town was preserved and treated as a picturesque silhouette to be enjoyed from elsewhere in the city – notably from Princes Street. It is characteristic of Edinburgh, as the authors of later chapters explain, to base the pattern of new development on the principles of the old, and in the process to ensure that artistic values balanced utilitarian ones. This is not to suggest that Edinburgh was conscious of creating a huge stage set of a city; but, generally speaking, civic leaders ensured that the direction taken learnt from the past.

Although Edinburgh is a remarkably coherent city, it is also an exceptionally legible one. The sense that one can readily navigate the city by the play of monuments, hills, streets and parks allows the urban historian and the tourist to read the city's growth as an unfolding chronology of political and artistic movements. Of course, the social values represented in the working-class housing schemes, the economy embodied in the city's banks, and the technologies employed above and below ground also play their part. But Edinburgh, more than any other city in the UK, is nurtured by a tangible sense of its own civilisation. To bring this to the fore is part of the justification for yet another book on Edinburgh.

As much as historians dismiss the typical 19th-century city as the product of rapid and often ill-coordinated development, in Edinburgh's case the Victorian city was based mostly on the values, ideals and spatial rules of the Georgian New Town. Similarly, the 18th century drew lessons from the 17th which itself was informed by artistic movements spreading northwards from Italy via France and the Low Countries. Edinburgh is thus largely a classical city – one where proportion, order and

FIGURE INT.4   The Castle provides Edinburgh with exceptional legibility, a point respected by centuries of growth.   *Brian Edwards*

harmony prevail. In this sense, it is fundamentally different from Glasgow with its tendency towards a modernistic loss of civic space, and London with its gothic prevalence. Edinburgh is not, however, without its occasional ugliness. But, at its worst, Edinburgh is certainly better than other UK cities and stands comparison with the best in Europe. Even London fails to hang its good parts together into a convincing whole; and smaller cities like Bath, Norwich and York do not produce the wider orchestration of urban effects found in Edinburgh. Neither are they so blessed with topography and landscape, nor do they bring them so effectively into play. So the historian of Edinburgh needs to be trained in the visual arts as much as the social ones to grasp fully the qualities of the city. As various authors contend, design (urban, landscape and building) played a large part in forging the city, and we need to continue to recognise its power in creating a sense of place.

Arguably (and the editors will develop this more fully in the Conclusion), one of the factors which has permitted Edinburgh to respond effectively and sustainably to the changing urban contexts has been the self-conscious analysis of its image, role and options. As a long-established seat of learning and intellectual development, Edinburgh has enjoyed a strong and largely fruitful relationship between the city and its educational institutions: 'town' and 'gown'. The city has provided an environment for reflection which has encouraged academics and other leading thinkers to input into the process of city change. This has permitted Edinburgh to learn continually from its own history – more so than many cities – and has been a critical factor in its success. The editors believe that this book will also serve in a modest way to continue this tradition through bringing a number of individual researchers together (academic and other), focusing on common themes, and thus further stimulate experiential learning from historical and contemporary urban analysis. It is our intention that this should influence the conscious development of the city, both directly through relevant political, civic and professional groups, but also indirectly through wider public appreciation of the city, whether by resident or visitor. In so doing, we believe we can not only enrich the debates on Edinburgh's contemporary urban change but also contribute usefully to better understanding of the role of design and town-planning in the renewal of cities in the 21st century.

A brief overview of the city's development

While we have structured the book in a generally historical sequence, as can be seen below, not all chapters deal with a specific period. In addition, they do not provide a seamless historical story of the city's development, as this has not been the major objective of the book. Rather, we have concentrated on bringing new and recent research of relevance to an understanding of Edinburgh's development – and the contextual relevance of this – to a wider public. However, we feel it is impor-

tant that the book should include a short overview of the city's development which will allow the siting of the chapters in a wider historical context. Necessarily brief, this obviously excludes as much as it includes for a city so deeply studied as Edinburgh, and so we can only assure those interested that there is much more available. Thus, for the reader who has a specific interest in themes or a wider historical or geographical overview, we have made some reference below to precedents in the literature that we would recommend.

In brief, the city first surfaces in written historical records in the first few decades of the 12th century, when it is referred to as a Royal Burgh. There is evidence of much older use and settlement in the area, and in fact the city's site is a direct descendant of hilltop forts of the Iron Age. The invading Romans, who did much for urban development further south, settled briefly in the area (at Cramond and Inveresk, for example), but never created any long-lasting urban settlement. Hence the first identification of the city as an urban area is generally taken as King David's grant of the Royal Burgh, essentially as part of the Norman consolidation of power in the area, because of its strategic position. The urban form of these small, local, market-focused burghs was influenced by their parallel strategic function and the early interest in establishing learning through the church as a means of wider development and rule. The town thus grew up in the shadow of the castle, around the market places and churches, with an organic structure which was underpinned by feudal land and other rights and responsibilities (for example, to undertake economic activity, provide public benefits and so on).

The general political and military instability of the wider national context, however, led to many setbacks, as did the problems of epidemics and other natural disasters (for example, fire), keeping the city enclosed and ever more densely occupied. What is today the Old Town is an amalgamation of the original Royal Burgh and the easterly religious Burgh of Canongate, based on monastic settlement but later the location of the royal palace, when this became fixed and a parliament created, thus creating the city as a capital. Not much of this medieval town remains intact – only some later (17th-century and thereafter) buildings and parts of fortifications – but its layout underlies most of the Old Town up to the present.

The town existed in this feudal, medieval phase for some six centuries, with increasing mercantile developments both in the surrounding countryside (i.e. links with other burghs) and by its seaport at Leith in the late 17th and early 18th century, by which time it was a major North Sea trading port and the second largest city in Britain (population 25,000). The development of early capitalism led to physical changes also, including urban renewal (e.g. Mylne's Court) and expansions of the walled area in the 17th century to include major new development (e.g. Heriot's Hospital), and then beyond this – mainly to the south – in the early 18th century. The Union with England at this time opened up new trading opportunities but undermined some of the administrative roles as the royal court migrated to London. The coming of more stable peace by the mid-18th century permitted the eventual reconfiguration of the urban space. As land and property increasingly became commodities, the pent-up demand led to a series of new expansion and redevelopment projects, in the south initially, although soon afterwards the open fields to the north also became attractive.

Paradoxically, the town became a city and began its first major planned expansion at a time when its political and economic significance was waning – with the growth of the Atlantic trade being based in Glasgow to the west, and the key government functions in London. However, the strength of the early investment in education and financial capital had permitted a dominance of the professions in the city, and the Scottish Enlightenment was based here, as was much new intellectual pursuit such as scientific invention. While this vibrant intellectual life had its origin in the close physical and social confines of the Old Town, it soon relocated to the Enlightenment New Town with its physical and economic separation and strong socio-cultural rules – physically displayed in the planned and ordered urban spaces and landscapes and in its grand private and public buildings. However, some of the new urban capital investment was also located in the Old Town, with limited restructuring and new public building. The links between the Old Town – as the continued centre for professional, educational and much commercial life – and the New Town (and continuing more piecemeal southerly development) were facilitated by grand bridge-construction.

By the mid-19th century, the city had substantially remade itself from a provincial mercantile centre with European focus into a national (North British/Scottish) centre for capitalist, professional and cultural services, although the city council had more or less bankrupted itself in the process of underwriting this, and the grand designs had taken longer to be realised due to macro-economic setbacks such as the Napoleonic wars. The very nature of the new urban form, together with the continued growth of the overall urban population due to rural out-migration (rising from 49,000 in 1751 to 66,500 in 1801 and 136,000 in 1831), led to the development of new forms of urban services (e.g. policing, cleansing, water and so on) and eventually urban government, with more professional management and new political structures (and successive boundary extensions). In the mid-19th century, new interests came to dominate city politics, and the previous trade-based dominance was challenged by manufacturing interests. Thus during the latter part of the 19th century there was a growth of industrial activities, many relocating to the (then) periphery, where the newly developing railways could obtain better access. The relatively slow consolidation of the municipal services and forms of government was in fact often in response to pressure from strong lobbying groups – private and voluntary. However, it was only towards the end of this period that attention was paid to alleviating aspects of urban poverty.

Most of the urban expansion and restructuring of the mid-18th to mid-19th century (which continued to both north and south, being expressed in successive administrative boundary changes) had been to benefit either the moneyed classes or the city in general (e.g. new streets), with the poor being left to fend for themselves at the fringes of the market in housing, jobs, medical services and so on. Those with a foot in the door of this system

– such as skilled trades – had either managed to create better conditions (e.g. through co-operative ventures) or bought into new forms of market provision. Increasingly the municipality acted in the broader public interest in these areas for those who could not. By the turn of the 20th century, it had initiated a number of new social-welfare activities, many of them public-health-orientated with new medical knowledge, and soon afterwards had developed the first new redevelopment and lower-income housing schemes.

The provision of better housing for the majority of the city's poorer population took various forms. Part of this was through increasing publicly funded provision in new expansion areas, but also – crucially for the urban fabric – in the redevelopment of the inner city, where the city pioneered concepts of urban regeneration conceived as part of its intellectual heritage. Another large part of the new urban development was through mixed public–private ventures, with the use of subsidies for the growing specialised housing development sector. A further part was provided for lower-middle-income populations through expansion in low-density suburbs (following the middle classes outwards) or infill higher-density tenements. This part of the housing sector benefited from the growth of the financial-services industry and its application to the housing market through building societies, which quickly eclipsed simpler co-operative forms of finance as house-production became more specialised. The overall effect for the city was a massive outward expansion, yet with much infill and continued inner-city living (which remains a key feature of the city today). Thus, while up to the First World War Edinburgh had a dense medium-rise character, it also quickly assumed the lower-density suburban spread of other British towns.

These trends led to reinforcement of the need for mechanisms which would safeguard not only public interests but also private ones from encroachment. So early forms of urban planning were developed in more sophisticated and grandiose development schemes, although often not being realised due to the lack of balance between national legislation, local political and economic interests and public perceptions. By the end of the Second World War, new national legislation permitted more comprehensive planning, but there was no real governance structure to permit the main stakeholders in the city to produce consensus. Attempts to plan the city in its wider city region, produce city-wide development plans and also comprehensive area redevelopment plans all seemed to result in only acrimony, distrust, shelved plans and blighted areas, although major new post-war housing development continued – upwards in high-rise as well as outwards to peripheral estates. This meant that, in Edinburgh, the regional-dispersal versus city-peripheral development debate that had dogged development in Glasgow for years was more muted, and more development took place within the city, although this was ring-fenced with a clear green belt.

The city continued to grow within this through the 1960s, but available land was rapidly being used up by both the government and the private sector. The green belt then began to be leapfrogged as the city's demand for labour surpassed the supply and the possibility of housing this in existing housing areas. Increasingly, the city was subject to redevelopment – more piecemeal than originally planned for, but often as controversial (e.g. the St James Square development and Dumbiedykes housing estate at the foot of the Salisbury Crags). The property boom collapsed, however, in the late 1960s and early 1970s, at a time when increasing public pressure for conservation and redevelopment grew. As such, there was limited new building in the 1970s, although some strategic preparation was undertaken for a revitalised boom in building thereafter, including a strategic view of government-owned sites and their use in new commercial urban development though new forms of public–private partnerships. The 1980s saw a revitalisation also of new house-building, increasingly by voluntary-sector entities in the social sector (housing associations) and large-volume private-sector developers. While the former usually redeveloped inner-city land, the shortage of sites for the latter led to their expansion into the region (as well as some green-belt erosion), thus following the government's lead in develop-

a

b

Figure INT.5   Housing in the High Street from the 17th century (a) and the 18th (b). Height and skyline are enduring features of urban housing in the city.   *Brian Edwards*

ing Livingston New Town to the west of the city. The result was a net loss of population in the 1970s, mostly young families.

Planning eventually caught up with these developments in the late 1970s and early 1980s with a structure plan for the region. This aimed at stabilising the population within the region at some 500,000 while facilitating inner-city regeneration (economic and residential). It effectively recognised the growing disjuncture between residence, employment and social facilities and provided for this partly through an early vision of 'polycentric' growth in the region. This process has, however, produced both growing transport problems in the city and region and the growth of 'dormitory' towns in the region as economic development has concentrated in the city. The location of this began

to change also in the 1980s and 1990s, with a trend to the periphery (the Gyle and Leith) despite some high-profile inner-city sites being made available by the city for public–private partnership in major commercial developments. These have been crucial in a remaking of the city's economic base to retain its service-sector importance in new internationally competitive markets. In the 1990s, these trends continued, with major new master-planned areas – increasingly for mixed use – at the periphery (e.g. Edinburgh Park, the Southeast Wedge and the Waterfront) but also smaller areas in the existing urban fabric. These latter included some key sites with a high public value (especially Holyrood and the new parliament building), so polemic debate on innovation and conservation in the built environment of the city continued to be a feature

FIGURE INT.6   Housing in the High Street from the 20th century designed by Basil Spence, to left and right (a) and the 21st by Richard Murphy (b). In their way, each maintains the Edinburgh urban tradition.   *RIAS and Brian Edwards*

of urban life. In recent times, the city has refocused its attention on the importance of design and place identity, mainly to retain its international standing. Whether this is the best strategy for a north-British city with a strong regional role and national status, but at the periphery of Europe, perhaps needs more attention in the future.

Summarising, then, Edinburgh has always had distinctive physical features which have been important elements of its development. Starting with its location and topography, it developed over time as seat of government and learning and as an important trading town with British and European status. The changing form of international mercantile capital expansion led to a significant shift to stress the services basis for economic life, and the city remade itself in a grand way as the seat of Scottish national pride, continuing to have European influence as its international economic influence waned somewhat. The transition to industrial capitalism did not leave the city untouched, but its self-conscious attitude to identity ensured that its physical image remained an important aspect of its character, with manufacturing and associated development subordinated to this. The impact of rapid urbanisation was similarly dealt with in planning and housing, with the city remaking itself yet again in a manner which carefully retained the unique physical attributes, despite various major restructuring proposals. As the city entered the post-industrial and post-modern age, it has been continuing to remake itself through a proactive entrepreneurial attitude to economic, political and cultural life. The city is unique in the range and quality of the functions and services it offers for an urban area with a population of some half a million inhabitants, taking into consideration its international standing. However, the resurgence of its international role needs careful assessment in relation to its local, national and European context, especially its increasing role as the focal point of a networked city-region.

Literary precedent and authors' focus

Inevitably, this book draws on the scholarship of others. Mention in particular should be made of Sir John Summerson, who, familiar with the city as a member of staff at Edinburgh College of Art in the 1930s, was one of the first architectural historians to discuss artistic movements in the context of urban development. His publications on Edinburgh and London – particularly those dealing with the circle of land-owning politicians and their architects – have been an inspiration for the authors here. Similarly, Edinburgh University's A. J. Youngson's enduring masterpiece *The Making of Georgian Edinburgh* – with its focus on the political context, development practices and designers of the 18th century – has provided a bedrock for this book, although the basic arguments have been adjusted in the light of more recent scholarship. The example of Summerson and Youngson in seeking to link intellectual, political and design movements remains valid, even if this book seeks to explore the connection in the light of a wider frame of historical and intellectual reference.

As noted previously, there is a wide range of books about the city's development and physical aspects (or which include writing on this), reflecting the extent of intellectual interest the city has generated. While it is not the intention to provide an exhaustive and comprehensive bibliography, we feel it useful to site this book within this literary tradition on the city, as we believe we contribute something unique to this. Some of these books are focused on Scotland as a whole, but include substantial references to Edinburgh, such as Adams' *The Making of Urban Scotland*, or Gordon and Dicks' *Scottish Urban History*, both of which review urban development in Edinburgh in a wider Scottish context. General books on Scotland with substantial reference to Edinburgh's architecture include Glendinning et al.'s *A History of Scottish Architecture*, MacInnes et al.'s *Building a Nation: The Story of Scotland's Architecture*, McKean's *The Scottish Thirties: An Architectural Introduction* and Glendinning and Page's *Clone City: Crisis and Renewal in Contemporary Scottish Architecture*. A Scottish focus on housing would include Glendinning and Watters' *Home Builders* and Currie and Murie's *Housing in Scotland*, with a wider historical view in Carruthers' *The Scottish Home* and a specific study in Rodger's *Housing the People: The Colonies of Edinburgh*.

Specific historical studies of Edinburgh's development include Lindsay's *Georgian Edinburgh*, McKean's *Edinburgh: Portrait of a City* and Rodger's *The Transformation of Edinburgh: Land, Property and Trust in the Nineteenth Century*. Books which develop an intellectual theme but draw their empirical material from Edinburgh include Hague's *The Development of Planning Thought* and Morton's *Unionist Nationalism: Governing Urban Scotland 1830–1860*. There are also a series of guidebooks to buildings and places in Edinburgh, some historic and some contemporary: Smith's *Historic South Edinburgh*, Baldwin's *Edinburgh, Lothian and Borders*, Cant's two volumes on the *Villages of Edinburgh* (and also a series on specific suburbs), Gifford et al.'s *The Buildings of Scotland: Edinburgh*, McKean's *Edinburgh: An Illustrated Architectural Guide*, McMillan et al.'s *Building Stones of Edinburgh* and J. Rodger's *Edinburgh: A Guide to Recent Architecture*.

As can be seen, a number of the above authors have contributed aspects of their recent research to this book, which thus has a wider-than-normal focus on urban development than has generally been published on the city in the past in one volume. These include Miles Glendinning, researcher in architecture at the Royal Commission on the Ancient and Historical Monuments of Scotland; Charles McKean, Professor of Scottish Architecture at Dundee University; Richard Rodger, Professor of Urban History and Director of the Centre for Urban History at Leicester University; and Cliff Hague, Professor of Planning at Heriot-Watt University, Edinburgh. Other authors are also active in research development in their fields, albeit not having published books specifically on Edinburgh. These include Ian Campbell, Reader in the History of Architecture; Margaret Stewart and Lou Rosenburg, architecture-school staff members; Julian Holder, former architecture-school staff member and Director of the Scottish Centre for Conservation Studies, and John Stuart-Murray, head of the landscape architecture school – all at Edinburgh College of Art, where book co-editor Brian Edwards is Professor of Architecture. Other academic authors include Derek Kerr, lecturer at the School of the Built

FIGURE INT.7   The new Scottish Parliament signals the re-emergence of Edinburgh as a capital city. Here the design of this important institution functions well in engaging in questions of meaning at a deeper level. In this, it is continuing a pattern witnessed in the city for at least 300 years.   *Adam Elder/Scottish Parliamentary Corporate Body 2004*

Environment, Heriot-Watt University, where book co-editor Paul Jenkins is a Reader and Director of the Centre for Environment and Human Settlements (seconded part-time as a Senior Associate Research Fellow to Edinburgh College of Art). Authors not based in academia include Peter Robinson, previously of the Scottish Executive, and Jim Johnson, architect, previously Director of the Old Town Renewal Trust.

Briefly, the book is structured in four broadly historical sections and has been edited in two main parts. The first part, under Brian Edwards' editorial guidance, focuses on the more historical development of the city and its physical attributes. Chapter 1, by Ian Campbell and Margaret Stewart, examines the early beginnings and growth of the city up to the union with England, focusing on the

evolution of the medieval and Renaissance city in terms of urban and architectural form. Chapter 2, by Charles McKean, deals with the first major expansion of the city after this period, and studies the impact of the Scottish Enlightenment on the form that this took. Chapter 3, by John Stuart-Murray, covers a wider period and examines the impact of topography and hydrology on the city's structure and vice versa – in essence, how landscape and urban form have affected one another through time. These three chapters are grouped in a section entitled 'The Athens of the North', which was the appellation given to the city in its initial enlightened expansion. The following section is entitled 'The city in the industrial age'. It comprises Chapter 4, by Richard Rodger, on the industrial basis for the city through the 18th and 19th

FIGURE INT.8   The façade of the Scottish Parliament building. The design is challenging at many levels and it may take a generation before the building's architectural qualities are fully accepted.   *Brian Edwards*

centuries – something often underrated in importance – and Chapter 5, by Peter Robinson, which examines the development of the tenement-house typology, distinctive to Scottish cities in the UK, and mainly associated with this period also.

The second part of the book, under Paul Jenkins' editorial guidance, also has two main sections based on historical significance. The first of these focuses on urban management in the early 20th century, and documents the growth of municipal government in urban development. This includes Chapter 6, by Lou Rosenburg and Jim Johnson, on how innovation in conservation and regeneration in the medieval Old Town began and developed under voluntary and municipal initiatives in the late 19th and early 20th centuries in the city, becoming a model for other cities, as well as start-

ing a continuing trend in Edinburgh itself. Chapter 7, by Miles Glendinning, then looks at how government involvement in housing provision developed and expanded in the city from the early 20th century through to about the 1960s. This is paralleled to a great extent by Chapter 8, by Cliff Hague, on how the role of planning also developed in this period, and its effect (or lack of this) on the city's form. This leads on to the final section, which brings the reader up to date, with Chapter 9, by Paul Jenkins and Julian Holder, reviewing trends in new building and urban design as well as the rise of conservation issues in the city from the 1960s to recent times, followed by a more in-depth analysis in Chapter 10, by Derek Kerr, of some more recent urban expansions. This section also brings in wider international political and economic analysis to the understanding of development of urban form, a theme which is further expanded in Chapter 11, by Cliff Hague and Paul Jenkins, who examine the concept of place identity and its relevance to the city, especially in the light of the growing importance of the European context. These three chapters fall within a section focusing on the city in the post-industrial and post-modern age, querying the relevance of these concepts for the city's future.

As noted above, our objective in this book is not to have a narrow physical focus on Edinburgh's development but to take a wide view of this, both historically and contemporarily, as well as relating the physical with other aspects of urban analysis. This was the basis for the selection of the chapter authors, given the nature of their research. However, as editors, we also wish to present some major issues throughout the book, hence the definition by the authors of the key themes mentioned above in this Introduction, to which the editors return in the Conclusion. In doing this, we hope to achieve something which is more than the sum of the parts and which will interest not only a wide range of different people with a concern for Edinburgh's future, but also urban analysts in general. We also hope to provide new insight for urban managers and urban developers in Edinburgh, Scotland and the UK, while at the same time providing a readable and interesting text for students and city visitors. These multiple objectives are not necessarily easy to achieve, but we hope we have largely managed this through the presentation of a variety of in-depth research and understanding which a collection of expert authors can bring together in one volume.

Notes

1. J. Burckhardt, *The Civilisation of the Renaissance in Italy* (New York, 1958), in particular Chapter 1.
2. D. J. Olsen, *The City as a Work of Art: London, Paris and Vienna* (New Haven and London, 1986).

PART I

The Athens of the North

Introduction

Edinburgh is a very long-lived city; its origins are ancient even by Scottish standards. Part I examines Edinburgh's 1,000 years of recorded existence and the early influences that shaped the city. As a Pictish settlement, Edinburgh was subject to the forces which ruled at the edge of modern-day Europe. Chapter 1 suggests that it was a Celtic–Welsh foundation which led to the embryonic settlement we today call Edinburgh. But, as the chapter explains, the true inheritance in terms of street layout and urban form is in fact that of Norman Europe. As such, Edinburgh embodies the values and ideas of mainland European culture. These found their way into the early Scottish burghs via royal and monastic foundation. Chapter 1 draws parallels in the layout of early Edinburgh (what we now call the Old Town) with the Vatican Borgo and other medieval European settlements. Why this is so and how the feudal culture shaped the city is explored.

The first footprint of Edinburgh follows naturally the dictates of topography and the discipline of burgh institutions. The need for defence, then for trade, led to the construction of an enclosing wall, gates (or ports, as they are ambiguously known), market squares, crosses and tolbooths. These are found throughout early Scotland but survive better in Edinburgh than generally elsewhere. Some indication of the purpose of the urban spaces in medieval Edinburgh can be gleaned from their names – Lawnmarket [land market], Grassmarket and Cowgate. Putting aside the mercantile origins of the city, there was another ancient foundation known as Canongate. Again the name tells us a great deal, as Chapter 1 elaborates. The monastic origins of the area around Holyrood contrasted with those further up the Royal Mile, where trade and then the disciplines of law, government and

education were centred. How these forces became generators of urban form is discussed.

Part I seeks to explain the medieval and Renaissance origins of the city, not just in terms of urban layout but also with regard to the design and construction of individual buildings. As a capital city, Edinburgh drew aristocrats and successful merchants into the compact streets and wynds of the Old Town. How, where and when they built their town houses is explained, especially in the context of practice elsewhere in Europe. Again, the message seems to be that Edinburgh was a city with European aspirations up to the Act of Union (with England) in 1707. Its terms of reference and its sources of architectural inspiration were with the cities of Denmark, Sweden and Holland. The trading cities which fringed the North Sea provided both the wealth and the artistic ideals for a flourishing Edinburgh. In this sense, London, York and Newcastle were not exemplars; on the contrary, there was little competition with England until the 18th century. How the dialogue between local references and wider European ones was acted out architecturally forms a recurring interest.

Part I also traces the emergence of the tenement – the characteristic flatted buildings of the four main Scottish cities – and its adoption by all social classes. The compact, mixed-use, high-rise block had its origins in 16th- and 17th-century Edinburgh. The sustainable city, if such a term can be used, had its precursor in the cliffs of tenements with shops beneath and gardens behind of old Edinburgh. Why and how the tenement evolved is discussed.

Part I also traces the origins, growth and subsequent decline of the Old Town. Constrained by topography and an engulfing landscape of bogs and precipitous hills, Edinburgh became overcrowded and increasingly insanitary as the 18th century unfolded. Political upheavals had starved the capital of investment, with the result that pressure grew to undertake improvements just when the city lacked the means to carry them out. Eventually new roads, bridges, sewers and public buildings were constructed in the Old Town; but, as wealth returned on the back of a revival of trade (mainly with the newly discovered Americas), so too did new ideas on urban reform. These mainly involved the concept of the 'new town' – self-contained urban growth at the edge of older settlements. Again the concept was mainly European in origin, perhaps in Edinburgh's case inspired by the example of Lisbon (see Chapter 2). The Enlightenment cultivated a climate of improvement based upon rational thought and largely rational processes. As a centre of learning, Edinburgh became a place where political, economic, philosophical and aesthetic debate converged and, as Chapter 2 explains, found their expression in the design of the New Town: the embodiment of the Age of Reason.

Central to the ethos of improvement was a complementary relationship between landscape and city. Rural areas were replanted with enclosures, woods and avenues. Roads, bridges, reservoirs and villages were built – all on regular geometric lines. Vistas to old buildings or landscape features were brought into play by landowners and their designers familiar with practice in France and Italy. The New Town of Edinburgh reflects in its various guises the Scottish Landscape Movement on the one hand, and the political ideals of order and democracy on the other. A largely gridded New Town with its internal hierarchies of wide streets and squares mirrors the mood of the Enlightenment. Both Chapters 1 and 2 bring new perspectives to bear on the relationship between the Old and New Towns and on some of the machinations surrounding the intellectual gestation of the New Town. In this regard, the poorly understood and somewhat neglected Mar Plan has been reconstructed here for the first time.

Landscape is a recurring feature of Part I. Edinburgh is a city of greenery, hills, deep valleys and rushing rivers. Chapter 3 sets the urban changes into the wider landscape context and asks how nature and the city were reconciled. However, it is not just the quality of Edinburgh's landscape which matters but also the ways the natural landscape has been preserved and exploited to enrich urban and architectural design. One has only to look at views of the city in the 18th century (and postcards today) to realise the importance of landscape to the image of the city. It was not only the architects who brought landscape into play as part of their visions for an expanded or improved Edinburgh but also the civil and municipal engineers. Many engineers worked for the city council on street-building and other infrastructure projects. As Chapter 3 explains, their efforts to bring clean water to the city or to cross the deep valley of the Water of Leith or to drain the Nor' Loch resulted in a symbiosis of engineering and landscape design. As with urban architecture, the landscape designers of the period were closely in touch with philosophical or literary movements, with the result that the city's parks embody ideas from well beyond horticulture.

Part I takes a long historical perspective, maybe 800 years from Edinburgh's origins to the expansion of the city in the 19th century. The three chapters explore certain themes, each perhaps expressive both of Edinburgh and of the spirit of the age. However, putting the themes together – political as well as aesthetic – provides insights into the basic chemistry of Edinburgh's urban character. How certain interests interrelate, how government, the aristocracy, trusts, the arts, religion and education co-operated in the making of Scotland's capital is the main focus. The city was as much the result of co-operation as of competition. In this, it is unlike Glasgow and London but not dissimilar to Amsterdam or Paris, where municipal endeavour joined forces with key stakeholders to produce the 'Athens of the North'.

1 *The evolution of the medieval and Renaissance city*

Ian Campbell and Margaret Stewart

This chapter falls into two parts, the first tracing the development of Edinburgh up to 1603, when James VI inherited the English crown and Edinburgh lost its resident monarch. The second takes the story up to the creation of the New Town in 1760.

The history and form of the Old Town

The first mention of a settlement within the vicinity of Edinburgh is in the Old Welsh poem *Y Gododdin*.[1] The poem is an elegy for a war band comprising native Britons, who mounted a heroic (or reckless) raid on the Angles' stronghold of *Catraeth*, probably Catterick in North Yorkshire. The band was assembled by Mynyddog the Wealthy, king of the Gododdin, at his stronghold of *Din Eidyn*, 'the fort of Eidyn' (or Edinburgh), about AD 600.[2] *Gododdin* is cognate with 'Votadini', the Latin name of the predominant tribe in south-east Scotland during and after the Roman occupation of Britain, whose capital had been Traprain Law in East Lothian.[3] Perhaps by the late sixth century, the threat from the invading Angles had caused the Gododdin élite to settle further west. Although Din Eidyn, where the war band feasted in Mynyddog's great hall, is usually assumed to have been on the Castle Rock, excavations in the 1990s failed to find significant traces of Dark Age occupation, and it is possible that it was actually on Arthur's Seat, which has earthworks dating from the Dark Ages.[4]

The Angles finally conquered Lothian in the 630s and extended Northumbria to the shores of the Forth. The dedication of a church to St Cuthbert, the premier Northumbrian saint, just north of the Castle Rock, has led to speculation that it was an Anglian foundation and perhaps served a settlement before the Scots took over Edinburgh in the mid-10th century.[5] Certainly, the influence of Durham masons is apparent in the earliest upstanding building in Edinburgh, the small chapel of St Margaret at the summit of the Castle Rock, which is thought to have been erected by Alexander I (reg. 1107–24) or David I (reg. 1124–53).[6] Under these kings and their successors, Scotland participated in the 12th-century Renaissance, which swept western Europe and included the revival of old Roman towns such as Florence and the creation of hundreds of new towns in areas where urban life had either been lost or never previously existed.

Early urban form

The old view, that Scotland before David I was entirely pre-urban, is now being revised. David was responsible for the establishment of about twenty Scottish *burghs*, the technical term for settlements, usually fortified, where trade and markets were permitted. However, some existing settlements such as Dunfermline and Aberdeen appear to have been raised to burghal status during this period, whereas others were completely newly planted.[7] Which category Edinburgh fell into is unclear. While the site of the Old Town, a glacial tail stretching east of the volcanic crag of the Castle Rock, dictated its form to a large extent, the plan also conforms to the commonest type for medieval new towns from the south of France to the north of Scotland – the single main street, wide enough to accommodate markets, with building plots or 'tofts' of uniform width and length (25 by 450 feet in the case of Edinburgh). These 'tofts' determined by burgh officials, *lineatores*, extended from the main street as far as back lanes or the town defences.[8] The closest Scottish parallel is Elgin, on a relatively level site, with a main street running east–west, a castle at the west end, and the street widening in the middle to accommodate a market and the parish church which, like Edinburgh, is dedicated to St Giles.[9] Elsewhere, Pembroke in Wales, founded about 1110, that is, just before Edinburgh, has a strikingly similar plan, again with the castle at the west end of a long single street running east–west.[10]

The parallels are explained by Anglo-Norman influence. David, himself earl of Huntingdon in England, encouraged Norman nobles such as the Bruces and Stewarts to migrate to Scotland to create a feudal society, at least in the eastern and southern parts of his kingdom, while his new burghs were settled by English, Normans and Flemings already familiar with urban life.[11] Such towns were not a Norman invention but had been borrowed from the Holy Roman Empire established by the Frankish king Charlemagne in 800. Throughout the empire, thousands of *Straßendörfer* (literally 'street-villages') were created in areas previously sparsely settled, and from these the typical burgh plan developed.[12] This explains the similarity between the Old Town, with the Castle at one end and Holyrood Abbey at the other, and the Vatican *Borgo* (= burgh), with the Mausoleum of Hadrian converted into Castel San Angelo at the east end and St Peter's at the west, with two parallel streets running between the walls built by Pope Leo IV (reg. 847–55).[13] From the 12th century, Edinburgh has been recognisably a European city.

However, it should be explained that the Old Town for 500 years technically consisted of two burghs. Edinburgh proper extended halfway down the ridge. The lower part of the ridge belonged to the burgh of the Canongate, which Holyrood Abbey, founded by David I in 1128, was allowed to establish between that date and 1153. Never large, the Canongate still remained a thorn in the flesh of its rival up the hill until Edinburgh bought its feudal superiority in 1636 and ended Canongate's independence.[14]

When a burgh was founded, the tofts were let to tenants, who undertook to build a house towards the front of the site, the 'foreland', within a year, and, after a few years' grace, to pay ground rent or burgage tenure to the feudal superior, that is, the king (in Edinburgh) and the abbot of Holyrood (in the Canongate). Tenure was heritable and later became transferable by selling. The backland behind could be used as a garden or smallholding to provide food for the owners until there was a demand to extend the front house or erect other buildings. Once the backlands were built up, paths along the boundaries of the tofts provided access. Thus the 'closes' so characteristic of the Royal Mile developed and have survived, despite almost total subsequent rebuilding.

Both burghs grew slowly at first. In 1385, the French chronicler Jean Froissart (1337–?1410) recorded that Edinburgh had only about 400 houses.[15] The earliest indication of expansion is a reference to a new street which became the Cowgate in 1335; but development was hampered by the bogginess of the site, some buildings being founded on wooden piles.[16] Even a century later, it cannot have been densely settled, since it was left outside the King's Wall, erected from 1427, which ran halfway down the southern slope of the ridge, parallel to the High Street, parallel to an earlier wall.[17] We know Edinburgh had at least two gates or ports – the Over Bow to the west halfway up what is now Victoria Street, and the Netherbow (Fig. 1.1) to the east on the High Street near[18] the crossing of the present St Mary's Street and Jeffrey Street.

By 1503, we can surmise that settlement had reached up the southern side of the Cowgate valley, since Margaret Tudor's entry into Edinburgh for her marriage to James IV began at a temporary wooden arch where the Franciscans of Greyfriars monastery greeted her.[19] The site was probably where the Bristo Port was erected as part of the new fortifications constructed after the disaster of Flodden in 1513. The Flodden Wall extended west beyond the Franciscan monastery (founded 1443) to enclose the Grassmarket (where we have references to building from 1363), making a new western entrance to the burgh, the West Port (Scots, meaning a town gate). East of Bristo Port, the wall enclosed the church of St Mary's in the Fields and the Dominican monastery of the Blackfriars (both founded in the 13th century). The wall then turned north at the Pleasance, running as far as what is now Waverley Station before turning west towards the Nor' Loch.[20] The Netherbow

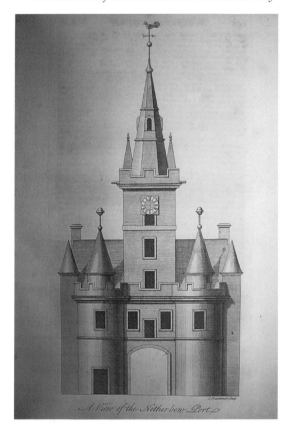

A View of the Netherbow Port

FIGURE 1.1   The Netherbow Port was remodelled in 1606, but demolished in 1764 to widen the High Street. *Margaret C. H. Stewart*

remained the principal port of the burgh, though there were several others. Apart from the growth of Portsburgh, the suburb beyond the West Port, this broadly remained the extent of Edinburgh until the 18th century.

The earliest representation of Edinburgh, a drawing contemporary with the Earl of Hertford's sack of 1544 (Fig. 1.2), confirms the extent of the two burghs in general, although it cannot be relied on in detail. The bird's-eye view from the north shows clearly the broad High Street running down from the Castle to Holyrood. In Latin documents, it appears as the *via Regia*, the King's Street or Way, paved at royal expense in the early 16th century and an object of admiration for many visitors, especially for its breadth and length. The English poet John Taylor in 1618 declared it 'the fairest and goodliest

streete that ever mine eyes beheld', while his compatriot William Brereton in 1636 exclaimed that it was 'the best paved street with bowther [boulder] stones (which are very great ones) that I have seen . . .'.[21] The other main street, the Cowgate, runs parallel as far east as St Mary's Wynd and marks the boundary between Edinburgh and the Canongate. Several other wynds (wide paths) break up the continuity of the tofts, whose backlands already appear densely developed on the High Street and on both sides of the Cowgate. In the Canongate, density is greatest nearest the Netherbow, but then it rapidly declined down the hill to tofts that had only the forelands built up. A low continuous wall is depicted along the northern edges of the tofts of both Edinburgh and the Canongate. The only port visible is the Netherbow with its two flanking round towers, prior to its 1606 rebuilding when it gained a tall square tower over the arch, reputedly echoing the Porte St Honoré in Paris.[22]

Early religious buildings

Like most Scottish burghs before the Reformation, Edinburgh had only one parish church, St Giles' (St Cuthbert's retained the landward parish outside the burgh). This was a consequence of its foundation with the burgh and is paralleled by examples in other medieval new towns such as Amsterdam.[23] The first St Giles' was damaged so severely in Richard II of England's attack in 1385 that the opportunity was taken to rebuild it completely. The cruciform core of the plan is still discernible despite the distortion of additional later aisles and chapels, which accommodated many different interest groups in the late Middle Ages and Renaissance. In 1581, the requirements of the new Protestant liturgy meant that St Giles' was divided into three separate parish churches. Charles I removed the partitions on elevating St Giles' to cathedral status, but they were rebuilt in 1639 and remained until 1882.[24]

By way of contrast, the nave of the church of the Augustinian canons of Holyrood served as the parish church of the Canongate until the late 17th century (it survives as a ruin), while St Cuthbert's served the landward parish of Edinburgh and was wholly rebuilt in the 18th century.[25]

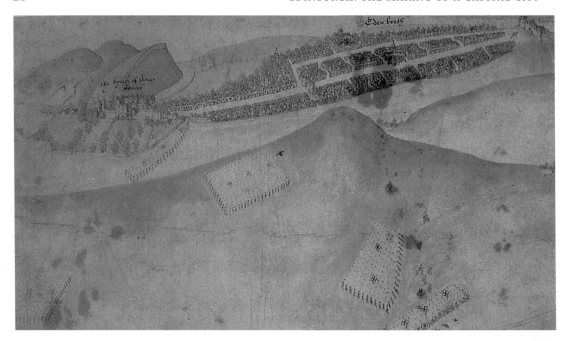

FIGURE 1.2   The Earl of Hertford's sack of Edinburgh, 1544.   *British Library*

All other churches in the vicinity were non-parochial. Blackfriars and Greyfriars, the monasteries of the two main mendicant orders, the Dominicans and the Franciscans, were built – as already mentioned – outside the city in a similar pattern to elsewhere, for instance at Florence and Venice. Both monasteries were attacked at the Reformation, and nothing survives of either (though the former is visible on the 1544 view).[26] The present Greyfriars Kirk is a new building dating from 1620 and up the hill from its medieval namesake. The chapel of St Mary's in the Fields, to the west of Blackfriars, was of uncertain function; but it had been raised to collegiate church status by 1511. It was sacked by Hertford in 1544 and became redundant at the Reformation. [27] It soon fell into ruin, although its ancillary buildings were used for housing the new university founded in 1582. Another collegiate church, Trinity, stood in the valley at the head of the Nor' Loch. Mary of Gueldres, wife of James II, had founded it in 1460 and so introduced the latest Burgundian Gothic architectural ideas into Scotland.[28] At the Reformation it passed to the city, becoming a paro-chial church until 1848, when it was dismantled to make way for the railway lines entering Waverley Station.[29] By the time of its re-erection in 1872 on its present site in Chalmers Close, many of its stones had disappeared, which accounts for its present forlorn appearance. Trinity College had an attached hospital, in the medieval sense of alms-houses, whose residents prayed for the souls of the founders in return for their board and lodging. Eight other similar hospitals existed in and around Edinburgh, all with chapels before the Reformation, of which the only survivor is the Magdalen Chapel at Cowgatehead (founded 1537).[30] After the death of one of its founders in 1553, it passed to the Incorporation of Hammermen (metalworkers), who maintained it until the 20th century. As well as a fine tower and spire, the chapel boasts the only surviving fragments of pre-Reformation stained glass in Scotland.[31]

Early public buildings

Besides the parish kirk, the three essential burghal structures were a tolbooth (town hall), a tron

THE OLD TOLBOOTH, EDINBURGH, FROM THE SOUTH (1817).
After a Drawing by D. Somerville.

FIGURE 1.3   By the 18th century, the Old Tolbooth of Edinburgh had become an urban and social anachronism. It was demolished in 1817 to create a square in front of St Giles' High Kirk, which is to the right.   *Margaret C. H. Stewart*

(weigh station) and a mercat cross (signifying the right to trade). The tolbooth accommodated the council chamber, and could accommodate courts and prison cells. Edinburgh had to build a new tolbooth, at the north-west corner of St Giles', soon after the English sack of 1385. Its old 'Bellhouse' survived until the 19th century and was a gabled steeple decorated with niches for statues. The rest of the medieval tolbooth was dismantled in 1562–3 when the council took over the west end of St Giles', where it remained until a rather utilitarian new block was built on to the Bellhouse in 1609–10 (Fig. 1.3). The whole was demolished in 1817.[32]

The Canongate Tolbooth was built to a similar formula in 1591 but had more architectural pre-tension, being built from ashlar, and is still handsome despite a radical 'restoration' in 1875. The bell tower, with its pend below leading to the road to Leith, and conical spire with four similarly capped bartizans, prefigures the Netherbow. The rest accommodated cells at ground level. The council chamber above was lit by an oriel window and reached by an external forestair, originally at right angles to the street. Above the chamber runs a parapet punctuated by four pedimented dormers.[33]

Nothing is known of the Canongate's tron; but James Gordon of Rothiemay's 1647 map (Fig. 1.4) shows us that there were two trons in Edinburgh proper. One is the simple weighbeam out in the street just west of the Tron Kirk; the other is the

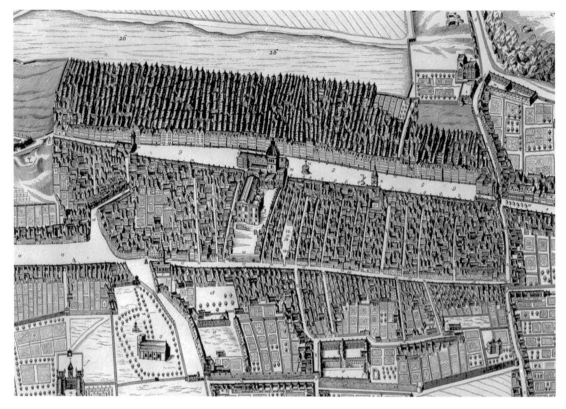

FIGURE 1.4   James Gordon of Rothiemay's 1647 map of Edinburgh.   *RCAHMS*

grand hall of the Over or Butter Tron at the head of the Lawnmarket. The latter was rebuilt in 1612–14 and, with its balconied steeple and symmetrical forestairs, rivalled the great town weigh houses of the Netherlands, then Scotland's major trading partner. Nevertheless, its predecessor must have been to a similar scale, since David II gave the burgh the building plot, 32 by 100 feet, in 1365.[34] Rebuilt less grandly after Cromwell's destruction, it was demolished in 1822.[35]

The early 15th-century capital and shaft of Edinburgh's mercat cross survive on top of the present impressive platform, a reconstruction of 1885 of the Jacobean mannerist remodelling of 1616–17, which had been removed from the vicinity of the tolbooth to the east of St Giles' until its demolition in 1756.[36] The pre-1616 cross must have already stood on an elaborate platform, since at the entry of Mary, Queen of Scots in 1561, allegorical figures stood on it to welcome her, and wine

flowed from its gargoyles. The shaft of the Canongate cross, possibly early 16th-century, survives in the Canongate Kirkyard.[37] On the Rothiemay map, it appears in the street on a platform resembling that of Edinburgh's.

Early domestic architecture: typical dwellings

Little is known of the earliest houses; but archaeological and documentary evidence suggests that they were largely constructed of wood.[38] By 1498, however, the Spanish ambassador to James IV was telling Ferdinand and Isabella of Spain that 'The [Scottish] towns and villages are populous. The houses are good, all built of hewn stone and provided with excellent doors, glass windows and a great number of chimneys.'[39] Physical, pictorial and documentary evidence confirms the ambassador's perception. The physical evidence consists of an apparently unique survival in Edinburgh from the late 15th century, No. 8 Advocate's Close.

Built of rubble with ashlar dressings, it has vaulted chambers at ground level, used as shops or stores, either by the owner of the floor above or sublet to tenants. The principal floor, the first, was originally entered through an external door (the surround is still visible at mezzanine level) via a timber forestair rising from the close. The first floor now consists of two rooms. Two tall cross-windows (i.e. single mullion and transom, the most fashionable domestic type across Europe from the mid-15th century) light the larger room. Their upper lights were probably fixed glazed panes with wooden shutters to the lower. The fact that the windows are not the same size and that the room has two large fireplaces implies that it was originally two spaces, which accords well with what we know to be the typical hall-and-chamber urban house across Britain at this date.[40] The jambs of both fireplaces, richly decorated with Gothic capitals and mouldings, again consistent with a late 15th-century dating, might suggest that this was a superior residence; but it appears to have been built by an ordinary Edinburgh merchant burgess, one Thomas Harvey. Over this room, there would probably have been lofts in the roof space and thatch on the roof.[41]

It is not clear whether the smaller first-floor room, which would have served as a closet or private study, was part of the original house or incorporated later. Its fireplace, though simpler than those next door, is generically similar. The ceiling beams are painted with Renaissance grotesques, a later 16th-century fashion that Scotland shared with France.[42] The ends of the beams are visible on the exterior and probably extended to support a jettied gallery on an upper floor, which may be part of the alterations when No. 8 was linked to the adjacent property to the south, No. 6, at which time upper floors were added, each a separate dwelling. A turnpike stair in No. 6, probably incorporating an earlier stone forestair, which projected into the close, provided access to both buildings. On the lintel over the entrance is the date 1590, along with a Latin motto and the initials of the then owners, Clement Cor and Helen Bellenden – all characteristic features of contemporary Old Town houses.[43]

The town house at 8 Advocate's Close appears typical for its date in Edinburgh.[44] Most of the houses in the Canongate in the 1544 view have two storeys with a door at ground level and two windows above, while in Edinburgh proper many rose to three storeys. The horizontal banding appears to represent coursed masonry, which is confirmed by the English traveller Fynes Morison in 1598:

> The houses are built of unpolished stone, and in the faire streete good part of them is freestone, which in the broade streete would make a good shew, but that the outsides of them are faced with wooden galleries, built upon the second story of these houses, yet these galleries give the owners a fair and pleasant prospect, into the said faire and broad streete, when they sit and stand in the same.[45]

No such galleries are visible on the 1544 view, but they must have already existed: William Dunbar (c. 1460–c. 1520) complains in a poem to Edinburgh merchants that 'your foirstairis makis your housis mirk', which makes more sense if 'forestair' is understood as a generic term to include all the timber protusions on the façades.[46] A good example is seen in the drawing illustrating the murder of Lord Darnley in 1567 (Fig. 1.5), which took place in the house of the former Provost of St Mary's in the Fields: to the left, the house has a stone forestair leading up to an open gallery. The same drawing is notable for giving us firm evidence of the popularity of crow-stepped gables by this date, a fashion borrowed from the Low Countries, where such gables appear on brick buildings from the late Middle Ages probably as a response to the difficulty of cutting bricks to match the angle of the gable. The 1544 view also shows that many houses already had gables to their front façades, again recalling contemporary houses across the North Sea.

Later in the 16th century, partly as a response to the 1544 fire following Hertford's sack, when much of the external timber was burnt, the city council began to encourage the enclosure of open galleries and stairs, preferably in stone like the

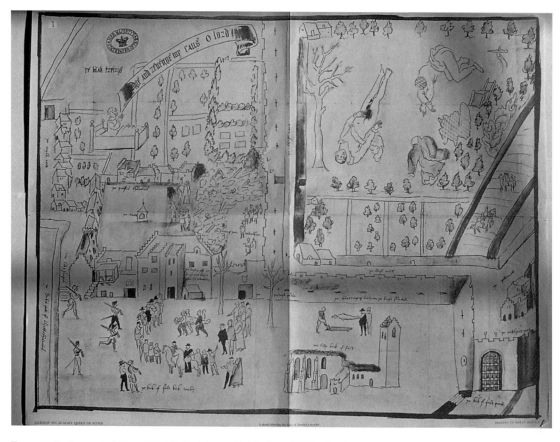

FIGURE 1.5   Provost of Kirk o' Field's Lodging.   *Public Record Office, London*

turnpike at 6 Advocate's Close, but often with lath and plaster as at the so-called John Knox House in the High Street, misleading some visitors, such as the French duke of Rohan, to believe that Edinburgh houses were predominantly timber.[47]

Early domestic architecture: grander houses

The Cowgate and the Canongate were areas favoured by the aristocracy during the 16th century primarily because of the lower density of building. Little pre-1600 construction survives in either area: the former because it declined socially as its population increased, while the latter saw much rebuilding in the 17th century, since James IV and V's palace of Holyroodhouse proved too small to accommodate the larger court of the later Stuarts. It is likely that the commonest type of mansion was the tower house, with bartizans and battlements to display their baronial status.[48] We have references to 'battling' and know from 19th-century photographs that the house said to be built by James Beaton, archbishop of Glasgow (1508–24) in the Cowgate, was three storeys and had a corner turret corbelled out from the first floor.[49] However, John Taylor remarked that in the 'closes each side of the way [High Street] are gentlemens houses, much fairer than the buildings on the high-street, for on the high street marchants and tradesmen do dwell, but the gentlemens mansions and goodliest houses are founded in the aforesaid lanes'.[50] It is here that we have the best pre-1600 survival, namely Riddle's Court, on the south side of the Lawnmarket, built by Bailie John McMorran around the time he was city treasurer (1589–91), and where he entertained James VI and his queen to a banquet in 1598.[51] It consists of two L-plan three-storey houses built around a rectangular court. The exterior has pedimented dormers and moulded door pieces that are recognisably classical, as well as a baronial cannon-shaped waterspout. Inside are painted timber ceilings as well as plaster ceilings of the 17th century, marking the yielding of French fashions to English.

Even these few physical survivals of pre-1600 Edinburgh confirm that the town was a place of peculiar magnificence, despite its small size in European terms, and that the foundations for the golden age of the 17th and 18th centuries were already well laid.

From the Union of the Crowns in 1603 to 1760

Later public buildings

Habitual reconstruction of the city's fabric continued in the early 1600s, when the town fitted itself out with several new public buildings. Their designs show a tendency to repeat and reinvent traditional forms – a kind of eclectic traditionalism; the self-referential nature of Scottish architecture in the period was combined with the desire for better amenity. In the early 1600s, the imagery of public buildings was the result of combining traditional forms, European influences and dynamic architectural planning to create large, robust structures of a deliberately historicist character. The later period sees the adoption of Scottish Classicism, a style that had been pioneered in the country house. Edinburgh's transformation was a stuttering progress, yet a remarkable achievement as the Interregnum, three Jacobite risings, economic deprivation on the heels of the Darien Disaster, the Union of the Crowns and Union of the Parliaments all combined to threaten the civil and economic security of the nation and its capital.

Compared to the public buildings discussed already, the Parliament House (1632–40) (Fig. 1.6) presents a more classical horizontal silhouette; but its downsized pepperpot tourelles have more in common with Murray of Kilbaberton's and Wallace's King James VI palace in the Castle (remodelled 1615–17) and Wallace's design for George Heriot's Hospital (1628). In the 18th century, the Tolbooth, the Netherbow Port, the

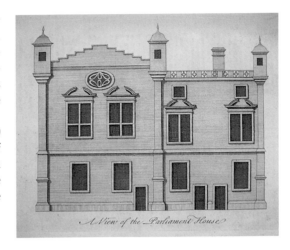

FIGURE 1.6   New Parliament House.   *Margaret C. H. Stewart*

mercat cross and the Gothic porch of Holyroodhouse were all sacrificed to the expediency of traffic flow, and, in the case of the Tolbooth, to the more scrupulous standards of 18th-century 'polite' society.[52] To the Edinburgh 'gentils' (as the higher social classes were known) of the Age of Reason, these structures, and much of the city's domestic architecture, were regarded as shambolic and decayed examples of Scotland's old architecture.

Initially, expansion continued within the city's walls, but it was led by the educational institutions. One of the earliest developments was the building of the College of Edinburgh (later University). This was a roughly quadrangular conglomeration of lecture rooms, residences and service buildings, the finest of which was the hall and library (1617). A New Library of three storeys with leaded roofs, ornamental door pediments and dormers was constructed in 1642. The College's best asset was its extensive gardens that probably gave it a pleasantly airy and secluded feeling; the gardens eventually became the site of William Adam's imposing Scottish Classical-style Royal Infirmary in 1738–48. However, it was the charitable foundations that led new construction: the paragon of private founders was James VI's extraordinarily wealthy banker, George Heriot. George Watson, Mary Erskine, the founders of the Orphan Hospital and, outwith Edinburgh, Robert

Gordon in Aberdeen all followed Heriot's example.

Out of these projects, there emerged a type of institution that set new educational and architectural standards both for the new purpose-built High School (Alexander Laing, 1777) and for schools throughout the whole of Scotland. William Adam became the leading designer of institutional buildings – he designed the Infirmary, George Watson's, the Orphan Hospital, the Royal Infirmary, and Robert Gordon's in Aberdeen.[53] Heriot's (1628) was, however, destined to have a greater impact on Edinburgh's cityscape and on Scotland's architecture as a whole for the next ten generations. Heriot's is ample evidence that, in the early 17th century, Scotland was undergoing its first baronial revival.[54] The potential of the site, between the Old Town wall and the Castle, must have been evident on that bright morning when the provost, magistrates and bailies in civic dress, with the architect, masons and surveyors, walked out onto the High Riggs and traced out the 'founds' of the 'Great Wark'. Within their view was the four-square block and gilded finials of the newly completed King James VI Palace in the Castle, the turreted form of which Wallace imitated for Heriot's.

There was, however, another architectural idiom in old Edinburgh – modest in form, and of simpler materials such as harl-dressed rubble. It was largely used in domestic architecture, but is interestingly also found in Edinburgh's post-medieval churches. This modesty was assertively different from the monumental and expensive European church – the Tron Kirk (1636–47, 1671). With its Dutch Reformist imagery, it is the only example of this type of church in Scotland at this date. Greyfriars (1602–20) and its progeny, the Canongate Kirk (James Smith, 1688–91), reflect in plan and organisation the more austere liturgical needs of post-Reformation worship, as do the later additions and alterations to Greyfriars in 1718–21. Both churches are uncomplicated basilica-type auditoria for hearing the Scriptures and sermons. Both also have white harled walls and simple stone dressings of the sparest form around the doors and windows, flattened gothic or semicircu-

lar arches, and imposing Dutch curvilinear gables on their entrance fronts. At first, it might be thought that their architects were mimicking vernacular structures; but we see the same treatment used on the west façade of the new Parliament House, and it was also widely employed for prestigious domestic architecture, for instance, at Huntly House (1671 additions), at Queensberry House (1681) and at Chessel's Court (c. 1745). Harled finishes on these important churches should not be mistaken for meagre vernacular; rather, they may have been influenced by the pioneering Burntisland Church in Fife, as well as by a desire to give the churches an association with the property of the people as opposed to the property of the state.

Later domestic architecture

The most profound change to domestic architecture in the period was the introduction of the French *hôtel* into the Canongate. This was a town house characteristically U-shaped and built around a courtyard. The side of the court to the street was usually a low screen that allowed a restricted view of the *corps de logis* beyond. This provided the characteristic urban pattern of two rectangles divided by a suite of apartments one room deep – the 'court and garden' arrangement of Paris's aristocratic suburbs. An embryonic version is the Bakehouse Close elevation of Acheson House (1633) for Charles I's Secretary of State.[55] Queensberry House in the 1680s is another example influenced by Sir William Bruce's remodelling of Holyroodhouse in the 1670s.[56] Holyroodhouse is the grandest of the Canongate *hôtels* – innovative in plan, but traditional in that it continued the Edinburgh tradition, which we have already noted, of copying formal elements of public buildings such as the Netherbow Port and the Tolbooth. Holyroodhouse was tricky: how to retain the historic James V tower and the great gallery extending behind it while providing sufficient comfort for king and court, and the mandatory mid-17th century suite of state apartments? In addition, contemporary classicism demanded axiality, symmetry and the expression of palatial grandeur. Bruce's ingenious solution was to use the historic structures as the elevation of one side of a court-and-garden arrangement – a French *hôtel* – and to build a duplicate of the James V tower for the opposite elevation. Between the two towers, the court is closed off by a screen and honorific baroque gateway, with giant orders of sufficient scale to compete with the paired circular towers on either side – the combination of enriched volumes, variable planes and fluctuating outline bears comparison with the robust silhouette of Heriot's. Though of considerable architectural interest, these examples had little impact on the Old Town as a whole.

However, changing tastes also meant that by the early decades of the 18th century timber-jetted lands such as the mid 16th-century John Knox House (Fig. 1.7), or the harled rubble of the Cannonball House, must have seemed shabby things; that generation aspired to build cities of smooth stone like those of the ancients – aping the cities they saw in the engravings of Poussin or Claude. Scotland's is traditionally a stone architecture, and ashlar had always been the material of choice for royal palaces. We have also seen that it had been part of the imagery of the city before timber fronts were added to tenements in the intervening centuries. However, it re-emerges in new buildings in the 17th century, with prototypes such as Gladstone's Land (1617–20) and later Mylne's Court (1690). These ashlar lands designed in the Scottish Classical style gave Edinburgh its most enduring physical characteristic. Masonry affects design and form: Scotland's rubble-and-timber tenements, though harled white or other cheerful tints, nevertheless possessed the characteristics of masonry construction – sturdy mass, volume and deep shadows cast in embrasures. When uniform ashlar frontages were introduced, the tenements retained these characteristics, but they also acquired a more dour aspect.

The multi-storey tenement provided high-density accommodation and a highly economical plan with vertical communication that resembles the rural tower house – a typology that offered a whole range of advantages from fireproofing to associations with high social status. Edinburgh's

FIGURE 1.7   The John Knox House (right) represents the older tenement with timber jetties that was succeeded, to the relief of the Town Council in its campaign for less flammable building materials, by ashlar and slate tenements. A good example is Moubray House (left) (c. 1630) – a more modest version of Gladstone's Land (1617–20) in the Lawnmarket. *Margaret C. H. Stewart*

freestones – Hailes and Craigleith sandstone – were the perfect materials for carving the Orders, for measuring out unit and sub-unit of proportionality and the internal coherence of classical symmetry and regularity. The complete union of material and form was fulfilled in the neo-classical monotony of the New Town. Most European cities metamorphosed into classical cities in the course of the 17th century. However, while Paris and Turin dressed their tenements in delicate and cheerful stucco, and opulent Rome combined stucco with carved stone dressings, or even curved its façades, Edinburgh abandoned colour and soft-textured harl for a bald and unadorned ashlar, polished but smoothly chased, or droved like the burin marks on an engraving. Nevertheless, these austere structures retain a close relation in plan, functionality and form to their 16th-century forebears.

The Dean of Guild Court and the early city improvements

The reputation of Edinburgh as smelly may have had less impact than we imagine on the motive for modernisation. After the introduction of clean drinking water from the Pentland Hills in 1675, Edinburgh rarely suffered waterborne infectious diseases – unlike London, where water was drawn from wells beneath burial grounds. Though live-stock was kept in Edinburgh's back courts, along with the mandatory tenement dung heap, this was probably fairly standard practice for most European cities. Old Edinburgh may have been a decaying and filthy blot on the landscape and the reputation of Scotland, but the Town Council's minutes record continuous repairs and improve-ments to its building stock. However, the measures invoked to reduce the 'puddle of filth and filthi-ness' of the town in the 1620s were inadequate to deal with the rise in population at the end of the century.[57]

Decayed properties were removed by order of the Dean of Guild Court (abolished 1975), an elected body of the Town Council that was origi-nally concerned with overseeing trade. By the 17th century, it was also charged with ensuring compli-ance with property boundaries and hence with building and planning controls. It monitored structures for stability and safety, inspected plans for new buildings and introduced bye-laws.[58] In Edinburgh, the principal hazard to the wellbeing of its citizens was not disease but fire. An Act of Parliament of 1621 required roofs of slates or tiles on new properties and on replacement roofs. In 1674, following the destruction by fire of several tenements in two parts of the town, the Parliament of Scotland and the Town Council acted not only to improve urban safety but also to renovate the appearance of the city. In 1674, the Town Council appointed a committee to investigate building

materials and draft an act for stone construction. The Town Council adopted their recommenda-tions in extraordinary session: all ruinous and burnt tenements were to be removed and rebuilt of stone, and all forestairs were also to be rebuilt in stone. Generous tax inducements were offered to proprietors of timber-framed tenements to recon-struct their properties. Consequently, the town was surveyed and all ruinous buildings listed for demolition, with confiscation threatened to those proprietors who failed to comply.[59]

Associated with safety was a uniform aesthetic appearance. The Town Council declared that all new tenements were to be built in a straight line, of equal height and with regular fenestration. Those facing the principal streets were to have piazzas (Scots, meaning open arcades) with shops at street level; and, to avoid defacing the regularity of the frontages, entrances at the front were forbidden.[60] Gladstone's Land, and its imitator Moubray House (Fig. 1.7), was the model recommended by the Town Council, and it set the pattern for the earlier part of the 17th century.[61] Thus the modern image of regularity, of tenements lining the street like books stacked on a shelf, dates from the acts of 1674 and 1675, and they were still being con-structed to this pattern in the West Bow in the first decades of the eighteenth century (Fig. 1.8).

Older properties remained a problem, and it was not until 1681 that all proprietors were obliged to reroof with lead, slates or tiles within one year of the act. However, stone tenements were clearly costly to build; and some proprietors, particularly on the south side of the High Street, were capitalising on property values by building high in spite of the 1675 Act restricting properties to five storeys above the street. In 1680, the Town Council waived duty on carts with loads of build-ing stone as a further incentive to reconstruction.[62] For the first time, all domestic buildings, what-ever their status, were roofed with pantiles or slates, and straw-thatch on outhouses and work-shops also began to disappear.[63] It is in this con-text of experimentation and aesthetic concerns that Robert Mylne's speculative development at Mylne's Court (Fig. 1.9) marks a turning point away from the piazza-tenement-shop type to the

FIGURE 1.8 Crockett's Land (c. 1705) and Johnston's Land (1729) in the West Bow. Most tenements continued to be built on narrow feus that did not even allow space for a close to a rear access stair: the forestairs were neatly tucked in off the pavements behind the front walls.
Margaret C. H. Stewart

purely residential type of tenement. Mylne's flats are entered by their main façades and have internal staircases. He dispensed with the need for space occupying outrig stairs at the rear, or pends that interrupted classical harmony and symmetry. Mylne's Court provided the pattern for one of the types of New Town Georgian tenements. The inspiration for this new tenement was an evolved variant of the traditional 'land'. Arguably, tenements such as Crockett's Land (see Fig. 1.8), Gladstone's Land and Mylne's Court had slipped into the thin interstices of the Old Town so successfully that they ameliorated the need for a New Town for some decades.

Despite this, the after-effects of the Union of 1707 increased local opinion in favour of a capital city that could restore the nation's self-esteem: the re-creation of Edinburgh became linked with the idea of the Scottish nation as a participant in Great Britain. It was Baroque grandiloquence that had created the new European city – expanding, penetrating into its hinterland, outward-looking, the state capital symbolic of national venturing in trade and colonisation. Urban development was also a means of improving national economies: this was the type of city that Edinburgh wanted in order to step up on to the world stage.

Urban transformation

Throughout the 17th century and right up until the mid-18th century, the city remained a thriving mercantile and social centre.[64] Between the Castle and Holyroodhouse, its stone façades, historic monuments, ornamental water fountains, the Tron Kirk and the mercat cross provided a visually interesting if antiquarian Scottish urbanity. There were also opportunities for outdoor activities at several public and private bowling greens such as Society Green and at Heriot's Hospital, where also the orchards and gardens were open to the public on Sundays. Another Sunday-afternoon outing was to walk in the Orphan Hospital's gardens and to hear the children singing. Golf was played on Bruntsfield Links and Leith Links; there was walking on Arthur's Seat, the Pentlands, across the Meadows or up Calton Hill, and skating at Duddingston Loch in winter: the places for outdoor recreation have remained largely the same as they were before the advent of the New Town.

However, increasing population density was causing serious problems. With only piecemeal additions to its area, Edinburgh had nearly doubled its population to around 20,000 in 1600, which further increased to nearly 30,000 by the 1690s.[65] In addition to poor cleanliness and overcrowding, there was traffic congestion. Until the completion of the South Bridge in 1788, the port of Leith was accessed from the precipitous Leith Wynd, or further down the Royal Mile through the bottlenecks of the Netherbow Port and the Canongate Tolbooth pend.

FIGURE 1.9   Large-scale developments built around an internal courtyard, as at Mylne's Court (1690), required a combination of feu amalgamation and retention of existing structures. The result was tall, largely symmetrical frontages to Lawnmarket.   *Margaret C. H. Stewart*

The first attempts to deal with housing congestion were largely directed towards the creation of new squares on the model of the Parliament Close (now Square), based on the French *place*. On the eastern side, facing Parliament Hall, were fine tenements with handsome doorcases. The south side was largely lawyers' chambers, and along the wall of St Giles' were stock offices and goldsmiths' shops; in 1685, the Town Council erected Grinling Gibbons' equestrian statue of Charles II at its centre. In 1748, it was described by the *Gentleman's Magazine* as 'beautiful and magnificent' and the 'best work in lead of its date' in the United Kingdom.[66] On the other side of St Giles' in the early 18th century, Allan Ramsay the poet and bookseller had his shop near the ramshackle wooden luckenbooths that lined the south side of the High Street. The Town Council removed them

along with many of the forestairs that gave direct access to the first-floor flats over the shops along the length of the Royal Mile. Only two examples of forestairs have survived in the Royal Mile (see Fig. 1.7). Though praised for its beauties, Edinburgh also had drinking dives and bagnios. Footpads and pickpockets lurked in dark closes and made social life in Edinburgh hazardous – burly Highland caddies escorted partygoers with lanterns, even carrying them to save their good shoes from the glaur, along closes too narrow to take a sedan chair. Even a visit to the doctor might be hazardous; Dr Archibald Pitcairne, the most distinguished physician of his day, held his surgery in a dark cellar in the Lawnmarket known locally as the 'grope shop'.

Social inconvenience alone did not give rise to the need for a New Town. Economic decline after the royal court had gone to London in 1603 was probably more important. The economy revived while James, Duke of Albany and York (later James VII), was Royal Commissioner to the Scottish parliament and resident at Holyroodhouse from 1679 to 1682. The Town Council improved the sanitary arrangements with the relocation of the fleshmarket and slaughterhouses to the Nor' Loch side; the new water supply of 1675, street-cleaning, lighting and paving were more systematically enforced, and a new merchants' exchange was established in the Parliament Close.[67] The departure of the king and court at the Union of the Crowns of 1603 had caused some economic distress, but the departure of the governmental classes after the Union of the Parliaments in 1707 had a greater impact, as did the aftermath of each of the Jacobite wars. Empty houses were leased to poorer tenants who were unable to repair them, and subdivision led to overcrowding and spates of fires. The most serious fires occurred in 1700 and 1708. The Town Council asked their representatives in London to appeal to the new King George I to take measures to alleviate 'the sad ruin and desolation come upon this city by the Union in its ceasing to be the Metropolis of our nation, the meeting place of the House of Parliament, Privy Council, resort of our peers, gentry and others'. The situation was so serious that the staunchly pro-Union Town Council threatened to take measures for the dissolution of the Union.[68] However, nothing happened because the Town Council, though keen to act, lacked the finance for compulsory purchase and reconstruction.

The success of Mylne's Court was imitated in the Old Town only at James' Court (1722). All other private initiatives were outside the burgh boundary, where regulation was more relaxed. The new developments at Nicolson Square (1765), George Square (1766) and along the Pleasance on the south side of the Old Town marked a fresh approach to urban development. Wide feus created by private developers in streets like Buccleuch Place resulted in the emergence of another tenement typology – massive four- or five-storey multi-bayed tenements with central staircases lit from above. In many ways, these provided the precedent for subsequent expansion to the north.

New visions of Edinburgh

When, as we might imagine, James 'Athenian' Stuart stood on one of Edinburgh's rocky outcrops and declared that here there might be an 'Athens of the North', the city obtained, at last, the confidence to realise a latent Hellenism that had been an aspect of Scottish culture from at least the late 17th century.[69] For example, Professor Thomas Blackwell (1701–57), who drew analogies between the Celts and the Homeric Greeks, had taught Greek to James 'Ossian' Macpherson at Aberdeen University. Even earlier, around 1700, Andrew Fletcher of Saltoun (1653–1716), a political pamphleteer and theoretician in the circle of the sixth Earl of Mar (1675–1732), had speculated on the form of Greek houses, and compared Roman Republican civic virtue with the cultural outlook of the modern Scots. Saltoun and Mar hoped for a reform of architecture away from the 'Gothick' and the 'gimcrackery' of the early 18th century, and Mar believed that the customs of the ancient Scots were 'alike to the Greek'.[70] What this educated élite inherited from Saltoun was the dream of a renewed city – noble, classical and modern, the civic virtue of its citizens reflected in academies, schools, theatres and bridges.

The idea of a new town had its origins in the 1670s. The earliest 'advocate for bridging the valley of the Nor' Loch' was the Duke of York:[71] like his brother King Charles II, who had personally overseen the rebuilding of London after the Great Fire, James saw himself as a European *urbaniste*-prince. However, Edinburgh's topography was difficult and the best site (Fig. 1.10) for the new town was Bearford's Parks to the north side of the town's cesspit. To achieve this, the Nor' Loch required a bridge of access. Undoubtedly, the bridge would have been begun in 1688 if the Glorious Revolution had not removed James VII from the throne.[72] Further delays were due to the failure of the Darien scheme, followed by several years of famine that devastated Scotland's economy.

The Mar plan

Andrew Fletcher of Saltoun dreamed of 'framing Utopias and new models of government'. He

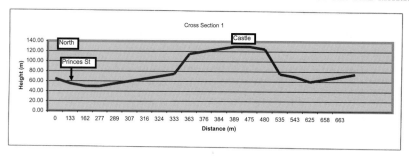

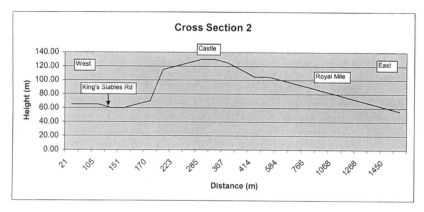

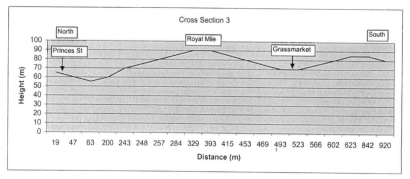

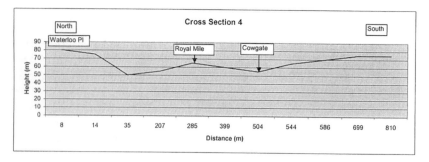

FIGURE 1.10   Edinburgh's development depended upon the bridging of the canyons of the Cowgate and the Nor'
Loch. The north–south sections graphically illustrate the problem that confronted the 17th and 18th century's planners.
Jack Gillon/City of Edinburgh Council

revived the idea of a new town.[73] In comparing London and Edinburgh, he stated that cities should be sufficient in scale and grandeur to bear the symbolic image of the state, and they should possess the physical criteria of the metropolis. In 1723, the Town Council proposed to canalise the north side of the Nor' Loch, make other 'sanitary arrangements', build bridges for access from north and south, purchase the Calton Crags (Calton Hill) and construct new public buildings.[74] Shortage of cash prevented these plans; but in 1728 the Earl of Mar produced, during his exile in France following his failed leadership of the Jacobite Rising of 1715, a detailed plan for Edinburgh that was clearly a response to the Town Council's proposal.

Mar's plan (see Plate 3) was also to be a 'great advantage to the convenience, beauty, cleanliness, and healthfulness of the town.' He tackled congestion, transport, public amenity, hygiene and the need for suburban housing.[75] This document formed the basis of the New Town as described in the Town Council's *Proposals* of 1752.[76] Stylistically the plan is baroque, with its creation of urban space and perspectives by circuses, *étoiles* and extended tree-lined vistas in the French classical tradition. In addition, there was the idea of the controlled vista as used in papal Rome to direct attention to ecclesiastical monuments. In baroque planning, monotony became an aspect of monumentality; but, as Louis XIV had discovered at Versailles, boredom could be alleviated by the refocusing of scale on smaller intimate elements such as gardens or fountains.

However, Mar was not the only exponent of formal planning in Edinburgh at the time, as Thomas Hope of Rankeillor's transformation of the common grazing at the Meadows into a public park had created an Edinburgh 'Bois de Boulogne'. In 1722, Hope partly drained the Borough (or South) Loch and formed Middle Meadow Walk with a double row of lime trees with canals along each side. The perimeter walks were planted with a hedge and rows of trees (see Plate 3).[77] Middle Meadow Walk terminated at its southern end on a large octagonal pavilion called 'The Cage' – possibly an aviary – and at its northern end on the medieval steeple of St Giles' High Kirk.[78]

Highlighting an ancient monument in this way is wholly in keeping with the principles of the Scottish Historical Landscape – a style of formal landscaping initiated in the 1660s by Sir William Bruce. Before his exile, Mar had been the greatest practitioner of this uniquely Scottish form of landscaping at his own estate at Alloa in Clackmannanshire (developed from 1702 to 1715). The Scottish Historical Landscape can be summarised as an acknowledgement of the historic nature of a locality by focusing views on ancient monuments, natural features and, as at Alloa, on industrial developments. These focal references created a dynamic relationship between past, present and future, and suggested renewal through economic and cultural development.[79]

Mar's plan would have encouraged peripheral growth, and traffic circulation around, rather than just into and out of, the city centre.[80] He also suggested a northern suburb (at Bearford's Parks in a grid pattern) and southern suburbs of villas with gardens. The pattern of straight intersecting streets would encourage new building between the Pleasance and the rear of Heriot's Hospital, and the city's markets were to be resited away from residential areas. These developments would have relieved pressure on the Old Town and helped to preserve it as the administrative, fiscal and mercantile centre. Broad, tree-lined avenues and circuses, gardens and plantations would endow Edinburgh with the imagery of a dynamic modern European metropolis. The plan resembled Mar's equally ambitious unrealised proposals for London and Paris. His intention was to create three cities that would be the capitals of a pan-Celtic Federation of Scotland, Ireland, France and England as an alternative to the incorporating Union of 1707. To Mar, the city was the microcosm of the nation. Scotland's macrocosm – its lochs, castles and mountains – is represented in the Edinburgh plan by activating the visual role of Edinburgh Castle, Arthur's Seat, the Nor' Loch and the woodland plantation of Calton Hill.

The impact of Mar's plan on the New Town, as finally built, is worth stating, as it underlies the coherence of the visions of the 1720s and the 1760s. The linking figure in this is Lord Provost

Drummond, who had set his sights on reconstruction since his election in 1725, although he seems to have taken little action until many years later.[81] Bridge-construction was essential for successful development of the north and south districts in the city, and the North Bridge of 1763 was constructed more or less on the site suggested by Mar (see Plate 3). Though Craig's plan (see Chapter 2) realised only a fragment of Mar's scheme, it nevertheless adhered to the same theoretical concept. As Youngson has noted, the streets 'terminated in impressive, monumental vistas'.[82] These focused on the Old Town, the Firth of Forth and Edinburgh Castle. When Craig drew a line from Calton Hill to form Princes Street (originally to have been named St Giles' Street), and another intersecting with it on the castle to form Castle Street, he was following the criteria of earlier generations of Scottish historical landscapists, of which Mar was a prime exponent.[83]

A major outcome of Craig's plan is that the city grew on the north and west sides. In Mar's plan, wealthy citizens would have migrated to the new suburbs which he designated on both the north and south sides of the Old Town.[84] Eventually, the southern districts did evolve in the 19th century at Newington and Marchmont, though not in response to Mar's proposals. However, Princes Street Gardens (from 1821), the focused vistas of the New Town as a guiding formal element in the laying out of new streets, the siting of monuments and the northward view to the coast of Fife along the terrace of Queen Street all conform to the principles of the Scottish Historical Landscape. Craig's and Mar's plans were both open plans that took full account of the dramatic interaction between hills, crags, seascapes and medieval and honorific structures. The formality, manipulation of scale and distance, and exploitation of monumental scenographic effects makes Mar's plan of 1728 one of the most visually exciting urban designs of the baroque age. Mar's aristocratic vision was unique in the British Isles but not so in Europe, where, for instance, Count Nicodemus Tessin the Younger planned the reconstruction of Stockholm in 1718 on similar lines. Lewis Mumford has commented that 'Baroque planning was usually at its best when it

had most to contend with', and that on easy terrain it can easily become 'pompous and empty'. Henry-Russell Hitchcock described Edinburgh as the 'most extensive Romantic Classical city in the world'.[85] Of course, neither Craig nor Mar could have imagined Romantic Classicism; but, by activating historic and undeveloped landscapes with their man-made schemes, they created dialogues between the ages and styles. The introduction of neo-Greek and neo-gothic structures in the early 19th century was, in these terms, a highly coherent response to the scenography of Mar's and Craig's visions.

Notes

1. A. O. H. Jarman (ed. and tr.), *Aneirin: Y Gododdin*, 2nd impression (Llandysul, 1990), p. 61.
2. Ibid., pp. xviii–xxi.
3. Michael Aston and James Bond, *The Landscape of Towns*, 2nd edn (Gloucester, 1987), p. 40.
4. Leslie Alcock, *Kings and Warriors, Craftsmen and Priests in Northern Britain AD 550–850* (Edinburgh, 2003), p. 41.
5. Christopher Wilson, 'Medieval churches', in John Gifford, Colin McWilliam and David Walker (eds), *Edinburgh* (Harmondsworth, 1984), p. 31.
6. Ibid., p. 32.
7. E. Patricia Dennison and Grant G. Simpson, 'Scotland', in D. M. Palliser (ed.), *The Cambridge Urban History of Britain, Volume 1: 600–1540* (Cambridge, 2000), pp. 718–22.
8. D. M. Palliser, T. R. Slater and E. Patricia Dennison, 'The topography of towns 600–1300', in Palliser (ed.), *Cambridge Urban History 1*, pp. 162–4; and the Royal Commission on the Ancient Monuments of Scotland, *An Inventory of the Ancient and Historical Monuments of the City of Edinburgh . . .* (Edinburgh, 1951), p. xl.
9. W. Mackay Mackenzie, *The Scottish Burghs* (Edinburgh and London, 1949), p. 58, fig. 2.
10. Aston and Bond, *Landscape of Towns*, p. 83, fig. 16.
11. Michael Lynch, *Scotland: A New History*, rev. edn (London, 1992), p. 80; and Mackenzie, *Scottish Burghs*, pp. 36–9.
12. E. A. Gutkind, *The International History of City Development, Volume I: Urban Development in Central Europe* (New York, 1964), pp. 108ff.
13. F. Castagnoli, C. Cecchelli, G. Giovannoni and M. Zocca, *Topografia e urbanistica di Roma*, Storia di Roma vol. XXII (Bologna, 1958), pp. 237–43.

14. Royal Commission, *Edinburgh*, pp. xxxviii and liii–liv.

15. Ibid., p. xlii.

16. Ibid., p. xli; and D. Tait, 'Excavations in the superficial deposits in the Cowgate', *Transactions of the Edinburgh Geological Society*, 13 (1936), p. 289.

17. Royal Commission, *Edinburgh*, pp. lxii–lxiv; and John Schofield *et al.*, 'Excavations south of Edinburgh High Street, 1973–4', *Proceedings of the Society of Antiquaries of Scotland*, 107, (1975–6): 155f.

18. Ibid., p. lxiii, fig. 35.

19. Ian Campbell, 'James IV and Edinburgh's first triumphal arches', in Deborah Mays (ed.), *The Architecture of Scottish Cities: Essays in Honour of David Walker* (East Linton, 1997), p. 26.

20. Royal Commission, *Edinburgh*, pp. lxiv–lxv.

21. Both cited in A. Riches, 'The teeth of an ivory comb: travellers' observations of Edinburgh and Glasgow, 1548–1830', in Mays (ed.), *Scottish Cities*, p. 35f.

22. W. D. Cullen, *The Walls of Edinburgh* (Edinburgh, 1988), p. 4. It has to be said that any resemblance was far from exact: see the 1630 view reproduced in B. de Andia et al., *Rue du Faubourg-Saint-Honoré* (Paris [1994]), p. 24, fig. 9.

23. Ian B. Cowan, 'The emergence of the urban parish', in M. Lynch, M. Spearman and G. Stell (eds), *The Scottish Medieval Town* (Edinburgh, 1988), p. 90.

24. Gifford et al. (eds), *Edinburgh*, pp. 102–6.

25. Cowan, 'Urban parish', p. 89.

26. Ian B. Cowan and David E. Easson, *Medieval Religious Houses, Scotland*, 2nd edn (London, 1976), pp. 118 and 131.

27. Ibid., p. 220.

28. Richard Fawcett, *Scottish Architecture from the Accession of the Stewarts to the Reformation 1371–1560* (Edinburgh, 1994), pp. 175–7.

29. Cowan and Easson, *Medieval Religious Houses*, p. 221.

30. Ibid., pp. 175–8.

31. Gifford, *Edinburgh*, pp. 163–6.

32. Deborah Howard, *Scottish Architecture from the Reformation to the Restoration, 1560–1660* (Edinburgh, 1995), pp. 116f. and 121f.

33. Ibid., p. 118.

34. John Maitland Thomson (ed.), *The Register of the Great Seal of Scotland*, 11 vols (Edinburgh, 1882–1914), vol. 1, p. 64, no. 207.

35. Royal Commission, *Edinburgh*, p. 126f.

36. Howard, *Reformation to Restoration*, p. 126f.; and Gifford, *Edinburgh*, p. 183f.

37. Gifford, *Edinburgh*, p. 152.

38. Palliser, 'Topography of towns', p. 182f.

39. Cited in P. Hume Brown, *Early Travellers in Scotland* (Edinburgh, 1891), p. 47.

40. Royal Commission, *Edinburgh*, p. lxvi f.; Geoffrey Stell, 'Scottish burgh houses 1560–1707', in *Town Houses and Structures in Medieval Scotland: A Seminar* (Glasgow, 1980), pp. 3–5; John Schofield and Geoffrey Stell, 'The built environment 1300–1540', in Palliser (ed.), *Cambridge Urban History 1*, pp. 385–7.

41. The significance of 8 Advocate's Close has only been recognised in the last decade.

42. Michael Bath, *Renaissance Decorative Painting in Scotland* (Edinburgh, 2003), p. 239.

43. Gifford, *Edinburgh*, p. 201f.; and for inscribed lintels see Royal Commission, *Edinburgh*, plate 7.

44. Royal Commission, *Edinburgh*.

45. Cited in Riches, 'Teeth', p. 35.

46. For the poem, see *The Poems of William Dunbar*, ed. Priscilla Bawcutt (Glasgow, 1998), p. 174. On forestairs, see John G. Harrison, 'Wooden-fronted houses and forestairs in early modern Scotland', *Architectural Heritage*, 9, 1998: 71–83. A mid-15th-century drawing of Stirling already shows galleries in house fronts: see Schofield and Stell, 'Built environment', plate 25.

47. For John Knox House, see Gifford, *Edinburgh*, p. 207f.; for the enclosure of galleries, see Royal Commission, *Edinburgh*, p. lxviii f.; for the Duke of Rohan, see Riches, 'Teeth', p. 35f.

48. Geoffrey Stell, 'Urban buildings', in Lynch et al. (eds), *Scottish Medieval Town*, pp. 70–2.

49. For 'battling', see Royal Commission, *Edinburgh*, p. lxvii. For Beaton's house, see Thomas V. Begbie, *Thomas Begbie's Edinburgh: A mid-Victorian portrait* (Edinburgh, c. 1994), plate 65.

50. Cited in Hume Brown, *Early Travellers*, p. 110.

51. Royal Commission, *Edinburgh*, pp. 81–5, no. 18; and Gifford, *Edinburgh*, pp. 198–200.

52. W. Forbes Gray, 'Edinburgh in Lord Provost Drummond's time,' *BOEC*, 27 (1949): 14.

53. George Watson's endowment was modelled on that of Heriot, while the Infirmary and the enlargement of the university were projects of Lord Provost Drummond. For Drummond, see W. Baird, 'George Drummond: an eighteenth-century Lord Provost', *BOEC*, 4 (1912): 1–53.

54. Castellation in country houses in this period is discussed by Charles Wemyss in 'Paternal seat or classical villa? Patrick Smyth, James Smith and the building of Methven 1678 to 1682', *Architectural History*, 46 (2003): 109–25.

55. Gifford, *Edinburgh*, p. 214.

56. Ibid., pp. 141–8 and 217.

57. R. H. Stevenson, *Chronicles of Edinburgh from its Foundation . . .* (Edinburgh, 1851), p. 138.

58. Iain M. Gray, 'A journey of discovery: surveying Scotland's Dean of Guild Court records', *Architectural Heritage* 7 (1996): 44–9.

59. M. Wood (ed.), *Extracts of the Records of the Burgh of Edinburgh, 1642–1655* (Edinburgh, 1936), pp. 176, 177–8, 227.

60. Ibid., p. 197.

61. M. Wood (ed.), *ERBE, 1681–9* (Edinburgh, 1936), pp. 277–9, and cited by Marguerite Wood, 'Survey of the development of Edinburgh', *BOEC*, 34 (1974): 31.

62. M. Wood (ed.), *ERBE, 1604–46* (Edinburgh, 1931), App., xxxvi, pp. 215, 319, 394, 425; *Acts of the Parliament of Scotland*, Vol. 6 (1), p. 227, and Vol. 7, p. 457, and Vol. 10, pp. 150–1.

63. This narrative is indebted to Helen Armet, 'Notes on rebuilding in Edinburgh in the last quarter of the seventeenth century', *BOEC*, 29 (1956): 111–42.

64. Defoe, for one, commented that the Royal Mile was the 'largest, longest and finest Street for Buildings and Numbers of Inhabitants, not in *Bretain* [sic] only, but in the World'; and its pavements were said to be superior to those of Lincoln's Inn Fields in London. Daniel Defoe, *Tour through Great Britain*, vol. 52, p. 29f. London description from the *Gentleman's Magazine* (1748), quoted by W. Forbes Gray, 'The Royal Exchange and other city improvements', *BOEC*, 22 (1938): 168–9.

65. Helen M. Dingwall, *Late Seventeenth-century Edinburgh: A Demographic Study* (Aldershot, 1994), pp. 9–33.

66. Quoted by Gray, 'Royal Exchange. D. Howarth, 'Sculpture and Scotland 1540–1700', in F. Pearson (ed.), *Virtue and Vision: Sculpture and Scotland, 1540–1990* (Edinburgh, 1991), p. 29 and n. 9. Our thanks to John Gifford for this last reference.

67. Helen Armet, 'Notes on rebuilding', p. 111. The loch's level was controlled by a sluice at its western end; see William Cowan, 'Bearford's Park', *BOEC*, 12 (1924), 79–91.

68. John Reid, *New Lights on Old Edinburgh* (Edinburgh, 1894), pp. 20–1.

69. For further discussion of the origins of Greek revivalism, see John Lowrey, 'From Caesarea to Athens: Greek revival Edinburgh and the question of Scottish identity within the Unionist state', *Journal of the Society of Architectural Historians*, 60 (2001): 136–57.

70. Historical Manuscripts Commission, *Portland*, X, p.

269. Letter from the sixth Earl of Mar to [Earl of Oxford], 28 May 1712.

71. First noted by William Maitland in *The history of Edinburgh, from its foundation to the present time . . . together with the antient and present state of the town of Leith . . .* (Edinburgh, 1753).

72. On 12 October 1688, the Town Council had successfully petitioned the king and had been granted permission to purchase land outwith the bounds of the Royalty and tenements within it to make the alterations necessary for constructing bridges. See Gray, 'Royal Exchange', pp. 170–2.

73. Saltoun made no distinction between economic, mercantile and civic functions. He regarded them as interdependent aspects of a complex organism. His ideas on urbanism are described in two pamphlets, *The Second Discourse concerning the Affairs of Scotland . . .* (1698) and *An Account of a Conversation concerning the Right Regulation of Government* (1703), from which the quotation is taken.

74. The Town Council obtained the permission of parliament in London to extend the ale tax to underwrite the costs of these projects. See Wood, 'Survey of the development of Edinburgh', pp. 34–7; and A. J. Youngson, *The Making of Classical Edinburgh* (Edinburgh, 1966), p. 13.

75. Hon. Stuart Erskine, 'The Earl of Mar's "legacies" to Scotland and to his son, Lord Erskine, 1722–27', with an introduction and notes by the Hon. Stuart Erskine, *Scottish History Society*, 26 December 1896, pp. 138–247, especially pp. 201–3. Article 36, entitled 'The Jewels of Scotland', is Mar's constitution for a federal union of Scotland, England, Ireland and France. Edinburgh was to be upgraded for its new role as the federal capital of Scotland.

76. *Proposals for carrying on certain Public Works in the City of Edinburgh*, 1752, drafted by Sir Gilbert Elliott and revised by Lord Kames in 1766, fully described in Youngson, *Classical Edinburgh*, pp. 4–17.

77. Maitland, *The History of Edinburgh*, p. 173.

78. The Cage was removed in 1821–8; see W. Moir Bryce, 'The Burgh Muir of Old Edinburgh', *BOEC*, 10 (1918): 258.

79. For a discussion of the Scottish Historical Landscape and its impact on Edinburgh, see Margaret C. H. Stewart, 'The metaphysics of place in the Scottish Historical Landscape: patriotic and Virgilian themes, *c*. 1700 to the early nineteenth century', *Studies in the History of Gardens and Designed Landscapes: An International Quarterly*, Autumn 2002, pp. 240–64.

80. This shift away from a single orientation is also

evident in Wren's plan for London with its three great intersecting half-circuses.

81. W. Forbes Gray, 'Edinburgh in Lord Provost Drummond's time', *BOEC*, 27 (1949): 12.

82. Youngson, *Classical Edinburgh*, pp. 73–4.

83. The way in which Craig generated his plan in the context of the principles of what we now recognise as the Scottish Historical Landscape is described by John Lowrey, 'Landscape design and Edinburgh New Town', in W. A. Brogden (ed.), *The Neo-classical Town: Scottish Contributions to Urban Design since 1750* (Edinburgh, 1996), pp. 70–2.

84. His model for this may have been the migration of the Parisian upper classes across the Seine from the Marais to Saint Germain in the 17th century.

85. H.-R. Hitchcock, *Architecture: Nineteenth and Twentieth Centuries*, 4th edn (Harmondsworth and New York, 1977), p. 112.

2 Twinning cities: modernisation versus improvement in the two towns of Edinburgh

Charles McKean

Perhaps nothing is more irrelevant to architecture than the notion that it is the realisation of a design *qua idea*. Far more dominant factors are the dialogue with and persuasion of the client and ... collaboration. The design as initially conceived is destined to be transformed during the course of its execution.

(Kojin Karatini, *Architecture as Metaphor*, transl. M. Speaks, MIT, 1995, p. 126)

Architecture has its Political Use: publick buildings being the Ornament of a Country; it establishes a Nation, draws People and Commerce; makes the People love their native Country, which Passion is the Original of all great Actions in a Common-Wealth.

(Sir Christopher Wren, *Tracts on Architecture*, Appendix to *Parentalia*, p. 351)

The great cities of an empire are, at least equally with its great men, a species of public property. In the history of both, that of their country is involved.

(John Britton, 'Introduction' to *Modern Athens*, London, 1829)

It is perhaps time to query the perception that the New Towns of Edinburgh exemplify the magnificent realisation of a great Enlightenment experiment in town-planning – to move, as A. J. Youngson put it, from a 'small, crowded, almost mediaeval town ... to become one of the enduring beautiful cities of Europe'.[1] The implication is that the city as we see it now is the result of heroic

efforts over seven decades and through many vicissitudes – two major wars, for example – to persist in the realisation of an unparalleled vision of neo-classical urban design. Indeed, the experience of walking through extensive streets and buildings holding fast to a similar architectural canon appears to justify such a view. Moreover, it is arguable that, until the present, it was only during this period that there was a successful attempt to create a British architecture. This chapter will consider whether Edinburgh's new towns were indeed the consequence of visionary control or rather of competing political objectives, muddle, commercial competitiveness and institutional lack of nerve. Put another way, was the powerful architectural homogeneity attributable less to the vision of the city fathers than to the pragmatic reinvigoration of Edinburgh's feuing conditions that governed New Town construction?[2]

Improving the Old Town

The glories of Georgian Edinburgh have tempted many an unwary person to dismiss the anterior state of Scotland. Youngson proclaimed: 'It is hardly too much to say that until the middle of the eighteenth century, Scotland was a small country on the fringe of civilised Europe [true], poor, little known, and of little account [questionable]'.[3] Studies of the Enlightenment, and of 18th-century and earlier Scotland, have since 1966 revealed the extent to which that view is misconceived. One starting point is the belief that, in 1752, there was a huge pent-up demand to quit the Old Town of Edinburgh. But was there? Our perception of

FIGURE 2.1   John Elphinstone's drawing of the High Street, c. 1760 (from Maitland's *History*).   *Charles McKean*

the condition of the Old Town of Edinburgh derives from 19th-century improvers like Robert Chambers who, with an intended audience of tourists coming to enjoy the Modern Athens,[4] denigrated 18th-century Edinburgh as 'a narrow, filthy, provincial town'. Most subsequent writers followed suit. However, as has been shown in Chapter 1, the Old Town of Edinburgh remained perfectly fashionable for at least twenty years after the New Town was begun. No Enlightenment Club, for example, met in the New Town.

Yet the Old Town in 1752 was not 'improved' in a contemporary sense, for there were three pressing, unresolved issues. First was its method of sewage disposal, which had remained unchanged since medieval times. When the Netherbow bell tolled 10 o'clock, inhabitants (or their servants) had become entitled to tip all household refuse into gutters in the High Street and side closes for scavengers to clean away. When houses were limited to 20 feet in height, that worked satisfactor-

ily, and the country's wet weather would combine with the steep wynds to sluice any residual ordure downhill. But as Edinburgh's buildings became higher, it was jettisoned from the windows, hitting passers-by and adhering to the walls. The increasingly polite Scottish society became impatient with such antediluvian procedures – ashamed at what John Taylor had, in 1705, described 'the nastiness of the inhabitants' that '*makes this country so much despis'd by the English*'.[5]

Since the generally lower-built English cities had no comparable problem, such complaints – as Smollett was to observe – emanated mainly from Londoners. Edinburgh's refuse disposal was typical of the high-density cities of medieval Europe, still practised by Spain, Portugal and some parts of France and Italy.[6] But Amsterdam, for example, had modernised by the addition of downpipes, while Edinburgh had not – and it remained a problem for Edinburgh in 1752. Seventeen years later, Thomas Pennant commended the assiduously cleaned streets, noting that anybody unlucky enough to be hit by the filth was encouraged to sue. He witnessed that 'utmost attention [was] given to cleanliness' in Edinburgh,[7] implying that effective action had taken place.

A growing demand for greater privacy than that provided by an apartment facing the High Street or one of the closes was being met in a new type of house in, for example, Alison's and Argyll's Squares. The *Gentleman's Magazine* in 1745 observed: 'on Society Green . . . they have lately begun to build new houses there after the fashion of London, every house being designed for only one family. . .'.[8] 'The fashion of London' did not mean an overblown comparison between these two small Edinburgh aneurysms and the expansive layouts of Hanover or Grosvenor Squares. Rather, the term referred to the fact that the houses took the form of individual houses in a terrace rather than the traditional form of a block of tenements. That the occupiers of the eighteen houses of Argyll's Square were far from the aristocracy of the town – two titled occupants, merchants, brewers, a wright, stabler, bookbinder and lint merchant – implies that the élite were not yet entirely convinced of the need to change.[9] Yet John Adam's subsequent Adam Square[10] (lacking the London concept of uniformity, with its florid central bow fronted and adorned with a Serlian window) implies an emerging market for houses rather than apartments.

The final impulse for change was probably urban rivalry. Edinburgh lacked the requisite grandiose architecture increasingly required for a modern city. It had nothing to compare John Wood's achievement in Bristol – broadcast as 'A Description of the Exchange in Bristol' in 1745. Edinburgh was frankly old-fashioned. Its symbol of justice was the outmoded and vandalised Tolbooth. Its principal church was infested by the myriad small booths – the 'Krames' – clustering between its crumbling buttresses. The High Street was cluttered with the city guardhouse, the weigh house and the luckenbooths. Even the 17th-century Scots architecture of Parliament House was alien to British eyes. Above all, the High Street was so physically inaccessible that its economic potential was constrained. A very good case could be made for improving the Old Town – but that would require capital and good allies.

The modernisers

The improvers were to find an unlikely ally in the modernisers. When Edinburgh had sought to defend itself against the Jacobites in 1745, the First or College Company of the Corps of Volunteers had comprised many men in their early twenties who were ministers of the church or otherwise intellectuals, marching down the Bow exchanging classical tags. These were not the sort of people whom nations normally had manning the barricades in 18th-century warfare.[11] Although they astutely managed to avoid too much action, it was a profound statement by people who were committed to defend the Glorious Revolution of 1688,[12] rejecting the superstitious days of royal autocracy and aristocratic disdain. These modernisers (Moderates or Whigs) were attracted by an altogether more civilised future. From the *Autobiography* of Alexander 'Jupiter' Carlyle emerges a strong sense of their networks – represented perhaps through membership of clubs like the Select Society or the Revolution Club.[13] The latter probably met in the 'loyal Smieton's' Netherbow Coffee House (since the satirical anonymous poet Claudero suggested that it should be retitled the Revolution Coffee House[14]). It was a fine time, Carlyle wrote, 'when we could collect David Hume, Adam Smith, Adam Ferguson, Lord Elibank, and Drs Blair and Jardine on an hour's warning'.[15] Others members of the Club included Gilbert Elliot Junior of Minto, Robert and John Adam, their cousin Dr William Robertson, Provost George Drummond, Adam Dickson, George Logan and Andrew Pringle. The Revolutionaries' agenda was to devise a modern country that would deliver social and commercial benefits to North Britain, so as to wean backsliding Scots away from their retrospective tendencies. *Theirs* was to be the idea for a New Edinburgh.

An ecumenical group chaired by a Revolution Club member, the modernising cleric Dr Alexander Webster,[16] went busily to work. 'The business was all done in the tavern, where there was a daily dinner.'[17] 'While Dr Webster and Provost Drummond were regarded as political adversaries, they consulted and co-operated in the promotion of the city's interests.'[18] The group was fronted by Gilbert Elliott, and, to judge by the language and clues left in Sir David Dalrymple's satirical pamphlet (see later), probably included Adam Smith (then in Edinburgh delivering his first lectures), Adam Fergusson, John and Robert Adam, David Hume and William Robertson. The outcome was the publication in 1752 of the *Proposals for Undertaking Certain Works in the City of Edinburgh*.[19]

The proposals of the modernisers

For the improvers, the Old Town was to be given bridges for easier vehicular access from the countryside, the obligatory Exchange, a new library for the advocates, and a building for the public records. They must have welcomed the plans to rebuild the university mooted in 1767–8. However, the modernisers grabbed the lion's share of the document and presented the biggest idea: the construction of a suburb on Bearford's Parks to symbolise Scotland's new role in North Britain. It was not a new idea (see Chapter 1); but the essential *new* argument was the *British* agenda, with the need to staunch the flight of Scottish aristocrats to London. The *Proposals* maintained that they were driven from Scotland's capital by the unsophisticated nature of its living conditions.

The authors both denigrated and falsified Scottish history to make their case, and certain parts of the *Proposals* imply the identity of their author. For example, William Robertson's hand appears to underlie the statement: 'few persons of any rank, in those days, frequented our towns. The manners of our peers, of our barons, and chiefs of families, were not formed to brook that equality which prevails in cities.'[20] It was arrant nonsense, as a glance at the countless aristocratic and gentry town houses in all towns of substance might demonstrate. *The Proposals* continued: 'The revolution opened to us a fairer prospect. Liberty was ascertained and established, our grievances redressed, and many excellent laws enacted.'[21] Likewise, Adam Smith's hand may underlie the vision of an aristocracy 'engaged in every useful project'[22] in

the workings of the country and its capital rather than remaining remote in London or isolated in their country seats.[23] Since Edinburgh needed to retain 'people of rank and of a certain fortune',[24] it required an aristocratic suburb exclusively for them. Men of professions and business of every kind would 'still incline to live in the neighbourhood of the exchange, of the courts of justice, and other places of public resort'[25] so that the two parts of the city could work in harmony.

The reason given to Edmund Burt as to why the Corporation would not allow houses to be built upon Bearford's Parks, back in 1733, was that 'if they did, the old City would soon be deserted, which would bring a very great loss upon some, and total Ruin upon others'[26] The *Proposals* argued that, since the New Town would be an isolated, élite enclave, its construction would benefit rather than harm the old city, which would end up even busier than before.[27] Yet, that the modernisers were probably secretly aware the new town might become a *substitute town* is implied by mapmaker John Laurie's designation of it as 'New Edinburgh' in 1766. Adam Smith, who believed that the Old Town had given Scotland a bad name,[28] would not have been disturbed by such an outcome. He moved to the New Town.

The *Proposals* were accepted (not without demur and procrastination from the heritors of Midlothian), and John Adam sketched a stumpy new bridge (perhaps a proposal for the North Bridge) upon his copy.[29] Conceivably, he or his brother might also have sketched out a concept for the new suburb at the time. Soon after its publication, Sir David Dalrymple lampooned the *Proposals* in a pamphlet that Robert Chambers, in his po-faced way, found disgusting.[30] To subvert the entire rationale behind the modernisers' argument for a new suburb, Dalrymple elaborately parodied the *Proposals* word for word, to argue that if the Old Town had problems, they should be remedied. By comparison with London, what Edinburgh so sadly lacked were not just great squares but sufficient Houses of Office – namely lavatories. Dalrymple suggested that priority should be given to making the old city work before diverting attention and investment to a grandiose new one. Convenient streets and open squares, he wrote, were not where money was made, but rather where 'the wealth of the nation is squandered'.[31]

For the next fourteen years, the focus was on improving the Old Town, for anything northwards hinged on building a bridge. The natural rhythm of the market was revealed in the development of new squares on the more accessible slopes to the south culminating in George Square. The modernisers kept their nerve and continued to purchase land contiguous to Bearford's Parks, apparently *in realisation of a plan that already existed*. For, in 1760, Bishop Pococke was informed that the hill to the north was 'to be divided into three streets from East to West, and the houses to be only three stories high, which will make it a most noble city'[32] – as, indeed, it was to be. When work on the North Bridge began in 1763, the elderly Lord Provost George Drummond revealed his hand to Dr Somerville, as they gazed down upon the final draining of the Nor' Loch from inside his son-in-law Dr John Jardine's apartment in the new Exchange Square. Drummond observed: 'look at these fields. You, Mr Somerville, are a young man, and may probably live, though I will not, to see all these fields covered with houses, forming a splendid and magnificent city.'[33]

The New Town plan

'A splendid and magnificent city', by implication a substitute for the existing Old Town, was a concept wholly divergent from the self-contained aristocratic suburb of the *Proposals*, and once the bridge was almost complete in 1766 – the heritors of Midlothian bribed, pacified and placated – even the language began to change. The bridge was no longer just a more level route to Leith; it had become the access to New Edinburgh. An architectural competition for the layout of regular streets and squares was duly advertised. There was no mention of any public space, commercial activity or place of entertainment. By the civic standards of the time, it was to be a suburb.

The winner was James Craig (1739–95),[34] a member of Edinburgh's professional establishment. Nephew of the poet James Thomson, Craig

adorned his final plan with a cartouche containing an extract from Thomson's *Prospect of Britain*:

> AUGUST, around. What PUBLIC WORKS I
>   see!
> Lo!: stately Streets, lo! Squares that Court the
>   breeze,
> See! long Canals and deepened Rivers join
> Each part with each, and with the circling Main
> The whole enliven'd ISLE.

Such an explicit British agenda was eventually underpinned by a dedication to the king, in which the plan is offered up as one of 'the New Streets and Squares intended for HIS ancient CAPITAL of NORTH BRITAIN'. Only an ardent North Briton would ever have risked perverting Scottish history to that degree. So how had he expressed his Unionist enthusiasm in his plan?

To gauge from the outline of 'New Edinburgh' contained in John Laurie's *Plan of Edinburgh and Places Adjacent* in 1766, Craig's design took the form of a Union Jack, hung across the line of an existing road running between the Long Dykes.[35] Unfortunately, the sharply triangular building blocks of the Union Jack were not only contrary to the competition requirement for 'regular squares', but were also unbuildable, and the plan extended far outside the site boundaries (compelling the Council to purchase the necessary properties). Either the other competition designs were truly dire, or the outcome was prejudged.

The plan was twice sent for refinement to John Adam and William Mylne.[36] They first attempted a rectilinear approximation of Craig's concept – three equal, double-sided streets and a square at each end instead of in the middle as implied by the original. However, the adopted plan, engraved in draft in February 1767, was different in kind, and strongly resembled Pococke's prophecy. Here was pure overarching form within which considerable variety would be permitted. Thus it appeared to exemplify the Enlightenment aesthetic ideals of Francis Hutcheson – namely unity within diversity.[37]

Its heart was a single, inordinately long and inordinately wide urban boulevard (100 feet wide,

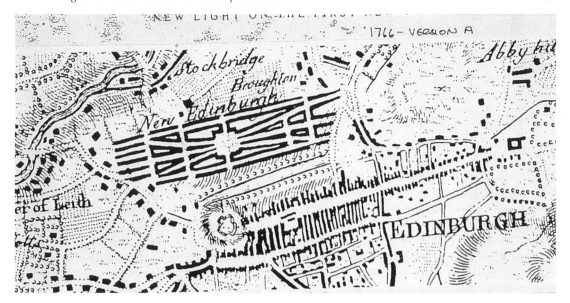

FIGURE 2.2 The 'Union Jack' plan of 1766, from John Laurie's *Plan of Edinburgh and Places Adjacent.* *National Library of Scotland*

like the High Street) joining two squares, with a monumental church closing the vista at either end. It provided the opportunity for what Roy Porter has described as 'the poised presentation of self . . . on an urban stage in which all doubled as actors and audience'.[38] A vignette on the plan depicts a vista of regularly windowed, three-storeyed terraced houses focused upon a domed church – the concept of what became George Street. In homage to the High Street, it ran along a ridge, with streets declining on each side.[39] But only in George Street could this plan be considered urban. In that the two other principal streets, and the cross-streets, looked over trees and parkland, it was fundamentally rural. Narrower back streets provided for service functions; and the only access to the Old Town was by the new bridge abutting its eastern extremity.[40] It was the epitome of a closed community. No public spaces whatsoever: no place to riot in.

A hunt for classical or Renaissance precedents to this plan obscures the fact that, in essential respects, the approved plan of Edinburgh's New Town was a larger and more sophisticated variation of the plans for the hundreds of new rural towns and urban suburbs founded in Scotland between 1735 and 1800.[41] Typically, a grid-iron new town would be laid out on either side of a straightened and widened road, usually with a square where the new church, market and possibly the laird's inn would be located. Feuing would be in rectangular blocks on either side of the spine, sometimes with parallel back streets. Given that Edinburgh's central spine followed the line of the ancient 'road betwixt the Long Dykes from the Kirkbraehead to St Ninian's Row',[42] rectangular blocks laid out to either side, the concept itself was not particularly novel for 1766. However, if it had originated in 1752, it would have been pioneering.

Compared to mainstream contemporary Scottish urbanism, Edinburgh's plan was distinctly English. Contemporary rebuilding in the lower new town west of Glasgow's High Street followed a modernised European pattern, namely apartments above arcaded commercial premises in a lower-scaled version of Lisbon's. Robert and James Adam's designs for the Professors' Lodgings in the High Street, the Trades House in Glassford Street,[43] Stirling's Square, and various schemes in Ingram Street and George Square were similar. So were early plans for Aberdeen east of the Denburn Bridge.[44]

An urban or suburban vision?

The essentially suburban nature of Edinburgh's plan can best be understood through a comparison with the Marquis of Pombal's plan for central Lisbon, rebuilt from 1757 after the devastating earthquake and fire, with the superficial similarity of a grid-iron plan with a square at each end. Lisbon's two squares – the Praca da Figueira and the Praca Dom Pedro IV – at one end, and the enormous Praca do Comercio for the royal palace open to the sea at the other, are of entirely differing shapes, scales and status. The latter rather resembles a Place de Vosges or a Covent Garden, with two or three storeys of accommodation above an arcaded ground floor. Although the Rua Augusta leads from the Praca do Comercio to Praca Dom Pedro IV, the two squares are not on axis. The urbanism of Pombal's new Lisbon is dense and European, its grid-iron streets narrow and commercial, their names reflecting their original artisanal purposes – silversmiths', cobblers' and goldsmiths' streets.

The scale and low density of the Edinburgh plan, by comparison, was breathtaking. Craig's urban vision was one of élite three-storeyed houses facing a long central vista terminated by a church in a square on axis at each end, whereas the narrower Rua Augusta was lined with four or more storeys of apartments above shops, with a giant triumphal arch at one end and nothing at the other. The squares at each end of Pombal's design were public, civic and ceremonial, whereas those in Edinburgh were private and railed to exclude non-residents. The length and width of George Street was so great that only excessively large churches could have fulfilled Craig's concept of churches closing the prospect. The lesser service streets have no parallels in Lisbon; and the single-sided flanking streets facing gardens were paralleled in Lisbon by further dense streets flanked by steep cliffs. Even the geometry of Edinburgh's design was more rigid than Lisbon's. Edinburgh's cross-streets rise and fall straight up and down steep hills, whereas Lisbon's grid mutates into curves where necessary to allow streets to rise up to the Bairro Alto.

Replanning Lisbon attracted the attention of Robert Adam while he was still in Rome. Probably collaborating with L.-B. Dewez, he prepared an esquisse in 1757 for an imaginary Lisbon that did not really fit its site. Its principal objective appears to have the ordered disposition of society in a baroque plan – separating nobility from burgesses, and them from the artisanal suburbs. Markets and public buildings were carefully located, with formal public parks to each side.[45] In key respects, Adam's plan resembled more what came to be built in Edinburgh than in Lisbon – perhaps not surprisingly, if he had had a hand in preparing the plan witnessed by Pococke.

The comparison with Lisbon (see p. 54, Fig. 2.8) accentuates the extent to which Edinburgh's was *not* a new town but, rather, a realisation of almost all the objectives of the *Proposals'* concept of a select suburb of houses. Yet whereas the squares of Mayfair might have provided the model for urban living, they were most magisterially improved upon in this plan for Edinburgh. London's Grosvenor, Hanover and Berkeley Squares are discontinuous, reflecting competing landownerships, whereas the thoroughgoing geometry of 'Mayfair on Forth' demonstrated what could really be achieved if you sought a rigorous application of Enlightenment principles within a single land-ownership. Clamped firmly upon the concept of North Britain, Edinburgh's New Town plan turned its back on the evolving European tradition within Scotland, and substantially improved upon the English model.

North British aspiration also inspired the original street names: St Andrew's Square joined by George Street to St George's Square, Forth Street facing the river, and St Giles' Street facing the Old Town with its crown steeple. Unfortunately, when Sir John Pringle sought the king's patronage for the plan, he 'objected to the name of St Giles's Street'. Pringle added: 'I need not tell your Lordship how liable to objection the name St Giles was; if you will be pleased to recollect that a Quarter of this city [London], always infamous for its low and disorderly inhabitants, is so called'.[46] So street names became Hanoverian – Queen, Charlotte, Princes, George, Frederick and Hanover

FIGURE 2.3   The formidable parade of George Street in the mid-19th century.   *Charles McKean*

– leaving a residual Scottishness only in St Andrew Square. The celebration of the Union was relegated to the naming of the two artisanal streets – Rose and Thistle – in the 1780s. Their narrowness, lower scale and poorer quality of masonry was evidence that class distinction was now being horizontally rather than vertically organised.

Aesthetic control

It is not as though aesthetic control in the New Town would have been a novelty. For example, Bristol Council, almost seventy years earlier, had required those building Queen's Square to use brick with stone dressings. Yet on 24 February 1768, Edinburgh's Council decided that it would control only scale and height (albeit permitting the banker and principal investor in the New Town, Sir William Forbes of Pitsligo, to erect a house of only two storeys on Princes Street as a reward 'for so hazardous and difficult' an undertaking.[47]) Judging from the variety of façades – some harled

rubble, some coursed rubble, some ashlar and some polished ashlar – it would control neither façade materials nor the size of each lot, 'as people's taste of building is so different'.[48]

In further variation from the presumed order, the Council itself permitted people to buy the three central stances in each plot for the creation of larger buildings.[49] It was being either libertarian or pusillanimous – and pusillanimity is more likely. For it was complicit in the principal departure from Craig's plan – the sale of the site dedicated to the eastern church to Sir Laurence Dundas, so that he could build his grandiose mansion designed by Sir William Chambers. It was the Council itself that sold the land.

Craig himself proposed to break with the regular ranks of houses implied in his vignette. For the houses which he proposed should flank his Physicians' Hall in George Street (shown in the Allan portrait), he planned a raised principal storey, and an attic, with an octagonal bay projecting into the street, not unlike the three terraced houses in John Adam's Square, of which Craig, like Adam, proposed to be the developer.[50] Craig further distanced himself from the New Town concept when, in 1773, he produced a plan to build St James' Square at its east end. He boasted the congeniality of this strange place, with a 'bason' at its centre and short, narrow streets of tall buildings leading off to nowhere at each corner: 'buildings will be sheltered by the New Town from the westerly winds *which blow near half the year with the greatest Violence* [author's italics] from that Quarter'. Perhaps he felt that the geometry of his original Union Jack plan might have been better in addressing practicalities like the weather. Indeed, had Craig proposed a tower at the centre, his plan would have been similar to Vitruvius' plan for a city laid out to control the wind.

Initially, adherence to Craig's approved plan maintained order and yet permitted variety; but its power to govern change was challenged in the courts.[51] It had proved insufficient as a mechanism of control, since it did not prohibit alterations to the external appearance or changing uses. There was much greater latitude than was permitted in Glasgow's George Square, whose three square-storeyed houses had to be built of ashlar work and roofed in slate.[52] Lengthy clauses specified prohibited businesses or industries.[53] In 1785, Edinburgh's Council duly tightened its aesthetic regulations. Height was limited to 48 feet or three principal storeys in the main streets, and two storeys in Rose and Thistle Streets. Gables to the street, and dormer windows, were now prohibited.

These new controls began a process whereby, over the following fifty years, increasing conditions over the design of individual buildings would be counterbalanced by greater variety in urban layout;[54] and it was to the precise feuing conditions imposed by each landowner that the discipline and the approximate visual homogeneity of the New Towns could be attributed.

An uncertain start

The focus of social, business and intellectual life in Edinburgh remained in the Old Town until the 1780s. Far from Old Town residents flooding across to the new houses, the New Town remained largely unbuilt for its first two decades. It competed for occupants with 'the small but commodious' George Square 'in the English fashion', as Pennant put it in 1769;[55] and, for some time, it appeared that George Square was winning. But Chambers also thought that people of moderate means feared that the greater stateliness of living in the New Town would be beyond their means.[56] To some extent, that is confirmed by John Ramsay of Ochtertyre's subsequent disparagement of New Town inhabitants as 'Edinburgh's swaggering misses and their *mummified* effeminate beaux'.[57] By the 1780s, the New Town barely extended to Frederick Street – even though the full street plan was marked on the ground in 1788, long before construction began.[58] The acceleration of New Town construction occurred with the ending of its western isolation by the construction of the Earthen Mound,[59] which appears to have been usable by January 1787.[60] Symbolically, the capital's principal Assembly Rooms moved to George Street in 1787; and, as new developers followed, the first New Town appeared to be moving to a conclusion.

One such developer was the Canongate mason Alexander Reid, who used the New Town for the social elevation of himself and his son Robert into architects. He first took sasine of land in Princes Street in 1771,[61] but it was ten years before he took his next two.[62] Thereafter the rate accelerated, presumably using the sales of one building to finance the next. By 1818, he and his son had constructed approximately thirty properties for lawyers, the Deputy Clerk of Session, military men, merchants, widows – and a number of people whose status was not identified. Perhaps they were the 'sons of nabobs' so sourly identified by John Symonds, Regius Professor of Modern History at Cambridge, perplexed by who could afford expensive New Town houses in 1790: 'It is the consequence of Oriental wealth . . . Their younger sons, having no house or property of their own, sought for a residence in the Capital, which could not be furnished by the ordinary building.'[63]

English houses and Scottish tenements

Craig's plan of August 1767 did not specify what type of building he proposed;[64] but, from the careful delineation of each garden, we may surmise that the intended buildings were individual terraced houses – and that is what observers like Thomas Topham thought that they were looking at: 'built after the manner of the English, and the houses are what they call here "houses to themselves" . . . In no town that I ever saw, can such a contrast be found betwixt the modern and antient architecture.'[65] The expectation of such town houses throughout Britain was the provision of a dining room on the entrance level, and a suite of reception rooms on the first floor that would open into each other for a *levée*. But the activities of Reid *père et fils*, in feuing the same address to four separate purchasers, shows just how cleverly appearances deceived. For what they were building at the western end of Princes Street were blocks of flatted apartments with the façade of a complete house, the communal staircase concealed in the mews to the rear.[66] Some purchasers bought in advance, some during construction, and some upon completion.[67] It was very similar in the cross-streets, albeit entered from the front rather than the rear. Sir Walter Scott's, at 39 Castle Street, was a classic example of a spacious apartment grouped with others behind a pilastered, pedimented classical façade resembling a grand villa.[68] So it was the *physical appearance* of the New Town buildings that represented the novelty, rather than the living patterns contained within them.

Charlotte Square and its challengers

As George Street surged westwards, individual houses became increasingly elaborate, each vying with its neighbour in jangling decoration. Only the scale of the street itself, and the use of large stone blocks, maintained a broad homogeneity. It was a poor advertisement for the Council's tightened process of design control. Probably in reaction to the emerging classical *pot pourri*, the Council required purchasers of plots in Charlotte Square to conform to the palace-fronted façade and plan that it had commissioned from Robert Adam.

FIGURE 2.4   Robert Adam's 1791 proposals for the north side of Charlotte Square.   *Soane Museum*

Unfortunately, where architectural grandeur costs too much, people go elsewhere. Although designed in 1792, building in Charlotte Square stuttered to a virtual halt after the completion of its northern wing. After 1803, it was speedily outstripped by the construction of smaller houses in the Second New Town downhill (demonstrating that the principal market for New Town houses was less the élite than the middling ranks). Since feu duties in the latter were, on average, just under double those of Charlotte Square,[69] this reversal cannot be explained by cheaper feus. The evidence points instead to the size of Charlotte Square houses and the cost of the architecture. Feuars had to conform to Adam's plan and elevation, use Redhall stone ashlar façades, 'Sphinx, Bulls head, Swag husks and Ribbon knots',[70] and also share the burden of maintaining the gardens. The square remained incomplete until at least 1816–20, only reinvigorated by the personal intervention of the Lord Provost, Sir John Marjoribanks of Lees, who took feus of nos 28–31 in 1817.

The five phases of the New Town were far from sequential. They were, rather, highly competitive. In 1785, before the first New Town was even half-built, the Governors of Heriot's Hospital considered how to profit from their lands to the north. The plan to which William Creech referred in 1793, making, when complete, 'Edinburgh [into] the most beautiful and picturesque city in the world',[71] was probably the somewhat incoherent plan produced for the Governors by William Sibbald that year. It echoed Craig's 1774 New Town plan with a circus and a 'Bason' at its centre, reached by extending Castle Street downhill.

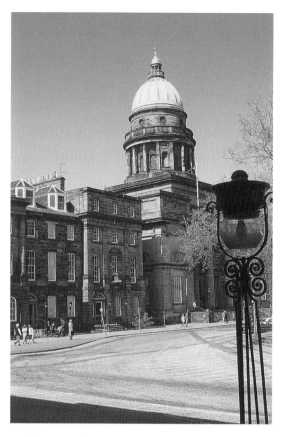

FIGURE 2.5 St George's West Church (now West Register House): the termination of George Street to the west. *Charles McKean*

A design competition held in 1800 awarded premia to John Baine, Robert Morison, William Sibbald and James Elliot. The latter three all signed a single drawing[72] in 1801 that incorporated, as instructed, the best features of their three proposals. At this point, Robert Reid, busy as a fashionable architect/developer in York Place, appears to have supplanted two of them, and was paired with Sibbald for the execution of a revised plan. Sibbald's circus was moved westwards to terminate King Street, and forfeited its connection with a northward Castle Street. Heriot Row and Dublin Street were largely complete by 1808;[73] and, qualitatively, the magnificent austerity of Great King Street bade fair to outstrip anything uphill.

Competitive construction and social segregation

In 1825, different parts of Edinburgh had moved into close combat with each other as adjacent estates sought to cash in. An anonymous diarist recorded:

> the number of houses building in Edinburgh this season probably exceeds that of any former year . . . The great increase is in the west and north-west Lord Murray's ground . . . extensive building in Parkside Street . . . 25 houses building in Melville Street . . . Moray Place is all built except a few stances . . . Royal Crescent is just beginning . . . Claremont Street . . . has 13 new houses,

and there was building in Gardner's Crescent, Randolph Crescent, Cumberland Street, Fettes Row, Leith Walk, Elm Row, Leopold Place, Hillside Crescent, Royal Terrace and Gayfield Square.[74] So construction work was proceeding in what we tend to call the Second (northern), Third (eastern), Fourth (Moray Estate) and Fifth (Walker estate, or western) New Towns simultaneously.

The *Proposals* had intended that the New Town be inhabited solely by persons of rank, with professionals and commercial people remaining behind in the Old Town. All places of commerce and entertainment were likewise to remain behind in the Old Town. Reality proved otherwise. The first new building across the bridge (although technically lying beyond the boundary of the New Town) was the blowsy Theatre Royal, whose foundation was laid in 1767. Four aristocrats initially inhabited St Andrew's Square, but the remainder were gentry or professionals. David Hume built himself a house on the south-west corner of St Andrew's Square, and was tickled when Alexander Webster chalked the words 'St David's House' on its wall, satirically in the light of Hume's reputation as 'The Atheist'.[75] Princes Street was under commercial pressure almost from the very beginning,[76] for a haberdasher had built the first house on it.[77] 'The fate of [the New Town's] magnates', observed Robert Chambers, 'is, every few years, to be expelled from their appropriated districts by the intrusion of the trading classes.'[78]

FIGURE 2.6   Great King Street: arguably the most handsome single street in the New Town.   *Charles McKean*

FIGURE 2.7   St Colme Street, 1825, forms the southern side of the Moray Estate. Such streets represented a harmonious balance between Enlightenment values, social ideals and nature.   *Charles McKean*

FIGURE 2.8   Lisbon: the Arco da Rua Augusta. Note the similarities in proportion and composition to the New Town of Edinburgh.   *Charles McKean*

Within five years of Charlotte Square having been completed, Oman's Hotel was already spoiling the exclusivity of its north side, the British Hotel having invaded Queen Street the year before.[79]

By the time that the Earl of Moray began to develop the Moray Estate in 1822, the battle was lost. Intended as the élite enclave of this élite New Town project – and the imposing scale and grandeur of James Gillespie Graham's designs confirm that aspiration – the only aristocrat to take a feu was the Earl of Moray himself.[80] Most feuars bought houses for themselves, although the dowager Lady Ramsay bought two, and Sir Patrick Murray of Ochtertyre three. Of the 189 first-time feuars, there were no other titled people, and barely ten military chaps; but there were forty-five lawyers including three law lords, thirty-two

lairds for whom these were probably their town houses, eleven doctors, twenty-one assorted other professionals, and forty-six individuals of independent means. Lairds dominated Moray Place, and lawyers Albyn Place, St Colme Street and Great Stuart Street.[81] The Earl managed to restrict the service businesses for the new community – milliner, tailor, hardwareman and spirit dealer – to Wemyss Place on the perimeter.[82] Youngson suggests that the aristocrats for whom the New Town had been intended had quit Edinburgh for a London town house and an improved Scottish country house by the 1820s.[83] The occupancy of the Moray Estate supports that analysis. So, in the critical respect of exclusivity, the New Town reality failed the *Proposals*.

Classical romanticism

The austere rectangularities of the First New Town no longer matched the growing taste for picturesque sensibility of the later 18th century. Romantically inclined aesthetes of the next generation found much to disdain in its topographically independent plan. Lord Cockburn disliked the unthinking stamp of a rational idea upon a natural landscape; and, for his London audience, the bitter expatriate Scot, Robert Mudie, decried it as a 'cold eternity of stone and lime'.[84] John Ruskin would eventually pace remorselessly along Queen Street counting 678 identical windows 'altogether devoid of any relief by decoration' as proof positive of the unnaturalness of the design.[85] Although the Second New Town enjoyed geometrical loosening in the gentle curves of Abercromby Place and Royal Circus, the transformation of Georgian Edinburgh occurred in the Third or Eastern New Town, which the Town Council initiated even though Charlotte Square remained unfinished.

Partly impelled by the need to regularise the principal entry from the east, it was the Council's second New Town project, running from the slopes of Calton Hill downwards. It hardly lent itself to the levelling and bridging that characterised Enlightenment urban planning in, say, Aberdeen. Yet the inspiration to break with precedent, by responding to the landscape rather than

FIGURE 2.9   Scotland's Acropolis: Thomas Hamilton's proposal of 1825 for Calton Hill.   *Royal Scottish Academy*

dominating it, came from William Stark – developed, after his death in 1813, by his former pupil William Playfair. The Council had followed its old pattern of holding a competition, then having the entries assessed; and Stark's recommendations were contained in his assessment of the competition designs. He elevated the values of landscape, contour, prospect and trees far above the seductions of geometry. 'Beauty of site will be found most probably a vendible commodity', whereas the beauties of a symmetrical geometric plan were more difficult to perceive on the ground.[86] The principal consequence was Royal Terrace – architecturally the single grandest phenomenon of New Town Edinburgh with a strictly controlled architecture to match, well worthy of its outstanding view over Leith to the sea.

The liberating geometry of the eastern New Town probably enabled James Gillespie Graham's sequence of polygon, ellipse and crescent for the Moray Estate axially focused upon Moray's house, then sited in front of Randolph Crescent Gardens. Yet, ironically, the Moray estate turns its back upon nature to create an intensely urban experience (providing an equally intense romantic experience only from the rear windows to the north). Moreover, in two specific ways, it was a masterly fusion of the old and the new worlds. Accommodation was in an invisible mixture of (Scottish) tenement flats and (English) terraced houses, and the streets were so aligned as to inhibit the wind from howling through. It still encloses the most sheltered spaces of classical Edinburgh.

A classical building site

One of the penalties of living in a town undergoing major construction over eighty years is that *their* experience of incompleteness and uncertainty is entirely at odds with *our* perceptions of a grand plan magnificently executed. Observing the twenty-year-old skeleton of a half-built university in 1806, James Stark concluded that

> The Scottish national character is vanity . . . most conspicuous in the public buildings. When forming the plans of many of these, it was on a scale of magnitude which the poverty of the country prevented them from executing . . . the

FIGURE 2.10   Thomas Hamilton's elevation of the east side of the West and Upper Bows prior to demolition and replacement by Victoria Street.   *RIAS*

small part built of the new university stands an immense ruin, a monument to vanity of which poverty has prevented the completion.[87]

For many decades – as the 1791 sketch by Major-General John Brown illustrates – purchasers of Princes Street property were facing a large mud-hole with dead dogs,[88] and it was not until the second decade of the 19th century – fifty years after the beginning of Princes Street – that the Mound began to acquire its present dignity.[89]

It must have been less like polite living than a noisy, dirty building site, where you ran the risk of losing the prospect from your windows. Thomas Carlyle moved lodgings because his ratiocination had been so disturbed by the noise of building work next door. Scott observed ruefully in his *Journal* how the smoke from the increasing chimneys of the later New Towns downhill from his Castle Street house was turning the air thick with yellow fog.[90] Ramsay of Ochtertyre advised his friend 'while south sea prices continue, sell your house [in St Andrew Square] and buy one in some of the new streets, where if you have a less elevated view, there is little chance of having it extinguished or contracted'.[91] But the real gauge is how long it took to build. Charlotte Square was almost thirty years a-building; and, in the grandiose, terraced

Great Stuart Street, two stances lay vacant for over twenty years after the rest of the street had been occupied. Greater delay in the completion of the corners of St Colme and Glenfinlas Streets with Ainslie Place was the consequence of significant errors in the layout discovered in 1831. Threats of lawsuits between Moray's Commissioners and the architect James Gillespie Graham led to the architect having to buy the disputed feus himself (albeit the Earl waived four years' feu duty) and build what he could.[92] Only one of the seven properties was developed before Graham's death in 1855.[93] One consequence of perpetual non-completion was vividly illustrated by Scott in November 1825: 'I had a bad fall last night coming home. There were unfinished houses at the east end of Atholl Place, and as I was on foot, I crossed the street to avoid the material which lay about; but, deceived by the moonlight, I stepped ankle deep in a sea of mud . . . and fell on my hands . . . I was absolutely rough-cast.'[94]

Modernising the Old Town

The improvers had not sought to replace the Old Town. They desired, instead, to make it more accessible, more fashionable, and adorned with the civic monuments expected of a major mid-18th-century city. The creation of the North and

South Bridges, Hunter Square and Blair Street, the creation of Bank Street, the demolition of ancient structures like the Black Turnpike in 1788[95] and the construction of new apartments around the fashionable coffee-house quarter by the Exchange (now occupied by the City Council) were aspects of the Old Town's modernisation. But those professional and well-to-do people destined to occupy new town houses – and those who serviced them – had to come from somewhere; and the Old Town began to haemorrhage population from the late 1780s. By the 1820s, even respectable families of the middle class had quit, although there were still 'some first rate shops in the old town but these are gradually moving off to the northwards'.[96] The loss of the old city's social cachet was so complete that even the stonemason, Hugh Miller, who came to Edinburgh in 1841 insufficiently wealthy to live in the New Town, opted to live in cheaper accommodation just off Lauriston Place rather than in the Old Town. The last persons of quality to quit – Governor Fergusson of Pitfour and his brother – had held a valedictory party in their luckenbooths apartment twenty-two years earlier, whereafter 'the veil had rent and the lintol crack'd'.[97]

The Old Town's character changed. The luckenbooths were cleared, Archibald Elliot's 1819 Midlothian County Hall replaced the demolished Tolbooth, and the weigh house was removed for George IV's visit in 1822. Robert Reid's 1808 refacing of Sir James Murray of Kilbaberton's Parliament House turned the once thronged Parliament Square into a virtual private enclave for lawyers. Opportunity was taken of a series of fires – culminating in the great fires of June and November 1824 – to rebuild the tenements, and then to propose 'the most magnificent series of improvements ever planned for the advantage and embellishment of our northern metropolis'.[98] Two new bridges south over the Cowgate – one from Parliament Square[99] and the other south from Bank Street – would open up the High Street from the south, and two new roads – the first up the Castle Hill itself, and the second from the Grassmarket up to the new Bridge – would open it up from the west. A crescent from Parliament Square was to curve into the High Street by Old Assembly Close.

FIGURE 2.11   View today of Victoria Street.   *Charles McKean*

The Lawnmarket was to be lowered by at least 20 feet and 'the ugly range of old buildings' on its north removed. It could be said that, in the seventy years from 1752, all traces of distinctiveness were being systematically eliminated from the Old Town.

The adopted slimmed-down plan by Thomas Hamilton destroyed the West Bow, lowered the Lawnmarket, smashed Johnston Terrace through into Castlehill, and created Victoria Street and George IV Bridge. Among the losses were Robert Gourlay's great house behind the Lawnmarket, the Upper Bow, much of the Cowgate and Johnny Dowie's tavern in Libberton's Wynd. In one of Scotland's first exercises in homage to heritage, Hamilton prepared detailed elevational records of the buildings he was removing in the West Bow.[100]

FIGURE 2.12   The Mound, c. 1870, showing the city ennobled by its temples to the arts.   *RIAS*

FIGURE 2.13   Waterloo Place, c. 1910, the gateway to Princes Street from the east.   *Charles McKean*

Had it not been for its continued occupation by the Scottish legal profession, the Old Town of Edinburgh might have vanished as completely as Glasgow's High Street. Its survival was assisted by a growing antiquarianism and by the evolution of a new role as the setting for Scotland's romantically tragic myths, and a picturesque backdrop and a primitive counterbalance to the classical regularities of the New Town. The contrast was symbolised in Alexander Naismith's painting of its craggy skyline under an appropriately savage sky, contrasted with the regularities of the New Town bathed in golden Attic sunshine. This was the contrast also enjoyed by the German architect Schinkel in 1822. This all suggests that, by the early 19th century, the Old Town had become a thing to view from the handsome promenade of Princes Street rather than a place in which to live.

Modern Athens

The New Town's new role as New Edinburgh, or substitute city, presented some difficulties, since the principal monuments of a capital city – the principal church, law courts, town hall, exchange and university – all lay behind in the Old Town, and there were no plans to move them. Moreover, the New Town's plan and buildings were those of an overblown suburb; and its streets, being designed for parade and suburban intercourse rather than for commerce, were too wide, too narrow or too short to make efficient shopping parades. There were no civic monuments and no urban meeting spaces. Indeed, the only empty space for the construction of new civic monuments lay around its rim: on Calton Hill and – particularly – on the Mound.

Coincidentally, the artist Hugh 'Grecian' Williams[101] painted the resemblance between Athens on the Gulf of Corinth, and Edinburgh on the Firth of Forth; and Edinburgh began to acquire the sobriquet 'Athens of the North', or 'Modern Athens', during the first decade of the 19th century.[102] For this child of the Enlightenment, it was apposite that its principal civic monuments celebrated not power or religion but ancient intellectual values – an observatory, classical tombs to a poet, mathematician and two philosophers, a

FIGURE 2.14   The Mound, showing planned contrast between the classical and medieval worlds.   *Charles McKean*

Valhalla to the memory of the Glorious Dead, a high school for the instruction of youth, a government institution dedicated to a drawing school and to a museum, and an art gallery. No other city in the world could boast of a comparably cultural collection, nor of such homogeneity in their architecture. Save the imposing High School and Burns Monument by Thomas Hamilton, and the proposed (but abortive) triumphal arch at the west end of Princes Street by Gillespie Graham, they all displayed the hand of William Playfair.

For all its glory, New Edinburgh never became a substitute city, since the legal, administrative and religious motors remained behind in the Old Town. Neither town was self-sustaining or self-contained, and the split between them acted

FIGURE 2.15   View of Edinburgh, c. 1880, showing the picturesque skyline of the Old Town above the rooftops of Charlotte Square.   *Edinburgh World Heritage Trust*

against their economic potential. The vision of a blessed conjunction between an ancient city and an enormous neo-classical city gave considerable aesthetic pleasure, but it masked fundamentally damaging economic and social divisions.

Conclusion

The two agendas for Edinburgh in 1752 had been the improvement and appropriate aggrandisement of the Old Town, and the creation of an urban exemplar symbolic of the Union. During the following thirty-five years, the Old Town gradually improved, and the New Town slowly expanded. It was a period of equilibrium. But, since the desired aristocrats never returned to occupy the New Town, its survival came to depend upon attracting those professional classes originally intended to stay in the Old Town. Once the Mound had opened in 1787, and feuars failed to prevent commerce from invading the residential suburb, the flood northwards became unstoppable.

The modernists – Drummond, Robertson, Fergusson, Adam, Carlyle, Home, Smith, Blair and Elliot – would probably have been delighted that their concept of North British living should attain

international recognition as the 'Athens of the North'. More extensive than Bristol or Bath, more coherent even than London, more British than the British, Edinburgh boasted of wide streets of dignified houses (or classically disguised tenements), with primacy given to churches and buildings of culture and intellect. They might have found the move of commerce to the New Town irrational (in that the physical plan was unsuited to such activity, and it would erode the intended social distinctions), but would have accepted it. The improvers might have lamented the loss of Scottish living patterns and then of the Old Town itself, but then been reassured by the subtle assimilation of Scottish and English ideas exemplified in the later New Towns.

But there had been a large element of luck. Through their failure to complete the first New Town with clarity, vigour and expedition, the city fathers lost the initiative, which passed to the private estates. Moreover, essential features of the New Town concept were cheerfully discarded more on less on whim, with little thought for the impact that they might have upon either the New or the Old Town; and the latter came perilously close to accidental death. Yet, even though the New Towns of Edinburgh were the product of accident, chance and commercial opportunity rather than of a grand plan consistently pursued, they achieved a unique and serene classical consistency – a result achieved not through planning but through feuing controls. Perhaps the greatest lesson of all is that though the city fathers proposed, the people disposed. Those who conceived New Edinburgh had a clear but narrow vision, and the inhabitants found the means to broaden it. *C'est tout.*

Notes

1. A. J. Youngson, *The Making of Classical Edinburgh* (Edinburgh, 1966), p. v.
2. R. Rodger, *The Transformation of Edinburgh* (Cambridge, 2001).
3. Youngson, *Classical Edinburgh*, p. 20.
4. R. Chambers, *Walks in Edinburgh* (1825), p. 117.
5. John Taylor, *A Journey to Edenborough in 1705* (Edinburgh, 1903), p. 134. See also R. Houston, 'Fire and filth', *BOEC* New Series, 3 (Edinburgh, 1994).
6. T. Smollett, *The Expedition of Humphrey Clinker* (London, n.d.), vol. 2, p. 60.
7. T. Pennant, *A Tour in Scotland 1769* (London, 1776), p. 62.
8. F. C. Mears and J. Russell, 'The New Town of Edinburgh', *BOEC*, (1939), p. 169.
9. J. Gilhooley, *A Directory of Edinburgh in 1752* (Edinburgh, 1988).
10. I. Mowat, 'Adam Square', *BOEC* New Series, 5 (2002).
11. *Autobiography of Dr Alexander Carlyle*, ed. J. H. Burton (Edinburgh, 1910), pp. 121–5.
12. R. B. Sher, *Church and University in the Scottish Enlightenment* (Edinburgh, 1985), defines the Enlightenment as 'the culture of the literati' (p. 8); this chapter prefers 'a way of doing things'.
13. With a membership of 666, the Revolution Club was not an ordinary Enlightenment Club. Edinburgh University Library Special Collections, DC 8.37 (thanks to Bob Harris for the transcription).
14. Chambers, *Traditions of Edinburgh* (Edinburgh, 1825), vol. 11, p. 89.
15. Carlyle, *Autobiography*, p. 288.
16. Webster produced Scotland's first parish census in 1755.
17. Carlyle, *Autobiography*, p. 252.
18. T. Somerville, *My Own Life and Times* (Edinburgh, 1861), p. 104.
19. *PROPOSALS For carrying on certain PUBLIC WORKS In the CITY of EDINBURGH* (Edinburgh, 1752).
20. Ibid., p. 12.
21. Ibid., p. 14.
22. Ibid., p. 23.
23. Brian Bonneyman's suggestion.
24. *Proposals*, p. 31.
25. Ibid., p. 32.
26. *Burt's Letters from the North of Scotland*, ed. R. Jamieson (repr. Edinburgh, 1978), p. 22.
27. *Proposals*, pp. 31–2.
28. Cosh, *Edinburgh in the Golden Age* (Edinburgh, 2003), p. 112.
29. Ranald MacInnes considers it early Robert Adam ('Robert Adam's public buildings', *Architectural Heritage*, 4), but Ian Mowat sees no reason to believe it is not John's: 'Adam Square', *BOEC* New Series, 5.
30. Chambers, *Reekiana: Minor Antiquities of Edinburgh* (Edinburgh, 1833), vol. 1, p. 24.
31. [Sir David Dalrymple] *Proposals for carrying on certain PUBLIC WORK In the CITY of EDINBURGH* (Edinburgh, c. 1752), p. 4.
32. Bishop R. Pococke, *Tours in Scotland 1747, 1750, 1760* (Edinburgh, 1887), p. 306.
33. Somerville, *Life and Times*, pp. 47–8.
34. C. Cruft, 'James Craig, 1739–1795: correction of his date of birth', *BOEC* New Series, 5.
35. First observed by M. K. Meade, 'Plans of the New Town of Edinburgh', *Architectural History*, 14 (London, 1971), pp. 40–52, analysed by Stuart Harris, 'New light on the first New Town', *BOEC* New Series, 2 (1992) and A. Fraser, 'A re-assessment of Craig's New Town plans 1766–1774'.
36. The rectified plan was produced by William Mylne. See Fraser, 'Re-assessment'; A. Lewis, 'Works and projects by James Craig', *BOEC* New Series, 5.
37. See A. Broadie, *The Scottish Enlightenment* (Edinburgh, 2001), chapters 3 and 6.
38. R. Porter, 'Enlightenment', in *Britain and the Creation of the Modern World* (London, 2000) p. 195.
39. William Mylne's principal street was some way down the southern slope: A. Lewis, 'Works and projects', *BOEC* New Series, 5.
40. P. Reed, 'Form and context: a study of Georgian Edinburgh', in T. A. Markus (ed.), *Order in Space and Society* (Edinburgh, 1982), pp. 123–4, suggests erroneously that Craig envisaged his town as part of some 'infinitely extensible network'.
41. D. Lockhart, 'The evolution of the planned villages of North-East Scotland: studies in settlement geography, c.1700–c.1900', unpublished PhD thesis, University of

Dundee (1974); P. Nuttgens, 'The planned villages of North-east Scotland', in W. A. Brogden (ed.), *The Neo-classical Town* (Edinburgh, 1996).

42. March 1766 plan of the ground from the Bodleian Library, reproduced in *BOEC*, 23 (1941).

43. This had been required by the Council ordinance of 1652, and seems not yet to have been repealed.

44. W. A. Brogden, *Aberdeen: An Illustrated Architectural Guide* (Edinburgh, 1986), p. 39.

45. See A. A. Tait, *Robert Adam – the Creative Mind* (London, 1996), p. 37: Soane Museum, vol. 9/56. Also A. A. Tait, *Robert Adam – Drawings and Imagination* (Cambridge, 1993), pp. 43–5. I am much indebted to Stephen Astley.

46. Quoted in F. C. Mears and J. Russell, 'The New Town of Edinburgh (continued)', in *BOEC*, 23 (1941), pp. 13–14.

47. Chambers, *Traditions*, vol. l, p. 65.

48. Act of Town Council of Edinburgh, 24 February 1768.

49. Town Council Minutes, 29 July 1767, cited in P. Reed, 'Form and context'.

50. See I. G. Brown and A. Lewis, 'David Allan's portrait of James Craig', in K. Cruft and A. Fraser, (eds), *James Craig, 1744–1795* (Edinburgh, 1995).

51. Rodger, *Transformation,* chapter 2.

52. Even the feuing conditions for Dundee's Tay Street in 1793 had these stipulations.

53. *Copy Restrictions as to Buildings in the New Town of Glasgow* held in Aberdeen, New Street Trustees NSET/4/12. Undated, but c. 1780s.

54. ACT OF COUNCIL containing RULES with regard to FEUING OUT the GROUND of the EXTENDED ROYALTY of the City of EDINBURGH and regulating the MANNER of BUILDING, etc. (29 June 1785). See also the Act with regard to ELEVATIONS OF HOUSES in the NEW EXTENDED ROYALTY (15 September 1784).

55. Thomas Pennant, *A Tour in Scotland 1769* (London, 1776), p. 68.

56. Chambers, *Traditions*, vol. l, pp. 49–52. The New Town engendered a growth in snobbery: viz. the description of James Hogg's visit to Walter Scott in Castle Street in Lockhart's *Biography*, or Elizabeth Grant of Rothiemurchus' description of Scott's wife in *Memoirs of a Highland Lady*.

57. *Letters of John Ramsay of Ochtertyre*, p. 123.

58. *Diary of George Sandy, Apprentice WS*, ed. C. A. Malcolm (Edinburgh, 1943), refers to 'the area marked out for Charlotte Square', p. 45.

59. Scott loathed this (Chambers, *Traditions*, vol. 1, p. 61): he called it an 'enormous deformity'. In November 1782, the Council had decreed that rubbish and spoil were to be placed there.

60. Chambers, *Walks*, pp. 37–8; M. Cosh, *Edinburgh*, p. 101. The streams feeding the Nor' Loch were culverted in brick-lined tunnels.

61. Register of Sasines, Midlothian: PR 247140, 17.5.71.

62. Ibid., PR 17177, 19.1.81.

63. I. G. Brown, 'An East Anglian visitor's report of 1790', *BOEC* New Series, 4 (1997), pp. 113–18.

64. Reprinted in *BOEC*, 23.

65. E. Topham, *Letters from Edinburgh* (London, 1776), pp. 12–13.

66. Chambers, *Traditions*, vol. 1, p. 76.

67. Register of Sasines, Midlothian: Tenement in Princes Street disponed before completion by Alexander Reid to Laurence Hill on 20 September, to W. Bethune on 21st January 1785, David Reid the following August, and J. Russell WS in September (when we might suppose it was occupiable): 1062 PR 820–180, 1151, 1231 PR285.68, 1483 PR 291 214, 1512, PR 292 162.

68. See Peter Robinson, 'The tenement story', unpublished PhD thesis, Strathclyde University (1986).

69. Rodger, *Transformation*, p. 62; for Charlotte Square, see NTS, '26–31 Charlotte Square: Ownership History', 1999.

70. Cited in Youngson, *Classical Edinburgh*, p. 101.

71. W. Creech, *Letters addressed to Sir John Sinclair respecting the Mode of Living, Arts, Commerce, Literature, Manners etc. of Edinburgh* (Edinburgh, 1793), p. 6.

72. NLS Map Library, Inv. TS 3.

73. C. Byrom, 'The Development of Edinburgh's Second New Town', *BOEC* New Series, 3 (1994), pp. 37–62.

74. Anon., 'Extracts from an Edinburgh Journal', *BOEC*, 29 (1956).

75. Chambers, *Traditions*. The name is commemorated in St David's Street.

76. Chambers, *Walks*, pp. 32–3; also p. 184. Cosh, Edinburgh, p. 19.

77. Chambers, *Traditions*, vol. 1, pp. 65–6.

78. Chambers, *Walks*, p. 200.

79. Ibid., p. 199.

80. A. Mitchell, *No More Corncraiks* (Edinburgh, 1998).

81. Ibid.

82. Extracted from ibid.

83. Youngson, *Classical Edinburgh*, p. 237.

84. The disenchanted, disenfranchised Dundonian in exile, R. Mudie, *Modern Athens* (London, 1825), p. 319, had presumably written to subvert the sycophancy of his *His Majesty's Visit to Scotland* (Edinburgh, 1822).

85. John Ruskin, *Lectures in Architecture and Painting*, delivered in 1853 (London, 1907), p. 6.

86. William Stark, *Report . . . on the Plans for laying out the Grounds for Buildings between Edinburgh and Leith* (Edinburgh, 1814).

87. J. Stark, *Picture of Edinburgh* (Edinburgh, 1806), p. 436.

88. NLS MS 8026 f.53 (Courtesy of Dr Iain Brown).

89. Chambers, *Reekiana*, vol. l, p. 312.

90. *Journal of Sir Walter Scott 1825–32* (Edinburgh, 1927), p. 342, 18 January 1827.

91. Ramsay, *Letters*, p. 86.

92. NAS GD314/582: letter to Gillespie Graham, 18th November 1836.

93. Based upon the feuing lists in *Corncraiks*.

94. Scott, *Diary*, pp. 17–18.

95. Ibid.

96. Anon., 'Extracts', p. 166.

97. Chambers, *Traditions*, vol. 1, p. 312.

98. Chambers, *Walks*, p. 263.

99. Ibid., p. 265.

100. Published in the *Transactions of the Architectural Institute of Scotland*.

101. An examination of Stuart and Revett's *Antiquities of Greece* does not reveal the comparison to originate from James Stuart.

102. The title inflamed Londoners: see Mudie's vitriolic *Modern Athens* and Thomas Love Peacock's *Crotchet Castle*.

3 *Landscape, topography and hydrology*

John Stuart-Murray

Authors through the ages have been moved to write about Edinburgh's distinctive urban profile. For MacDiarmid, in his poem 'Edinburgh Midnight', the city is 'a mad God's dream, fitful and dark . . . wildered by the Forth . . . cleaving to sombre heights . . . til stonily earth eyes eternity'. Less metaphysically, Scott's hero Marmion, approaching from the south, sees 'the huge castle . . . and all the steep slope down, whose ridgey back heaves the sky' as 'mine own romantic town'. Stevenson, however, is one the earliest writers to understand the importance of contrast afforded by context in any appreciation of the city's townscape. In his *Picturesque Notes*, he observes:

> The old town depends for much of its effect on the new quarters that lie around it, on the sufficiency of its situation, and on the hills that back it up. If you were to set it somewhere else by itself, it would look remarkably like Stirling in a bolder and loftier edition. The point is to see this embellished Stirling planted in the midst of a large, active, and fantastic modern city, for there the two react in a picturesque sense, and the one is the making of the other.[1]

Not surprisingly, the city has also provided both a fertile seedbed and empirical evidence for the emergence of many eminent geologists. Chief among these was James Hutton, who was born in Edinburgh in 1727 and is widely recognised as the founder of modern geology. When he wrote his *Theory of the Earth* in 1785, some geologists, known as Neptunians, believed that rocks like basalt, on which the castle sits, were formed by cold precipitation in primeval seas. Others like Hutton, who were called Plutonians, believed that such rocks had risen in molten state from the earth's interior

to solidify in its crust. He deduced this by observing the metamorphosing effects on carboniferous sediments by the intrusion of basalt sills at what became known as Hutton's Section below Salisbury Crags, in Holyrood Park.

This chapter will examine how the forces of both rock and water have shaped the city's form. It will analyse the effect that geomorphology and hydrology had and continue to have upon its patterns of space and building. Finally, it will assess how architectural and landscape architectural precedent have influenced some current developments and issues.

Geology

Several hundred million years ago, what is now Scotland's central belt lay below a shallow tropical sea between mountains to the north and south. Active erosion of these mountains, which were reduced to what we now know as the Highlands and the Southern Uplands, formed a fluvio-deltaic complex of continental scale. The area has been likened to the Gulf of Mexico today.[2] Sand and mud were deposited close to sea level. Limestone was laid down in clearer, deeper water where coral reefs accumulated. Forests developed on emerging sand and mudbanks. When these were flooded, the precursors of coal were buried. Thus the whole spectrum of carboniferous, sedimentary geology was slowly built up.

Igneous activity also occurred intermittently at this time. The Arthur's Seat volcano was small in comparison to Mauna Loa in Hawaii, which rises 10,000m above the sea bed and is 300km in diameter. When active, Edinburgh's volcano was about 450m high and 5km in diameter. At first, it erupted below water. In time, however, the cone emerged above sea level, and fossil remains interspersed between ash and agglomerate deposits show that it was colonised by plants between its thirteen eruptions. Upon extinction, the volcano was buried under subsequent depositions of shale sediments, uplifted above sea level and tilted 25 degrees to the east, which prompted erosion and re-exposure of its cone. Faulting dispersed the cone into the fragments of the Castle Rock and Calton Hill we see today and allowed the later intrusion of dolerite sills such as Salisbury Crags.

Geomorphology

Stevenson compared the Castle Rock to 'a Bass Rock upon dry land'.[3] For, despite its small stature, Edinburgh's igneous, miniature mountain landscape is striking in profile. It has been made so by glaciation. Indeed, such an argument could be made for much of Scotland's glacially reduced mountain landscape.

Between two million and 12,000 years ago, northern Europe was subject to periods of glaciation. During the last ice age, major glaciers formed in the north and west of Scotland, where precipitation was and still is higher, and flowed south and east, as most of the country's major rivers still do. Moving ice moulded the surface geology according to the directions of its flow and the resistance of the rock types it encountered. In Edinburgh, ice moved from west to east, and the vicinity of the city provides many examples of resultant crag-and-tail landforms such as Salisbury Crags, Craiglockhart Hill, Calton Hill and Blackford Hill. Perhaps the most renowned in geological literature, however, is that which supports the castle on its crag and the 'ridgey' Old Town on its tail.

Here, ice moving from the west was diverted around either side of the hard dolerite crag and excavated hollows to its north, west and south. Allowing for the accumulation of loch deposits, peat and rubbish, it has been estimated that over-deepening occurred to a depth of at least 65m. To the east, softer carboniferous sediments were protected from glacial erosion by the harder igneous rock and formed a tail extending eastwards for one mile in length. Some writers have mistakenly assumed the tail to consist solely of glacial debris. While this may be so to some extent at its Holyrood

terminus, borehole studies have shown otherwise.[4] Indeed, the junction between igneous and sedimentary rock can be seen just inside the castle portcullis. To the north-west, the cliffs below the castle show glacial grooving and striae, while the uneven bank below and to the north of the Esplanade, which has never been developed, has been over-steepened to such an extent that a landslip has taken place. It has been estimated that 105m of rock was removed from the Castle crag, which is now 138m above sea level.

As Stevenson noted, Stirling provides another example of a town built upon a crag-and-tail formation. Here, however, the direction of ice movement created a landform with a more north-south orientation. Elsewhere, and in the absence of protective dolerite, the ice-moulded landscape is more gentle and rolling, but no less influential on city development. Across the Waverley Valley, for example, a series of drumlin ridges almost a mile in length was formed. To the south of the Meadows, which once was the site of a shallow glacial loch, a series of gentle yet long drumlin ridges runs from west to east. Indeed, most of urban Marchmont is organised around the long west–east roads, which are aligned with these landforms.

Landscape, form and pattern

Arthur's Seat, Salisbury Crags, Calton and Dunsapie Hills all bear the outlines of prehistoric ramparts. The tail or east side of Arthur's Seat also once supported arable crops grown on cultivation terraces. Only upon the Castle crag and its tail, however, has human settlement lasted to the present day. The castle, on its volcanic plug, unassailable on three sides, formed a nucleus for the development of the original city down a tail of carboniferous sediments to the east. The limit of the walled city at the Nether Bow Port was determined by a slackening of gradient, where the High Street ends and the Canongate begins. This was the limit of King David's original burgh (see Chapter 1).

In 1385, there were still only 400 houses in the city. In the 16th century, however, population growth in Scotland was one of the highest in

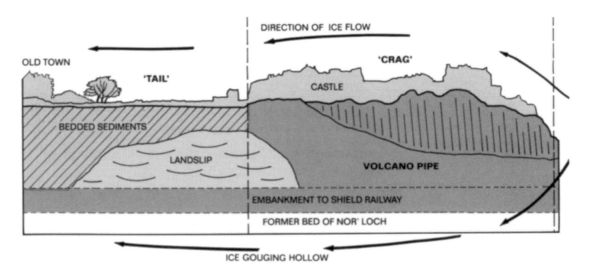

FIGURE 3.1   Section through crag and tail of Edinburgh.   *D. McAdam*

Europe and twice that of England. In quantitative terms, Edinburgh could now be compared to Norwich – England's largest provincial city.[5] Between the mid-16th and mid-17th centuries, the population more than doubled, rising to 20,000. However, the people were still contained within the original burgh bounds – an area of 54ha. Originally, the urban pattern of the Old Town was formed by burgage plots (8 x 150m long) set at right angles to the High Street. Initially, only the frontages of these plots were developed; but, as population density increased, so too were the backlands. Properties there were accessed by wynds or closes at intervals which often reflected original ownership boundaries. The urban pattern created by this process has prompted the habitual comparison of the Old Town to a fishbone, usually and fittingly a herring, with its head as the castle and its spine formed by the High Street and Canongate and the ribs by the many wynds running north and southwards either side of the glacially formed tail.

Such densities gave rise to some of the first pre-industrial tenement buildings. However, as overcrowding grew worse, so too did the problem of sanitation and waste disposal. Streets became open sewers at the shout of 'gardyloo' from a tene-

ment window (French – *gardez l'eau*) as night soil was tipped from upper floors into the narrow closes below. (*Gardyloo* was the name of the ship that dumped sewage into the River Forth until the mid-1990s.) Much of the filth slid off the ridge into the Nor' Loch. Many writers and visitors to the city over the ages commented on the conditions underfoot. The rich could travel in sedan chairs. A storage shed for these conveyances can still be seen in World's End Close. It was Daniel Defoe, however, whose hero Robinson Crusoe longed for an escape from barbarity to rationality, who anticipated the long-term solution to overcrowding in the Old Town and its attendant problems. He remarked that if the 'Lough' were filled in, the city could 'run out of its gates to the North' to the 'spacious, rich and pleasant plain' across the valley. Under Provost George Drummond in 1752, proposals were made 'to enlarge and beautify the town, by opening new streets to the north and south'. To facilitate this vision, what eventually proved to be the slow process of draining the Nor' Loch began, and the building of the North Bridge over its valley commenced in 1767. The route of the new bridge paralleled the line of the dam, which had contained the flow of the Tummel or Craig burn to form the Nor' Loch. This had been accomplished

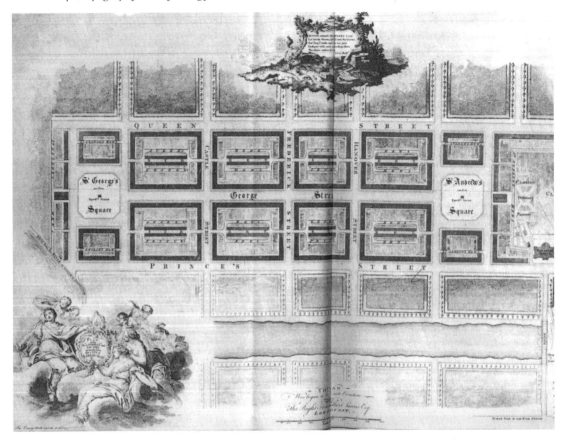

FIGURE 3.2 James Craig's competition plan for the New Town of Edinburgh, 1767. *RCAHMS*

as early as 1450 in order to add to the defences of the castle. The original South Loch in the Cowgate had been drained in the 15th century – so, when the South Bridge was constructed in 1788, it spanned a dry valley.

A competition for the layout of residential development to the north, in Barefoot's or Bearford's Parks, was held in 1766 and won by James Craig, an unknown Edinburgh architect. However, the plan originally submitted by Craig was not the design implemented subsequently. Walker considered that the 18th-century urban predilection of Scotland was for a disciplined classical arrangement of grid and tripartition.[6] Indeed, McKean has pointed out that such designs already existed for several towns in north-east Scotland, such as at Keith in 1750, Aberchirder in 1760 and

Strichen in 1764.[7] It may be that Craig was also aware of precedents for axial layouts terminated by squares in the design of the French towns of Nancy or Richelieu. He may also have known the one-sidedness of Royal Crescent in Bath opening out on to views over a valley to the south. However, as Walker[8] also argues, idealised abstractions of neo-classical form can only take material form in the unique topographical context of a particular place. Whatever the precedents, native or mainland European, this species of design had never been seen on such a scale before in the UK. Neither had a site been so well used.

George Street, the main and central axis of the three axes about which the first New Town is disposed, lies on the approximate line of the Lang Dykes, a walled track which ran along the length of a rolling drumlin ridge whose form was as much the product of west–east ice movement as the Old Town's crag and tail. To the north and south, Queen Street and Princes Street were defined by open spaces and the more distant panoramas that these allow, to Fife across the Firth of Forth and to the castle across the valley of the Nor' Loch. Like a good landscape architect today, Craig, in the adopted plan, looked beyond the boundaries of his competition brief and accommodated the borrowed landscape of the context. Thus, New and Old Towns are visually conjoined, but physically separate. Craig's plan has attracted criticism on several counts, however.

Firstly, Youngson[9] and Whyte[10] have both criticised the adopted plan for its failure to connect axially with the line of the North Bridge, which was already under construction. They also point out that the line of the then Queensferry Road created an awkward relationship with Charlotte Square. In both cases, however, it can be argued that Craig was aiming for as complete a consistency of his plan with landform as possible. For, to the east of St Andrew's Square and to the west of Charlotte Square, the drumlin ridge of the Lang Dykes begins to fall away.

Whyte also argues that Craig's New Town was a self-contained upper middle-class suburb which did not allow for expansion, as evidenced by the lack of access to east and west from its two main squares.[11] However, the architect Robert Reid easily expanded the town to the north, in a second orchestration of grid and tripartite form, terminated by the two squares of Royal Circus and Drummond Place. Moreover, this form represented by Reid's Second New Town was again simply added to by James Gillespie Graham on the Earl of Moray's estate to the north-west of Charlotte Square. In contrast, this development took the form of an axial arrangement of 'duodecagon, oval and crescent at once linear and introspective', as Walker puts it.[12] As in Queen Street Gardens, open spaces took up the levels of the sloping site, and distant views to the valley of the Water of Leith were retained by restrictions on building height. Indeed, Walker argues that the great charm of the various phases of developments

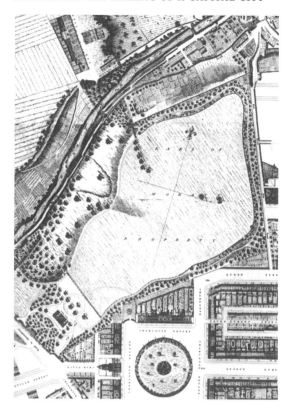

FIGURE 3.3   Plan of the Earl of Moray's estate before designs by James Gillespie Graham.   *RCAHMS*

in the New Town is that they are a succession of domains each with its own path and focus, skilfully stitched together at the edges.[13]

More fundamentally, in 1814 the architect William Stark, referring to Craig's plan in his *Report on the Plans for laying out the grounds for Buildings between Edinburgh and Leith*, thought that it was attractive on paper but monotonous in reality. He considered that scenic values were of greater importance than symmetry. Although he recommended that streets should follow natural contours, he failed to recognise that Craig's layout achieves precisely this. More generally, Stark argued for a combination of trees and architecture. Trees, he considered, should be used to adorn townscape and give a picturesque effect. In contrast, Craig's drawings depict the open spaces of the plan as hard continental piazzas with statues as focal points and devoid of subsequent picturesque embellishments.[14] William Playfair, of course, developed Calton Hill in 1813 according to picturesque principles set out by his mentor Stark. Stark considered the Hill to be 'a leading feature in the general scenery of Edinburgh . . . affording a succession of the most splendid and diversified views that are assembled in the vicinity of any fine city . . .'. There is no doubt that the unrivalled collection of monuments and the dominance of space between them provides as distinctive a skyline as the Castle rock.

The landscape style of the New Town spaces

Whether it is an apocryphal story or not, it is significant that, as a child, Robert Louis Stevenson played with a model boat on the pond in the middle section of Queen Street Gardens and was later inspired to write his romantic tale of *Treasure Island*. It is also significant that the functional farm pond of Mr Wood's steading was informally reshaped and an island added on its incorporation into the Gardens.

Rather than reflecting the architectonic form of the New Town that surrounds it, as Robert Chambers observed in 1825 in his *Walks in Edinburgh*, the gardens are laid out in the landscape style, with labyrinthine walks. Their atmosphere of romantic mystery is further heightened by the almost complete absence of views in or out. The same style applies to Moray Place, Princes Street Gardens and George Square in the Southside. Unlike in London or Paris, Edinburgh's squares departed from plan and developed into gardens of informal character with an atmosphere of Palladian rural retreat.[15] They became a scene of *rus in urbe*, with idealised nature sweeping up the thresholds of Georgian architecture. It is significant, although nothing remains of his work, that William Sawrey Gilpin, a nephew of William Gilpin, well-known writer on the Picturesque movement, was commissioned to produce plans and a model for Princes Street Gardens East.

While it would be invidious to employ stylistic preference as a means of analysis, it could be argued that the city's picturesque spaces are most successful when set in landscapes which are dominated by geological and geomorphological features, such as on the basalt rock of Calton Hill or in the river gorge of Dean Gardens. In the absence of such fundamental defining elements, an oasis of informality set in a context of formality can only be successful if it is of sufficient size to sustain the delusion. Arguably, Princes Street Gardens in its hollow, out of sight of the street and dominated by the Castle Rock, achieves this, albeit at the expense of the natural axiality of the site. Paradoxically, the design of the Meadows, one of the largest spaces in the city, has ignored its potentially romantic antecedents of a tree-fringed glacial loch and opted for a formal layout of single, double and triple avenues based simply on direct circulation routes. As a result, the Meadows is composed of a series of interlocking triangular spaces originally developed for an international exhibition of science and industry in 1886, but now providing a series of fields for sport and circuses.

Hydrology, water supply and flooding

The Water of Leith, which flows north-eastwards for 35km from the Pentland Hills to the Firth of Forth at Leith, was too distant from the Old Town to be influential in its development. It was only the 30m-deep Dean Gorge, formed after post-glacial land uplift, which limited the expansion of the Third New Town development on the Earl of Moray's estate. Unlike London or Paris, Edinburgh is an unusual example of a pre-industrial settlement which has never had easy access to a navigable river. This has caused problems of both water supply and waste disposal for both industry and domestic purposes. The sheer density of the Old Town exacerbated these problems, although the city's climate also mitigated them.

However, in the 16th century, Edinburgh was set among expanses of water. A view from Corstorphine Hill would have shown the castle and the Old Town like a beached boat, keel up, set in the midst of several shallow, inland lochs, rather than the sea of suburbs we observe today. Only two of these lochs survive today, at Lochend and Duddingston. The latter, much reduced in area, once extended to Cameron Toll. At the foot of Corstorphine Hill, the eponymous village was

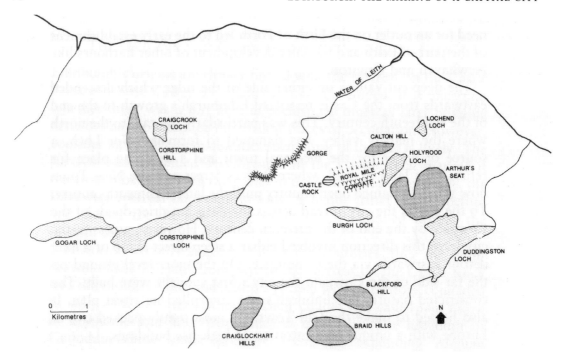

FIGURE 3.4   The site of Edinburgh and the adjoining landscape.   *Ian Whyte*

built on a strip of land between Corstorphine and Gogar Lochs. The former was the largest of the glacial water bodies remaining after the ice retreated, reaching 5km from Haymarket to Broomhouse across Roseburn and Murrayfield, and 1.2km wide from Corstorphine to Gorgie. It was fed by the Water of Leith, which now wanders across what is left off the alluvial floodplain reclaimed by the digging of drainage ditches between 1670 and 1763.

Its neighbour Gogar Loch was the last to be drained, in the late 18th century. It once extended from Corstorphine to what is now the City Bypass and was 2km long by 0.8km wide. In 1826 it consisted of 20ha of marsh still prone to periodic flooding, which in 1960 had shrunk to 12ha. The Gogar Burn was its source of water at a point where the Edinburgh Business Park has been built.

Holyrood Loch, in the glacial hollow at the foot of Salisbury Crags, covered an area between Meadowbank, Canongate and Abbeyhill. It was finally drained in the Middle Ages to create a

garden for the palace. Water came from springs issuing from Arthur's Seat, which also fed a small loch in Hunter's Bog. The much smaller and artificial St Margaret's Loch makes use of the same source.

Earlier still, in prehistoric times, lochs existed at Turnhouse, where the airport is sited, and to the south of Craigmillar Castle in the valley of the Burdiehouse Burn, where the new Edinburgh Royal Infirmary is now located. Only the Borough or South Loch, which inherited the name from a water body in the Cowgate and was drained in the Middle Ages, was used as a water supply for the Old Town. Once that use was superseded, it too was progressively drained between the mid-18th century and 1847 to form the Meadows.

Although its basalt crag provided the castle with a superb defensive site, as a rock type it contains no aquifers. As a consequence, those under siege often ran short of water, having to make an exposed descent to the Wellhouse Tower, at the foot of the rock where springs emerge. The Old Town, although it is built on permeable strata and despite being surrounded by glacial lochs and marshes in the 16th century, also suffered severe water shortages. At that time, most of its supply came from the Borough Loch. Like the Nor' Loch, it had a dam and sluice at its outflow, the Lochrin Burn, controlling water levels. Even so, extraction by brewers caused levels to fluctuate, and the watering of stock and washing of linen in a reduced water volume created a pollution risk. Sweet water was already being carried from springs in the Pentlands. The next step was to construct a 6km pipeline from Comiston in 1676. Water ran by gravity to a new reservoir at Castlehill (1681, rebuilt in 1851), which supplied five wells in the High Street and a further nine elsewhere in the Old Town. Edinburgh was one of the first towns in the UK to be provided for in this way. A cannonball in the west wall of Cannonball House marked the gravitation height inside the reservoir. Springs at Swanston were piped in 1760 from a small, suitably classical pump house in the form of a pavilion. With the growth of the New Town, however, demand rapidly outstripped what the springs could supply.

Although the Water of Leith was too distant to be influential in the city's development, its catchment was useful in the further exploitation of water supplies. The first reservoir was built in the Pentlands at Bonaly in 1785 and extended in 1853. It is paradoxical that, while from the Middle Ages to the end of the 18th century Edinburgh was draining its lochs, from then until the late 20th century it was creating artificial lochs to supply the increasing water requirements of an expanding conurbation. Moreover, new housing and industry has often been built on floodplains once covered by glacial water bodies.

The diminutive river also provided energy for industry. In the late 19th century, there were about eighty mills of various roles, such as papermaking, fulling and linen-making, which were reliant on waterpower. With so much water now being withdrawn from the catchment, this source of power became prejudiced. As a result, reservoirs which compensated for loss of river flow were built at Threipmuir in 1847 and Harlaw in 1848. Following a major drought in 1847, further drinking-water

reservoirs were also built at this time in the northern Pentlands, at Clubbiedean in 1850 and Torduff in 1851.

The growing demand for water meant that the city had to cast its net progressively wider to source catchments and hill ranges far-flung from its marches. On the eastern flank of the Pentlands, water destined for the River North Esk was first impounded at Glencorse in 1819 by one of the earliest earth dams of its type in Britain. Just upstream, Loganlea followed in 1847. Further afield, the headwaters of the River South Esk supplied new reservoirs in the Moorfoot Hills at Gladhouse, Roseberry and Portmore. Water from these was piped to another storage tank at Alnwickhill, which was built in 1876. Today however, only 5 per cent of Edinburgh's water supply comes directly from reservoirs within its boundaries. Most of the city's thirst is now slaked by the remote catchment of the upper Tweed, where three large reservoirs were built in the late 19th and 20th centuries, Talla (1895), Fruid (1968) and Megget (1981).

There are only two mills left on the Water of Leith, and neither makes use of waterpower. There is now no conflict, therefore, between the supply of drinking water and the supply of compensation water to industry. The role of the early reservoirs has changed from one of supply to one of ecology, scenery and recreation. They have in a sense come to resemble, in functional terms, St Margaret's and Dunsapie Lochs, designed by Prince Albert in 1856 as part of a beautification plan for Queen's Park, or the lochans designed by contemporary landscape architects at Edinburgh Park (see p. 75, Fig. 3.7) on the site of the Gogar Loch.

Today, growing urbanisation coupled with increased and more intense winter rainfall arising from global warming, now presents the city with a different challenge for the management of its hydrology. During the 20th century, the Water of Leith became more prone to flash floods. There were major floods during 1927 and 1948, and the largest ever was recorded in April 2000. In this last inundation, 112mm of rain fell over forty-eight hours, causing a one-in-200-year flood. The average monthly rainfall is 39mm. With flood

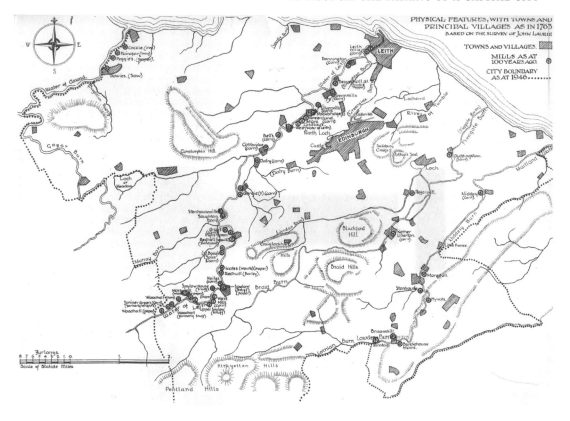

FIGURE 3.5   The Water of Leith: 19th-century mills.   *E. J. MacRae*

defences designed to withstand a one-in-fifty-year flood, the Braid Burn and the Water of Leith burst their banks. The latter rose to a maximum of 3m above normal levels. At one time, the rugby pitch at Murrayfield Stadium was under 1m of water. Around 150 people in Gorgie, Peffermill and Liberton had to be evacuated, and £14 million of damage was caused to 750 properties.

It is thought that by 2080, with a 20 per cent increase in rainfall, the equivalent of a one-in-eighty-year flood will occur every decade.[16] The pattern of individual floods has also changed. Hydrographs of floods now have two high points – an urban peak followed by a rural peak, reflecting more rapid run-off times from newly developed areas such as Wester Hailes and Baberton Mains. It is estimated that the City Bypass alone, with 2km of drain discharging into the Water of Leith, accounts for 2 per cent of the flow at Juniper Green.

After the waters receded in April 2000, the City Council recognised that it had no adequate flood-control policies in place.[17] It recognised that undeveloped floodplains were important as means of storing floodwater, and development on them should be discouraged. Indeed, in 2000, it was thought that flooding at Murrayfield, even though a rugby fixture the following day was nearly called off, prevented greater damage from occurring downstream. Flood studies of the Braid Burn and the Water of Leith were commissioned, and it is proposed that the levels of compensation reservoirs at Harlaw, Harperrig and Threipmuir should be permanently lowered.[18] Secondly, where watercourses habitually overflow their banks, flood-attenuation areas have been proposed in areas such as Roseburn Park, Saughton Cemetery and Murrayfield and elsewhere in the catchments of the Almond, the Water of Leith and the Braid and

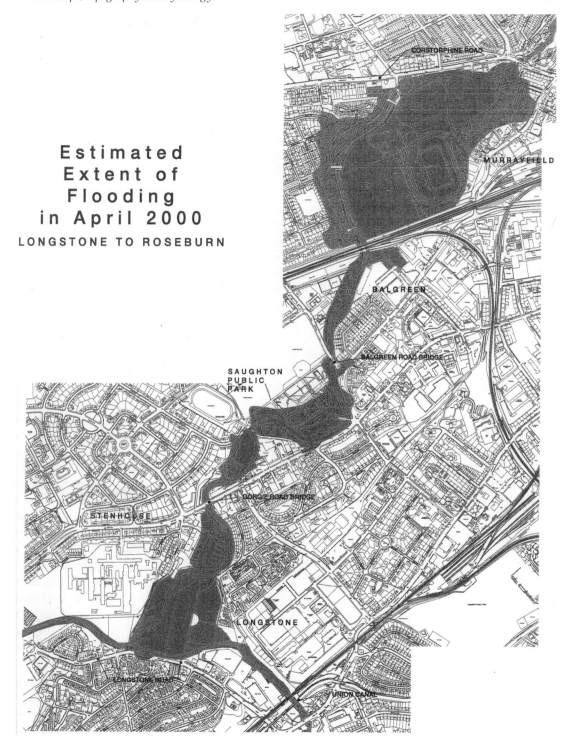

FIGURE 3.6   Estimated extent of April 2000 flooding.   *City of Edinburgh Council*

74

Gogar Burns. It is significant that many of the attenuation zones were in areas once occupied by drained glacial lochs. Thirdly, existing flood-prevention walls and bunds are to be increased in height and strength. However, it is intended to minimise the scale of engineering works by the efficient management of water levels in compensation reservoirs. The scheme is designed to withstand a one-in-200-year occurrence.

Many of the flood-attenuation areas are proposed on areas of existing open space. Currently, these consist of informal layouts of grass and trees, which are of little interest ecologically. Clearly, when such areas come to be inundated regularly, there is an opportunity to rethink the rather traditional approach to recreational provision. In so doing, their ecological value could be greatly enhanced. Grass and trees could be exchanged for water meadow, fen and alder carr. However, despite the recognition of the Water of Leith as a major ecological and recreational corridor, there has been little attempt to marry flood-prevention strategy with environmental management policies.

Recent developments

Edinburgh Park

This 57ha business-park development lies adjacent to the City Bypass, five miles to the west of the city centre. The scheme was master-planned by the American architect Richard Meier and Scottish landscape architect Ian White. They aimed for a different approach to the usual suburban business park with its campus style, which they criticised for its lack of cohesion between landscape and architecture. Instead, they sought to achieve a common, overarching identity by the consistent use of architectural form and materials.

Rather like Queen Street Gardens, landscape is concentrated in an urban context, which is aligned to take advantage of long-distance views – in this case, to the Pentlands to the south, rather than the coastline of Fife. The idea of open space shared by the different building-users also reflects the origin and spirit of gardens in the New Town. The importance of formal parkland is shown by the fact that it occupies approximately 10 per cent of the devel-

opment area, the same as that devoted to the pleasure gardens within the New Town Conservation Area. However, the development differs from other design aspects of the New Town in three important ways.

Firstly, the landscape architecture is modernist rather than romantic in character. Tree-planting is not decorative as recommended by Stark, but provides spatial structure and relates to circulation, infrastructure and functional demarcation. Individual trees set within blocks and avenues are spaced according to the same grid system as that used to organise the architecture. Indeed, many trees are genetically identical, so that differential growth in design elements such as avenues will not be visually disruptive. Here, there are no labyrinthine paths articulated by informal clumps of trees positioned to create mystery and surprise. Instead, a limited palette of species is planted for a purpose, rather than for their gardenesque qualities.

Secondly, Edinburgh Park has a very different relationship to landform than the New Town. It is not built on a drumlin ridge and aligned west-to-east. In contrast, it is built around the former valley of the Gogar Burn and Loch, and aligned north-to-south. Its western boundary is also enclosed by the man-made element of the City Bypass embankment. This alignment means that both architecture and structure-planting shelter the central parkland from prevailing south-west winds and traffic noise from the road, in contrast to the New Town, whose long axes invite the prevailing wind and caused Stevenson to term them 'draughty parallelograms'.[19] Also, rather like Craig's original proposal to canalise the Nor' Loch in Princes Street Gardens, the designers intended to dam the waters of the burn to create a series of formal descending lochans. Like the Nor' Loch, however, the Gogar Burn proved to be too polluted with effluent for this to be a success, and the supply for the water features now comes from distant reservoirs in Tweedsmuir.

Finally, the residents of this rational composition of architecture and communal parkland are office workers who commute to their place of work, rather than upper middle-class families and their servants. Indeed, this New Edinburgh,

FIGURE 3.7   Richard Meier's perspective sketch of proposals for Edinburgh Park (1989).   *Richard Meier and Partners*

like other peripheral developments such as the new Royal Infirmary at Little France, is only walkable within its own boundaries. Although it possesses its own domain with a path and focus, it is not stitched together with earlier, neighbouring industrial developments. Furthermore, it is not connected to the city centre by efficient public transport systems. In these terms, it can be likened to out-of-town shopping malls so prevalent in North American cities. As a result, congestion and pollution have grown measurably at the Bypass interchange of the Gyle. It may be, however, that such a large-scale removal of business from the city centre to the periphery encourages a reoccupation of residential property in the New Town.

Waverley Valley, Princes Street Gardens and the Playfair Galleries

It has been argued that a glacially formed west–east landform has been influential in the development of both the Old and New Towns of Edinburgh. The axes of their major streets are predominantly west-to-east. This is also true of open spaces such as the Meadows, Princes Street and Queen Street Gardens. However, with the construction of the North Bridge in 1767, the South Bridge in 1788 and the Mound, which started life as Geordie Boyd's Mud Brig with material excavated from foundations and cellars of houses in the New Town, a north–south orthogonal tension has been progressively introduced into the city.

In the Old Town, usage, particularly during the Festival, shows that the long, swelling, downhill-sloping, egg-timer shape of the Royal Mile Plaza[20] (as McKean puts it) has withstood the puncturing of its envelope from the north and south, even though the south aisle of the Tron Kirk has suffered a glancing blow. The same cannot be said for Princes Street Gardens and the rest of the Waverley Valley. Division of the East from the West Gardens by the Mound, later reinforced by the construction of Playfair's Royal Scottish Academy from 1822 to 1826 and the National Gallery in 1854, ensured their separate development. In the West Gardens, the siting of the Ross Concert Hall on the long axis and a diverse and amorphous replanting policy, which has obscured the original spatial structure, have further exacerbated the loss of west–east emphasis. A recent landscape management study[21] has recommended the removal of the concert hall and a return to clarity in the planting structure.

To the east of the Mound, the railway, which to the west is unobtrusive, widens and feeds into station platforms, which dominate the gardens. The station to the east of Waverley Bridge, and its associated car park and storage yards, completely fill the valley of the former Tummel Burn. It is not surprising, therefore, that in 1949 Abercrombie was the first to propose roofing it over to support lawns and terraced gardens.

Indeed, the City Council, in its tourism strategy of 2000, observed that 'Edinburgh has conquered the valley with bridges, railway tracks and station, and the Mound – the cumulative effect of which is to reduce the Old Town setting'.[22] They proposed that 'a green landscape should be developed to restore the original character of the valley space with the sense of visual separation between the Old Town and New Town being enhanced'. The proposal envisages an extension of the green valley eastwards as a garden deck over the station. However, while this might alter the colour of the valley in plan, it is difficult to see, without demolition, how the depth of the valley could be restored. This is substantial, and was made more so by the draining of the Nor' Loch. The eastern gardens are 9m below Princes Street and 17m below Market

Street. The western gardens, which were not subject to infilling with railway spoil, are deeper, 15m below Princes Street and 60m below the Castle Esplanade.

People-movement along the valley could, however, be facilitated, as Byrom[23] and McGowan[24] have suggested. Citing the Grand Parade in Bath as a UK precedent, Byrom proposes a 'Mediterranean paseo' along the line of what he calls the Mar/Craig axis. This would pass underneath the Mound and through the Playfair Gallery development and be aligned on a re-creation of Craig's canal. Byrom sees this new Nor' Loch as being more than merely a compositional element. It would also be linked to the city's sustainable urban drainage strategy. Both Byrom and McGowan propose a second pedestrian tunnel to the south of the National Gallery.

In the light of this new thinking, it is surprising, therefore, that the underground linking extension between the two Playfair Galleries by John Miller Architects, while including an entrance and glazed interface with the eastern gardens, does not match this with equivalent transparency to the west. It also does not tackle how the new interface might readdress the eastern gardens, which could have been remodelled to accommodate different and more intense functions.

Conclusion

The landscape architect Meto Vroom uses a model of three interacting layers to analyse landscape.[25] These three layers from base level upwards are: abiotic or physical, biotic, and finally the occupation pattern or cultural level. Layers in the model can articulate vertically, that is between layers; or horizontally, that is within any one layer. It can be argued that, as human society has moved from hunter-gatherer tribes to the global village of mass communications, occupation patterns have become less vertically determined by living and non-living processes and more horizontally driven by the physical expression of cultural activities. Human geography has superseded physical geography – or so we think. The modernist liking for universal rules and solutions would favour horizontal articulation, while the post-modernist,

FIGURE 3.8 Artist's impression of the Waverley Valley, Princes Street Gardens and the Playfair Galleries. *John Miller and Partners*

responding to the nature of place, would favour vertical articulation. There is of course no reason why both processes cannot occur simultaneously. However, it can be argued that the cultural layer is now so fragmentary that landscape evolution at this level has become increasingly disarticulated. Edinburgh offers very clear examples of the results of such processes.

The development of the castle and the Old Town provides a dramatic example of a vertically articulated response to geology and geomorphology. The necessary north–south connections, which stimulate an orthogonal tension with the west–

east axes, are examples of horizontal articulation at the cultural level. The New Town shows a subtler vertical articulation with geomorphology than the Old Town. At the same time, however, it also provides an example of horizontal articulation at the cultural level, by adopting an architectural style and urban design model which, like modernism today, in the 18th century could be said to be international. The New Town thus represents an adaptation of concept to context.

However, this marriage of form to physical or intellectual precedent is less evident in the subsequent evolution of the city. To the west of the city

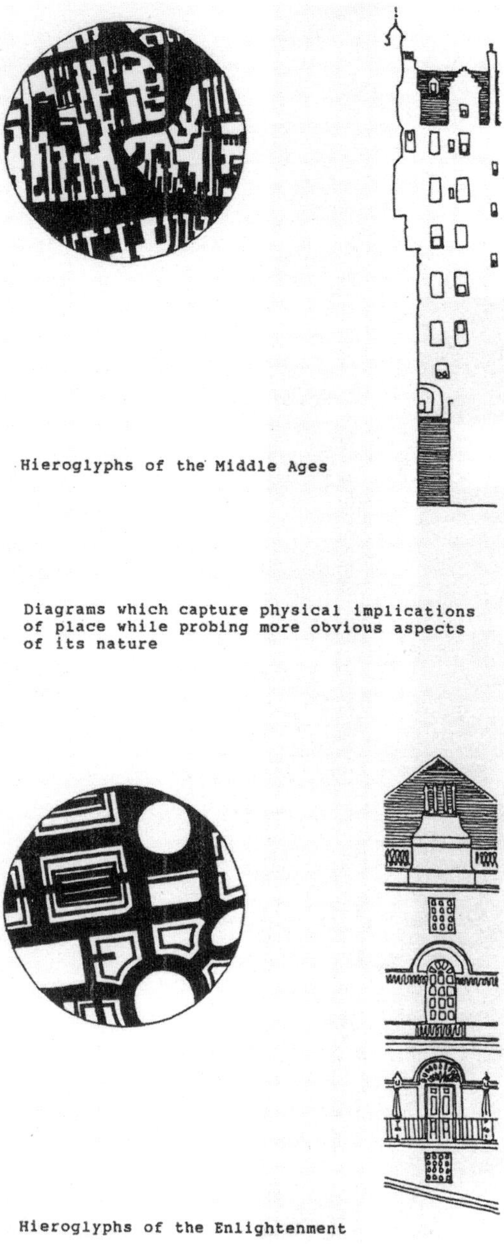

Hieroglyphs of the Middle Ages

Diagrams which capture physical implications
of place while probing more obvious aspects
of its nature

Hieroglyphs of the Enlightenment

FIGURE 3.9   Schemata of the medieval and
Enlightenment.   *A. MacAlistair*

centre, industrial and business development have
been a response to railway and canal transportation systems that enter the city from the central
belt. This represents fragmented horizontal articu-

lation at the cultural level. As one moves further
west, associations between built forms become
more incoherent in their contextual associations.
Witness the juxtaposition of the various forms, patterns and styles prevailing in Saughton, Sighthill,
Wester Hailes and the Gyle. McKean describes the
approach of the visitor from the west: 'They are
presented with a superabundance of supermar-
kets, bypasses and bungalows, tawdry industrial
estates, filling stations, brick rejects from Welwyn
Garden City, glass slabs and spotty construction'.[26]
Mischievously, he suggests: 'It was a subtle idea to
embody tawdriness in the outer stages of entry
into Edinburgh, so that a visitor's reaction when
the castle heaves in sight would be enhanced'.[27]

The influence of modern transportation systems
such as the bypass, first mooted in the 1940s by Sir
Frank Mears, has also been influential in the development of many out-of-town developments such
as Heriot-Watt University, the airport and the
Edinburgh Business Park. The latter two examples, like much inter-war housing in Roseburn and
Murrayfield, and like the Royal Infirmary and the
Cameron Toll shopping centre to the south-east,
have also been constructed on floodplains. It can
be argued, therefore, that the articulation of the
city's built form up to the early 19th century,
whether at the cultural or the physical level, was a
clear and connected response to the contexts and
concepts prevailing at the time, although the
designs of its picturesque open spaces are perhaps
less homogeneous in this respect. However, the
incidence of flooding, and its anticipated increase
in frequency, shows that in the late 19th century
and throughout the last century the city has been
less sure-footed in its response to natural form and
process.

The historian Duncan Macmillan has suggested
that Stevenson's characters Dr Jekyll and Mr Hyde
can be seen as a metaphor for the Old and New
Towns in the mid-19th century – when the former
was a festering slum.[28]. The two towns, while
dependent upon one another and essential to the
city's completeness, represent divided and divergent aspects of the one individual. With the reinvigoration of the fabric and society of the Old Town
initiated by Patrick Geddes and continued by

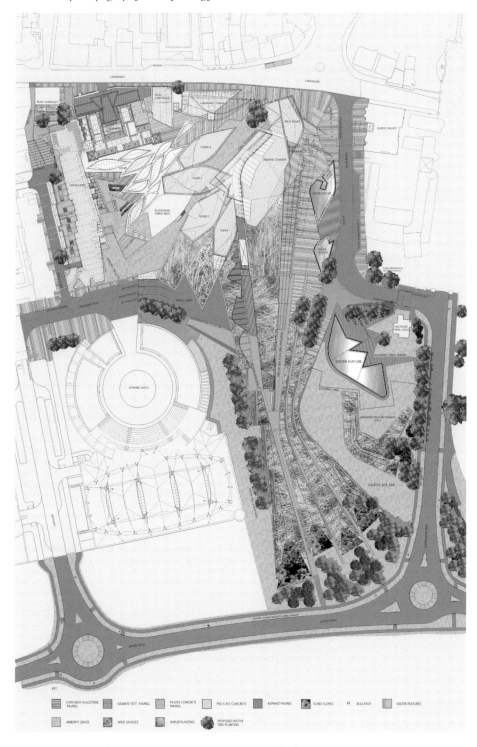

FIGURE 3.10   Plan of the Scottish Parliament.   *Enric Miralles/RMJM*

Robert Hurd, Stevenson's metaphor can now be attached with more justice to the relationship of the city centre with its peripheries and outer suburbs.

In this light, it is heartening therefore that Enric Miralles, architect of the Scottish Parliament, sought to root architecture in the striking igneous landscape of Holyrood Park. One of his initial presentations to the client involved a collage of leaves and a bundle of twigs. The former representing the flowing and folding roofscape and the latter the landscape 'tail' which mirrors the linear form of Salisbury Crags. The architect's idea was that the Parliament Building and adjoining landscape should be seen as an extension to the debating chamber. Here is a building, therefore, which in physical dialogue with its context expresses the 21st century's relationship with nature in much the same way that the New Town Gardens reflected an 18th-century interpretation of nature.

Notes

1. R. L. Stevenson, *Edinburgh Picturesque Notes* (Edinburgh, 1878), p. 16.
2. D. McAdam, *Edinburgh: A Landscape Fashioned by Geology* (Edinburgh, 1993), p. 5.
3. Stevenson, p. 12.
4. J. B. Sissons, *The Evolution of Scotland's Scenery* (Edinburgh, 1967), p. 89.
5. I. Whyte, *Edinburgh and the Borders Landscape Heritage* (Newton Abbot, 1990), p. 178.
6. F. A. Walker, 'Urban form', in D. Mays (ed.), *The Architecture of Scottish Cities* (East Linton, 1997), pp. 58–60.
7. C. McKean, 'James Craig and Edinburgh's New Town', in K. Cruft and A. Fraser (eds), *James Craig 1744–1795* (Edinburgh, 1995), p. 53.
8. Walker, 'Urban form', p. 58.
9. A. J. Youngson, *The Making of Classical Edinburgh* (Edinburgh, 1966), p. 92.
10. Whyte, *Landscape Heritage*, p. 195.
11. Ibid.
12. Walker, 'Urban form', p. 60.
13. Ibid.
14. C. Byrom, 'The pleasure grounds of Edinburgh New Town', *Garden History*, 23(1) (1995): 70.
15. Ibid.
16. *The Scotsman*, 27 April 2000, p. 4.
17. City of Edinburgh Report, *Planning and Flooding*, August 2001 (no publisher).
18. City of Edinburgh Report, *Flooding*, June 2001 (no publisher).
19. Stevenson, *Notes*, p. 15.
20. C. McKean, *Edinburgh: An Illustrated Architectural Guide* (Edinburgh, 1992), p. 1.
21. P. McGowan, *Princes Street Gardens Conservation Management Plan* (n.p., 2003).
22. City of Edinburgh, *Waverley Valley Redevelopment Strategy* (n.p., 2000).
23. Byrom, 'Pleasure grounds', p. 70.
24. McGowan, *Princes Street Gardens*.
25. M. Vroom, K. Kerkstra and P. Vrijlandt, 'Mergelland: the impact of limestone quarrying on a rural scenic area', in D. Lovejoy (ed.), *Landscape and Landscape Planning* (Aylesbury, 1979), p. 270.
26. McKean, *Edinburgh*, p. 239.
27. Ibid.
28. D. Macmillan, 'A single-minded polymath: Patrick Geddes and the spatial form of social thought', *Edinburgh Review*, 88 (1992): 85.

PART II

The City in the Industrial Age

Introduction

The main focus of Part II is the 19th-century city. A map of Edinburgh today would suggest that about 40 per cent of the urban area was constructed between 1800 and 1900. Part II seeks to explain what the forces were that found expression in the countless streets of tenements, the pockets of industry, new institutions and areas of housing constructed by railway companies and working men's co-operatives.

Edinburgh is not a city associated with industry – yet manufacturing companies, their factories and the canals and railway lines that served them left a bigger mark on the city than many realise. Local manufacturers were often involved in urban development around embryonic suburban railway stations, resulting in housing closely integrated with public transport and industry. In this (as Chapter 5 explains), Edinburgh differs to a degree from 19th-century cities such as Glasgow, Leeds and Manchester. In Edinburgh, while new neighbourhoods such as Dalry and Fountainbridge were built to serve the interests of local manufacture, establishing cohesive working-class districts, smaller manufacturing concerns from earlier centuries survived as businesses closely integrated into the fabric of older residential areas. Shops with workshops beneath or behind existed on the ground floors of tenements in the fashionable New Town or as more ancient survivors in the Old Town. Here, industrial processes on a limited scale were conducted, adding to the social vibrancy and economic diversity of inner-city neighbourhoods. Activities like bookbinding, printing, upholstery, cabinet-making and tailoring were undertaken on the doorstep of the banks, university and City Chambers. The analysis should dispel the myth that Edinburgh was not an industrial city in the modern sense of the term.

Why industrial Edinburgh developed in a fashion unlike that elsewhere in the UK is discussed – for, although the city had big industrial concerns such as brewing, it never sought to disperse manufacturing to the outer suburbs. That is, not until the 20th century, when the waterfront of Granton and Leith became the location for large-scale industry. Until then, manufacturing was closely integrated with residential areas in a fashion perhaps unique in the UK.

How the medieval, Renaissance and Georgian city was adapted to meet the modern demands of the 19th century is explored particularly in the context of housing intervention by the City Council. Remarkably, the city absorbed manufacturing industry and its infrastructure demands with little adverse aesthetic impact. Canals, railway marshalling yards, harbour facilities and working-class housing were built without the kind of social polarisation and urban disruption found elsewhere. As in much of Edinburgh's history, this owed a great deal, as Chapter 4 explains, to enlightened private patronage and partnership between public bodies, trusts and commercial developers.

The housing constructed to meet a growing and often industrialised city is explored in Chapter 5. The ubiquitous tenement, whose origins were ancient (see Chapter 1), was gradually improved and standardised to satisfy both middle-class and working-class needs. Unlike in England, where the terraced house (for the poor) and suburban villa (for the rich) were the dominant housing typologies, in Scottish cities the four-storey tenement block served a variety of social-class needs. As Chapter 2 suggested, in the smarter areas of the New Town, middle-class tenement flats were disguised within what appeared from the outside to be town houses for the wealthy. But, by the 19th century, the tenement flat had enough style, swagger and convenience to suit the most discerning citizens. In this, Edinburgh was like other European cities where, from Paris to Madrid, apartments built in the city centre were preferred to villas built in the suburbs. The rise and eventual fall of the tenement forms a thread running through Part II.

The history of the tenement is explained in detail in Chapter 5 against a background of innovation in construction, design and patronage. Controls by the Dean of Guild Court over building heights and street widths are discussed, as is the influence of private feuing plans on tenement design. Compiled by some of the city's most eminent architects for the new landowning class of the Victorian age, the feuing plan became an important instrument of urban design in the city. The façades of tenement blocks, their dressed stone finish, height and skyline were dictated across large tracts of the city by often self-made business people who had worked their way from the trades into Edinburgh's new ruling class. They realised that tenement development was good investment as long as it was properly regulated – socially and visually.

Industry, tenements, schools, churches and public libraries were the principal legacy of the 19th century. Part II seeks to redress the balance in writings on Edinburgh in favour of the early modern period, when so much of today's infrastructure was constructed. Although the emphasis is upon landowners and their architects, the role of the City Council and its team of municipal engineers is also discussed. For, whereas the Georgian New Towns of Edinburgh were mainly the result of private endeavour (though with significant political support), the success of the Victorian city owed a great deal to the new powers (over water, sewage, streets and transport) vested in the Town Council. It is this theme which is explored in Part II and which forms the thematic connection to Parts III and IV.

4 Landscapes of capital: industry and the built environment in Edinburgh, 1750–1920

Richard Rodger

Edina! Scotia's darling seat!
All hail thy palaces and tow'rs,
Where once, beneath a Monarch's feet,
Sat Legislation's sov'reign pow'rs:

Here Wealth still swells the golden tide,
As busy Trade his labour plies;
There Architecture's noble pride
Bids elegance and splendour rise:
Here Justice, from her native skies
High wields her balance and her rod;
There Learning, with his eagle eyes,
Seeks Science in her coy abode.

(Robert Burns, 'Address to Edinburgh', 1786)[1]

Burns knew Edinburgh. He identified key characteristics in the distinctive townscape: kirk and castle – 'palaces and tow'rs'. He reminded Scots generally, and Edinburgh citizens particularly, of the loss of 'sov'reign powers', keenly felt even eighty years on, by reference to the former parliament building and an independent legislature prior to the Union of 1707. Burns also knew that the wealth of the city was based on 'Science', 'Learning', 'Justice' and, in the heady days of New Town development, 'Architecture', with lip service also paid to 'Trade', meaning industry, not overseas commerce. But it was the castle that took pride of place in Burns' address to Edinburgh:

There watching high the least alarms
Thy rough, rude fortress gleams afar;
Like some bold veteran, grey in arms,

And mark'd with many a seamy scar:
The pond'rous wall and massy bar,
Grim-rising o'er the rugged rock,
Have oft withstood assailing war,
And oft repell'd th' invader's shock.

Most great cities have a dominant image. The Brandenburg Gate in Berlin, Red Square in Moscow, the Empire State Building in New York – each has the status of icon. The reaction to the assault on another, the Manhattan skyline, on 11 September 2001 was due to the loss of such an old friend, the icon that was a signature for New York.[2] Worldwide, dominant images stand as representatives of the city. Edinburgh is known for its ancient castle, high above the city, on a great volcanic rock. It dominates the skyline and makes its presence known each day with a cannon now fired electronically from the ramparts. Beneath the volcanic crag, the tourist thoroughfares are no less saturated with its presence, represented heavily on the postcards sold on pavements and in the newspapers shop lining the tourist's progress along Princes Street and the High Street.[3] As if it needed marketing, tourists and residents alike were assailed in 2002 with an image of Edinburgh Castle on the panels of local bus shelters, underneath which were captions: 'You wouldn't go to Paris without visiting the Eiffel Tower?' and 'You wouldn't go to New York without visiting the Empire State Building?' By 2003, the marketing strategy had moved on, as the caption to a poster in bus shelters proclaimed: 'You can't miss it' and exhorted the tourist to 'Take the free Castle bus from Hanover Street'.

Though representations of the castle take pride of place, a 'second image of Edinburgh is formed around the New Town as both a physical reality . . . and also as an ideal and aspiration towards a new type of polite, civilised urban living consistent with the Enlightenment'.[4] The association with élite and high culture, as represented in the castle and the Georgian New Town, is a powerful one, and 'gives rise to a third image of Edinburgh, the Festival City' – festivals of international jazz, film, book, mela, music, drama and art.

This international version of the city has been promoted by means of powerful logos using either the castle in conjunction with the Edinburgh skyline or by a grid-plan representation of the New Town, as instantly recognisable as the satellite pictures of the River Thames' serpentine course through central London. Even the University of Edinburgh unashamedly employs the image of the castle, with which it has no connection, to promote its 'positions vacant' website. The promotional message has been of Edinburgh as a cultural capital, as a place of sophistication and consumerism, and as a World Heritage City. Year-round visitor attractions are packaged so that Edinburgh has become the runner-up to London as the most visited place for tourists to Britain.

Industrial Edinburgh rediscovered

Robert Burns' 'Address to Edinburgh' pandered to Edinburgh citizens and their sense of self-importance. In the 20th century, marketing and public-relations specialists enthusiastically re-peated his message of architectural splendour. Even the National Library of Scotland, unwittingly, has been complicit in projecting this view of élite Edinburgh. Its accompanying text to the splendid Ordnance Survey digital maps of Edinburgh employs 400 words to describe architectural and planning excellence, with just sixty-eight words devoted to trade and industry.[5]

Aided by assurances under the Act of Union 1707 concerning the independence of banking, the church, education and the law in Scotland, the concentration of legal, financial, religious and educational interests was unparalleled elsewhere in urban Britain.[6] Edinburgh became the natural

Table 4.1 *Male employment in the professions (as a percentage of total male employment)*

City/town	1861	1911	1951
Edinburgh	14.5	13.0	17.0
Oxford	8.8	11.3	17.0
Ipswich	7.4	7.2	10.6
Bristol	6.7	6.5	12.8
Derby	5.2	5.2	8.5
Manchester	5.1	5.3	10.4
Glasgow	5.1	5.7	10.9
Liverpool	4.9	5.9	11.3
Cardiff	4.5	6.6	14.7
Coventry	4.5	3.7	5.3
Newcastle	4.5	6.6	15.4
Birmingham	3.8	4.3	7.4
Sheffield	3.8	4.6	7.7
Dundee	3.7	5.4	10.1
Leeds	3.6	5.0	10.6

Sources: Based on census data for each city in 1861, 1911 and 1951.

headquarters for such institutions. As a result, the hospitals and schools, workhouses and charities, courts and kirks scattered around the city produced a distinctive and dense institutional topography in the built environment of Edinburgh. For over a century, about one in six employed Edinburgh men found work in the professions from c. 1841 to c. 1951, although other towns and cities began to catch up during the 20th century as the orbit of government, local and central, expanded under pressure of budgetary control and accountability (see Table 4.1).[7]

The professional caste in Edinburgh was highly influential – disproportionately so. As one English observer commented when explaining the prosperity of different cities: ''twas pig-iron that did it for Glasgow . . . 'twas cotton that did it for Liverpool and Manchester' but 'twas quarrels that did it' for Edinburgh.[8] Litigation and professional opinions were the stock in trade, with 'almost every house in the New Town . . . occupied by some person connected with the law'.[9] However, the view prevailing in the 1840s that 'Edinburgh has never been famous as a great manufacturing city' (1845) and that 'Edinburgh's manufactures are few and on a limited scale' (1849) was false.[10] If one man in six in the capital obtained a living by

Table 4.2   *Employment by sector, Edinburgh 1861–1951*

	Men			Women		
	1861	*1911*	*1951*	*1861*	*1911*	*1951*
Engineering & metals	8.9	7.6	12.6	0.2	0.3	3.8
Textiles & clothing	9.8	4.1	1.6	22.9	12.3	4.9
Food & drink	5.6	5.7	10.1	4.8	4.1	15.2
Other manufacturing	14.7	11.7	9.5	2.9	4.5	6.4
Manufacturing	39.0	29.0	33.7	30.7	21.3	30.2
Building & non-manufacturing	18.6	17.2	16.9	4.8	7.9	7.5
Total industrial	**57.6**	**46.3**	**50.6**	**35.5**	**29.2**	**37.7**
Professional/government	14.5	13.0	17.0	3.7	8.5	26.7
Commerce	14.4	20.0	15.4	6.2	21.4	23.3
Transport	7.4	15.1	13.6	0.5	1.2	3.8
Domestic	2.4	2.9	0.6	52.3	39.4	7.8
Total non-industrial	**38.7**	**51.0**	**46.6**	**62.7**	**70.5**	**61.6**

Source: as for Table 4.1.

professional duties – lawyers, accountants, military personnel, ministers, teachers and professors – then five in six did not.[11] For a century, approximately 50 per cent of the male workforce were employed in industry; some 30–40 per cent were in manufacturing industry itself (see Table 4.2). Among women, about one-third were industrial workers while 60–70 per cent were in non-industrial pursuits, mostly in domestic service in the half-century before the First World War. Edinburgh was an industrial city. It just was not a heavy industrial city dominated by a single industry and a few powerful industrialists in the way that Sheffield was, or by innumerable small industrial units as was Birmingham.[12] The capital city differed fundamentally, therefore, from Sheffield or Coventry, where four in five men worked in industry, but was not very different to Bristol, Liverpool, Cardiff or even Glasgow in the proportion of men who worked in industry in Victorian times.[13]

Beneath these figures are characteristics that are not unimportant in relation to the nature of the built environment. For example, if the proportion of male professional employment placed Edinburgh at the top of the British league table, the reliance on a staple industry placed it in the relegation zone. An index of concentration, a measure of the proportion of workers employed in the largest single occupational category, reveals Edinburgh (and Oxford before the Cowley car plant got under way in the inter-war years) to be at the bottom of a table of major towns and cities.[14] This dispersal of the workforce across a number of industries affected the urban landscape in various ways. There were few very large plants; workshop production was squirrelled away among tenements and back lanes, and with the fragmentation of capitalist production came diversity in the socio-spatial structure of Edinburgh. Residential, commercial, distribution and service sectors co-existed and provided a varied, even integrated, local landscape.

Two myths can be dispelled. Firstly, the landscape of the Edinburgh bourgeoisie with its symbols of religious, financial and state power enshrined in the courts, kirks and castle, while powerful, was not all-powerful. Industry and commerce, manufacturing and services, increasingly assumed prominence in the 19th-century landscape, especially as the spatial extent of the city was extended significantly after 1856. Secondly, to neglect the manufacturing and wider industrial base of the city is to misrepresent the balance of the local economy. There were areas of manufacturing industry that were strongly represented in the local economy and were distinctive to the Edinburgh economy. Printing, brewing and distilling specifically came into this category. Yet in various other industrial specialisms, for example in precious metalworking, hatmaking,

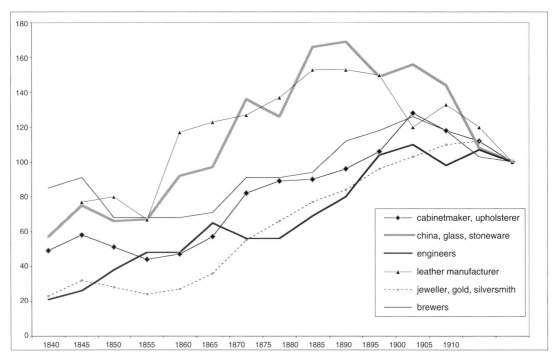

FIGURE 4.1   Growth in selected Edinburgh industries, 1840–1910 (Index: 1910 = 100).   *Edinburgh and Leith Post Office Directories, 1840–1910*

chemicals, tobacco, dressmaking, leatherworking, non-ferrous metalworking, brick and glass manufacture, and the furniture trades, in that order, there were areas of employment that were more prominent in Edinburgh than in the Scottish economy overall. It was in high value-added industries, therefore, such as scientific instrument-making, cabinetmaking and bookbinding rather than in iron manufacture, shipbuilding and textiles of all kinds that Edinburgh industrialists concentrated their enterprise.

Like most settlements in modern times, Edinburgh was a city with its own specialist activities, driven partly by consumption-led demand and also by high value-added to the products of science, technology and a knowledge-based economy. Edinburgh was the quintessential instance where 'the talk of the bourgeoisie, not the smoke of the factory, was the defining characteristic of the modern city economy',[15] but significantly the presence of the chimney, warehouses, mills, malt houses and other physical features in the

industrial landscape were central to the daily experience of the majority of the citizens of the capital.

Of the expansion of the industrial sector in Edinburgh between 1840 and 1910 there can be little doubt. With population doubling from 83,000 in 1811 to 161,000 in 1851 and doubling further to 320,000 in 1911, the number of businesses also increased significantly.[16] The long-run trends in firms active in brewing, glass and stoneware, engineering, leather manufacture, precious metal-working and brewing are shown in Fig. 4.1. In addition, and as a reflection of the different specialist processes, there were many subtleties within industrial classifications and a multitude of small-scale firms that existed within an industrial sector. Nowhere is this better illustrated than in one of the premier industries in Edinburgh, the printing industry, where there were over forty different types of firms. By 1910, there were more than 1,250 drapers, hatters and tailors, 400 booksellers and stationers, 400 dairies, 800 bakers and

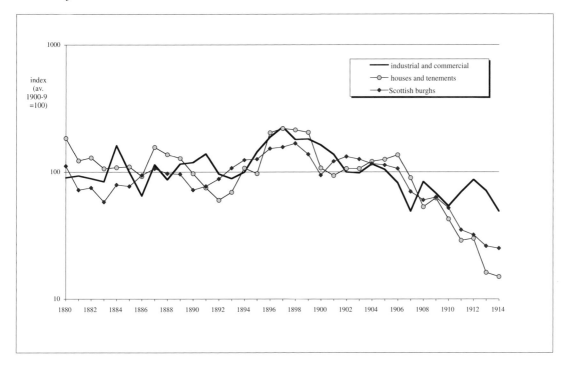

FIGURE 4.2   Industrial and residential building fluctuations, Edinburgh, 1880–1914.   *Edinburgh City Archives, Dean of Guild Court Registers 1860–1914, R. Rodger, 'Scottish urban housebuilding, 1870–1914', University of Edinburgh PhD thesis, 1975*

confectioners, 600 grocers and 560 spirit dealers, many of whom combined their manufacturing and retailing roles from workshops scattered throughout the city and frequently operated from a New Town address.[17]

In short, Edinburgh was much more than its professions and institutions. The built environment was saturated with the micro-organisms of industrial and commercial life. The atomistic structure of firms in Edinburgh contrasted with most cities where powerful manufacturing agglomerations existed. Accordingly, the multiple sinews of the local Edinburgh economy produced a measure of stability through its numerous and complementary activities. As in anatomy or civil engineering, the intertwined strands of muscle or steel, though individually weak, collectively enhanced strength. So it was with the economy of Edinburgh. Unlike those Scottish burghs and English cities heavily dependent on the fortunes of a narrow industrial base, for example Dundee, Sheffield, Preston and

Paisley, the diverse strands in the local Edinburgh economy insulated it against the vagaries of the business cycle and international fluctuations.

These local economic circumstances produced two influences of considerable importance for the built environment in Edinburgh. Firstly, and as a result of its reduced susceptibility to business cycles, periods of boom and bust in the Edinburgh building trades were also less pronounced than elsewhere; and the building industry itself, though notorious for its stop-go cycle, was less affected than in any other Scottish burgh in the forty years before the First World War. Indeed, the Edinburgh construction industry, both residential and industrial, was rather similar to the overall performance of the largest thirty burghs in Scotland (see Fig. 4.2).[18] Greater predictability had an impact on the quality of materials and standards of workmanship, and thus in the long-run quality of the built environment.[19] Less exposed to the severity of building cycles, the speculative builder was determined to wrest a profit when the property boom was in his favour, whilst a more orderly building industry discouraged scamping and avoided the worst consequences of materials shortages.

Secondly, small units of industrial production meant that no quarter of the city was entirely exempt from industrial activities, although there were noted clusters of activity too. The scattered distribution of industrial firms was heavily dependent on workshop and artisanal production and so was insinuated in the interstices of the built environment: in back courts, accessed through pends, wynds and lanes intended as the carriage houses of the wealthy New Town residents. Every square mile of Edinburgh contained industry, as the first large-scale Ordnance Survey maps show. This, then, was the urban landscape that most Edinburgh folk knew as they went about their daily business. Their knowledge of the High Street, of the New Town and its open spaces and architectural splendour, was *terra incognita* to them. It was the immediate vicinity of their tenement flat, the cobbled streets and familiar sights, smells and sounds of the trek to school or work, or to the corner shop and occasionally to the church and its city mission, that were the landscapes of the majority of Edina's citizens, not that of Burns' rendition of the brooding castle. Even in the 1950s and 1960s with Corporation buses and 'transfer' tickets, many Edinburgh citizens knew only certain well-defined routes and sub-areas; everything else was an adventure with risk and uncertainty associated with it.[20] These landscapes of the mind were defined by the rhythms of the day – school, work, church and sociability – and, in turn, social and spatial knowledge and exploration were limited.[21]

The industrial landscape before 1850

The neglect or downgrading of industry by early Victorian observers, noted earlier, is all the more surprising since the *Statistical Account of Scotland*, published between 1791 and 1799, specifically identified industrial growth and even calculated rates of expansion. Thus, in the thirty years between 1763 and the date of publication, the printing, brewing, buttonmaking, wig, perfume,

hat, glove and shawlmaking, starch manufacture and distilling industries are each stated to have enjoyed considerable expansion in Edinburgh.[22] Indeed, Heriot's Hospital trustees, the major landowner in the north of the city, recognised the industrial development potential by swiftly making plots of land available for development along the banks of the river to take advantage of its water-powered milling, washing and bleaching potential so sought after by 18th-century industry. The first two of these developments were at Silvermills in 1714, just seven years after the Heriot's trustees had completed their land-consolidation strategy, and over the next thirty years another five important sites were released in the Stockbridge and Canonmills areas. These decisions to develop industry alongside Edinburgh's only river provided a platform for the spurt of industrial development noted in the *Statistical Account*, and persuaded the Heriot's trustees to release further properties in 1781 and 1786 to enable Dunbar Pringle to develop 'Tanfield' at Canonmills and, just upstream, James Haig to develop his whisky-distilling business.[23] These 18th-century property-development decisions cast the die in terms of industrial development in north Edinburgh; and for ever afterwards the Water of Leith, later described as a 'gigantic nuisance',[24] was an open sewer containing the pollutants of industrial dye, bleach, papermaking and other noxious effluents, as well as residential waste.[25] The contamination of Edinburgh's water supply did not escape the prime minister, Lord Palmerston, on a visit to Edinburgh in 1861, when he punned: 'The Water of Leith! Would it were the Water of Lethe!'[26] Four years later, Henry Duncan Littlejohn,[27] newly appointed Medical Officer of Health, identified a number of environmental hazards associated with the Water of Leith, and even John Fulleylove's idyllic painting of stream, weir and mill captures something of the brooding river and industrial landscape, if nothing of its polluted character (see Fig. 4.3).

Distinctive north-Edinburgh industrial building along the Water of Leith was consciously developed in the 18th century. 'Craft manufacturing', however, remained the dominant business form in

FIGURE 4.3   The Water of Leith from the Dean Bridge (c. 1890).   *John Fulleylove*

Edinburgh. In 1812, for example, craft manufacturing accounted for about 130 enterprises or almost 32 per cent of all Edinburgh businesses, and an eclectic category of thirty-seven 'manufacturers' constituted the larger industrial enterprises and 8 per cent of Edinburgh firms.[28] In the post-Napoleonic years, craft activity in tailoring and in the clothing trades generally was much more numerous than the larger enterprises associated with the printing industry; and this persistence of small-business organisations in Edinburgh, and in other Scottish burghs, continued in the last quarter of the 19th century.[29]

While small-scale consumer-based industries continued to be a significant source of employment in Edinburgh throughout the 19th century, their rate of expansion was less than in some sectors of industry, notably chemicals, glass, rubber, brewing and heavy engineering, where

technological advances meant that significant levels of capital investment were imperative to maintain and develop market shares. By 1851, a strong degree of industrial dualism was already evident, with 2.3 per cent of firms employing 30 per cent of the workforce.[30] Despite the observation by H. D. Littlejohn in 1865 that 'Edinburgh . . . has no pretensions to be a manufacturing city', he analysed the geographical distribution of 220 'manufactures and trades' throughout the city (see Table 4.3).[31] From the 1860s, therefore, larger manufacturing concerns were beginning to make an impact on the Edinburgh landscape.

Redefining the industrial landscape

By 1871, industrial dualism in Edinburgh was yet more pronounced. An average of fewer than ten employees in jewellery, precious metalworking, shoemaking, watchmaking, baking and several of the building trades contrasted with the sizeable concerns such as Morrison & Gibb, R. & R. Clark, Constable and Bartholomew in printing, each of which employed over 100 workers where the industry average workforce was forty-seven employees.[32] In engineering, the mean workforce was eighty-three, in glass 119 and in rubber over 300. To a degree, the larger scale reflected a greater integration of the manufacturing sector into national markets and the development of branded goods such as Jacob's biscuits, Ballantyne's 'Hovis' bread and Stewart's whisky, each supplied through improved transport links to distributors throughout the British Isles. The growth of industrial units was also a reflection of the wider diffusion of steampower in the production processes associated with baking, stationery and printing, glass-making, brewing and, in a more limited way, in the building trades too.

One consequence of the increasing scale of production in the second half of the 19th century was the migration of many sizeable firms between 1860 and 1900 from the Cowgate, Old Town closes, St Leonard's and Causewayside, and the Water of Leith to the urban fringes (Fig. 4.4). At Moray Park Maltings (Abbeyhill), a brewery, foundry complex and the innovative electric-turbine engineworks of Carrick and Ritchie were relocated in the 1860s. On

Table 4.3 *Tabular statement of the number and distribution of manufactures and trades*

No.	Names of the districts	Population in 1861	Printing Establishments	Breweries	Distilleries	Tanneries	Cabinetmakers	Coach Works	Foundries	Workers in Metals	Workers in Glass	Tobacco Manufactories	Hat Manufactories	Pipe Manufactories	Marble Cutters	Flour Mills	Oil Manufactories	Dye Works	Chemical Works	Cat-gut Manufactories	Gas Works	Builders	Saw-mills	Gutta-Percha Works
1	Upper New Town	10,930	17							9														
2	Lower New Town	14,024					2	2		4												1		
3	West End	7,748	1		1		4	2		6						1			1			2		
4	Upper Water of Leith	12,332				1										4		1						
5	Lower Water of Leith	3,866		1		3										1		1	1	1		2		
6	Broughton	5,672						1							1									
7	Calton and Greenside	10,984	7				2			12	11			1	2							1		
8	Abbey	2,237		3					1	1									1				2	
9	Canongate	12,200		8		3			2	7	2										1			
10	Tron	11,636	4	1		2				1		1	1	1										
11	St Giles	15,967	9	2						3			1					1						
12	Grassmarket	5,227				3						2								1				
13	Fountainbridge	9,880		2				1	1	6						1	2							
14	George Square and Lauriston	6,593																				2		2
15	Nicolson Street	18,307		1					1	7		1	1				1							
16	Pleasance and St Leonard	11,104	1	3				2	1	1				1								1		
17	Newington	4,955		2		1																1		
18	Grange	1,886			1																	1		
19	Morningside	2,573								3														
	Totals	168,121	39	24	2	13	8	8	6	60	13	4	3	3	3	7	3	3	3	2	1	11	2	2

H. D. Littlejohn, *Report on the Sanitary Condition of the City of Edinburgh: with relative appendices* (Edinburgh, 1865), p. 47.

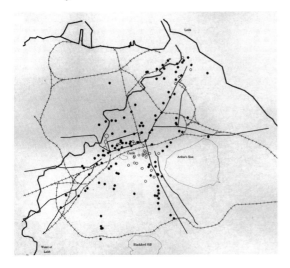

FIGURE 4.5   The growth of Edinburgh and the Municipal Extension Act, 1856. (Note: the built-up area of the Old and New Towns, together with some minor outlying developments, is surrounded by the expansion brought about by the 1856 Act.)

FIGURE 4.4   The deconcentration of manufacturing in Edinburgh, 1861 (○)–1911 (●).   *Edinburgh and Leith Post Office Directories, 1861 and 1911*

the same site, Thomas Miller established his London Road Foundry in 1867, specialising in 'chilled' rolled steel and a variety of castings.[33] The manufacturers of gas meters and governors, Bruce Peebles & Co., moved from Fountainbridge to Bonnington so as to be able to expand their capacity in response to increased domestic usage of gas; and, though the move to Sciennes by the heavy engineering firm of Bertrams hardly seems a development on the fringe, at the time they undertook the transfer from Eskbank, it was.[34] Somewhat later, two breweries and a creamery migrated to Craigmillar, where they employed 600 workers in what passed for a Victorian industrial estate.[35] In the loops and vectors created by the spaghetti of railway lines in Dalry (Fig. 4.4), distilleries, breweries, biscuit factories and the rubber companies either migrated or expanded their operations. Seven acres on the shores of the Forth at Caroline Park, Granton, were required to relocate the firm of A. B. Fleming & Co., 'the largest printing-ink business in the world', while two of their customers also relocated: the cartographic firm of W. & A. K. Johnstone re-established their Edina Works to the north of Holyrood Park at Easter Road, and, across the park to the south, Nelson's resited their printing works alongside Usher's Park Brewery, which had

moved there in 1862 from George IV Bridge. Undoubtedly, city-centre congestion and the council's slum-clearance strategies after 1867 were push factors in some decisions to relocate; but the migratory impulse of employers in search of greenfield sites for their increasingly capital-intensive and land-hungry factories was a crucial centrifugal force in the relocation of the population of Edinburgh. Important, too, was the response of the railway companies in opening new lines from Slateford to Granton in 1861 and to Leith in 1864, and new passenger stations at Abbeyhill, Piershill and Trinity in 1868.[36] The Edinburgh Co-operative Building Company also captured the momentum of industrial relocation and constructed new and substantial quantities of housing specifically intended for skilled workers at Abbeyhill and Haymarket in the late 1860s and 1870s following their earlier successes at Stockbridge.[37]

The greenfield expansion of industry was assisted by the geographical extension of the city itself (Fig. 4.5). In a sense, it was because of the physical constraints on industrial and commercial development themselves that the largest percentage expansion of the area of Edinburgh took place as a result of the Edinburgh Extension Act, 1856.[38] Any geographical expansion had administrative costs and benefits. The town clerk and burgh chamberlain had to make careful assessments of the implications for the city's finances. Policing, cleansing, firefighting services, markets, public health, building control and a multitude of additional responsibilities applied to the extended urban area as statutes and local bye-laws took effect. For business enterprises of all kinds, there were considerable advantages in boundary extensions. 'External economies' operated within the administrative jurisdictions. That is, businesses, like residents, benefited from the water and gas supplies, sanitary and public-health provisions, road improvements and tram routes, and many other municipal services that applied to the area embraced by boundary extensions. When combined with cheaper land for building, less congestion and the stimuli to private developers to undertake housebuilding, the appeal of industrial estates to Victorian entrepreneurs was obvious.

As a result, the landscape of Edinburgh changed after 1856. Land-extensive construction, including institutional building, was increasingly attracted to the urban periphery. In Edinburgh, as elsewhere, the ring of poor-law and fever hospitals, prisons and asylums, slaughtermarkets and wholesale produce markets generally moved out of city-centre locations to take advantage of cheaper land costs on the urban fringes.[39] City-centre access commanded a very low premium for such users. The same applied to many Edinburgh manufacturers, especially when combined with satisfactory rail links to bring in raw-materials supplies and to distribute finished products. Edinburgh's expanding rail network in the 1860s provided a spur to the migration of industry.

The specific locations for this emerging industrial landscape were in large measure determined before the passage of the 1856 Act. Railway access to Edinburgh was along an east–west axis. From the west, the route of the Caledonian Railway ran parallel with the Union Canal through Fountainbridge, converging on the west end of Princes Street at Lothian Road. This approach route was already defined by custom and use as industrial, commercial and distributive. The North British (NB) Railway also gained western access to

the city through Dalry, with a station at Haymarket connecting beneath the castle to link with the NB's Waverley Station at the east end of Princes Street. This station was also the point of eastern access to the city for the NB, approached by way of the marshalling yards and engineering works at St Margaret's. Superimposed on this Y-shaped pattern of main-line access were many additional spur lines, for example, connecting Leith and the docks from both east and west. Topography and landed interests defined that this east–west axis was for industrial and commercial use. In addition, the east–west railway axis was constructed on relatively flat terrain, and this topographical characteristic provided the easiest engineering access and thus the most economical approach to the 'Athens of the North', where on the surrounding hills powerful landowning interests saw greater advantage in developing residential construction.[40]

In short, when market conditions, technological change and manufacturing interests dictated that larger plants and land-hungry premises necessitated a move away from the congestion of the ancient thoroughfares of Edinburgh, then districts along the existing railway routes provided flat, well-serviced sites with good communications (Fig. 4.4). Spaghetti-like spurs and branch lines developed from the original railway framework so that the east–west industrial corridor was essentially preserved, with some important suburban clusters emerging at Granton, Craigmillar and Slateford. This was the context for the industrial and residential expansion that developed from the late 1850s; and, largely though not exclusively from this decade and the 1860s, many breweries, dyeworks, printing firms, bakeries and biscuit manufacturers and foundries re-established their operations on the margins of the built-up area – actually in green fields in many cases. An added stimulus was also given by university-based research and development in the 1840s and 1850s into the diverse properties of rubber, and this appliance of science combined with American inward investment resulted in 1855 in the foundation of the North British Rubber Company.[41] The firm took over the derelict Castle Silk Mills at

Fountainbridge and redeveloped them into a plant to manufacture a variety of rubber products. The factory treated not just all types of clothing, gloves and footwear for industrial and sporting purposes but also vulcanised mats, tubing and industrial belting and had branches in Leeds, Bradford and Belfast, in each of which they won lucrative contracts with the town council for the supply of rubber-based products. Several North British Rubber shareholders combined in 1861 to form the Scottish Vulcanite Company and built another substantial factory for the manufacture of rubber products for machine-belts, tyres and consumer items, including combs, adjoining Castle Mills (see Fig. 4.6a).[42] In quick succession, these new factories transformed Edinburgh, and Fountainbridge specifically, into a world centre of manufactured rubber products from the 1860s.

The scale and mass of the rubber companies was matched by others nearby. Another industrial pairing, Wm McEwan's Fountain Brewery established in 1856, and Lorimer and Clark's Caledonian Brewery (1869), also represented significant capital investments in plant and machinery, cooperages and maltings (see Fig. 4.6a). Though the Caledonian Brewery was a relatively low-rise structure of four storeys, the scale of these and the Grove Bakery, also in Fountainbridge, meant that the area was dominated by substantial structures, impenetrable perimeter fences, gatekeepers' surveillance and the heavy traffic associated with each, despite the railway sidings at the rear of their properties. It is likely that these industrial developments would have materialised in any event; but the extension of the Edinburgh municipal frontier certainly facilitated the process, and both owners and shareholders benefited from the City Council's decision, as did private builders and developers. Edinburgh was an industrial and manufacturing city throughout the 19th century, and in the last third it was experiencing fixed investment in plant and buildings on the scale seen in Fig. 4.7. Where there were major plants of the kinds illustrated, workforces were numbered in hundreds rather than thousands, and there remained a very strong commercial office-based and professional layer to employment in the city.

a

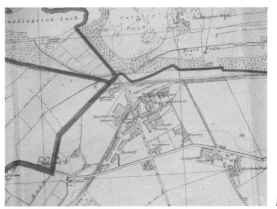

b

FIGURE 4.6   Late 19th-century industrial estates, Edinburgh: (a) Fountainbridge; (b) Craigmillar.   *Based on the Ordnance Survey Map, 1876–77, and J. G. Bartholomew's Chronological Map of Edinburgh showing expansion of the city from earliest days to 1911 (reproduced by permission of the National Library of Scotland)*

The impact of industry on the landscape of Edinburgh

How did the 19th-century landscape change? Standing at the factory gates of the vacant Castle Mills in Fountainbridge in 1856 and looking north, it was possible to see Corstorphine Hill and, to the north-west and across the Firth of Forth, the Cleish Hills on the Fife–Kinross border. A generation later, following the development of the Vulcanite Rubber works, Fountain Brewery and other industrial

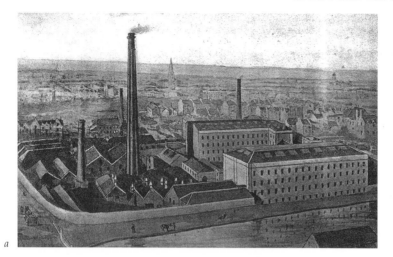

a

b

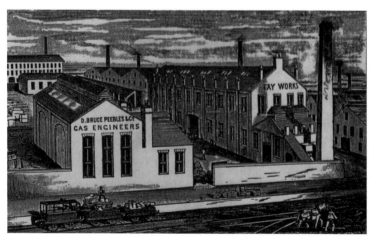

c

FIGURE 4.7   Industrial expansion, 1860–1900:
(a) North British Rubber (Castle Silk Mills), Fountainbridge, 1855.
(b) Grove Biscuit Factory, S. Henderson & Sons, 200 employees, established c. 1860, Fountainbridge.
(c) D. Bruce Peebles & Co., Bonnington, established c. 1860 at Fountainbridge, moved to Bonnington, Edinburgh–Leith boundary, 1873.
(d) John Ford & Co., Holyrood Flint Glass Works, established 1815, extended 1871.
(e) Royal Blind Asylum, bedding and brush works, established 1793, extended c. 1870 at Abbeyhill; over 200 blind employees, 1888.
(f) A. B. Fleming & Co., Caroline Park Works, Granton, established 1852, 1875. Printing-ink manufacturers, oil refiners. Considered the largest printing-ink manufacturers in the world.
(g) Bertrams Ltd, Engineers and Millwrights, St Katherine's Works, Sciennes, established 1821.
Edinburgh Post Office Directories, 1870–1914

d

e

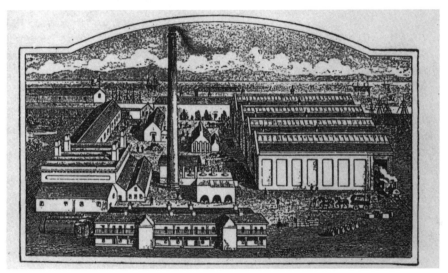

f

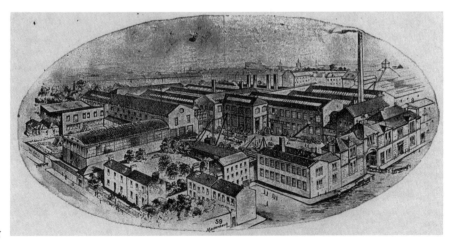

g

premises in the vicinity, both views as well as the easterly vista to the castle were blocked. Large industrial complexes at Parkside, Dalry, Holyrood and Abbeyhill also obliterated the horizons formerly visible to local residents. Even the top of Arthur's Seat, a hill 250m high, could be removed from the landscape of local residents when tall, bulky buildings were constructed behind perimeter walls themselves over 2m high and intended to restrict both pilfering and prying eyes. What psychological effect, if any, this had on residents of these areas is difficult to say, though the reverse process, the demolition of large industrial complexes in the 1980s and 1990s in these same areas, revealed remarkable new perspectives in late 20th-century Edinburgh. Once-darkened streets, often in shadow as a consequence of the surrounding tall industrial buildings, were bathed in sunlight and presented with open views after demolitions had removed the factories and foundries.

Another consequence of mid-Victorian industrial development was the emergence of informal zoning in Edinburgh. Together, landowners and railways influenced the axis of industrial development. Without any formal decisions by Edinburgh City Council, and before the Burgh Police Act of 1862 encouraged municipalities to adopt building regulations, and even longer before the tentacles of building control as discharged by the Edinburgh Dean of Guild Court were extended to the margins of the city, Dalry–Fountainbridge–Gorgie–Slateford was defined as the vector for industrial development. Sandwiched between the two principal railway access routes from the west, this became *de facto* the principal Edinburgh industrial zone until after the Second World War.[43] The consequences of mid-Victorian industrial development, therefore, were very durable. A second, easterly industrial zone was developed at Holyrood–Abbeyhill–Easter Road. This industrial axis in Edinburgh prevailed because, in the east, landownership patterns were fractured, Heriot's trustees had no significant interest, and railway access was adjacent to a sewage farm at Craigentinny, a barracks at Piershill and the engineering depot. To the west, the Union Canal had already breached the defences of genteel development on Lothian Road by securing its terminus

nearby at Lochrin Basin in 1821 and thus contributed to residential property blight for almost thirty years in the Tollcross–Orchardfield area. Perversely, the line of the Union Canal itself provided a physical buffer to the southward drift of industrial development and so prevented any encroachment on the prime residential lands of the Merchant Company at Merchiston.[44]

Since the industrial zones were developed in a relatively short space of time, so, too, were many of the new housing estates that were built for workers in the area. Along Dalry Road, for example, first the Edinburgh Co-operative Building Company (ECBC) developed properties opposite Haymarket station, quickly followed by private developers, one of whom was James Steel. These properties were in easy walking distance of employment in the newly established Fountainbridge rubber, brewery, distillery and warehousing areas compressed between the Caledonian and the North British railway lines. A few hundred yards further west, the 'colony'-style flatted houses of the Edinburgh Co-operative Building Company were under construction at North Merchiston opposite Lorimer's brewery complex just as it was being built. Industrial zones, therefore, stimulated new housebuilding for the regularly employed working class; and, in turn, working-class organisations developed in these neighbourhoods. Of no little significance was the establishment of the Protestant Heart of Midlothian Football Club at Tynecastle in the west, and the Catholic Hibernian FC in the east, with their ground at Easter Road. The ECBC promoted savings clubs, while new churches were established in the Dalry area ministering to the parishioners and providing clubs and evening activities in the meeting halls bordering the main thoroughfares.

Along with zones for industry were zones for industrial workers. Edinburgh, the tenement city, congested and confined for centuries and only on the threshold of extending building for its aspiring suburbans into the northern and western New Towns in the early 19th century, experienced the development of consciously constructed working-class suburbs in the 1860s for the first time in its

history. The deconcentration of industry encouraged the decanting of this industrial workforce.
Social segregation was sought by the middle
classes and induced for the working classes.
However, though this trend towards residential
segregation gained momentum in the 1860s, it was
never uniform. As micro-studies of Edinburgh
streets demonstrate, the social mix within and
between tenements produced stark contrasts of
wealth and class.[45]

Nor was Edinburgh City Council neutral in its
promotion of industry in the city. By announcing
its intention to establish an industrial museum in
the high-profile and newly constructed Chambers
Street, the City Council showed its desire to raise
the profile of industry in the city almost as soon as
the slum-clearance programme initiated by the
Improvement Act of 1867 was under way. Soon
afterwards, the Watt Institute established itself
across the street with strong interests in applied
science and engineering, specifically with reference to the brewing and mining interests that were
so prominent in the local economy. The City
Council was part of the governing body of the
Watt Institute. In another promotional coup,
the International Exhibition of Industry, Science
and Art in 1886, suggested and sponsored by
Edinburgh City Council, was a major public-
relations success, with over 2.7 million visitors
to the exhibition.[46] The cultural credentials of
Edinburgh were explicitly subordinated to those
of industry.[47] The International Exhibition also
made a profit of £5,687, 14 per cent of which the
City Council decided to plough back into small
businesses in much the same spirit as it had
adopted for the Exhibition itself when it agreed to
fund a modest prize for artisan exhibitors to
encourage their participation.[48] A Ladies Section
used the International Exhibition to promote the
industries in which women were employed in the
city.[49] In a much more specific way, too, the City
Council used the Common Good Fund to attract
national conventions and international delegations of manufacturers to the city. The Institute of
Mechanical Engineers, the Iron and Steel Institute
and the Society of the Chemical Industry were all
hosted in 1893–5; between 1905 and 1907, there

were modest receptions for the Canadian
Manufacturers' Association and the American
Society of the Chemical Industry, and a more elab-
orate lunch for the Foreign and Colonial Electrical
Association; and in 1913–14 it was the turn of the
British Pharmaceutical Conference and the British
Carriage Manufacturers to enjoy the hospitality of
the Common Good, courtesy of Edinburgh City
Council.[50] In some, though not all cases, these
industrial delegations were wooed by the City
Council as it endeavoured to promote Edinburgh
as the intersection of science and technology,
knowledge and business. On other occasions, the
city fathers sent delegations to London to present
the case for improved infrastructural provisions in
the city, specifically as these related to electric
lighting, consolidation of railway lines, and tramways.

Conclusion

For Edinburgh, the industrial past has languished
in the shadow of the city's position at the epicentre
of the Scottish Enlightenment. Paradoxically, the
same spirit of enlightenment that embraced rational thought and recognised the legitimacy of alternative perspectives was blind to the relationship
between science and industry which elsewhere in
Britain was a central concern of the aspiring middle
class.[51] Compared to Edinburgh, the scale of professional middle-class engagement in economic and
social life was unparalleled in British cities. For the
majority of Edinburgh citizens, however, a very different perspective on the 19th century existed.
Their Edinburgh landscape was not the refined
architecture of Playfair, Adam, Gillespie Graham or
Rowand Anderson. Theirs was a vernacular architecture dominated partly by tenement housing
where closes and wynds were conduits of communication and interaction, and partly by the workshop and factory embedded in this setting. These
patterns of life and daily work persisted throughout the 19th century, but the physical and mental
landscapes changed – in some cases quite quickly.
Centrifugal forces projected land-hungry industrial plants into the greenfields while leaving large
numbers of manual workers in the city centre to
continue the trades and manufacturing processes

which had long been the mainstay of the Edinburgh economy. As the physical landscape of home and work, therefore, changed for some categories of workers who migrated to newly created industrial zones, such as Dalry–Gorgie, the mental landscape altered too, as social and political structures were redefined and large factories altered the nature of the wage bargain to one that would be instantly recognisable to employees in a Lancashire mill or a Sheffield foundry. The tyranny of the time clock and the physical rigour of system production imposed limitations on individual decisions and work patterns. By the late 19th century, therefore, the factory system had caught up with Edinburgh, and as a result the geometry of Edinburgh had changed fundamentally during the course of the Victorian age. From the irregular, porous street plans of the Old Town, the neat rectangles and crescents of the suburban New Towns emerged for, though not exclusively populated by, the middle classes. For the Edinburgh working class, this geometry also proved irresistible as four-storey tenement blocks developed, fortress-like, on each side of a small rectangular drying-green – an arrangement designed to maximise the development potential of a site. Informal spaces, previously used promiscuously in the Old Town, were replaced by the increasingly regulated city that developed from the 1860s and which was influenced by the economics of housebuilding and the economies of scale in industrial production. Systems defined behaviour. Regulation induced order.

Robert Burns' 'Address to Edinburgh' misrepresented the city. His characterisation, and others', constructed the myth of a non-industrial city. This was a myth in 1786, it was recycled throughout the 19th century, and it is still trawled out as a description of Edinburgh.[52] To deny the presence of industry suited, and continues to suit, some purposes, such as the sales pitch for a cultural city and its festivals. The danger is that, by reasserting it, the myth becomes the reality, and industrialists quit the city or cannot be attracted because they believe that the infrastructure, skills and housing market are unsuited to their purpose. So, for all concerned, it is time to deconstruct the myth.

Notes

1. Robert Burns, *The Poems and Songs of Robert Burns* (New York, 1909–14), vol. 6.

2. See, for example, http://911digitalarchive.org/

3. In a survey in 2000 of postcards of Edinburgh produced by Colin Baxter, a photographer noted for his postcards of Edinburgh, 52 per cent were of Edinburgh Castle.

4. Adapted from S. Nenadic, reviewing R. Rodger, *The Transformation of Edinburgh: Land, Property and Trust in the Nineteenth Century* (Cambridge, 2001). See http://www2.h-net.msu.edu/reviews/showrev.cgi?path=235471036740395

5. See http://www.nls.uk/digitallibrary/map/townplans/edinburgh1056_2.html

6. R. Rodger, 'Wages, employment and poverty in the Scottish cities 1841–1914', in G. Gordon (ed.), *Perspectives of the Scottish City* (Aberdeen, 1985), pp. 25–63, reprinted in R. J. Morris and R. Rodger (eds), *The Victorian City: A Reader in British Urban History, 1820–1914* (Harlow, 1993), pp. 73–113.

7. See S. P. Walker, 'Anatomy of a Scottish CA practice: Lindsay, Jamieson & Haldane 1818–1918', *Accounting, Business and Financial History*, 3(2) (1993): 127–54 for an account of the expansion in one sector of professional work.

8. *The New Statistical Account of Scotland* (Edinburgh, 1845), p. 738; J. Heiton, *The Castes of Edinburgh* (Edinburgh, 1861), p. 282.

9. Heiton, *Castes*, pp. 176–7.

10. T. McDowall and W. McDowall, *New Guide to Edinburgh* (Edinburgh, 1849), p. 10.

11. For women, employment in the professions was very limited initially, with only 4 per cent in 1861 and 9 per cent in 1911 obtaining a living this way, though by 1951 this had risen to 27 per cent.

12. For the implications of this see, D. Smith, *Conflict and Compromise: Class Formation in English Society 1830–1914: A Comparative Study of Birmingham and Sheffield* (London, 1982).

13. D. Reeder and R. Rodger, 'Industrialisation and the city economy', in M. Daunton (ed.), *Cambridge Urban History of Britain, vol. 3: 1840–1950* (Cambridge, 2000), p. 566.

14. Between 1861 and 1951, the index value averaged 14 for Edinburgh, that is, 14 per cent of male workers were in the largest single industrial sector (printing and publishing). In Glasgow, the index was just 17 in 1861, but rose to 28 by 1951, showing increasing concentration in the largest industrial activity. See

Reeder and Rodger, 'Industrialisation and the city economy', p. 570.

15. Ibid.

16. These population figures are based on parliamentary boundaries from 1881 and thus refer to an expanded geographical area including Portobello and Granton. See Rodger, *The Transformation of Edinburgh*, p. 23, for an explanation of the boundary changes.

17. S. Nenadic, 'Middle-rank consumers and domestic culture in Edinburgh and Glasgow 1720–1840', *Past and Present*, 145 (1994): 122–56 provides an account of consumption for an earlier period.

18. For full details of the method of calculation for the weighted series of building in individual and all Scottish burghs, see R. Rodger, 'Scottish urban housebuilding 1870–1914', University of Edinburgh PhD thesis (1975), pp. 39–141.

19. On the vagaries of the Scottish building cycle, see R. Rodger, 'Speculative builders and the structure of the Scottish building industry 1860–1914', *Business History*, 21 (1979): 226–46.

20. S. Damer, 'Memoirs of a Catholic boyhood: a map of Catholic Edinburgh, *History Workshop Journal*, 44 (1997): 189–96.

21. For an elaboration of this point, see R. Colls, 'When we lived in communities: working-class culture and its critics', in R. Colls and R. Rodger (eds), *Cities of Ideas: Civil Society and Urban Identities* (Aldershot, 2004), pp. 283–307.

22. D. J. Withrington and I. R. Grant (eds), *The Statistical Account of Scotland*, vol. 2, pp. 32–5.

23. National Archives of Scotland: George Heriot's Hospital and Trust; Treasurer's Accounts; Abstracts of Hospital and Trust Accounts; Financial Papers, GD421/5/7/1–1.

24. *The Builder*, 27 February 1864.

25. As a result, the Water of Leith became the subject of numerous vigorous campaigns to clean up the river and restrict usage along its course. See Edinburgh City Archives, ECA 175; National Archives of Scotland, RHP 83792–4; *The Builder*, 22 June 1861.

26. This refers to Greek mythology, where the Lethe is one of the rivers that flow through the realm of Hades. The river of Lethe was also called the river of Oblivion; the shades of the dead had to drink from the river to forget about their past lives on earth. See *The Builder*, 27 February 1864.

27. H. D. Littlejohn, *Report on the Sanitary Condition of the City of Edinburgh: with relative appendices* (Edinburgh, 1865), pp. 76–92.

28. A. J. A. Dalglish, 'Voluntary associations and the middle class in Edinburgh 1780–1820', University of Edinburgh PhD thesis (1992), pp. 36–7.

29. R. Rodger, 'Concentration and fragmentation: capital, labor, and the structure of mid-Victorian Scottish industry', *Journal of Urban History*, 14 (1988): 178–213.

30. R. Rodger, 'Business failure in Scotland', *Business History*, 27 (1985): 75–99; R. Rodger, 'Concentration and fragmentation', pp. 188–9; W. Knox, 'Between capital and labour: the petite bourgeoisie in Victorian Edinburgh', University of Edinburgh PhD thesis (1986), table 2.6.

31. H. D. Littlejohn, *Report*, Tabular Statement, p. 47.

32. R. Q. Gray, *The Labour Aristocracy in Victorian Edinburgh* (Oxford, 1976), pp. 18, 28.

33. Anon., *A Descriptive Account of Edinburgh Illustrated* (Brighton, 1891), p. 106.

34. *Ibid.*, p. 53.

35. A. J. Strachan, 'The rural–urban fringe of Edinburgh 1850–1967', University of Edinburgh PhD thesis (1969), p. 88.

36. J. Thomas, *A Regional History of Railways of Great Britain*, vol. 6 (Newton Abbot, 1984 edn), pp. 299–302.

37. R. Rodger, *Housing the People: The 'Colonies' of Edinburgh 1860–1950* (Edinburgh, 1999).

38. *19 & 20 Vict. c32*, Municipal Boundaries of Edinburgh Extension Act.

39. J. W. R. Whitehand, *The Changing Face of Cities: A Study of Development Cycles and Urban Form* (Oxford, 1987), pp. 11–59.

40. R. Rodger, *The Transformation of Edinburgh*, pp. 101–11, 211–21.

41. J. Grant, *Old and New Edinburgh: Its History, Its People and Its Places* (London, n.d.), pp. 219–20.

42. D. Bremner, *The Industries of Scotland: Their Rise, Progress and Present Condition* (Edinburgh, 1869), pp. 362–3; Anon., *Scotland of To-day* (Edinburgh, 1890), p. 9.

43. P. Abercrombie, *A Civic Survey and Plan for the City and Royal Burgh of Edinburgh* (Edinburgh, 1949), p. 47.

44. Rodger, *The Transformation of Edinburgh*, pp. 87–91, 99–101.

45. Rodger, *The Transformation of Edinburgh*, pp. 278–341.

46. *The Times*, 21 August 1886, p. 10, col. b; *The Scotsman*, 15 May 1886, p. 9. The subsequent Edinburgh International Exhibition held in 1890 drew 2.4 million visitors, about half the number who visited the Glasgow International Exhibition in 1888.

47. Edinburgh International Exhibition of Industry, Science and Art, *The Official Catalogue* (London, 1886).

48. Edinburgh City Archives, Town Council Minutes, Session 1885–6, pp. 45–6; ECA, ACC 378/1, Edinburgh Exhibition Trust, fos 1–41; *The Times*, 19 October 1889, p. 4, col. e.

49. K. Ingham, 'A capital exhibition', *Scots Magazine* (1986): 145.

50. R. Rodger, 'The "Common Good" and civic promotion: Edinburgh 1860–1914', in R. Colls and R. Rodger (eds), *Cities of Ideas: Civil Society and Urban Identities* (Aldershot, 2004), pp. 144–77.

51. R. J. Morris, 'Clubs, societies and associations', in F. M. L. Thompson (ed.), *The Cambridge Social History of Britain, vol. 3: Social Agencies and Institutions* (Cambridge, 1990), pp. 410–18.

52. C. McKean, *Edinburgh: Portrait of a City* (London, 1991), pp. 203–4, commented on the 'fragility of Edinburgh's industrial aspirations in the 1880s'.

5 Edinburgh – a tenement city?

PETER ROBINSON

By 1900 few towns, even the smallest, were without their quota of at least one large, metropolitan-looking flatted block . . . they provide the most characteristic experience of Victorian townscape. Round Edinburgh they form an almost continuous ring, well built in the main, and regularly planned.

(Colin McWilliam, *Scottish Townscape*, London, 1975, p. 151)

We associate tenements with Victorian Glasgow; but Edinburgh was building flats when Glasgow was little more than a village, with survivors spanning nearly 500 years. Tenements are found all over Scotland in one form or another – in contrast to England, where flat life has been a relatively recent experience and where, for most outside London and Tyneside, flats do not go back any further than the post-war multi. Living in a volume of space off the ground was well established in Edinburgh by 1500, and it is a practice that continues as vigorously as ever. In this respect, Scots' living habits are much closer to continental Europe than to the English.

This chapter explores why Edinburgh is a city of flats. It shows how tenements have played a crucial role in the physical development of the city and why they continue to leave their mark on the urban landscape. It discusses the relentless pressure for subdivision in what became the principal burgh in Scotland and the legal and institutional frameworks that developed to reinforce and intensify these practices; and it follows the changing forms of the buildings themselves to the great heyday of tenement development in the second half of the 19th century.

Tenements, houses and flats

McWilliam's flatted blocks are the familiar stone Victorian tenements found almost everywhere in Scotland. More usually between three and five storeys high, they can contain up to sixteen or so flats, sometimes with shops, with a common access and a stair leading to individual dwellings – access that is conveniently referred to as 'a stair' in Edinburgh and 'a close' in the west. There are many variations on this general theme. Glasgow's tenements tend to be a uniform four storeys, while Aberdeen's and Dundee's are three or four floors, often with an attic storey.

Edinburgh's Victorian tenements are taller, sometimes with five floors and generally with a dark internal common stair lit by a rooflight, or 'cupola' in local parlance. However, the earlier Georgian New Town flats have a straight common-access stair with landings set immediately behind the front elevation. These are picked out at night by the dull yellow glow of street lighting, lit because in Scotland access to individual flats is via a common landing seen as an extension of the pavement. A local feature is the 'main-door flat', that is, a ground-floor house accessed directly from the street. They are found in all classes of property in Edinburgh, attracting a relative premium for their convenience and privacy. Common-access stairs in Scotland's windy east tend to have doors, while Victorian practice in the west favoured a draughty doorless slot. Victorian tenements are almost always built of stone with slate roofs and partitions of plastered brick, conveying an often grim solidity. They are durable and tend to be reasonably uniform within well-defined local traditions. Expanding building regulation in the 19th century ensured that they were also of fire-resistant construction, adequately ventilated and well served by modern sanitation.

These are no more than sketches hinting at the formal consistency and stylistic variety found across the country. The real picture is complex, as local use of the word 'tenement' embraces most flatted buildings built before 1914, with physical forms evolving by place and through time. Two-storey and two-storey-and-attic 'cottage flats', sometimes with open stairs, are common in smaller burghs such as Arbroath, Dumfries, Kirkcaldy and Wishaw, where they can be mistaken for the English type of row or terraced house. City-dwellers may not recognise them as 'tenements' at all.

Outside Scotland, 'tenement' has a consistently downmarket overtone, corresponding to what Scots would call a subdivided or 'made-down' house; but, as most Scottish flats built before 1850 were intended for occupation by the relatively well-off, tenement life could be elegant and spacious. Purpose-built flats for occupation lower down the housing ladder appeared only when improving job security made new houses accessible to skilled working people. In Edinburgh, this occurred after 1850, first through the co-operative movement and then by the actions of the housing market.

Usage also changes through time. Originally, 'tenement' referred in Scotland to all forms of proprietorship or occupation of heritable property, so that both a piece of land and a building could be referred to as a 'tenement'. Only much later did it come to be applied more specifically to 'a building constructed or adapted to be let in portions to a number of tenants, with each separately occupied portion being considered as an individual dwelling'.[1] In a curious reversal of language, the word 'land' applied to a building, usually urban, and often with the prefix 'fore-' or 'back-' added, depending on its relationship to the street. These prefixes applied equally to stair position: a fore-stair is a projecting front stair. 'Close' initially referred to the enclosed and cultivated ground behind the 'foreland', or 'closour', literally an enclosure. It came to mean a passage only when

the long, narrow tofts or burgage plots were built up and filled with 'backlands'.

A similar change was going on with 'flat'. At the turn of the 15th century, 'flet' was being used in Scotland to describe the inner part of a house.[2] By 1800, 'flet' had come to mean the complete floor or storey of a building, and only more recently a suite of rooms forming a complete dwelling. As its use was confined to Scotland until well into the 19th century, 'flat' can be taken as a Caledonian contribution to our common Anglo-Saxon culture and language. In Edinburgh, 'tenements', 'houses' and 'flats' are interchanged in normal usage.

Why flats?

Whatever we call them, an intriguing question is why people should want to live this way at all. Stacking one household above another is not a natural way of living even now; and, in the more distant past, flat life was inconvenient, if not actually life-threatening through fire and collapse. There had to be powerful reasons to live in flats and for the practice to persist.

Crowding within a confined boundary is a useful starting point in seeking to explain the origins of the tenement idea, and it is tempting to look no further than Scotland's burgh traditions in developing this theme, although this may not be a complete explanation.[3] Burghs were privileged trading enclaves, deriving an income from the levying of customs and dues. They were part of an organised mercantile system, administered by burgesses whose rights depended on their living and working within fixed boundaries – barriers that were necessary to regulate trade. The word 'burgh' comes from 'burgus', literally a fortified enclosure.

It was through a combination of topography and circumstances that Edinburgh proved exceptional. The familiar crag-and-tail site of the Old Town would have been spacious enough in 1100, but by 1500 it had developed fixed boundaries. To the north was the so-called River Tumble, later dammed to form the Nor' Loch, and to the south were the large monastic institutions of Blackfriars, 'Kirk o' Field' and Greyfriars.[4] The only clear path to expansion was obstructed to the east by the separate burgh of Canongate, and to the west development was hindered by the steep slope down to the Grassmarket through the West Bow.

The English wars after 1285 led to enclosure behind a succession of walls and to significant changes in status as Edinburgh became the permanent seat of Scottish government in the course of the 1400s. By 1535, the Court of Session met in Edinburgh regularly, and noblemen, landowners, judges and lawyers became a significant element of the population to compete for houseroom with those merchants and tradesmen whose livelihoods depended on residence. Edinburgh was where the fashionable lived for a least a part of the year as it developed into the principal burgh of Scotland. Changing status was reflected in the population figures within these relatively fixed boundaries. Evidence is scanty, but by making crude assumptions it is possible to follow a striking upward trend as circumstances changed. At the Sexcentenary celebrations in 1929, Frank Mears estimated the population of Edinburgh at the time of the Bruce Charter in 1329 to be in the region of 2,000, based on a crude assessment of burgage plots in the area behind the Flodden Wall of 1514 roughly corresponding to the Ancient Royalty.[5] Using this simple baseline, by 1560 the population had risen to 10,000, a fivefold increase.[6] In 1635, there were nearly 4,000 entries recorded in the Stent Roll, representing a population of around 20,000, and an increase by a factor of ten.[7]

The division of a tenement of land on the south side of the Canongate in February 1491 into three equal parts is described in the *Protocol Book of James Young*.[8] This was typical of a continuing process of subdivision made necessary by a combination of pressure of numbers, inheritance and the impact of strictly enforced burgh rules insisting that burgesses should be property-owners. Here the tenement comprised a foreland, made up of easter and wester forebooths, and a foreloft, described as the 'upper storey', suggesting a two-storey structure. A backland, gardens and yards are also noted. Each party received an element of the foreland (the easter and wester booths and the upper storey respectively), and the back property was divided. This is clear evidence that subdivision was by then

taking place vertically as well as horizontally, even in the Canongate.

For merchants and tradesmen, the High Street was both the principal market and the main source of their wealth, and it was here that this crush became most intense. Thus it was not crowding within a confined boundary alone, but sustained competition for prestige frontages that created the relentless pressure for subdivision which ultimately led to the self-contained flat. Subdivision may have been haphazard and casual at first, gradually developing in formality as pressure of numbers grew and as occupation might go beyond the control of a single extended family. A similar process of competition for prestige sites was suggested by Sutcliffe as an explanation for the Paris flat.[9]

Height and density

More than 350 years later, Robert Chambers described houses in the Cowgate which he believed to date from 1490. The example he chose to illustrate, on the south side opposite the foot of Mint Close, was a two-storey building corresponding closely to the Canongate model. He noted that the 'two booths, or shops, with gallery above conforms to the description of a tenement in Perth which was granted a little before the year 1200 to the Church of Scone', suggesting that similar structures existed in other burghs at an early date. Chambers also refers to more prestigious houses surviving on the Canongate, described as being located 'next below the Horse Wynd'. 'Here, beside the ground accommodation and gallery floor with an outside stair, there is a contracted second floor, having also a gallery in front, with a range of small windows. On the gallery floor, at the head of the outside stair is a finely moulded door, at the base of an inner or turnpike stair leading up to the second floor.'[10]

Circular turnpike stairs made high levels of congestion possible in 16th-century Edinburgh, as they allowed the upward growth of Chambers' Horse Wynd tenement to continue as far as the technology of the day would allow. The commercial ground floor and cellars – the booths – were bypassed by an exposed forestair encroaching on the street and giving access to houses above. As repeated subdivisions occurred, at some point it became safer and more economical of space to build turnpikes springing from the first-floor level to give access to a succession of upper flats. By 1650, most Edinburgh lands had forestairs and followed this broad pattern. There were exceptions, like the Black Turnpike to the south of the city guardhouse, where a turnpike extended to street level; but this was a monastic house – the Auld Bishop of Dunkeld's Lodging – rather than a more usual commercial and domestic mix. The so-called John Knox House and the adjacent Moubray House are examples of lands from a period after the Hertford invasion of 1542, with the forestair and turnpike clearly visible (see p. 31, Fig. 1.7).

Once multi-occupation within a single vertically divided structure was established with separate titles for each 'flet' within the 'land', the tenement idea – for it is little more than formalised multi-occupation within a single structure – merely seems to have been refined, and it was a pattern reinforced as buildings became bigger. Successive generations had little choice but to accept growing congestion, faced with a continuing insistence that burgesses live and work within the Ancient Royalty. Compensating advantages of economy, shelter and warmth were a small comfort, as they became increasingly tolerant of their overcrowded, dirty and close-knit community.

The earliest burgh buildings were most probably built wholly of timber and thatch. Gradually, as timber grew scarcer, stone became the predominant building material, so allowing structures to be more massive and for hearths and flues to be built with reasonable safety. Fire was an ever-present risk when cooking, heating and lighting depended on naked flame. Old lands burned often, creating a cycle of destruction and rebuilding that allowed newer structures to become more massive and durable. Even so, there could be no absolute guarantees against fire, as successive conflagrations proved well into the 19th century.

What is abundantly clear is that formalised subdivision was almost universal in Edinburgh at the time of the Stent Roll in 1635, with tenants and landlords occupying a complex three-dimensional

warren of timber and stone lands. Flat life, as we would recognise today, was well established. We know that Gladstone's Land, then recently refaced in stone and incorporating a fashionable covered way or piazza in the Dutch style, was owned jointly by Thomas Gladstaines and David Jonkin, both merchants, with the front portion of the land divided into five taxable units. Four flats were valued at £150 Scots and the fifth at £160 Scots (£12 Scots was worth £1 sterling at that time), with Thomas Gladstaines occupying the double top flat and David Jonkin the first floor over the shop.[11] The relative status of the occupiers can be judged from other entries in the same Roll. Dwellings in the close behind were assessed at £20 Scots, while the wealthy Sir William Dick of Braid paid £500 and occupied a complete frontage on his own account, although his wealth and status were quite exceptional.

Gordons of Rothiemay's depiction of Edinburgh (Fig. 5.1) may be more illustrative than accurate, but it is a striking picture of how the burgage plots had by 1647 been built up and the extent to which the tenements facing the High Street had grown in height. The fragment of the map shown in the figure of the area around St Giles' shows a clear difference in scale between the High Street and the Cowgate. Contemporary descriptions leave no doubt that Edinburgh was a crowded tenement city: 'High and Dirty' was how Thomas Kirk described the town in 1679. A decade later, Thomas Morer, another English visitor, gave a fuller account of the buildings:

Their old houses are cased with boards and have oval windows (without casements of glass), which they open or shut as it stands with their conveniency. Their new houses are made of stone, with good windows modishly framed and glazed, and so lofty, that five or six stories is an ordinary height, and one row of buildings that is near the Parliament Close with no less than fourteen. The reason is, their scantness of room, which not allowing 'em large foundations they are forced to make up in the super structure, to entertain comers, who are very desirous to be in, or as near to as they can to the city ... Most of the

FIGURE 5.1   Detail of Gordon of Rothiemay's Map of 1647 showing the area around St Giles' in 1647. Note the difference in scale between the High Street frontages (top) and the Cowgate (bottom).   *RCAHMS*

houses are parted into divers tenements, so they have as many landlords as stories; and therefore have no dependence on one another, otherwise as they stand on the same foundation so that in this respect they may be compared to our student's apartments at the Inns of Court, which are bought and sold without regard to the chambers above or below.[12]

Evidence of purpose-built mansion flats for the well-to-do begins to appear in the second quarter of the 17th century. The rebuilding of the Parliament Close area following fires in 1674 and 1676 was acknowledged to be to the very highest standards, with lands occupied by some of Edinburgh's leading citizens.[13] These lands were in turn to burn down in 1700 and again in 1824. Few hints survive to show how the earlier replacements looked beyond the evidence of Morer, but their very massiveness set a pattern for the future.

Mylne's Court at the top of the Lawnmarket dates from 1690 and remains an isolated survivor from this period of intense building activity. In today's terms, we could describe Mylne's Court as a comprehensive redevelopment, created by amalgamating several burgage plots to form a courtyard offering privacy and enclosure. The wealthy were becoming more discriminating in their ways, and civic pride and fashion were beginning to show. Here, the turnpike was abandoned in favour of a generous straight stair with half-landings more typical of the later Georgian New Town. The Mylne's Court frontage to the High Street has a distinctly plain and classical look, sitting comfortably with the later James' Court. Fashion mattered less at the back overlooking the Nor' Loch. Here, the elevation remains craggy and medieval, retaining some of the haphazard character of Gladstone's Land. Fig. 5.2 shows the extent of Lawnmarket lands surviving in the 1880s.

Although Edinburgh's status diminished, first when the Royal Court left in 1603 for London and then in 1707 when it was followed by the Privy Council and Parliament, numbers continued to rise within boundaries that remained essentially unchanged from 1300. In 1694, the population was in the order of 27,000,[14] a thirteenfold increase over the notional 1329 baseline; and in 1755 Webster estimated the parish corresponding to the Ancient Royalty to contain approximately 31,000 people, a fifteenfold increase.[15]

Over a long interval, the pre-industrial burgh developed a legal and institutional framework capable of dealing with the complexities of tenement life and an outlook generally tolerant of flats. At some time between the refacing of Gladstone's Land in 1613 and the building of Mylne's Court in 1690, fashion, display, comfort and convenience became dominating forces, leading to the genesis of 'tenement' buildings that we can begin to recognise. This refinement was virtually complete by the 1790s, at which point quite different factors came into play in the period of town expansion and land speculation.

Town expansion: New Town tenements for the middle class

Agricultural improvements and the beginnings of industrialisation greatly increased the wealth of Scotland from the mid-18th century onwards. Textiles, iron, coal and, latterly, shipbuilding and engineering triggered migration from the land to the towns, stimulating urban building of all kinds, while a shift in trading patterns from Europe to America moved the commercial centre of gravity of Scotland from the Forth to the Clyde. The effect was to transform tenements from a minority building form, largely confined to the burghs, into a dominant one – initially as the prospering middle classes built bigger and better flats, and later as mass housing for an industrial workforce. Some of this first flush of wealth found its way to Edinburgh, stimulating suburban expansion on the south side and unlocking the development potential of the Heriot Trust lands immediately to the north.

Almost inevitably, there was a short-lived reaction to the congestion of the Ancient Royalty and to the entrenched tenement tradition, as a 'London model' of self-contained terraced house caught the imagination of the wealthier classes in Argyle and George Squares. To the south, the tenement was never seriously challenged as ribbon development edged down old roads, as in Buccleuch Street, and

FIGURE 5.2   North side of the Lawnmarket, Edinburgh, c. 1880, showing (left to right) James' Court dating from 1720, Gladstone's Land, 1617, and Lady Stair's Close, 1622. The tenement had clearly arrived by this time.   *RCAHMS*

elongated versions of Old Town lands lined new streets. In the New Town, terraces gained an initial hold in the new climate of formality based on Craig's rectangular blocks; but, as development advanced, plots were released in increasing numbers for flats, reflecting both a relaxed approach towards feuing and the possibility that these sites were seen as less desirable. Flats tend to occur in streets with a north–south axis, principally Hanover, Frederick and Castle Streets, where the stair doors can be traced even now from the Kirkwood Map of 1819. (Fig. 5.3). The proportion of flats increases westwards along Queen Street and by degrees northwards down the hill beyond Queen Street Gardens in what were relatively remote suburban fringes of the day.

Suburban expansion was a clear reaction by the better-off to the congestion and dangers of the Ancient Royalty and the way of life which it represented. The increasing proportion of suburban

tenements north and south could be seen as something of a contradiction, but a metamorphosis was under way. Far from abandoning the tenement, the emerging middle classes were experimenting with the flat idiom in new and exciting ways and transforming an essentially medieval building form into something that was culturally and socially acceptable. Over the period 1775 to 1825, the purpose-built middle-class tenement became elegant and respectable.

Georgian good manners dictated that stairs should be discreetly hidden, so enabling a more formal and unencumbered treatment of front elevations. Initially turnpikes, now relegated to the back, persisted on Edinburgh's south side. They lingered on in Glasgow and Dundee well into the 19th century to become the hallmark of the 'plattie' in the latter, but turnpikes were virtually abandoned in Georgian Edinburgh to the north. Figs 5.4 and 5.5 show the distinctive Edinburgh three-door

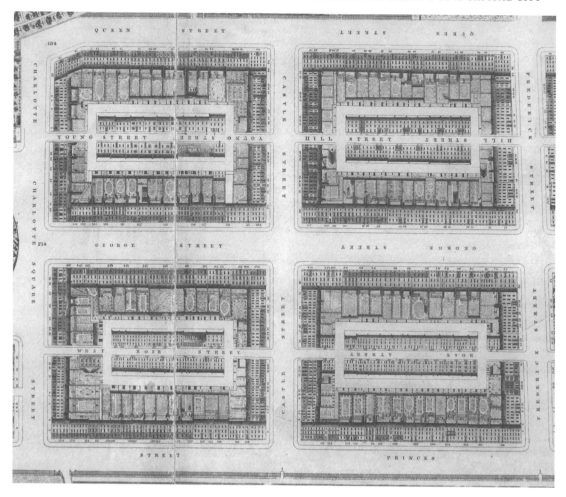

FIGURE 5.3   Fragment of the Kirkwood Map of 1819 showing street blocks and elevations to the west side of the Craig New Town. Tenement flats are mainly on the north–south streets.   *Edinburgh City Archives*

configuration of main-door flat, straight stair and main-door flat at 39–43 Castle Street, typical of that period. The main door to the right (No. 39 Castle Street), containing twelve rooms on three floors, is better known as the town house of Sir Walter Scott. In some later New Town streets, such as Albyn Place, Moray Place, Great Stuart Street, Heriot Row and Great King Street, flats are integrated into corners of grander formal designs, as at Drummond Place and London Street (Fig. 5.6). These flats were well finished, offering a convenient solution to the design difficulty of inserting a marketable property into a dark corner. Flats can occur almost anywhere in New Town street blocks:

sometimes hidden, as in Cumberland Street, and sometimes visible and oddly juxtaposed with terraces, as in Northumberland and India Streets. London Street is composed entirely of flats.

The closing years of the 18th century and the first of the 19th were a period of vigorous experiment and considerable refinement. Edinburgh's example of elegant town expansion was copied widely, as were the flats. Glasgow, Dundee, Aberdeen, Perth, Greenock and elsewhere all pursued their own variations of both, in turn providing inspiration and models for later developments. By the time building activity came to an abrupt halt in 1825, Edinburgh had also added to

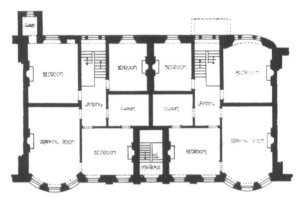

FIRST FLOOR PLAN

GROUND FLOOR PLAN

BASEMENT FLOOR PLAN

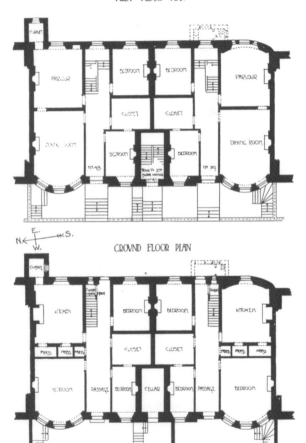

FIGURE 5.4   Nos 39–43 Castle Street, Edinburgh: built in 1794 as four flats: two main-door flats (nos 39 and 43) and two upper flats (no. 41 upper left and right). Sir Walter Scott owned and occupied no. 39 from 1802 to1826. Bow windows give views south to the Castle and north to the Firth of Forth.   *Peter Robinson*

FIGURE 5.5   Plans of 39–43 Castle Street showing the arrangement of main-door tenement flats. The common stair is to the front.   *S. Perks*

the legacy of development practices that were to influence the shape of the Victorian city.

Scotland's property laws were based on feudal principles governing the relationship between superior and vassal. Feuing was the process that allowed a landowner in Scotland – the superior – to sell the title to his land in return for a fixed annual fee, called the feu duty, a sum agreed at the outset and remitted to the superior in perpetuity by the feuar (more quaintly referred to as vassal). Over the period of Georgian expansion, feuing relationships were refined and developed to protect the long-term interests of property-owners, just as tenements adapted to suit changing circumstances.

FIGURE 5.6   Exterior (a) and interior (b) view of the corner of Drummond Place and London Street. An example common in the New Town of tenement flats disguised as a palace façade.   *Peter Robinson*

Feuing raised money for the development costs of drains and roads in the early years of the Craig New Town; but, as the plan was challenged repeatedly and as successive waves of development took place, superiors became more prescriptive. By 1820, feuing had become a device to preserve long-term amenity and value.[16]

Congestion, overcrowding and idealism

For more than 400 years, the entire burgh community shared the 130 acres of the Ancient Royalty; turnpike stairs amounting to vertical streets with a gradation of classes living within the same structure. In later days, one commentator noted that the very highest and lowest flats were 'possessed by artificers, while the gentry and better sort of people dwelt in fifth and sixth stories'. Rents varied considerably even within the same structure, but they were all generally low. 'When incomes were meagre, life was plain.'[17] Some of this flavour lingered on to impress an American visitor in the early 1830s:

> You may call on a friend of note, and discover
> him
> With a shoemaker under, a staymaker over
> him.
> My dwelling begins with a periwig maker:
> I'm under a corncutter, over a baker;
> Above, the chiropodist; cookery too;
> O'er that is a Laundress – o'er is a Jew:
> A painter and tailor divide the eighth flat,
> And a dancing academy thrives over that![18]

These relatively genteel arrangements did not last. By the time this was written, bankers, professional and other educated individuals had very largely decamped to the New Town. They were replaced by successive waves of poorer incomers, and the Ancient Royalty declined into what could be described as a romantic slum.

Edinburgh's population rise in the first half of the 19th century was spectacular. Numbers more than doubled from 67,300 in 1801 to 160,500 by 1851.[19] Much of this expansion was absorbed into the Ancient Royalty, where squalor of a truly horrific kind took over as migrants, often from rural

areas and unaccustomed to the disciplines of high-density life, crowded into decaying and obsolete lands. Contemporary accounts describe unspeakably degrading conditions for many. When William Chambers reported to the Poor Law Commissioners in 1840, he noted: 'Society, in the densely peopled closes which I have alluded to, has sunk to something indescribably vile and abject. Human beings are living in a state worse than brutes.'[20]

Collapses continued. Thirty-five people died and many more were injured on 26 November 1861 when the High Street frontage of Chalmer's Close fell without warning. The much-quoted inscription 'Heave awa' chaps, I'm no deid yet!' survives above Paisley Close as a testament to the dead and injured. A more enduring memorial was the attention which this collapse focused on conditions in the High Street, leading to the appointment in 1862 of Dr Henry Duncan Littlejohn, the City's first Medical Officer of Health. Municipal action was at first modest and concentrated on sanitation, overcrowding and health. At a government level, the General Police and Improvement (Scotland) Act of 1862 gave burghs enabling powers to appoint commissioners to improve the regulation of lighting, cleansing, paving, draining, water supply and other related factors including street layout. This was a useful start, although adoption was discretionary.[21] The Act also endorsed the authority of the Dean of Guild Courts, institutions for resolving neighbour disputes going back to the earliest days of the burghs; but again this was of little use, as the authority of the Edinburgh Court was confined to the Ancient Royalty. Boundaries had failed to keep pace with suburban growth, excluding significant areas of building activity at a critical time. Leith took independent action as a burgh in its own right from 1833 to 1921.

Meanwhile, a combination of general improvements and commercial intrusion, principally from the railways, was forcing a steadily increasing workforce into a diminishing number of decayed and subdivided lands, so driving up rents. In 1829, the Improvement Commissioners cleared an area of the West Bow, and between 1830 and 1841 railway improvements systematically removed the back of the Canongate and Abbeyhill. At the same time, vacant spaces in the centre were taken up by industrial and commercial use or developed with public buildings. Edinburgh was not unique in this respect. Much the same was happening in Dundee, and in Glasgow the coming of the railways had a similar effect in the High Street area.

As if all this was not bad enough, property in Scotland was let for a year, with only one annual date for removals on Whitsunday, while in England accommodation could be found on a weekly basis. The balance of legal powers between landlord and tenant also differed, with the balance in favour of the landlord in Scotland, including powers to seize a tenant's goods in anticipation of rent due – the so-called law of hypothec. It was small wonder that tenants were reluctant to take on any more than they could reasonably afford and were forced in hard times to take in lodgers to share the rent. It was a system guaranteed to encourage overcrowding. Some contemporaries at least were sympathetic. 'We had often wondered', said one observer, 'how the Lowland Scotch mechanic retained his virtue and his courage, when so many malign influences are at work, whose tendency is to destroy both.'[22] Neither was overcrowding confined to the older areas. William Chambers was able to point in 1840 to a house in Jamaica Street in the heart of the New Town 'which a few years ago contained, and probably still contains, 150 persons'.[23] This was, quite literally, on the doorstep of some of the most fashionable houses in the city. Small wonder that well-meaning and idealistic gestures by the better-off were generally hostile to the tenement life represented by the overcrowded and squalid lands, just as the emerging middle classes had themselves sought radical change in the 1760s.

Model working-class tenements

Between 1825 and 1860, virtually no new houses were built that could be regarded as remotely suitable for Edinburgh's growing workforce. There were, however, several local philanthropic gestures, including Ashley Buildings, built in 1851 just behind Moubray House and long cleared. Chalmers Buildings was another, dating from

1854, and newly exposed in the area of the Lochrin canal basin. Both were small-scale affairs. Of more interest are the Pilrig Model Dwellings started in 1852 as a partly philanthropic venture on cheap land owned by Mr Balfour of Pilrig, just on the Edinburgh side of the Leith boundary. This was a deliberate attempt to try something different, being described at the time as occupying 'a kind of intermediate character between the town and country house'.[24] The cottage-flat solution chosen was not new, reflecting smaller burgh practice. Key features were that each house had its own front door and a small garden, and flats were so arranged that the upper and lower floors were approached from opposite sides of the building. Houses were small, but most had an internal toilet, a rare luxury in the mid-19th century even in superior accommodation. Typical is Shaw's Place, a short row built end-on to the street (Fig. 5.7). It is less densely built than adjoining tenements in James Street, developed two decades later as a product of the market. Rosebank Cottages, now visible from the West Approach Road, refined the idea on a larger scale in several rows in the mid-1850s. Here, flats are accessed from opposite sides of the building; but, unlike Pilrig, upper flats shared an external stair and balcony.[25] This general arrangement was borrowed in turn in 1861 by the Edinburgh Co-operative Building Company for the well-known and widely copied 'Colonies' development in Stockbridge.[26]

Although similar in general layout and appearance to Rosebank, the Colonies was a radical experiment in home-ownership based on the same co-operative principles of mutuality and participation that drove the better-known co-operative retail movement. The Company's founding group was encouraged by the newly independent Free Church of Scotland and backed by men who saw improved housing conditions as a crucial first step towards moral reform. This was a new departure in the drive for better housing, introducing working people to home-ownership and to wider responsibilities of participation in the local community. The Edinburgh Co-operative Building Company built 2,300 houses over the following five decades, using the 'Colonies' pattern of

FIGURE 5.7   Nos 1–17 Shaw's Place, built in 1852 by the Pilrig Model Dwellings Company. The upper flats and lower flats are accessed from opposite sides.   *Peter Robinson*

uniform rows rather than street blocks in early years. Some of this idealism waned in time, and the impact of ownership would always be limited while a majority of working people led insecure lives. These distinctive rows became a popular local variant of the cottage-flat theme and, like the Pilrig Model Dwellings before them, in Abbeyhill and Haymarket the Company anticipated the activities of the free market.[27]

The operation of the housing market, 1860–1900

Well-meaning as these experiments were, there was little chance that any could make a real impact on the overwhelming problem of accommodating a burgeoning urban workforce. It was a point recognised fully by the remarkable Committee of the Working Classes of Edinburgh. Set up in July 1858, this Committee took a fairly blunt view: 'The most enthusiastic philanthropist will one day tire of building houses for the working classes when he discovers that such investments are unrenumerative; and that, after all, the people whom he intends to benefit were unconscious of the good

intention'.[28] The Report was critical of early local experiments, and their examination of real options came down firmly in favour of the traditional four-storey tenement financed by private capital and built for rent. The reasons they gave for what might seem an unimaginative conclusion revealed both pragmatism and a depth of local prejudice in favour of what they described as 'the Scottish system of building':

There can be no doubt that a Scotchman is quite as wedded to his flats as an Englishman to his floors . . . His ideas of the importance of his native country are always enhanced by his comparison of the substantial Scotch structures of stone with the slight buildings of brick which grow up around Manchester and Birmingham . . . where ground is scarce and feu duties are high – the Scottish system possesses the advantage in points of economy, in durability, in substantial appearance, in warmth, and capacity for standing tear and wear, there can be no comparison whatsoever.[29]

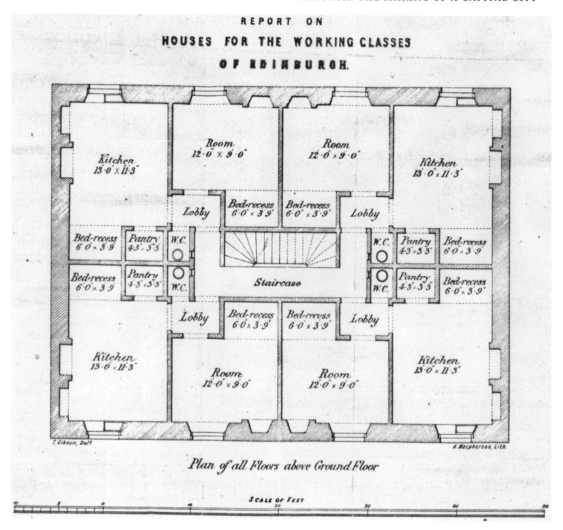

REPORT ON
HOUSES FOR THE WORKING CLASSES
OF EDINBURGH.

Plan of all Floors above Ground Floor

FIGURE 5.8   Model tenement plan from the Report of a Committee of the Working Classes etc., 1860. The arrangement shows four room-and-kitchen houses on each of four floors. The committee estimated that the probable cost of such a tenement 58 feet by 38 feet was £1,350. The rent of sixteen houses at £7.10.0 came to £120 p.a., less £26 feu duty. Factorage, repairs, taxes and insurance gave an annual profit of £94, or a rate of interest of 7 per cent per annum. *Edinburgh City Archives*

The model plan put forward by the Committee in Fig. 5.8 shows a conventional four-storey arrangement with four back-to-back 'room-and-kitchen' houses on each landing, each equipped with a pantry and WC. What is not clear is the extent to which this report merely reflected prevailing views or whether it represented more radical thought.[30] Irrespective of the origins, it was a plan that was adopted widely over the next forty years

in blue-collar developments in the city. Fig. 5.9 shows an improved version incorporating baths and WCs on external walls as personally approved by James Steel for 17–18 Downfield Place in Dalry in 1887. Downfield Place was in the heart of Steel's working-class suburb, reflecting the bottom rung of new tenements constructed for the rental market of the day (Fig. 5.10). It is worth noting that the single-roomed house – the 'single-end', so preva-

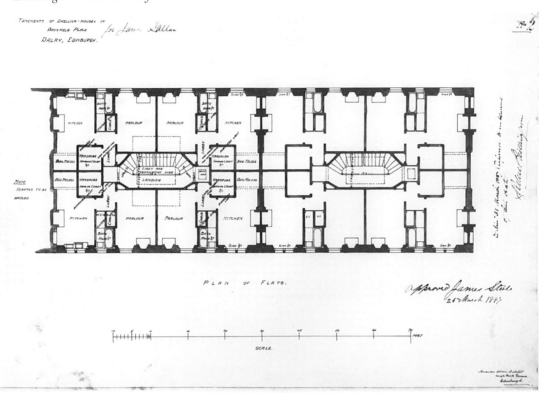

FIGURE 5.9 Upper-floor plan submitted to the Dean of Guild Court in 1887 by James Allan for two working-class tenements in Dalry. The plan is clearly influenced by the 1860 Report. *Edinburgh City Archives*

lent elsewhere in Scotland – is relatively rare in Edinburgh. Room-and-kitchen houses like these were generous and well equipped when compared to equivalent accommodation in Glasgow, Paisley and working communities that lacked the stability of Edinburgh's employment base.

Edinburgh's population almost doubled from 1851 to 1901, growing from 161,500 to 317,000, and increasing by a factor of almost five over the century from 1801.[31] Edinburgh had the advantage of a significant professional and white-collar presence arising directly from capital functions, plus a varied industrial sector. Both guaranteed a measure of stability favouring investment. Another key factor was that by 1870 the release of development land was determined by a handful of professionally managed major trusts and institutions.[32] This was a period when property investment was familiar to the small saver looking for a

safe income. Described by one contemporary as 'the shopocracy', these were tradesmen and others interested in a steady return who might be equated now to building-society savers.[33] Neither professionally managed institutions drip-feeding land supply with an eye to the long term, nor small savers seeking security, favour innovation. They were innately conservative in their choices. Their actions reinforced whatever local prejudices prevailed, preferring proven designs that could be adapted to new market conditions and multiplied in a formulaic way on a predictable, industrial scale.

Other powerful influences reinforced successful local practice. The rate of interest on flat-building, the 'bond rate', was lower than for terraced development because the risk of empties was much reduced.[34] Typical financing involved the borrowing of something like two-thirds of the cost of a

FIGURE 5.10   Tenements with shops hard against the pavement in James Steel's blue-collar suburb of Dalry. *Peter Robinson*

working-class tenement containing around a dozen houses for rent. This produced a return of 5–7 per cent per annum as a minimum after all risks and maintenance were covered.[35] The conventional wisdom of the day was that, while the prevailing rate of interest dictated the tempo of building, the level of feu duty dictated the density.

The feuing system created what amounted to a self-fulfilling prophecy operating through the mechanisms of potential value. The system of fixed payments in return for rights in perpetuity induced a reluctance to release developable land; and, when sites were released, superiors drove a hard bargain. Congestion bred congestion, as adjacent land values reflected the possibility of an equivalent density of development. Feus were also valued as security, which made them attractive

commodities in their own right and a useful instrument for raising building capital. This was achieved through a process of sub-infeudation, that is, creating a pyramid of responsibility through a chain of vassals, each paying duty to his immediate feudal superior and each with an interest in a property. A chain might involve the original landowner, a developer, one or more builders and a landlord, so allowing a succession of interests access to a source of finance, while giving superiors a strong measure of control over building form and future use. The downside was that every aspect of feuing added significantly to land costs, with the predictable consequence that Scottish land had to be densely or profitably developed to cover land charges.[36] It was the operation of the feu system, coupled with a long-standing tolerance of high densities and innate investor conservatism, that created the Victorian tenement suburb. The 1918 Royal Commission on Housing in Scotland reported:

> When industrial activity became pronounced in the middle of the last [19th] century, towns began to expand rapidly, and it was found by owners of ground that a great deal of money could be made by such owners in selling or feuing their ground for housing purposes. With the example of housing people in tenements before them, their calculations were naturally based upon what was the utmost number of people who could be housed on a given area, so that from the total earnings of the people so housed on that area the largest possible sum could be extracted as cost of ground in the shape of ground rent. This practice has developed, and it has become practically universal in large towns to build on the intensive system.[37]

A tenement legacy: feuing plans and aesthetic conditions

The pace of residential development in the last forty years of the 19th century more than made up for the lean years from 1825 to 1860. Between 1811 and 1911, Edinburgh's housing stock increased fivefold, doubling between 1871 and 1911, largely

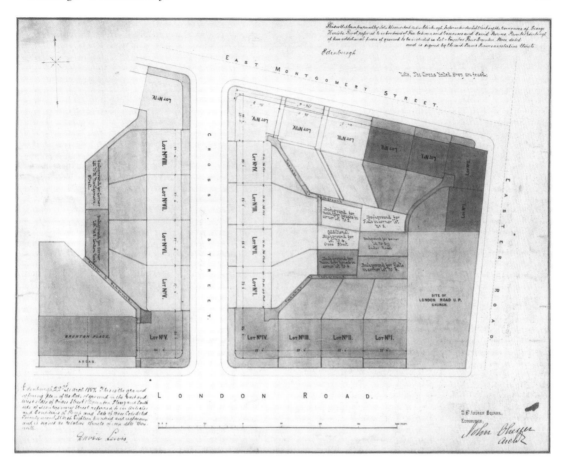

FIGURE 5.11 Heriot's Trust Feu Plan for East Montgomery Street, Cross Street and London Road of 1887. *RCAHMS*

through suburban expansion.[38] Industrial relocation encouraged blue-collar building, as factory-owners shifted from congested city-centre sites to relatively spacious greenfield premises better suited to industrial production and more directly accessible to railways. Newly built room-and-kitchen flats in Dalry and Easter Road attracted working populations away from subdivided lands, although many families still found it necessary to take in lodgers to help pay the rent. Overcrowding often remained, being merely displaced from the centre to new working communities that survived almost intact until the 1950s.[39]

James Steel's rags-to-riches story, from bankrupt incomer to knight and Lord Provost, is the stuff of legend. Active in several parts of the city from 1862 to 1904, and latterly the city's largest single landowner, he was directly responsible for developing Dalry and Comely Bank in the course of his colourful career, stamping his mark through a combination of sub-infeudation and business skill. When James Allan undertook to build in Downfield Place in 1887, he accepted feu conditions from Steel that defined the physical characteristics of the proposal from overall height and building lines to details of elevation and materials, right down to specifications of boundary walls and outbuildings. He also accepted limitations on use to protect amenity.[40] There was little room for manoeuvre.

The Heriot Trust was just as prescriptive in the London Road area. Fig. 5.11 shows the feuing

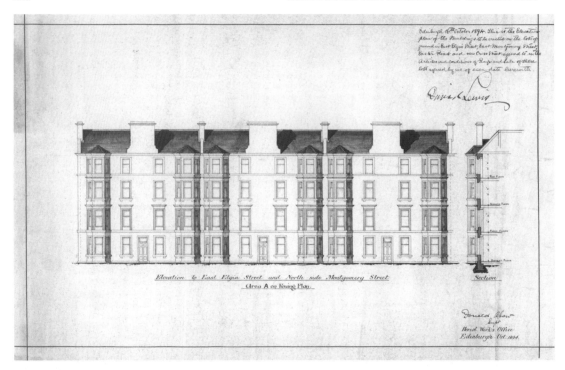

FIGURE 5.12   Heriot's Trust elevations relating to the feuing of East Elgin Street and Montgomery Street. Developers who bought feus were required to comply with the overall design.   *RCAHMS*

plans and Fig. 5.12 the elevations used by the Trust when releasing land for auction – and they are exactly contemporary with Downfield Place. In Edinburgh, the most instantly identifiable difference between white-collar and blue-collar developments was the use of the bay window. Here, the street elevations and sections were drawn by Heriot's own Works Office for the avoidance of any doubt over letting intentions or compliance. Dean of Guild plans submitted later for East Montgomery Street show two flats to a stair, with main-door flats on two levels. Each upper flat had four rooms with a bathroom and a generous access stair lit by a cupola. Main doors had four rooms on two levels linked by an internal stair, plus access to a private drying-green in the middle of the enclosed street block (Fig. 5.13). Steel's own development in Comely Bank in the 1890s followed the white-collar example while showing more imagination in the configuration of street blocks. Contemporary developers like Steel had an inti-

mate knowledge of their markets, adjusting the number of flats on a stair to reflect subtle changes of status. Gradations also occur within each stair, from prestigious main-door to less attractive top flat – pale reflections of the social mix of earlier times, and differences hard to detect from the street.

The same careful response to market needs and class occur in the Warrender estate, developed from the late 1870s to the south of Bruntsfield Links. These feus took on a distinct character deriving from the generous size of the ten or so street blocks comprising the estate and their architectural treatment, borrowing the baronial style used by Peddie and Kinnear in Cockburn Street over the period 1859–64 and by David Cousin and John Lessels in St Mary's Street in 1869. Warrender was baronial on a grand suburban scale. McPherson and Calvert's 1880 tenement at 17–19 Warrender Park Terrace has five floors and a basement. Containing ten flats, each with a large bathroom

FIGURE 5.13   Nos 1–21 Wellington Street adjacent to Montgomery Street, built as a single unit in 1890 to the Heriot Trust conditions.   *Peter Robinson*

(rather than just a WC), it was a considerable undertaking in its own right even by today's standards, yet it is only one segment in a street block that is itself part of a grander planned scheme. Three street blocks create what amounts to a massive boundary wall to the south of the Meadows. The scale is more modest on the southern edge of the estate at 111–114 Marchmont Road, where the Strathearn Building Company built sixteen flats on two stairs in the same year. Here, the flats are much smaller, reflecting proximity to shops and the less private setting of a main-road frontage (Fig. 5.14).

Baronial was well suited to the vagaries of feuing. It offered a way of accommodating different builders by making a virtue of small differences as development proceeded incrementally along street faces. Individual addresses are, when viewed from the front, very different within an overall discipline of height and materials along the length of Warrender Park Terrace, and yet the whole composition conveys the impression of being built at the same time as a single structure. From the back, each segment is virtually identical and indistinguishable from other contemporary tenements almost anywhere else in Edinburgh (Fig. 5.15). Baronial also made a virtue of verticality – very convenient in flats, as each floor plan repeats itself one above another; but the remorseless verticality becomes boring and clumsy in long vistas, in contrast to earlier and more modest Georgian development relying on formal composition.

There is little in Edinburgh to compare to the Haussmann-like refinement of the Glasgow tenement ranges of the 1850s and 1860s, where architects began to explore the visual potential of vertical balance and horizontal rhythm in the

FIGURE 5.14   Tenements at 111–114 Marchmont Road,
built in 1880 by F. James Hay for the Strathearn Building
Company.   *Peter Robinson*

increased scale of Victorian tenement developments. Neither is there much in the city to match
the Glasgow tenement corners of the 1890s; but
Edinburgh has some magnificent oddities. There
are Thomas Pilkington's ponderous 1864 gothic
tenements in Grove Street. Ramsay Gardens, built
in stages between 1892 and 1909 just below the
castle to designs by Sydney Mitchell for Patrick
Geddes, is a conspicuous landmark; and there is
what must be the most luxurious tenement in
Scotland at 17–25 Rothesay Terrace, built in 1908
with lifts, service entry and dumb waiters.

Whatever the treatment of the street face or
quality of the building, the Edinburgh tenement
street block has a well-defined public face, usually
viewed obliquely in perspective. The passage
leading through the depth of the building to

drying-greens at the back signals a hierarchy of
order from the public to the private, with the street
door as the demarcation point, often accompanied
by a striking contrast of colour from the grey man-
made street face to a lush green enclosure. In
better-class flats, public rooms were arranged at
the front and kitchens to the rear. Victorian tenement suburbs were more socially segregated than
their Georgian forebears, but both were based on
the street block. By 1900, the stage was set for the
introduction into Scotland of English-inspired
garden-city ideas that would challenge this hierarchy and lead to a move away from the regulated
uniformity that gives Edinburgh's tenements their
identity and character.

Five centuries of flats

Private investors lost interest in the lower end of
the housing market after about 1904 through
a combination of circumstances that led to a
paradoxical situation of both overcrowding and
overbuilding. Isolated 'upmarket' private-sector
building for rent continued until 1914 and resumed
on a limited scale in the 1920s and 1930s in
Learmonth, Ravelston and Morningside, but after
1919 the private sector became increasingly preoc-
cupied with building semi-detached and bungalow developments largely for owner occupation
(see Chapter 7). Thereafter, it was left to municipal
landlords to carry on building flats for rent (see
Chapter 6), although private-sector conversions
and 'making down' continued unabated. The collapse of the private-sector rental market ended a
long period of development and refinement.

In summary, Edinburgh's tenements have their
origins in modest burgh buildings fronting the
High Street and in the behaviour of the merchants
and tradesmen who were obliged to live and work
within the narrow confines of the burgh. They
competed for houseroom with landowners, judges
and lawyers as Edinburgh took on the functions of
a capital, creating a relentless pressure for prestige
frontages. By 1635, almost every property in the
burgh was a flat. Middle-class prosperity and
town expansion provided the climate for a crucial
period of inventiveness and refinement at the
close of the 18th century, leaving an institutional

a

b

FIGURE 5.15   Front (a) and back (b) of Warrender Park Terrace facing Bruntsfield Links. The feuing elevations normally applied only to the front façade, thereby allowing the rear elevation to be built more casually.   *Peter Robinson*

framework and models that were adapted and greatly multiplied in the great period of tenement-building between 1860 and 1900. The Victorian tenement suburb owes its homogeneity to the Scottish feuing system and to a handful of trusts working through a disciplined chain of individuals with a vested interest in the property and operating in a market that was essentially conservative in outlook.

Over a century on from the last great phase of Victorian building, Edinburgh's tenement suburbs are still dominant and important to the visual perception of the city. Their very solidity and coherence convey order. They are the uniform matrix that holds the town together – a regulated four-storey forest of chimney heads punctuated by spires: the 'almost continuous ring', giving shape and identity to each inner area.

Notes

1. *Scottish Judicial Dictionary* (Edinburgh: 1946), p. 299.
2. Warrack and Grant, *Chambers' Scots Dictionary* (Edinburgh, 1974 edn), p. 180.
3. Daniel Defoe, *Tour Thro' the Whole Island of Great Britain*, Vol. 3 (London: G. Strahan, 1727), p. 6, shows that sub-division was as much a characteristic of the Scots' way of life in small, almost rural communities as in the burghs. For burgess status, see W. M. Mackenzie, *The Scottish Burghs* (Edinburgh and London, 1949).
4. On the south side of Edinburgh, the Blackfriars founded a convent in 1230, and in the same century the 'Kirk o' Field' (the Church of St Mary in the Field) was established nearby. Two centuries later, the Greyfriars built a church and convent to the southwest. The three religious establishments formed a continuous southern boundary to the Cowgate, at that time an exclusive southern suburb.
5. Mears assumed there to be about 200 holdings fronting the High Street, with approximately 150 more in the Grassmarket and Cowgate. Six people to each plot gave a total population in 1329 of approximately 2,000. See Frank Mears, *City of Edinburgh 1329–1929* (Edinburgh and London, 1929), p. 375.
6. Dr Michael Lynch estimated the population at the time of the Reformation in 1560 at 10,000.
7. Estimated figures supplied by Dr Makey, based on the Stent Roll (City of Edinburgh: 1635).
8. *Protocol Book of James Young, 1485–1515*, ed. Gordon Donaldson (Edinburgh, 1942), item 410, pp. 95–6.
9. Anthony Sutcliffe (ed.), *Multi-Storey Living: The British Working-class Experience* (London, 1974), pp. 8–12.
10. Quoted from Robert Chambers, *Edinburgh Papers, Wm. and Robt. Chambers* (London and Edinburgh, 1861), p. 4.
11. Gladstone's Land, frontage to High Street. Extract from Stent Roll (City of Edinburgh: 1635), NW Quarter, p. 84.
12. Taken from Peter Hume Brown, *Early Travellers in Scotland*, facsimile edn (Edinburgh, 1973), pp. 279, 256.
13. See Dr Marguerite Wood, 'All the Statlie Buildings of . . . Thomas Robertson, a building speculator of the seventeenth century', in *BOEC*, 24 (1942), pp. 126–51. Also George Home, 'Notes on the re-building of Edinburgh in the last quarter of the seventeenth century', in *BOEC*, 29 (1956), pp. 111–42.
14. Estimated figure calculated by Dr Makey on the basis of the Poll Tax returns of 1694. The principal reference is Dr Marguerite Wood, 'Edinburgh Poll Tax returns', in *BOEC*, 25 (1945), pp. 90–126.
15. Estimate based on Webster's Census; but suburban expansion to the south and west makes the figures difficult to disaggregate. The total population of the city was calculated at about 66,000, with only a portion residing within the ancient boundaries: James Gray Kyd (ed.), *Scottish Population Statistics, including Webster's Analysis of Population 1755* (Edinburgh, 1975), pp. 14–15.
16. See Richard Rodger, *The Transformation of Edinburgh: Land Property and Trust in the Nineteenth Century* (Cambridge, 2001), pp. 59–68.
17. Henry Grey Graham, *The Social Life of Scotland in the Eighteenth Century* (London, 1909), chapter 3, 'Town Life – Edinburgh', pp. 81–126.
18. Philadelphia American Courier, quoted in John Heiton, *The Castes of Edinburgh* (Edinburgh, 1861), p. 225.
19. Figures are for the City and Extended Royalty, Census of Scotland 1911.
20. W. Chambers, *Report on the Sanitary State of the Residences of the Poorer Classes in the Old Town of Edinburgh* (Edinburgh, 1840), p. 3.
21. The General Police and Improvement (Scotland) Act 1862.
22. Quoted in Heiton, *Castes*, pp. 228–9.
23. Chambers, *Report* p. 1.
24. *Report of a Committee of the Working Classes of Edinburgh on the Present Overcrowded and Uncomfortable State of Their Dwelling Houses, with an Introduction and*

Notes by Alexander Macpherson, Secretary of the Committee (Edinburgh, 1860), p. 16; and see also 'Report of the Visiting Sub-Committee', pp. 2–24.

25. Rosebank Cottages were designed by Alexander McGregor, apparently under the instruction of (later Sir) James Gowans, the railway contractor turned architect and later Lord Dean of Guild of the City of Edinburgh. McGregor described the underlying philosophy behind the flatted design in evidence to the Royal Commission on Housing 1885.

26. The Edinburgh Co-operative Building Company Ltd was registered on 25 May 1861. See *Transactions, National Association for the Promotion of Social Science* (Edinburgh, 1863), p. 627.

27. For an explanation of the co-operative housing movement in Edinburgh, see Rodger, *The Transformation of Edinburgh*, pp. 353–414. See also Rosemary Pipes, *The Colonies of Stockbridge* (Edinburgh, 1984).

28. *Report of a Committee of the Working Classes*, p. 12. The Committee was set up on 15 July 1858 after a public meeting in Buccleuch Street Hall, reporting in 1860.

29. Ibid., pp. 16–17.

30. There is an uncanny similarity between the model plan, left hanging when the property market collapsed in 1825, and 17 Home Street built in 1826. The Drumryan Estate in Tollcross remained undeveloped for nearly forty years until completed by James Steel.

31. Figures from the Census of Scotland 1911 are for the City and Extended Royalty in 1851 and the Parliamentary Burgh in 1901.

32. Six of the seven largest landowners in Edinburgh in 1872 were institutions or trusts, all professionally administered: the Crown, George Heriot's Hospital, Edinburgh Town Council, Charles Rocheid's Trustees, Sir William Fettes' Trustees, and Alexander Learmonth's Trustees. See Rodger, *The Transformation of Edinburgh*, p. 8.

33. The term 'shopocracy' comes from the evidence of George Eadie, a Glasgow speculative builder from 1851. He had built 200 tenements of twelve houses each by 1902, mainly for shopkeepers: Glasgow Municipal Commission, Minutes, p. 339. Quoted in John Butt, 'Working-class housing in Glasgow, 1851–1914', in Stanley A. Chapman (ed.), *The History of Working-class Housing – A Symposium* (Newton Abbot, 1971), p. 74.

34. Cd 8731, Royal Commission on Housing in Scotland, *Report of the Royal Commission on the Housing of the Industrial Population of Scotland, Rural and Urban* (Edinburgh, 1918), para. 484, p. 62.

35. Scottish Land, *The Report of the Scottish Land Enquiry Committee* (London, 1914), chapter 24, pp. 325–31.

36. Ibid., p. 308.

37. Cd 8731, Royal Commission on Housing in Scotland, *Report*, para. 1,612, p. 245.

38. Rodger, *The Transformation of Edinburgh*, p. 492.

39. The impact of tenement life on women in Edinburgh's working suburbs is recorded in Helen Clark and Elizabeth Carnegie, *She Was Aye Workin'* (Oxford, 2003).

40. Edinburgh City Archives, James Steel's Trust, Conditions of Feu, Dalry, ACC 373.

PART III

Urban Management in the Early 20th Century

Introduction

Urban areas in Scotland began to grow significantly in the 18th century, peaking in growth terms in the 19th century. Until the middle of the 19th century there was limited urban management, with the role of urban legislation being mainly protective of individual rights, and urban government largely self-perpetuating. However, the results of relatively unchecked urban growth and development by the middle of the 19th century, despite the initiative of new-town development on the fringes of older urban cores, such as in Edinburgh, led to a mind-shift in terms of management of urban areas. This was expressed by a growth of municipal activity and functions, with much wider powers as well as wider geographical areas of action. This 'swelling tide of municipalisation' (Gordon and Dicks 1983: 18), or 'transition from oligarchic incompetence to bureaucratic omnipotence' (Adams 1978: 127), did not happen quickly, but evolved over time.

As with other urban areas, in the latter part of the 19th century and into the early 20th century the city of Edinburgh expanded its urban footprint, its city limits and the powers of its municipality. This was a gradual process, and one not without struggle. Although the functions developed became mainly proactive in their scope, they were mainly reactive when introduced initially. Starting with municipal fire brigades and policing in the early 19th century, this evolved after the Burgh Reform Acts of 1833–4 to include lighting, paving, cleansing, regulating slaughterhouses, naming/numbering streets and houses, and preventing infectious diseases. The next stage was provision of sewers and improved water supplies (1840–90), municipal involvement in gas and electricity supplies, and provision for public parks as well as increased poor relief, hospitals and prisons. During this period, attitudes to urban development changed, and while new urban expansion areas continued to be provided, as in the New Town, there was a growing focus on urban renewal. Initially a local initiative, this soon became a national concern and refocused attention on the Old Town. In time, the expanded role and area of the city's local authority once again became critical.

In Part III, we examine what these changes meant more specifically for housing and planning and how this affected the built environment of the city. The growing role of municipal government in regulating and then providing housing, as well as the growth of urban planning as an essential part of urban government, are the main subjects studied. In Chapter 6, Lou Rosenburg and Jim Johnson investigate the origins and ongoing implementation of a revolutionary approach to urban renewal pioneered in the city – 'conservative surgery' – first advocated by Patrick Geddes, but crucially consolidated by the City Architect, Ebenezer Macrae. In Chapter 7, Miles Glendinning reviews the provision of housing, with direct and indirect state involvement, and changing levels of engagement with the private sector, from early in the century to the 1960s, including the impact on the city's fabric. In Chapter 8, Cliff Hague looks at the early initiatives of urban planning in the city, and how these evolved through to the last quarter of the 20th century, when state involvement in urban development peaked and the role of the state in planning was publicly queried.

The overall theme of the three chapters in Part III is thus the emerging and growing role of the state in managing urban growth and development through the action of the municipality in practice – a situation which began to decline after the middle of the 20th century. Inherent is the fact that state power was not homogeneous but often contested – not only between political parties, but also between the national and local levels of government, and with social groups and strong lobbies. State power initially developed through close association with civil-society groups, such as the evolution of building and planning controls supported by civic action around public-health issues. However, with the growing dominance of the state and relatively stable agreement about roles of national and local government, the action of civil society was effectively subordinated. In its place rose more concerted private-sector activity, especially in housing provision, although the most contentious areas of engagement between the government, private-sector and civil society were probably around planning.

PLATE 1 Edinburgh, a landscape fashioned by geology: artist's impression of the Arthur's Seat volcano in Carboniferous times.   *D. McAdam/The Natural History Museum, London*

PLATE 2 Robert Barker's view of Edinburgh, 1792. Part of a panorama of the city showing the Old Town in relati◄ geology interact. *Edinburgh University Library, Special Collections*

the New Town, at that time under construction. Barker captures the wonderful contrast in the way city and

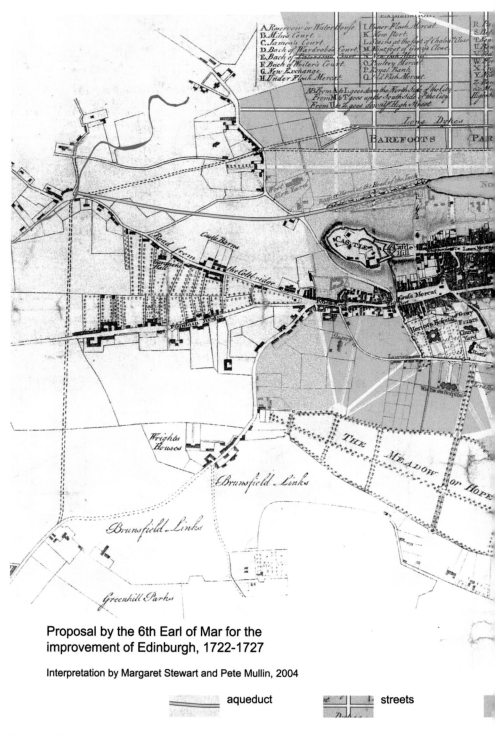

Proposal by the 6th Earl of Mar for the
improvement of Edinburgh, 1722-1727

Interpretation by Margaret Stewart and Pete Mullin, 2004

aqueduct   streets

PLATE 3   The sixth Earl of Mar's plan for the reconstruction of Edinburgh, 1728. In his proposals, Ma
one ever existed. However, the description is sufficiently clear and detailed to enable a reconstruction. Th
form, Scottish in its integration of landscape and historical imagery, and functional in its road network an
and the Royal Scottish Geographical Society

residential   bridges   plantation

ives only a suggestion for the disposition of the streets; and no plan on paper has survived, if indeed
econstruction is on a map of 1748, using Mar's written description. The design is essentially Baroque in
he distribution of new suburbs to the north and south of the Old Town.   *Pete Mullin, Margaret C. H. Stewart*

PLATE 4   The Old Town has inspired many, from Robert Louis Stevenson to Patrick Geddes. It continues to provide a landscape rich in memory and artistic potential.   *Brian Edwards*

Plate 5   New housing in Fishmarket Close, designed by Richard Murphy and Partners, reinforces the message of sustainable development through architectural design.   *Brian Edwards*

PLATE 6   The Scottish Parliament Building, designed by Enric Miralles with RMJM, provides a model of creativity which is anchored to a sense of place. The architecture is as much an interpretation of Scotland's landscape as an exercise in building design.   *Adam Elder/Scottish Parliamentary Corporate Body 2004*

6 'Conservative surgery' in Old Edinburgh, 1880–1940

Lou Rosenburg and Jim Johnson

Edinburgh may grow to be a larger and larger city, and add to herself model factories and garden suburbs in every direction, but she can never be a great city so long as the High Street, the Grassmarket, and the Canongate are accepted by either her taste or her conscience as slums. (Editorial Comment, in *The Blue Blanket: An Edinburgh Civic Review*, 2, April 1912, p. 83)

Introduction

The medieval quarter of Edinburgh, known as the Old Town, is currently perceived as a vibrant part of the city. Despite the loss of many ancient buildings over the centuries, the area has managed to retain much of its historic character. The present vitality of the Old Town is largely due to a series of successful urban-regeneration initiatives undertaken by public, private and voluntary bodies since the mid-1970s. With the mounting investment of recent decades, this remarkable piece of Scotland's urban landscape is no longer seen to be crying out for care and attention.

By and large, the recent phases of regeneration have treated the historic fabric of the Old Town with respect by making relatively small-scale changes within the existing street pattern. This pattern of gradual renewal, known as 'conservative surgery', has evolved from the earlier remedial initiatives of the period 1880–1940. The conservative-surgery approach was pioneered by Patrick Geddes (1854–1932), who lived and worked in the Old Town during the closing decades of the 19th century. The civic efforts of Geddes and his contemporaries were, in essence, a reaction against the more dramatic forms of inter-

vention carried out during the 1860s and 1870s within the medieval quarter of the city.

Living conditions in the Old Town declined significantly after 1775, as the wealthier residents moved to more salubrious accommodation in the New Town (as noted in Chapter 2). Over time, the concentration of impoverished households increased within the Old Town, and by 1850 the area was reputed to be among the worst slums of western Europe. The Town Council's first concerted attempt to remove these conditions was an area-based sanitary improvement scheme promoted in 1867. In physical terms, the 1867 Scheme can be seen as an example of the 'street improvement' approach, which had been introduced on the continent during the 1850s. The Edinburgh variant, involving large-scale clearance and redevelopment of entire street frontages, was carried out over a twenty-year period in selected parts of the Old Town. Although many of the new buildings were designed to a high standard, few steps were taken to preserve the historic fabric of the area. Also, the rehousing needs of local residents received little attention.

This chapter traces the early transition from comprehensive redevelopment to gradual renewal within the Old Town, and details how the conservative-surgery approach was applied in the municipal sanitary improvement initiatives of the 1890s and the 1920s. This facet of Edinburgh's experience in dealing with public-health problems was highly atypical. During the period under consideration, most British cities made little effort to develop area-based methods in the promotion of sanitary reform. In those cities where a genuine commitment was made to area-based measures, such as Glasgow, the usual form of physical treatment involved comprehensive redevelopment of relatively large sites.

Legacy of the 1867 Improvement Scheme

In November 1861, the need for remedial action in the Old Town was dramatised by the collapse of a High Street tenement resulting in thirty-five fatalities and 100 persons being made homeless.[1] A year later, the Town Council decided by a narrow margin to use the enabling powers of the General Police and Improvement (Scotland) Act 1862 (known as the Lindsay Act) to appoint a Medical Officer of Health. The appointment of Dr Henry Littlejohn was the first of its kind in Scotland; he was to hold this post until 1908. His pioneering study entitled *Report on the Sanitary Condition of the City of Edinburgh* was published in 1865. This research provided the first systematic body of evidence on the deplorable living conditions in the Old Town and other impoverished areas of the city.[2]

Informed by Dr Littlejohn's research, and aware of the potential health risks for the wider Edinburgh community, the publisher William Chambers (1800–83) took up the cause of sanitary reform.[3] Despite having no previous experience of public office, Chambers was invited to serve as Lord Provost. Under his stewardship, the Town Council secured parliamentary approval for private legislation known as the Edinburgh Improvement Act of 1867. Along with Liverpool and Glasgow, Edinburgh was among the initial group of municipalities in the UK that managed to obtain local statutes with explicit powers concerning area-based sanitary improvement.[4]

The 1867 Act was employed to carry out an extensive slum-clearance scheme within the medieval quarter. A total of thirty-four separate areas were designated for clearance on health grounds. Collectively, these sites contained more than 3,000 derelict properties on roughly fifty acres of land.[5] In the most congested locations, the population densities exceeded 600 persons per acre.[6] During the course of implementing the Chambers Scheme, over one-quarter of the Old Town's residents (equivalent to one-tenth of the total population of Edinburgh) were displaced from their homes involuntarily.

The municipality had wide discretion in determining the future use of cleared sites. There was no formal requirement to build any new housing, and the interests of displaced residents were largely unprotected. A new agency, the Edinburgh City Improvement Trust, was set up to implement a rolling programme of street improvement. Over a twenty-year period, a series of new and expanded streets were created with redeveloped frontages, including Jeffrey, East Market, Cranston, Blackfriars, St Mary's, Chambers, Guthrie and Lady Lawson Streets.[7] The construction of Chambers Street was seen as an opportunity to facilitate institutional expansion, and a number of prestigious buildings were provided for civic and educational bodies.

Generally speaking, the 1867 Scheme was perceived by Edinburgh's propertied classes as a questionable use of public-authority money and a serious drain on the local rates. Over the full period of implementation, a net operating deficit of £380,000 was funded through a local improvement tax.[8] In the end, more than 2,700 dwellings were demolished.[9] Most of the displacement occurred between 1868 and 1875, at a time when the general level of housebuilding in the city was relatively buoyant.[10] A total of 340 new dwellings were constructed on the cleared sites, representing a replacement rate of only 15 per cent. The new housing developments in St Mary's, Blackfriars and Jeffrey Streets were mainly built to accommodate skilled artisans; the rents were well beyond the means of impoverished residents. Under the terms of the local statute, the Trust was prevented from playing a major role in direct housing provision. In 1870, the Trust built two tenements in Guthrie Street on a cost-rent basis, but this accommodation also proved too expensive for any of the displaced residents. Nevertheless, the Guthrie Street development did establish a precedent for future municipal housebuilding in the city.

Pressures for further action

The next phase of area-based sanitary improvement in the Old Town was not implemented until

FIGURE 6.1   Chambers Street (c. 1903), the most prestigious example of street improvement carried out under the 1867 Improvement Scheme promoted by Lord Provost William Chambers. A statue of William Chambers was erected in the middle of the street in the year 1891.   *RCAHMS*

the 1890s. The municipality's second improvement initiative was shaped by various events at local and national levels. During the 1880s, a new network of local civic organisations emerged with specific interests in promoting sanitary reform and regeneration of the Old Town. At the national level, a Royal Commission was appointed in 1884 to investigate the general lack of progress in solving urban and rural housing problems. As a by-product of the Commission's work, the national legislation dealing with slum-clearance schemes was consolidated under Part 1 of the Housing of the Working Classes Act 1890.

In his evidence given to the Royal Commission, Dr Littlejohn argued that while significant progress had been made in Edinburgh, there was still a pressing need for further action on sanitary matters. During the period 1855–74, the city-wide death rate was reported to have averaged around 26 per 1,000 of population; over the next decade (1875–84), a decrease of nearly 25 per cent had been achieved.[11] Despite this overall progress, persistent disparities remained between the privileged and impoverished areas of the city; the crude death rate for the Old Town's St Giles Ward was double the corresponding figure for the New Town.[12]

The new network of local civic groups played important roles in raising awareness of the need for further municipal action and in defining appropriate forms of area renewal within the Old Town. These groups had relatively wide-ranging concerns including improved sanitation and public health, better housing provision for the city's poor, progressive approaches to social work, physical

FIGURE 6.2   The top of St Mary's Street, looking south
(c. 1995). Another example of street improvement carried
out under the 1867 Scheme.   *RCAHMS*

and cultural regeneration of the medieval quarter, and historic preservation of ancient buildings and monuments. Activists and supporters tended to be drawn from the professional classes including clergy, medical practitioners, educators, artists, architects, and in a few instances local politicians.

Two organisations were particularly instrumental in the development of the next phase of municipal improvement. The Social & Sanitary Society of Edinburgh was formed in 1884 as a vehicle for extending public-health reform in the city. That same year, the Edinburgh Social Union emerged with diverse interests in social work, housing reform, environmental improvement and community-based forms of art education.

The Social & Sanitary Society functioned primarily as a 'vigilance group' or 'civic watchdog'. Through a network of neighbourhood committees, volunteer members identified specific sanitary problems and reported the offending conditions to the responsible municipal officials.[13] This information was valued by the Medical Officer of Health,

since the municipality employed only a handful of sanitary inspectors at the time. Two elected members of the Town Council were actively involved in the Social & Sanitary Society, Dr James Alexander Russell and William Slater Brown. The former had trained in medicine and public health at the University of Edinburgh, while the latter had gained direct knowledge of the city's slums through his experience as a property factor (agent). These politicians provided valuable links between the Council and the body of interested civic groups. Both were associated with the Liberal Party, and both eventually held the office of Lord Provost.[14]

The Edinburgh Social Union evolved from a discussion group of young intellectuals including Patrick Geddes, who had recently joined the staff of Edinburgh University. The participants became interested in possible forms of direct action to improve living conditions in disadvantaged areas of the city. Visits were made to observe the work of the Toynbee Hall Settlement in East London, the Nottingham Town and County Social Guild, and various branches of the Kyrle Society. To explore the potential for useful activity in the housing field, a small delegation visited Octavia Hill's base of operations in the Marylebone area of London.

The main pressure for a more gradual approach to renewal in the Old Town came from the activities of Patrick Geddes and the Social Union's housing arm, which comprised volunteer housing managers trained in the methods of Octavia Hill. Owners of slum housing were encouraged to place their properties in the hands of the Social Union, in return for a reasonable rate of profit on their investment. Any surplus funds were used to upgrade the stock and to cover the costs of suitable recreational activities for deserving tenants.[15] The operation began with two blocks of property at James Court in the Lawnmarket, consisting of around thirty dwellings. In 1887, two members of the Social Union acquired Whitehorse Close, a historic courtyard complex in the Canongate, with a view to carrying out physical improvements. By the start of 1888, the Social Union was providing accommodation in seven different locations for nearly 200 families.[16]

The Social Union's profile within the Old Town was raised significantly in 1887, when the newly-weds Patrick and Anna Geddes took up residence at No. 6 James Court in the Lawnmarket.[17] With a deep commitment to voluntary civic action, the couple became involved in various local initiatives. Some of Patrick Geddes' projects were carried out within the formal framework of the Social Union, while others were undertaken in a personal capacity (often placing the family finances at serious risk in the process). Involvement in the activities of the Social Union, and the day-to-day experience of life in the Old Town, inspired Geddes to extend his thinking about the nature of cities and sustainable solutions to urban problems. In due course, he developed an integrated overview of city-regions. Within this broad framework, the concept of 'conservative surgery' was seen to be the appropriate means of regenerating older parts of cities.

For Geddes, the 'conservative surgery' approach was intended to adapt and improve older areas by minimising the destruction of existing buildings, preventing unnecessary upheaval in the lives of local residents, and respecting the social and cultural heritage of the locality.[18] In advancing this package of ideas, Geddes differed with the advocates of comprehensive redevelopment as well as those who were committed to the strict preservationist principles advanced by the Society for the Protection of Ancient Buildings (SPAB). There was a strong element of pragmatism in Geddes' approach. In cases where an older building could be upgraded to a reasonable standard, he generally argued for retention subject to contextual factors. But where an existing property was obstructing essential change to the surrounding environment, full or partial demolition could be justified. As a consequence, Geddes' most imaginative renewal projects in the Old Town were sensitive blends of rehabilitation and infill new construction.

Before long, Geddes' boundless energy was channelled in a number of new directions. He intended the wider regeneration process in the Old Town to serve as a focal point for the renascence of Scottish society.[19] Beginning in 1887, Geddes

FIGURE 6.3   No. 6 James Court (c. 1955), the tenement in the Old Town which became the home of newlyweds Anna and Patrick Geddes in 1887.   *RCAHMS*

embarked on an ambitious series of personal projects in the Lawnmarket area, of which the best known were: University Hall, a network of self-governing halls of residence for students; Ramsay Garden, a picturesque housing development for students and university staff, combining new construction with the refurbishment of Ramsay Lodge, the mid-18th-century home of the poet Allan Ramsay; and the Outlook Tower, a 17th-century tenement that had previously been converted as a public observatory with a *camera obscura*, which became Geddes' base for civic education and the promotion of regional concepts.

These specific initiatives were undertaken without any formal assistance from the Town Council; however, two of Geddes' other Lawnmarket projects were implemented in conjunction with the municipality's sanitary improvement scheme of 1893. The projects known as Wardrop's Court and Riddle's Court are detailed below.

FIGURE 6.4   Official publicity photo of the 1886 International Exhibition, showing The Old Edinburgh Street designed by Sydney Mitchell.   *RCAHMS*

Two older civic organisations – the Edinburgh Architectural Association (formed in 1858) and the Cockburn Association (formed in 1875) – provided general support for the extension of sanitary reform, but neither of these bodies played a leading role in pressing for the resumption of area-based improvement in the Old Town. It is likely that the Edinburgh International Exhibition of Industry, Science and Art, held on the Meadows in 1886, helped to raise public awareness of the loss of ancient buildings and the need for higher standards of housing provision. Two sections of the Exhibition, known as 'Model Dwelling Houses' and 'The Old Edinburgh Street', were particularly significant in this context.

The exhibit of model dwelling houses were designed by James Gowans (the serving Lord Dean of Guild) as a demonstration of the 'proper application of sanitary science to the flatted tenement'.[20] A two-storey structure was erected at the north-east corner of the Exhibition grounds, based upon model plans for flats within the ground and upper floors of a tenement.[21] In contrast, The Old Edinburgh Street was intended to depict the buildings and costumes of the 14th, 15th and 16th centuries.[22] This highly popular exhibit (seen by nearly three million persons) was designed by Sydney Mitchell, who was later to work with Geddes in the development of Ramsay Garden. A 'typical' medieval street was laid out, comprising facsimiles of actual buildings that had been demolished over the years in various parts of the Old Town.[23] Although not explicitly intended as a propaganda vehicle for either historic preservation or sanitary improvement, it seems likely that The Old Edinburgh Street would have enhanced the level of popular support for sensitive forms of physical and cultural regeneration in the Old Town.

The 1893 Improvement Scheme

The local authority's decision to resume area-based sanitary improvement in the 1890s was a major victory for the civic groups that were concerned about the need for regeneration of the Old Town. Officially, as the Edinburgh (Housing of the Working Classes Act) Improvement Scheme of 1893, this initiative can be seen as an important turning point with respect to both the physical renewal of the Old Town and the development of housing policy in the city. In effect, the 1893 Scheme represented a shift away from the earlier policy of large-scale clearance and redevelopment of entire street frontages toward a form of treatment that was more consistent with Geddes' concept of 'conservative surgery'. Relative to the 1867 Scheme, greater attention was given to the rehousing issue, and eventually the municipality decided to build directly in order to ease the pressures in the local housing market. Also, a different style of administration was adopted that involved working 'in partnership' with local civic groups to improve living conditions in the medieval quarter.

Formal approval of the 1893 Scheme by central government was granted in a Provisional Order dated 29 April 1893.[24] The full scheme covered ten separate areas that were designated by the Medical Officer of Health. Of this number, seven areas were located in the heart of the Old Town and one area was situated in Potterrow on the southern perimeter of the medieval quarter.[25] These sites were generally small in size. On aggregate, the eight sites amounted to roughly four acres, or less than one-tenth of the total land area cleared under the 1867 Scheme. The only site larger than one acre was located off Old Assembly Close, between the High Street and Cowgate.

Under the 1890 Housing Act, there was scope for the local authority to 'engage with any body of trustees, society or person' in carrying out a sanitary improvement scheme.[26] At the public inquiry for the 1893 Scheme, the Lord Provost (Dr J. A. Russell) drew attention to Patrick Geddes' recent activities in the Lawnmarket projects and indicated that the Council was intending to involve local civic groups and philanthropic organisations in the proposed initiative.[27] While this was clearly not envisaged as a way of empowering the Old Town's poor, it does seem to reflect a genuine interest in utilising the experience and resources of civil society. In this sense, the subsequent working relationships that were developed under the 1893 Scheme can be seen as an early example of 'public–private partnership' in area regeneration.

The municipality made a conscious effort to extend the application of 'conservative surgery' in the Lawnmarket. Geddes was given delegated responsibility for co-ordinating the projects in Wardrop's Court and Riddle's Court. The Social Union also became involved at Campbell's Close in the Canongate, where twenty-two flats were to be retained and upgraded.[28] The remainder of the designated areas were administered by the Council directly, although several other bodies assisted with rehousing.

A number of significant problems emerged in the course of implementation. One of the main difficulties was the high net cost of site clearance, which meant that the sites could not be redeveloped without some form of subsidisation. Although the 1890 Housing Act offered an improved framework for slum clearance and municipal housebuilding, there was still no financial assistance available from the Treasury for these activities. In the event, the combined costs of property acquisition and demolition greatly exceeded the potential market value of the cleared sites. According to official estimates, if residential redevelopment were assumed, a fair market price for the site would have covered less than 20 per cent of the expense incurred by the municipality; the remaining 80 per cent needed to be met from the rates.[29]

A serious problem was also encountered in the rehousing of local residents. At the public inquiry, the Lord Provost gave firm assurances that the municipality would take any necessary measures to ensure that those displaced were adequately rehoused.[30] Official surveys had revealed a total of 2,700 persons occupying around 800 dwellings within the designated areas.[31] It was anticipated that the vast majority of displaced households could be accommodated through the normal turn-over of vacant dwellings at the cheaper end of the housing market.[32] Thus, the Council initially had no plans to build any housing directly, and there was a presumption that outside bodies would provide any new accommodation should this prove necessary.[33]

Against official expectations, a severe shortage of alternative accommodation did in fact emerge. In the course of implementation, it became evident that the local authority had failed to consider the impact of other redevelopment initiatives in the immediate vicinity of the Old Town. These parallel activities included the widening of Bristo Street and major improvements to Waverley Station, which displaced an additional 1,500 persons.[34]

Initially, the local authority looked to outside organisations for assistance. The North British Railway Company, the developer of Waverley Station, was persuaded to build 116 workmen's dwellings at St John's Hill, near the northern end of the Pleasance.[35] A second development of 112 new and refurbished dwellings was provided in the Cowgate by a semi-philanthropic group called the St Giles Dwelling Company.[36] (Both of these developments are now demolished.)

When the problem persisted, the Council eventually decided to build directly. The question of municipal housebuilding was first raised within the Town Council as early as 1890, by the elected member for St Giles Ward, John Macpherson.[37] Although no action was taken at that time, Macpherson persevered over the next five years. In June 1894, he drafted a report arguing that the local authority should respond to the current rehousing needs by building a municipal housing development on the large clearance site at Old Assembly Close.[38]

Over the next year, letters of concern were received from various bodies including the Edinburgh Social Union, the School Board, Edinburgh Trades Council and the local branch of the Independent Labour Party.[39] In October 1895, the first formal commitment to direct provision arrived through a decision to earmark a Council-owned site in the Tynecastle area for future development as municipal housing.[40] Although the site was well removed from the Old Town, this commitment was clearly a response to the pressures generated by redevelopment activities in the city centre.

Several more years elapsed before any municipal accommodation was actually available for occupation. Between 1897 and 1902, six housing developments – providing more than 300 small flats – were completed in conjunction with the 1893 Scheme. Of these, one was a refurbished block of flats in the south back of the Canongate, whereas the other five provided new purpose-built dwellings.[41] Three of the new developments were located within the core of the Old Town at High School Yards (completed in 1897; fifty-six units and eight shops), Tron Square (1900; 105 units) and Portsburgh Square (1901; sixty-one units). The other two were situated in Potterrow on the southern edge of the Old Town (1902; thirty-one dwellings) and in McLeod Street within the Tynecastle area (1898; sixty-four dwellings).

These early municipal housing developments were at best a mixed success. Direct provision was originally justified by the Council as a measure to improve the housing conditions of the city's poor and to reduce the pressures that were created by the

FIGURE 6.5   Early photo of deck-access housing within the Tron Square development, built by Edinburgh Corporation and completed in 1900.   *RCAHMS*

various renewal activities.[42] In practice, however, very few of the displaced households were able to benefit directly from this new form of housing provision.[43] This was partly due to time-lags in the construction process; but the key factor was the rent levels, which were generally well beyond the means of those who required rehousing.[44]

The new developments were usually designed as 'balcony' or 'deck access' blocks with a view to achieving better standards of ventilation and daylight in the densely populated areas of the city. In resolving the physical specifications, the Council was faced with many of the same dilemmas that philanthropic providers had been facing since the 1850s. Compromise solutions needed to be found within the prevailing parameters of quality, cost and affordability. The question of standards had to be weighed against both the cost implications and the rent-paying capacity of prospective tenants. As in other British cities, the early municipal developments offered a narrow choice of either one- or two-apartment units, internal decoration and fittings were very basic, and shared sanitary amenities were fairly common.

To the Council's credit, the need to provide something more than 'bricks and mortar' was recognised at the outset. As a general policy, resident caretakers were to be appointed for the new developments.[45] For the delivery of basic housing-management services and other forms of tenant support, the Council looked to the Social Union.[46] This working relationship remained in place until 1904 when, to the regret of the municipality, the Social Union took a decision to terminate the arrangement.[47]

The three developments within the core of the Old Town have survived to the present day. Tron Square remains part of the local-authority stock, whereas High School Yards and Portsburgh Square were transferred to local housing associations for modernisation in the 1980s. This accommodation is generally popular among small households who prefer city-centre living.

Having discussed the handling of the rehousing issue, we turn to the Lawnmarket elements of the 1893 Scheme that were associated with Patrick Geddes. The improvement initiatives in Wardrop's Court and Riddle's Court were intended to be mutually advantageous. From the Council's standpoint, collaboration with Geddes meant that the sanitary measures would be carried out in a manner that respected the historic fabric of the Lawnmarket. From Geddes' standpoint, collaboration with the Council enabled him to apply 'conservative surgery' in two situations where compulsory purchase powers were essential to produce effective physical results.

The treatment of Wardrop's Court was a particularly complex example of the 'conservative surgery' approach. Although less well known than Geddes' development at Ramsay Garden, the initiative was perhaps even more important in area-renewal terms. Geddes was personally involved in the planning and administration of the project at a detailed level, including negotiating for property on the Council's behalf.[48]

The site in question is located at a vital junction along the Royal Mile, where Bank Street and the Mound are linked to George IV Bridge. Bounded by North Bank Street on the north and the Lawnmarket on the south, the designated area contained a dense warren of dilapidated buildings behind the main frontages.[49] The official proposal specified the retention of two ancient merchant's houses – Gladstone's Land in the Lawnmarket (dating from around 1550) and Lady Stair's House to the rear (built in 1622). The other properties in the interior of the block were scheduled for demolition to form an open court. Two new passageways were formed to provide access from North Bank Street and from the interior of James Court to the west (this opening required partial demolition of later additions to Gladstone's Land and Lady Stair's House).

Within the Lawnmarket frontage, a sizeable gap site was also created through the removal of a large tenement. This land was eventually transferred to Geddes, who built a striking infill development known as Burns Land, containing twenty-four relatively modest flats with shops at ground level.[50] The residential accommodation was intended mainly for skilled artisans, since the rents had be set at levels that would cover the necessary expenses including a reasonable rate of return for Geddes' financial backers. The architect was S. Henbest Capper, who had been involved with Geddes in the Ramsay Garden project. Capper's design for Burns Land was sensitive to the vernacular tradition along the Royal Mile. The wide Lawnmarket frontage was divided into three gabled bays, a feature that had been evident in the demolished timber-fronted façade.

Geddes also played a key role in securing the future of Lady Stair's House. In 1895, he persuaded Lord Rosebery, a direct descendant of the original owner, to purchase the property from the Council.[51] Under the terms of the sale, Lady Stair's House was to be reconstructed either for Lord Rosebery's personal use or for public use as a local museum.[52] G. S. Aitken was eventually appointed as architect; and, in 1907 when the upgrading had been completed, the building was gifted to the City. Lady Stair's House is currently the venue of

FIGURE 6.6   Infill housing fronting onto the Lawnmarket (c. 1920), which Geddes called Burns Land. Officially part of
the municipal improvement scheme for Wardrop's Court, this new development was designed by S. Henbest Capper.
RCAHMS

The Writers' Museum, which celebrates the lives and works of Scottish authors.

The treatment of Riddle's Court, on the south side of the Lawnmarket, was a less imposing example of what sanitary reformers termed 'opening out'. Behind the early 18th-century tenement facing on to the main street, there were two interconnected interior courts. Within the innermost court was Baillie McMorran's House, a late 16th-century mansion acquired by Geddes in 1887 as a base for summer schools and other 'town and gown' activities. In order to improve the basic standards of ventilation and daylight, the municipality removed a projecting building from the forecourt as part of the 1893 Scheme. The official plan called for retention of the tenement facing on to the Lawnmarket, and the flats above ground level were transferred to Geddes for upgrading.[53] G. S. Aitken designed a new system of access with open galleries at the rear leading off an original turnpike staircase. This refurbishment initiative provided a total of fifteen small flats with shared sanitary amenities.[54]

Despite the problems encountered in the course of implementation, the 1893 Scheme was seen by the Council to be successful in public-health terms. On the strength of the progress in the Old Town, two additional area-based sanitary schemes were promoted under the 1890 Housing Act, for Stockbridge and Portobello in 1898 and for

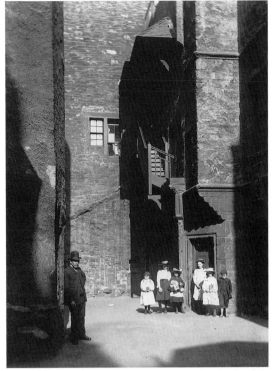

FIGURE 6.7   Lady Stair's House in Wardrop's Court (c. 1955), which was reconstructed by G. S. Aitken (on behalf of Lord Rosebery) as part of the 1893 Improvement Scheme.   *RCAHMS*

FIGURE 6.8   View of the forecourt of Riddle's Court (c. 1900–30), after the treatment known as 'opening out' was implemented as part of the 1893 Improvement Scheme. *RCAHMS*

Greenside and Simon Square in 1900. When these schemes were completed, the local authority decided to suspend this type of intervention because the financial deficits were regarded as excessive.[55] Consequently, several decades were to pass before the Old Town saw its next major phase of conservative surgery.

Improvement schemes of the 1920s

By the 1920s, various events had served to redefine the general context for municipal housing intervention. Prior to the outbreak of the First World War, two major investigations of Scottish housing problems were set in train – the Scottish Land Inquiry and the more influential Royal Commission on Housing of the Industrial Population of Scotland, chaired by Sir Henry Ballantyne. During the war years, popular protests against illegal evictions and

rising rents in Glasgow and other cities led to the introduction of rent control.[56] Conventional forms of residential development (and maintenance) were virtually suspended, and, at the conclusion of hostilities, severe housing shortages were apparent in many parts of the country. In the aftermath of war, there were serious problems in readapting the construction industry to peacetime conditions. Widespread shortages of labour and materials yielded a threefold increase in the average cost of residential construction between 1914 and 1919. So long as production costs remained abnormally high, there was little incentive for private investors to build any new housing for either rent or sale.

At a local level, the prospects for conserving the Old Town were enhanced by the formation of the Old Edinburgh Club in 1908, under the patronage of the Town Council.[57] The primary object of the

Club was to collect and disseminate material on the early history of Edinburgh; however, when sanitary improvement schemes were resumed after the First World War, a subgroup of the general membership gave advice to the Medical Officer of Health regarding the historical significance of designated properties.[58] Also, in the years prior to the First World War, the Cockburn Association was to become more proactive in its efforts to save important ancient buildings within the medieval quarter. In 1910, the Association took direct steps to acquire and preserve Moubray House in the High Street, and subsequently placed pressure upon public authorities to acquire Huntly House in the Canongate and Cannonball House in Castlehill.[59]

A revised statutory framework was introduced in the Housing, Town Planning Etc. Act of 1919, which contained a number of important new provisions. This legislation placed an explicit duty on local authorities to ensure that housing needs in their areas were being met. Through the Boards of Health, central government officials were expected to monitor the progress of local authorities in fulfilling this obligation. In addition, Treasury assistance was made available for both slum clearance and the construction of new housing for general needs. The provision of financial assistance for these activities was seen to be a temporary measure that was necessary in the prevailing conditions. There was an implicit presumption that central government support would be withdrawn, at least for general-needs housing, once the shortage of accommodation had been eased and building costs had fallen back to 'normal' levels.

Throughout the 1920s, the primary goal of national housing policy was expansion of the general supply of accommodation across the country. Understandably, removal of slum conditions was given a lower priority at a time of severe shortage. In the circumstances, only a small number of local authorities made a concerted effort to deal with substandard housing.[60] Glasgow Corporation and Edinburgh Corporation were among the most proactive authorities during this period.

Edinburgh's interest in resuming area-based sanitary improvement was indicated in an official response to the proposals contained in the 1919 Housing Bill. The local authority was particularly concerned to ensure that Treasury assistance would be available both for improving older areas as well as for providing general-needs housing on greenfield sites.[61] At that time, the Public Health Committee was already giving consideration to a list of priority areas drawn up by the Medical Officer of Health.[62]

The subsequent municipal improvement schemes were to continue the application of 'conservative surgery' within the Old Town and surrounding areas. There were, however, significant changes in the style and method of administration. The earlier practice of direct involvement of private and voluntary-sector bodies in implementing various improvement projects was not resumed after the First World War. By the 1920s, the municipality was in a stronger position to deliver public services, and the new legislation had placed a firm obligation upon local authorities to rehouse those displaced by slum-clearance initiatives. Through links with the Old Edinburgh Club, voluntary bodies with an interest in historic preservation of the Old Town were, however, still able to influence the Council's sanitary measures.

During the inter-war years, the various sanitary improvement schemes were administered by an experienced team of senior officials, including Andrew Grierson (Town Clerk, 1918–34), Allan W. Ritchie (Chief Sanitary Inspector, 1915–50), Ebenezer J. Macrae (City Architect, 1925–46) and William A. Macartney (Burgh Engineer, 1926–45). Each of these long-serving staff gained recognition in their respective fields of public service, and all were deeply interested in housing and town-planning matters. Macrae's contribution has a special significance for the Old Town, since his department was responsible for the infill housing developments that have played such a vital part in consolidating the historic fabric of the area.

In total, during the 1920s, five area-based improvement schemes were promoted for localities within the newly expanded city boundaries. Together, these schemes dealt with nearly 4,000 substandard dwellings, displacing over 12,000 residents in the process.[63] Four schemes focused (in whole or in part) upon sites within the Old Town and St Leonard's, the working-class area immediately to the south. The fifth scheme concentrated upon areas of Leith. The overall impact in the vicinity of the Old Town, in terms of dwellings and residents directly affected, was perhaps three to four times greater than the earlier experience under the 1893 Scheme.

For several years after the new legislation became available, the municipality gave priority to general-needs provision in various parts of the city (see Chapter 7). Area-based sanitary improvement was effectively resumed in 1922, when a scheme was promoted for the Grassmarket area of the Old Town. This initiative dealt with seventeen designated areas in the Cowgate, the Grassmarket and Candlemaker Row, which contained about 630 slum dwellings.[64] Most of the 1,500 occupants were rehoused on a purpose-built council estate at Lochend, about two miles to the north-east of the Grassmarket. The treatment of the small improvement sites varied: in some cases, new infill developments were preferred, and in others, steps were taken to refurbish or reconstruct existing buildings. The various projects were designed to provide mainstream housing, hostels for single men and women, community halls and commercial premises.

In 1927, the sanitary initiative known as the Canongate–Corstorphine scheme was promoted in order to carry out improvement work in six different parts of the city. A major element of this scheme was the treatment of eight sites in the Canongate. Since the Canongate properties were largely empty, it was possible to phase the improvements in a way that facilitated local rehousing.[65] One of the larger sites contained a group of properties dating from the 16th century, including Bakehouse Close and Huntly House. The architect/planner Frank C. Mears, who had close personal and professional ties with Patrick Geddes, was appointed by the Council to carry out this major restoration project. Huntly House has been used as a municipal museum since the work was completed in 1932.

Within the St Leonard's area, the sanitary improvement measures were administered in two

FIGURE 6.9   Huntly House in the 1880s. Under threat of demolition for many years, the building was eventually acquired by the municipality and restored by Frank C. Mears as part of the 1927 Canongate–Corstorphine Improvement Scheme.   *RCAHMS*

stages. An initial scheme involving fifteen sites in the vicinity of Howden Street and East Crosscauseway was confirmed in 1928. These sites contained a total of 750 slum dwellings and 2,600 residents.[66] In order to reduce the overall level of population density, one of the larger clearance sites was retained as open space, and the new infill developments were provided with generous back greens. Although some attention was given to local rehousing, the bulk of the displaced residents were allocated accommodation on the new Prestonfield estate (around a mile to the south-east).

The second St Leonard's scheme was confirmed in 1931. This ambitious initiative was roughly twice the size of the first stage. A total of twenty-four sites were to be improved, containing as many as 1,600 dwellings and 5,600 residents.[67] These sites were located principally along the Pleasance and Buccleuch Street. In two instances, at Richmond Place and Gifford Park, there was sufficient land to erect moderate-sized infill developments with their own distinctive architectural character. During the second stage, the displaced residents were usually removed to the new Niddrie Mains estate (around two miles to the south-east).

Implementation of the second St Leonard's scheme proved to be problematic. The rate of progress was highly dependent upon efficient completion of the new accommodation that was needed for rehousing. By the early 1930s, the demand for owner-occupied housing was rising to an unprecedented extent in Edinburgh. The added pressures of new speculative housing developments created labour shortages in certain building trades. As a consequence, the local authority was faced with serious delays in meeting its own housebuilding targets.[68] These difficulties were exacerbated by the reluctance of some residents to consider a move to an outlying location.[69] Elderly residents often had strong attachments to the St Leonard's area and were not likely to be tempted by the prospect of a larger house. For the younger households, relocation to an outlying council estate usually meant an increased outlay for rent, a lengthier journey to work, and greater external supervision of the home environment.

As noted above, one of distinctive features of the 1920s schemes was the general quality of the municipal housing developments on the designated sites within the Old Town and St Leonard's. This body of work by the City Architect can be seen as an important extension of the 'conservative surgery' approach. This accommodation has remained popular and well looked-after over the years, and as such it can also be seen as a genuine early example of sustainable urban renewal.

In his capacity as City Architect, E. J. Macrae (1881–1951) was responsible for the construction of various building types. From his papers and correspondence, however, he appears to have maintained a lifelong interest in housing design and Scottish history, as well as an abiding commitment to improving the living conditions of ordinary people. Macrae's concerns for preserving the charm and character of the Old Town were generally endorsed by the Town Council.[70] He advocated the use of stone in historic parts of the city, not only for major public buildings but also for the street façades of municipal housing developments. If available, redressed stone from recently demolished buildings was used; but, where this form of recycling was not feasible, new stone was specified at an added cost of around 15 per cent.[71] This extra expense was treated as ineligible for central-government assistance, but fortunately the Council agreed to provide the necessary funding from the rates.

The range of physical solutions in the Grassmarket area was achieved through detailed consideration of possible options. This is evident from the decision-making process for the site containing 74–82 Grassmarket. The main buildings at this location were two late 17th-century tenements with a pub and a restaurant at street level. An initial proposal to rehabilitate the existing buildings was rejected by the Medical Officer of Health on the grounds that the ceiling heights would not meet the current regulations. On the instructions of the Housing and Town Planning Committee, Macrae explored a more radical form of reconstruction.[72] The end result was a single tenement rebuilt in rubble stonework, incorporating many of the original features. The common stair was moved to a projecting bay in the centre of the plan, and two two-apartment flats with internal bathrooms were provided on each of the upper floors. The ground-floor space was designed to accommodate a public house, with a pleasant new neo-Georgian façade. Shortly after completion, fellow architect Robert Hurd praised Macrae's solution as 'sensitively reminiscent of its predecessor and very cleverly planned', with a 'charming elevation . . . full of interest and . . . an improvement on the old one'.[73]

Macrae's new-build solutions for two of the larger clearance sites in the St Leonard's area reflect an interest in adapting the designs for traditional Scottish tenements built around enclosed squares. At Richmond Place, a development of 113 flats and five shops was built on a three-acre site

FIGURE 6.10   Nos 74–84 Grassmarket *after* reconstruction by City Architect E. J. Macrae.   *Paul Jenkins*

FIGURE 6.11   The south-facing frontage of Macrae's Richmond Place development in 2004, which was constructed as part of the 1929 St Leonard's Improvement Scheme (Second Section).   *Paul Jenkins*

that had previously contained a dense mix of uses. The new design incorporated fifteen tenement stairs of varying height, arranged around the perimeter of the site. Three gaps were left between the buildings, giving access to the residents' drying areas and back greens. In order to protect the privacy of the interior spaces, a high stone wall with a gated opening was built within each gap.

The visual character of the development was enhanced by variations in roof-edge treatments and the provision of bold stone chimney stacks. In contrast, the internal planning of the dwellings was highly standardised. Each tenement had two flats per floor, approached off a common stair placed on the rear wall. The flats generally consisted of a living room, two or three bedrooms, a good-sized kitchen opening off the living room, and a bathroom with bath and WC.

At first glance, some of the basic elements of Richmond Place are suggestive of a continental influence, since Macrae had travelled extensively in Europe to observe innovative social-housing projects such as Karl Marx Hof in Vienna. However, the key features of the Richmond Place development, including the large internal communal grounds, the arched openings to the internal footpaths, and the setback within the Pleasance frontage, can also be regarded as pragmatic solutions to the particular problems of the site. In essence, the character of the overall design has

been achieved through skilful application of the language of the 'Traditionalist School' in Scotland.

At Gifford Park, Macrae replaced a crowded cul-de-sac of four-storey tenements with a less dense development of similar form. A total of thirty-eight flats were constructed on the designated site and an existing community hall was integrated within the new development. As at Richmond Place, the new structures were traditionally built, with front and gable walls of solid stone, and rear walls of cavity brick covered with harling. The buildings facing on to the cul-de-sac were a maximum of three storeys in height, whereas the corner block was increased to four storeys in order to match the scale of the late 19th-century tenements on the main road. Also, within the cul-de-sac, the tenements were set back from the street, to provide for small front gardens enclosed by low stone walls. Macrae's design for Gifford Park has created a pleasant pocket within central Edinburgh, almost 'garden city' in scale, yet tenemental in basic form.

The slow rate of progress in completing the St Leonard's work caused the Council to rethink its sanitary improvement strategy. Six years passed before any further area-based initiatives were promoted, and the new schemes were generally much reduced in scale. Between 1934 and 1938, fiteeen new schemes were promoted, covering a total of

FIGURE 6.12   The northern side of the cul-de-sac development in Gifford Park, as it appeared in 2004. These flats were also constructed as part of the 1929 St Leonard's Improvement Scheme (Second Section). Macrae's design allowed for the retention and upgrading of an existing recreation hall, which is now used by members of Edinburgh's Chinese community.   *Paul Jenkins*

1,450 slum dwellings.[74] Only four of these schemes had any direct impact upon the Old Town or its immediate environs (two dealt with sites in the Canongate, and the other two dealt with sites in High Riggs and Morrison Street).[75] Completion of these initiatives was probably interrupted by the onset of the Second World War, which effectively ended the second major phase of 'conservative surgery' in Old Edinburgh.

An unsteady path forwards

This chapter has examined the early development of area-based renewal in the Old Town, with a particular focus on the shift from large-scale redevelopment in the 1860s to a more piecemeal Geddesian approach in the 1890s and 1920s. We would not wish to give the impression that the process of 'conservative surgery' had become institutionalised by the end of the inter-war period. In fact, the commitment to this form of regeneration was rather insecure, and a return to large-scale redevelopment could well have occurred at various points.

By the end of the 1920s, Edinburgh's civic leaders were again considering the need for more comprehensive forms of renewal in the Old Town.

A prestigious committee was appointed by the Lord Provost in 1929 to examine the future development of the city centre.[76] Under the direction of F. C. Mears, a technical subgroup produced a report with various suggestions about the way forward.[77] Mears was very concerned to facilitate the expansion of higher-education institutions within the city centre. Towards this objective, an ambitious proposal was floated to create a wide boulevard from the McEwan Hall to the Pleasance, with new academic buildings on either side and a prestigious educational landmark on the designated clearance site at Richmond Place.[78] Ironically, this proposal, by Geddes' most apparent disciple, in effect would have heralded a return to the street, improvement approach of the 1860s. For better or worse, Mears' vision could not be taken forward in the depressed economic climate of the 1930s.

Shortly after the Second World War, the 'conservative surgery' approach was again threatened by bold planning proposals. The 1949 *Civic Survey and Plan for the City* (by Abercrombie and Plumstead) envisaged a radically improved road network for Scotland's capital, including a new link from Princes Street (across Princes Street Gardens) to the Old Town and the southern suburbs.[79] Had it been implemented, this proposal would have created serious disruption near the eastern section of the High Street and within the heart of the St Leonard's area.[80] Again, due to lack of resources – or perhaps lack of conviction – this dramatic vision was also never realised (see Chapter 8).

Eventually, in the post-war period, the municipality resumed the 'conservative surgery' approach in the Old Town. Between 1953 and 1966, Robert Hurd was commissioned to design three infill housing developments in the Canongate on sites that were very near to some of Macrae's inter-war efforts. In 1965, Basil Spence was commissioned to design another municipal housing development at the eastern end of the Canongate. During the 1970s, a variety of tenement-rehabilitation and environmental-improvement projects were undertaken throughout the Old Town by non-profit housing organisations and the Council. The sustained commitment of public funds in the area encouraged the return of private-sector investment in the 1980s and 1990s. When this occurred on a significant scale, the tide of regeneration had been well and truly turned in Old Edinburgh.

Shortly before retiring from the post of City Architect in 1946, E. J. Macrae prepared a report on the historic preservation of the Royal Mile.[81] In the introduction, the basic resilience of the Old Town was noted. Although little had survived from medieval times, the ancient part of the city had managed to retain its romantic character by accommodating a diversity of interesting buildings from each succeeding century.[82] Against the odds, Macrae's depiction of the Old Town still holds at the start of the new millennium. This favourable state of affairs has been strongly influenced by the wise endeavours of those who persevered with the 'conservative surgery' approach between 1880 and 1940.

Notes

1. *The Scotsman*, 25 November 1861, quoted in R. Rodger, *The Transformation of Edinburgh* (Cambridge, 2001).

2. H. D. Littlejohn, *Report on the Sanitary Condition of the City of Edinburgh* (Edinburgh, 1861).

3. P. J. Smith, 'Planning as environmental improvement', in A. Sutcliffe (ed.), *The Rise of Modern Planning* (London, 1980), pp. 99–133.

4. J. N. Tarn, *Five Percent Philanthropy* (Cambridge, 1973); W. Thompson, *The Housing Handbook Up-to-Date* (London, 1903).

5. Rodger, *Transformation*, p. 76.

6. P. J. Smith, 'The rehousing/relocation issue in an early slum clearance scheme: Edinburgh 1865–1885', *Urban Studies*, 26 (1989): 100–14.

7. C. McKean, *Edinburgh: Portrait of a City* (London, 1991), pp. 191–2; F. Walker, 'National romanticism and the architecture of the city', in G. Gordon (ed.), *Perspectives of the Scottish City* (Aberdeen, 1985), pp. 149–52.

8. Smith, 'The rehousing/relocation issue', p. 103.

9. The Royal Commission on the Housing of the Working Classes (1885), *Minutes of Evidence, Appendix, and Index as to Scotland*, C. 4409-I, vol. V, London: HMSO, p. 23.

10. Rodger, *Transformation*, p. 436.

11. Royal Commission (1885), op. cit. pp. 30–5. (Testimony of Dr Henry Littlejohn).

12. I. H. Adams, *The Making of Urban Scotland* (London, 1978), p. 170.

13. Social & Sanitary Society of Edinburgh, *Seventh Annual Report 1891*.

14. T. B. Whitson, *The Lord Provosts of Edinburgh 1296–1932* (Edinburgh, 1932).

15. Accounts of Octavia Hill's methods may be found in E. Gauldie, *Cruel Habitations* (London, 1974); Tarn, *Philanthropy*.

16. Edinburgh Social Union, *Fifth Annual Report*.

17. P. Mairet, *Pioneer of Sociology: The Life and Letters of Patrick Geddes* (London, 1957), p. 51.

18. P. Green, Introduction to reprint of P. Geddes, *City Development: A Report to the Carnegie Dunfermline Trust* (New Brunswick, NJ, 1973); V. M. Welter, *Biopolis: Patrick Geddes and the City of Life* (Cambridge, MA, 2002).

19. M. Cuthbert, 'The concept of the outlook tower in the work of Patrick Geddes', unpublished MPhil thesis, University of St Andrews (1987).

20. J. Gowans, *Model Dwelling-Houses* (Edinburgh, 1886), p. 12.

21. Ibid., p. 2.

22. J. C. Dunlop and A. H. Dunlop, *The Book of Old Edinburgh and Handbook to the Old Edinburgh Street* (Edinburgh, 1886).

23. S. Mitchell, *Report to the Old Edinburgh Street Committee* (1885).

24. T. Hunter, *City of Edinburgh Municipal and Police Acts* (Edinburgh, 1909), p. 300.

25. Ibid., pp. 298–303.

26. C. E. Allan, *The Housing of the Working Classes Acts 1890–1900* (London, 1901, 2nd edn), p. 19. The specific provision is contained in Part 1, Section 12 (3).

27. F. Bailey, *Inquiry re. Edinburgh (Housing of the Working Classes Act) Improvement Scheme 1893*, pp. 23–4 (testimony of James Alexander Russell).

28. Disposition by the Lord Provost, Magistrates and the Council of Edinburgh to George Kerr Esq., Bachelor of Medicine, 6 St Colme Street.

29. J. Cooper, *Annual Report of the Burgh Engineer for the Year 1899*.

30. Bailey, *Inquiry re. Improvement Scheme 1893*, p. 23 (testimony of James Alexander Russell).

31. Ibid., p. 57 (testimony of John Cooper).

32. Ibid.

33. Ibid., pp. 37–8 (testimony of James Alexander Russell).

34. J. Cooper, *Report of the Burgh Engineer's Department 1893–94*; J. Cooper, *Edinburgh Railway Schemes – Report by Burgh Engineer 1891*; Thompson, *Housing Handbook*, p. 47.

35. Cooper, *Annual Report of the Burgh Engineer 1899*, p. 6.

36. Royal Commission on Housing in Scotland (1921), *Evidence Given Before the Royal Commission*, Edinburgh, vol. 4, p. 1,715 (testimony of Johanna C. Ross and Margaret Salmon).

37. *Minutes of Edinburgh Town Council*, Meeting of 7 October 1890.

38. J. Macpherson, *Report on Dwellings of the Poor*, dated 20 June 1894.

39. *Minutes of Improvement Sub-Committee*, dated 17 June 1895 and 18 July 1895; Edinburgh Social Union, *Eleventh Annual Report – November 1895*.

40. *Minutes of Improvement Sub-Committee*, dated 18 October 1895 and 22 October 1895.

41. Information on the detailed characteristics of early municipal accommodation was obtained largely from annual reports of the Burgh Engineer.

42. Cooper *Report of the Burgh Engineer's Department 1893–94*, pp. 8–9.

43. Cooper, *Annual Report of the Burgh Engineer 1899*, pp. 6–7.

44. Ibid.

45. Cooper, *Report 1893–94*, pp. 8–11.

46. Edinburgh Social Union, *Thirteenth Annual Report – November 1897*.

47. A. M. Williamson and J. W. Smith, *Reports by Medical Officer of Health and Burgh Engineer as to Condition of Working-Class Properties Belonging to the Corporation*, prepared for the Treasurer's Committee in 1909.

48. *Minutes of Improvement Sub-Committee*, dated 9 January 1893.

49. *Report by Improvement Schemes Committee on Proceedings in Carrying Out 1893 Scheme*, 19 April 1900.

50. Bailey, *Inquiry re 1900 Improvement Scheme*, p. 23 (testimony of W. S. Brown). The name of Burns Land was chosen by Geddes because Robert Burns had stayed nearby in Lady Stair's Close during his first visit to Edinburgh in 1789.

51. T. B. Whitson, 'Lady Stair's House', in *BOEC*, 3 (1910), p. 244.

52. *Minutes of Improvement Scheme Sub-Committee*, 25 March 1895.

53. *Minutes of Meeting of Edinburgh Town Council*, 23 January 1894.

54. Bailey, *Inquiry re. 1900 Improvement Scheme*, p. 23 (testimony of W. S. Brown).

55. *Evidence Given Before Royal Commission on Housing in Scotland*, vol. 1, p. 739 (testimony of Adam Horsburgh Campbell).

56. M. Bowley, *Housing and the State 1919–1944* (London, 1945), p. 3.

57. *Minutes of Meeting of Edinburgh Town Council*, 4 February 1908.

58. Unpublished lists of properties referred by the Medical Officer of Health for comment are held in the Edinburgh Room of the City Library.

59. Article on the 42nd Annual Meeting of the Cockburn Association in *The Scotsman*, 14 January 1920.

60. P. Malpass and A. Murie, *Housing Policy and Practice*, (Basingstoke and London, 1999, 5th rev. and updated edn), p. 48.

61. A. Grierson, *Memorandum as to Draft Regulations under Clause 5 of Housing, Town Planning, Etc. (Scotland) Bill 1919*.

62. Ibid.

63. A. W. Ritchie (1930), *Housing: Improvement and Clearance Schemes in Populous Areas of the City*.

64. *Edinburgh (Cowgate, Grassmarket, Etc.) Improvement 1922: Report of Proceedings at Public Inquiry*, pp. 7, 9.

65. A. W. Ritchie, *Annual Report of the Sanitary Department 1927*; *Edinburgh (Canongate, Corstorphine, Etc.) Improvement Scheme 1927 – Report of Proceedings at Inquiry*, pp. 13–15.

66. Ritchie, *Housing: Improvement and Clearance Schemes*, p. 9.

67. Ibid.

68. These pressures were anticipated in a letter from E. J. Macrae to the Secretary of the Department of Health for Scotland, dated 18 April 1934.

69. Ritchie, *Annual Report of the Sanitary Department 1927*.

70. E. J. Macrae, *The Manner in which Edinburgh Deals with Their Ancient and Historical Buildings when These Have to Be Re-constructed and Adapted to Modern Requirements*, unpublished paper read to Edinburgh Women's Citizens' Association in November 1934.

71. This figure is based upon the Burgh Engineer's cost estimates for the St Leonard's Scheme – First Section, 17 June 1927.

72. *Minutes of Reconstruction Subcommittee of Housing and Town Planning Committee*, 12 April 1926 and 24 April 1926.

73. R. Hurd, 'Clearing the slums of Edinburgh', in *The Architects' Journal*, 2 April 1930, p. 542.

74. A. W. Ritchie, *Annual Report of the Sanitary Department 1938*, pp. 168–9. The overall reduction in scale was partially offset by increased use of closing

and demolition orders for individual properties.

75. Ibid.

76. F. C. Mears, *The City of Edinburgh: Preliminary Suggestions in regard to the Development and Re-Planning of the Central Area, March 1931.*

77 Ibid.

78. Ibid.

79. P. Abercrombie and D. Plumstead, *A Civic Survey and* *Plan for the City and Royal Burgh of Edinburgh* (Edinburgh, 1949).

80. Ibid.

81. E. J. Macrae, *The Royal Mile: Report by the City Architect* (Edinburgh, 1945).

82. Ibid., p. 3.

7 *Housing and suburbanisation in the early and mid-20th century*

Miles Glendinning

It was a magnificent thing to watch, as I did many times, whole streets of slum tenements being demolished – all those decades of human misery and degradation just vanishing into dust and rubble! (Councillor Pat Rogan (1987), Edinburgh Corporation Housing Chairman, 1962–5)

Historical accounts of early and mid-20th-century Scottish urban development have been dominated by a 'Glasgow-centric' tale of violent polarisations and fluctuations of policy, focused on the enthusiastic embrace of mass municipal housing. But this simplistic picture did not apply to Edinburgh, which saw a more complex pattern during the post-1914 era, constantly shifting between public and private agencies, and between the 'peripheral expansion' and 'inner regeneration' approaches to built form.

The inter-war years

In the revolutionary year of 1917, the government's Ballantyne Commission called for a radical reform of the existing organisational and architectural regime in working-class housing, replacing privately built tenements with state-built (or controlled) cottage garden suburbs. But a minority (Lovat) report warned that state intervention could become self-perpetuating;[1] and, although what followed was, ultimately, a 'revolution' in housing, the outcome was at first uncertain. Central government intervened, with wildly fluctuating subsidy policies, beginning with an open-ended 'general needs' subsidy (1919 Act) to kick-start local-authority building; then, as costs escalated, reining back council building to the field of low-cost slum

clearance and redirecting general-needs effort to the subsidising of private builders (1923 Act); and finally restoring subsidies for rental housing (public and private) at a higher rate in the 1924 (Wheatley) Act. But local authorities now had the key role in influencing both the supply of housing and the relative levels of council and private-sector building in their areas. This meant the constant involvement of local politics in housing – something virtually unknown in the 19th century.

In Edinburgh, the council was ruled until the 1970s by the 'Progressives', an anti-socialist coalition dominated by businessmen and landlords.[2] The stress on financial prudence ensured a cautious attitude towards building council housing, as higher property taxes ('rates') might hamper the city's favourable industrial position.[3] At first, the private-sector house-construction industry was very weak, as also across Scotland, although Edinburgh Corporation made a vigorous start in council housebuilding, producing as many as 1,300 houses under the 1919 Act and 6,400 under the 1924 Act. But thereafter, as private building recovered, the city became increasingly half-hearted in general-needs provision, preferring to support building by private enterprise. Of the private-sector housing constructed between 1918 and 1932, 75 per cent was built with Corporation assistance, the vast majority for owner occupation. The Corporation also provided low-interest loans for building and purchasing houses. Its officials came to believe that it should not, through large-scale council building, raise the prices of building materials and labour and thus damage the private-enterprise market. What is unclear is whether the strong late 19th-century contribution of voluntary housing societies in Edinburgh contributed to this bias against a dominant council sector. Despite its lower population, the capital built almost 50 per cent more private-sector houses between the wars than Glasgow – something that may also have been helped by the greater amount (proportionally) of suburban building land available within its boundaries (see Appendix 1).[4]

The architectural result of this approach was a mixture of change and continuity: the pre-war pattern of radial population movement set by the upper classes since the 18th century now embraced the lower middle class, who moved from vertically stacked single-storey houses (in tenements) to similar dwellings distributed horizontally (bungalows). At the same time, there was a focus on building cheaper council houses for the poorer classes, exploiting the slum-clearance powers of the 1923 Act. These programmes were inspired less by the sweeping Improvement Act redevelopment ethos of the mid-19th century than by the somewhat contrary ideology of conservative regeneration and rehabilitation of 'Old Edinburgh', developed by Geddes from its romantic roots in Stevenson and Scott (see Chapter 6). Geddes in 1915 had argued that 'the policy of sweeping clearances is one of the most disastrous and pernicious blunders in the chequered history of sanitation'. But although Edinburgh only built half as many general-needs council houses per head of population in 1919–38 as Glasgow, and although demolitions were kept on a piecemeal basis, it achieved proportionately more slum clearance and replacement council housebuilding.[5]

The distinctiveness of Edinburgh's policy was accentuated in the 1930s, which was a time of relative prosperity in the capital. Nationally, state subsidies for building for sale dried up: the 1923 Act grants were withdrawn in 1933 and the 1924 Act subsidies in 1935. However, to maintain a supply of general-needs rented housing, Edinburgh Corporation itself continued to help firms prepared to build low-cost houses for renting. To do this, it released land on favourable feuing terms and provided builders with cheap loans of up to 75 per cent of the houses' value, provided that rents were kept within regulated levels. A quarter of all new private-sector houses built in Edinburgh after 1933 were built for renting under such post-subsidy schemes. Of course, as a merely local equivalent to the national systems of regulation and cheap finance in other countries, such as Germany, this initiative could do nothing to slow the nationwide decline in the private rented sector. And all the time, the council continued with a strongly committed slum-clearance programme of flat-building.

1920s council housing

What were the consequences of these policies, in built form, 'on the ground'? From the beginning, low-density cottages of three or more rooms, favoured by all garden-city reformists, were balanced with moves to revive the building of traditional tenements on grid-iron layouts, albeit spaced out and reduced to three storeys.[6] Under the 1919 Act, Edinburgh Corporation set up a Housing and Town Planning Committee (HTPC), which proposed a 1,750-dwelling programme of garden suburbs. Three of these were actually completed: Gorgie (from 1919), and Abercorn and Wardie (from 1920). All featured a mixture of two-storey cottages and flats, and a predominance of rubble facing. But, by the time of opening of the first Gorgie houses in October 1920, efforts were already under way to cut labour costs, and experiments began with concrete blockwork. Despite reformists' opposition, pressure built up from government and ratepayer groups to recommence building small two-roomed flats, both in two-storey 'four-in-a-block' layouts[7] and as part of the revived building tenements for 1923 Act slum clearance.[8]

In his evidence to Ballantyne, A. Horsburgh Campbell, Edinburgh's Burgh Engineer from 1910 to 1926, had strongly advocated the continuing use of tenements. In the early 1920s, he had the opportunity to put his ideas into practice when he briefly became the central figure in Edinburgh's burgeoning slum-clearance programme and in 1920, despite architectural opposition, was appointed 'Director of Housing' by the HTPC. He exploited his overall responsibility for town-planning to carve out an autonomous field of design work, beginning with straightforward slum-clearance and rehabilitation work in the historic core (under the Grassmarket and Cowgate Improvement Act 1919), but soon extending into new building under the 1923 Act. He realised that the Geddesian small-scale redevelopment pattern could be maintained *ad infinitum* if the bulk of the inhabitants were 'decanted' to new suburban schemes. His first new projects (1923–4) were relatively small urban infill sites in Leith (newly absorbed by Edinburgh), at St Clair Place and Sheriff Brae. These established the principle of three-storey 'block dwellings' or tenements, containing only small flats and costing less than a third of the 1919 Act houses. In mid-1923, he submitted plans for a far larger (120-acre) slum-clearance scheme at Lochend, eventually comprising over 1,000 houses and combining a garden-suburb layout, with three-storey tenements and two-storey four-in-a-blocks – some in concrete or steel construction. Eventually, a succession of large, low-rise suburban estates was built under the two Acts: other large 1923 Act schemes included Niddrie Mains and Prestonfield, and purely 1924 Act schemes included Saughtonhall, Stenhouse, Whitson and Craigentinny.[9]

Following Campbell's retiral in 1926, the split between 'engineering' and 'architectural' factions in the Corporation was healed when a powerful new City Architect, Ebenezer Macrae (1881–1951), absorbed all aspects of council-housing design. He reinforced the philosophy of piecemeal redevelopment combined with new suburban overspill schemes. As described in Chapter 6, in 1927–8 an initiative to regenerate a number of slum pockets across the city – the Edinburgh (Cowgate, Corstorphine and so on) Improvement Scheme, 1927 – was begun, combining sanitary clearance with Geddesian enhancements of the Old Town with subtly 'artistic' traditionalist interventions: for example, at 100–110 Canongate, where an old tenement was demolished in 1929 and replaced two years later by a three-storey-and-attic rubble tenement containing seven flats.[10]

Private builders in the 1920s and 1930s

Overall, building in Edinburgh remained fragmented and lacking in mechanised modernity. Contractors of council housing still used the continental-style 'separate-trades system', partly because of union pressure. But this changed as a result of the stimulus of private speculative building. In the late 1920s and 1930s, larger firms employing all their tradesmen came to dominate subsidised private housing. The percentage of houses built as single commissions, rather than speculatively, slumped from 57 per cent in 1923 to less than 1 per cent in 1932, and the most successful speculative firms mushroomed in size. In Edinburgh, one builder, James Miller, rose to dominate subsidised housing for sale: between 1927 and 1934, he built 1,922 subsidised houses, over twice as many as the ten next largest firms put together, and accounting for 36 per cent of all subsidy applications in Edinburgh.[11] Miller was just 23 when he built his first, sixteen-house development at Blackhall in 1927. He recalled that when he put his advertisement in *The Scotsman* in March, 'the first pair were only being roofed. I hadn't time to eat or rest till after it was dark that night and practically every house was spoken for.' Initially, Miller's firm was a limited partnership, including his two brothers: its first subsidy application was for thirty-two houses in 1927, but five years later it was building no fewer than 1,224 houses (64 per cent of all applications for subsidy houses in the city). In 1934, it became a limited company, James Miller & Partners, with capital of £50,000. James Miller became an Edinburgh Town Councillor in 1936 and rose to become Lord Provost from 1951 to 1954 and Lord Mayor of London in 1964. The development of an integrated speculative building process was also extended to land acquisition, offsetting feuing restrictions; Miller had built up an extensive land bank, comprising 489 acres of land on seventy-two separate sites, by late 1939.[12]

Edinburgh Corporation's diminishing interest in general-needs building for rent, and its growing reliance on subsidised private-rental building – assisted by 1924 Wheatley Act subsidies until 1935, and by Corporation incentives after that – ensured a continuing large market for private-rental building. This gap was filled from 1932 by the large Glasgow building firm Mactaggart & Mickel, one of the largest producers of housing in inter-war Scotland, having built nearly 20,000 new houses between 1923 and 1939. In Edinburgh, attracted by the city's prosperity and the Corporation's favourable policies, it embarked on a series of large rental developments, totalling 3,356 houses between 1932 and 1939, and came to dominate the private rented sector in Edinburgh well into the 1970s. Mactaggart & Mickel's inter-war rental building in Edinburgh was concentrated in three large outer-suburban schemes, East Pilton (1932–8), Carrick Knowe (1936–9) and Colinton Mains (1937–9); another, at Broomhouse, was begun in 1939 but suspended by the war. Although subsidy levels shifted with successive legislation, the basic arrangement with the Corporation remained constant – that is, Mactaggart & Mickel feued land from the Corporation and employed a large Edinburgh house-factoring firm, Messrs Gumley and Davidson, to collect rents and service the estates.[13]

All these developments were built entirely of two-storey 'flatted villas' on low-density, simplified garden-suburb layouts, designed by Stewart Kaye (1891–1952), the firm's Edinburgh consultant architect. There were two basic house types (one of three and one of four apartments), arranged in uniform rows of four or eight, and constructed of roughcast brick.[14] Kaye's elevations also featured tile-hung bay windows and piended roofs of varying heights. But by then, Mactaggart & Mickel had decided to begin building for sale in Edinburgh, competing not only with Miller (who had twenty estates under way by 1935) but also with other active firms, such as Hepburn Bros, who were building large estates of bungalows at Glasgow Road, Corstorphine, Greenbank and Craigentinny (1933–8), designed by draughtsman Thomas Bruce of Inverkeithing. Mactaggart & Mickel's most 'upmarket' and individualistic inter-war development was Hillpark (from 1936), on the leafy edges of Corstorphine Hill. It was sold plot by plot for development with white, metal-windowed, Art Deco house types (designed by Kaye), all costing over £900, and was marketed for its combination of accessibility with rural exclusivity.[15]

Council and private flats in the late 1930s

By the mid-1930s, a strong architectural polarisation had emerged between the garden-suburb formula of these private estates and the denser

FIGURE 7.1   Advertisement for Hillpark, Mactaggart and Mickel's most ambitious speculative housing development of the late 1930s.   *RCAHMS*

flats associated with Corporation building. Private developments of tenements or modern 'service flats' were relatively rare, and mostly designed by Stewart Kaye: in the late 1930s and late 1940s, he built a conservatively styled tenemental extension to James Steel's Learmonth estate for the Dean Property Investment Company. More ambitious, in 1933–5, was his redevelopment of the Port Hopetoun canal harbour in Lothian Road in the form of a huge block of flats and shops. Architecturally, most precocious was Neil & Hurd's Ravelston Garden (1935–7), a row of three white, flat-roofed, Art Deco butterfly-plan blocks with a profusion of 'mod cons' in their six-roomed flats.

Under Macrae's direction, the Corporation's own flat-building programme had been developed in the mid-1930s, in developments such as Craigmillar Castle and Pilton/Royston Mains, so

FIGURE 7.2   Tenement housing designed by City architect Ebenezer Macrae and built in 1940. The development was typical of small gap sites in the Torphichen Street/Dewar Place area.   *RCAHMS*

as to exploit the slum-clearance subsidies of the 1930 Housing Act (which fuelled a total inter-war slum clearance of 7,000 dwellings) and the overcrowding subsidies of the 1935 Act. There was a feeling that the 'slum problem', and the 17,000 overcrowded houses revealed by the 1935 Act survey, constituted a soluble challenge. There was growing concern with architectural and planning 'quality', and a sense, emphasised in the official 1935 'Highton Report', that one could learn from the 'higher standards' of modern continental social housing and its provision of collective social facilities. A further report in 1937 argued for variegated modernist flats rather than 'traditional tenements'. Macrae, who made frequent European tours, played a key role in the Highton Report. He contrasted the utilitarian, official 'hack-work' of

Scottish housing schemes with the 'vital forces at work' in continental modernism, despite the latter's sometimes 'brutal . . . nakedness'.[16] Alongside modernist sympathies, Macrae also argued for the incorporation of overtly 'Scottish' features of a Lorimerian traditionalist kind.

Restrained modernist elements appeared in some of the large peripheral schemes of the mid- and late 1930s, such as Saughton Golf Course, Stenhouse (1933), with its grand crescent and banded windows in a somewhat Viennese manner, or West Pilton, designed by Macrae with Stewart Kaye from 1936, with a large central circus. Traditionalist and Geddesian elements predominated in Macrae's piecemeal inner-area improvement and clearance projects, such as the multi-phase St Leonard's redevelopment (see Chapter 6). In the ambitious redevelopment of the Piershill Barracks site with 342 flats in 1937–40, the 'Scots' Arts and Crafts element was clear in the rustic rubble (recycled from the barrack buildings) and the broken, dormered style, while the 'continental' influence was more indirect in the freely planned, open layout, with a continuous building strip looping around huge U-shaped courtyards, planted with flowers and over-looked by sun balconies.[17]

In the 1938 Housing Act, the building of more variegated flat schemes and sensitive housing set in historic courtyards was further encouraged, but the law's main aim was to cope with the mounting crisis of housebuilding resources. Private and council housing had always competed for labour and materials, but in post-1933 Edinburgh the buoyancy of 'spec' building abstracted workmen from lower-paid council contracts; by 1938, council building costs had shot up 38 per cent since 1934, and the 1938 Act introduced a new, generous sliding subsidy scale – although the outbreak of war, of course, brought all this to an abrupt stop.[18]

Postwar: introduction

The post-war period, with few but significant changes, broadly continued the existing general radial population movement and the correspond-ing conversion or intensification of the centre as a cultural and conservation zone. Now, however, municipal housing played, for two decades, the main role in this movement, which was dominated by housing the working class rather than the middle class. Where two-thirds of the 43,000 houses built between 1918 and 1940 had been privately built, and one-third by the municipality, from 1946 to 1963 the proportions were reversed, with 28,000 built by the Corporation. By 1958, 25 per cent of all dwellings in the city were owned by the Corporation. There was still an emphasis on mini-mising the financial burden on the local taxpayer: for instance, the average rent of a municipal house was £37 in 1962, compared with a £30 average for all Scottish cities. In addition, there were still subsidies for house-purchase or building: by 1962, the Corporation had lent over £6,000,000 in this way.

Despite these major changes in house tenure, the overall demographic trend, of the radial 'rippling

out' of social classes, stayed the same. The Civic Survey and Plan prepared by Patrick Abercrombie and the Corporation's consultant planner, Derek Plumstead – in contrast to the radical population overspill envisaged in Abercrombie's Clyde Valley Plan – proposed a far more conservative formula of internal population redistribution for Edin-burgh. The creation of a 'green belt' around the city prevented simple peripheral spread: instead, local-authority suburban housing was increas-ingly infilled within outer areas already partly developed with private bungalows. Thus the 1950s saw a partial reversal of the inter-war trend to class segregation through suburbanisation.

The years of rationing: 1945–53

The wartime coalition government's plans for a combined public and private-housing drive were abandoned by the incoming Labour administra-tion, which scrapped all private subsidies and introduced draconian licensing curbs.[19] By 1947, the worsening economy had sparked a crippling materials shortage and price inflation, with Edinburgh building costs nearly trebling since 1937; tenders for the new Inch and Liberton Corporation housing schemes were over 50 per cent above DHS guidelines. Further licensing curbs were slapped on new housing in 1947–8, provoking some councillors to unleash vain tirades against the advance of 'Socialism and Bureaucracy'.

Indeed, the Corporation's ethos was becoming more favourable towards city council housebuild-ing, and the overwhelming initiative now lay with the council-housing drive, which was first unleashed by the wartime emergency Housing (Temporary Accommodation) Act 1944, and redi-rected to the task of permanent building by the nearly doubled subsidies of the Housing (Financial Provisions) (Scotland) Act 1946.[20] Here, in contrast to the stress on slum-clearance flats in the 1930s, the emphasis was firmly thrown back to low-rise 'family houses'.

Under the 1944 Act, 32,176 lightweight prefabri-cated bungalows ('prefabs'), with an expected life of ten years, were built across Scotland by the Ministry of Works. Edinburgh, with its plentiful

FIGURE 7.3   'AIROH' aluminium prefab house (Mark 2 permanent version), built in 1949 at Moredun housing scheme. *Miles Glendinning*

outer-suburban sites, received by far the biggest allocation in Scotland – 4,000, compared to only 2,550 in Glasgow. The Edinburgh allocation was split between 2,206 houses of more conventional panellised concrete/steel construction (Arcon, Tarran, Uni-Seco) and 1,794 'AIROH' aluminium bungalows – a more advanced design which epitomised the scientific and organisational panache of the prefab programme, and which was hailed by one American academic as 'the largest single industrialised house enterprise in human history'.[21]

The bungalows were much more expensive than 'traditional' building, but their production was heavily subsidised by the government as a safeguard of future military-industrial capacity. The lavish internal amenities of the prefabs, including fitted kitchenette and background heating, coupled with their conservatively styled resemblance to pre-war bungalows, guaranteed them a rapturous welcome in Edinburgh. The first consignment was a batch of 193 Arcons assembled at Muirhouse,

from December 1945, on sites prepared by German prisoners working under armed guard: the first completed house, at 22 Pennywell Path, was occupied on 7 January by Mr and Mrs A. Fielding and two young children, residents for the previous eight years in a one-roomed slum 'single-end'. They hailed the Arcon as a 'housewife's delight', but criticised the lack of bus links to the city.[22]

When the emphasis shifted from temporary to permanent houses, from 1946 onwards, the strong central regime of the prefab programme began to dissolve. In 1944, a government-backed report on housing design, the Westwood Report (*Planning Our New Homes*), had not only demanded a vast post-war programme of over 500,000 new dwellings but also made it clear that these should be designed on totally new lines. Of course, the houses would have to be larger and better equipped than pre-war ones – that was a standard demand – but equally important was a new ethos of design and landscaping.

At first, the government interdepartmental committee (Burt Committee) formed in 1942 to investigate 'non-traditional' construction delegated much of its Scottish work to the Scottish Special Housing Association (SSHA), an autonomous government-controlled agency, which in 1944 began building an area of experimental house types at Sighthill in Edinburgh. For this site, in Sighthill Road/Neuk/ Loan, ten houses of five types were designed by the energetic Sam Bunton, a prefabrication-minded member of SSHA's consultant architect panel. Later, a range of other types was added, so that by 1964 there were sixty-nine houses of thirty different construction types. The two main methods of construction at Sighthill were concrete and steel. The first house built at Sighthill was commissioned by the SSHA for its own use from Weirs of Cathcart: the 'Paragon', a four-apartment, flat-roofed bungalow built of steel external walls and Gyproc (compacted gypsum-panel) internal partitions, for use especially in mining areas. Construction of the Sighthill prototype in July 1944 took only two weeks, and was followed by 100 elsewhere in Scotland.[23]

In Edinburgh, the new permanent housing programme was also eagerly taken up in 1946 by the Housing Committee, which now proposed to build 5,547 permanent houses in addition to the 4,000 prefabs, with most of the former using prefabricated systems too. But rapidly, it became clear that the non-traditional permanent-house programme would be a partnership between local authorities and private building firms which had developed their own 'proprietary' systems. A typical transitional episode which straddled the boundary of command production and proprietary production was the 1947–9 programme to build a permanent version of the AIROH bungalow with thicker walling panels (83mm). In Scotland, 2,504 were manufactured and supplied between 1947 and 1949, entirely by Blackburn, who designated it 'Blackburn Mk II'; in a dramatic last-minute gesture, the final batch of 145 was offered to Edinburgh Corporation in February 1949 at only a week's notice and was delivered to the Moredun scheme, where a 1946 garden-suburb plan by J. A. W. Grant for traditionally built houses

was developed instead, mostly using prefabricated types. The permanent AIROHs were delivered to Moredun at a rate of six bungalows daily; the contractors involved, Mowlem and Wimpey, could assemble a bungalow in just over half an hour after the four sections were hoisted up onto the site on gantries.[24]

By the beginning of the 1950s, the growing call for increased densities began to make lightweight prefabrication systems suitable only for one – or two-storey dwellings look less attractive; with the lessening of the materials shortage, there was a gradual return to conventional, non-prefabricated construction. A transitional stage in this process, at the time of severe steel shortages in 1951–2, was a shift towards greater use of concrete for two-storey houses, especially in composite systems combining precast concrete blocks with frame-like elements. These systems often worked on a licensing or franchise basis, administered by umbrella organisations. The Scottish Housing Group (SHG) was a Glasgow-based cartel of housing contractors built up in the mid-1940s with DHS and Building Research Station help. In Edinburgh and the east, more important was the Musselburgh-based Cruden Group, a new and thrusting firm set up in 1943 by engineering draughtsman Harry H. Cruden and focused on the licensing of house types. The first post-war Cruden house was steel-framed, with external concrete panels and prefabricated timber-framed interior: a prototype was built in 1946 in Milton Road, Edinburgh. Over the 1940s and early 1950s, the systems fluctuated in response to materials rationing, but the organisational method remained constant. From 1949, the Cruden programme concentrated on a traditionally built but dry-lined house type, the 'Dunedin'. During these years, another concrete specialist firm, Orlit, also became increasingly focused on Edinburgh and the east of Scotland, renaming itself in 1954 the Scottish Construction Company (Scotcon), and devising systems for three- or four-storey tenements using load-bearing precast blockwork.[25]

In Edinburgh itself, however, the consolidation of council-housebuilding contract operations in the 1950s was based around the revived dominance of

Miller, which now emphasised the manufacture of precast concrete blocks as a part of its operations.[26] Reinvigorated by wartime expansion and participation in the prefab programmes, Miller made vigorous efforts to standardise the components of more-or-less traditional (or, as they were often styled, 'new traditional') house types. The firm took over one of Scotland's leading builders' merchants, and by 1950 was employing 1,000 workers at factories at Craigleith and Granton, producing standard joinery and precast concrete elements. In the early post-war years, especially in Edinburgh, over 7,250 Miller houses in various systems were built. These showed a diminishing element of prefabrication but a continuing concern for systematised planning.

The 1950s and 1960s speculative-building revival

By the mid-1950s, the post-war revival of the private sector was well under way, following a step-by-step relaxation and (1955) abolition of the licensing regime. By 1962, the private sector's contribution to overall Scottish output had risen to 29 per cent, from its low point of 3 per cent in 1950. Although, politically, any revival of national government subsidies to private builders was impossible, something which encouraged the growing polarisation between rental public housing for the working class and owner-occupied private housing for the middle class, in Edinburgh the Corporation doggedly revived its policy of subsidising the private sector. By 1963, with over a third of the post-war housing stock privately built, over £6 million of local subsidies had been disbursed, and several large firms, such as Miller, Mactaggart & Mickel and Thain, were engaged on developments of significant size (of over 2,000 dwellings, in the case of Mactaggart & Mickel's Broomhall). Miller had returned to unsubsidised speculative building after 1955, with an expanded range of house types: this side of the business was James Miller's own special passion, and he controlled the programme personally. Architecturally, the new private developments rejected the bungalow pattern for a two-storey form, like their suburban council counterparts.

This private-sector revival was achieved only gradually and with many fits and starts. In 1950–1, there was a partial relaxation of controls, which continued chiefly to benefit firms which had secured bulk licences: for example, Miller or Mactaggart & Mickel were able to offer five-apartment villas for only £2,000, while excluded firms such as Hepburn Bros could only afford to build three- or four-apartment houses at that price. Yet even the large firms continued to rely on local-authority contracting to keep them afloat. What was clear was that, with the continuation of rent control, there was no future for the private rented sector within the increasingly polarised 'housing system'; and, from 1953, Mactaggart & Mickel began selling their rental properties as soon as they became vacant.[27] A large estate of three-storey flats and villas built from 1965 onwards, Forrester Park (designed by William Vannan), was entirely for owner occupation.[28]

Edinburgh's second council-housing boom

The recovery and reorientation of private building away from the low-cost and rental markets increased the pressure on the Corporation to become more active, not only in slum clearance but also in some kind of revived 'general-needs' building: Edinburgh's council-housing output dropped to as few as 788 dwellings in 1958, far below the Scottish, or even English, norm for a city of its size, and the 'waiting list' continued to rise, from 6,000 in 1958 to 11,000 in 1964. A succession of Progressive housing chairmen in the late 1950s, culminating in Tom Morgan in 1959–62, adopted more interventionist policies. But the figure who played the decisive role in triggering a key change in policy was a Labour councillor, Pat Rogan, a bricklayer who was elected and placed on the Housing Committee in 1954 and immediately began to follow the nationally well-trodden path of agitation on behalf of his constituents against 'poor housing'.

The arena of conflict was no longer the Old Town itself, where redevelopment was being tackled by 'conservative surgery' interventions of an increasingly architecturally complex character. James Miller, now Lord Provost, backed architect

FIGURE 7.4 Chessel's Court redevelopment, Canongate, by Robert Hurd and Partners, 1958–66. *Paul Shillaber*

Robert Hurd's three-phase programme for the rebuilding of the Canongate (Tolbooth area, 1953–8; Morocco Land, 1956–7; and Chessel's Court, 1958–66), whose mixture of preserved blocks and new, colourful, traditionalist infill set out to preserve the 'couthy, intimate quality of the street'. Similar picturesque principles informed Basil Spence's piecemeal redevelopment of the old village of Newhaven (1957–9), as well as his more flamboyant 79–121 Canongate project of 1965–9. Now, the focus of 'slum' agitation had shifted to the 19th-century tenements of Rogan's own ward, Holyrood, immediately south-east of the Old Town and facing Holyrood Park.[29] The crisis focused on a tenement in Beaumont Place whose owner, to emphasise the harmful effect of rent control on house maintenance, had in 1953 offered to sell it to a Glasgow Labour MP for one penny. Six years later, one night in 1959, part of the 'Penny Tenement' collapsed, and Rogan was able to

exploit this emergency to secure declaration of two extensive clearance areas (Carnegie Street 'A' and 'B') and the rehousing of 101 families in nine days – the beginning of a major slum-clearance drive. He recalled that 'at that time, a rather shocking story went the rounds in Edinburgh that I was seen running away from that tenement, armed with a pick and shovel!'[30]

Actually, this outcome did not yet in itself amount to anything to offend the Progressive Party, among whom slum clearance was seen as an eminently suitable activity for the Corporation. But how was a substantial programme of demolition and new building to be put together, given the increasing shortage of sites? During the late 1950s, the Corporation was still methodically developing the last of its big peripheral housing sites. But with the end of plentiful land in sight, the obvious next step was to begin building multi-storey blocks of flats. Isolated prototype blocks had been built earlier in the decade, establishing the norm of a high degree of internal services (including central heating and lifts). The first were two eight-storey blocks of a somewhat conservative, monumental character, and both built by Hepburn Bros as contractors: Westfield Court (1950–1), a 458-foot long, curved slab block designed by Williamson & Hubbard originally as a pre-war private project for property developer Alexander Glass, and innovatively containing a nursery school on its top floor; and Maidencraig Court, Queensferry Road, a curved, pitched-roof block by traditionalist architect Leslie Grahame MacDougall (from 1953).[31]

To extend multi-storey building on to a sufficiently large scale, not only modernist architecture was demanded but also contractual reform, since separate-trades builders were obviously unsuited to the scale of tower blocks. The opposite of separate trades was the 'package deal' (design-and-build), under which a single contractor's staff designed as well as built the development – like the 'proprietary' low-rise houses of the 1940s. In 1955, two pioneering infill schemes were started, both including tower rather than slab blocks: a single eleven-storey block by Scotcon at Spey Street, and a more complex development by Miller (with DHS architects) at Moat Drive, including two massive ten-storey towers. And two years later, at the instigation of Morgan, the Housing Committee began a more ambitious attempt to allocate package-deal contracts for up to eighteen tower blocks on four sites to a 'panel' of contractors including Wimpey and Scotcon (at Muirhouse), Crudens (Gracemount) and Laing (Comiston); these were mostly chunks of large suburban schemes. DHS architects fiercely resisted the package deals,[32] and had a measure of success in enforcing tailor-made design in the slum-clearance inner areas.

Councillors acknowledged that, unlike Glasgow, where a huge clearance programme was being adumbrated in 1957, 'all our history in Edinburgh left us much more limited scope for demolitions'. But this 'history' – as in Macrae's day – was seen as a positive factor, and the most prestigious projects were given to private architects.[33] The scope of the ethos of 'conservative surgery' had now spread beyond the Old Town to areas such as Leith, where the late 1950s saw the beginning of a succession of piecemeal redevelopments in the decayed industrial/housing belt south of the docks. Architects Alison & Hutchison & Partners designed a cluster of interventions, at around 160 persons per acre, north of Great Junction Street ('Citadel and Central Leith Area'), built from 1962 onwards. This included two slab blocks, one of them (at Cables Wynd) an ingeniously curved ten-storey deck-access block, to fit into the confined site; the area also included a shopping centre with integral tower block, built by private developers Murrayfield Real Estate Co. and designed by Ian Burke, Martin & Partners.[34] The most prominent of these redevelopments was slightly earlier: the Leith Fort project, built in 1960–6 following a competition of 1957 judged by Leslie Martin. The keyhole-shaped site, overlooking the docks, contained an old, classical barracks complex; the brief specified a fairly high redevelopment density, but left competitors free to decide how to divide it up.

The winners were newly graduated architects John Baikie, Frank Perry and Michael Shaw-Stewart. Their project retained the outer walls and gate lodges, giving a strong element of historic

context. They split the site into contrasting building types for each size of dwelling and household: the centre was occupied by a dense kasbah of two-storey 'courtyard houses' for large families, flanked to the north by a pair of concrete slab-clad tower blocks for small families, and a 'spine' of seven-storey deck-access blocks to the south. The monumental aesthetic of the towers (designed by Baikie; demolished 1994), with their massive stair towers studded with glass-brick windows, was intended by the architects to reflect the 'robust' industrial setting, and the contemporary architecture of Louis Kahn. In this, they were successful in unforeseen ways: when the housing-committee chairman at the time of their completion (1966) took his wife on a tour of the site, she remarked in puzzlement: 'Fancy putting the houses so close to those huge grain silos!'[35]

The Rogan–Theurer years: re-housing and re-planning in the 1960s

By the time the above idiosyncratic project was completed, it was almost beside the point. For, by then, a new and unprecedented situation had arisen: Edinburgh Corporation was engaged, with cross-party support, on a massive general-needs building drive – inspired partly by the policies of Glasgow Corporation! In 1962, political deadlock in the Council had allowed Pat Rogan, at last, to assume the chair of the Housing Committee – the first Labour member to do so. His inspiration was the 'crusading' work of his Glasgow counterpart, David Gibson, an idealistic socialist who pushed through – in defiance of planners' opposition – a massive housing drive of tower blocks on vacant suburban sites. Paradoxically, however, Rogan in 'Tory' Edinburgh was in an easier position than Gibson, because the Progressives' parsimony had left the financial resources to support a sudden boost to the housing drive, and the large, low-density schemes of prefabs had bequeathed him a tempting land bank to raid. An outline plan had already been drawn up in 1960 to demolish almost all of these, replacing 3,616 prefabs with 9,272 permanent houses, many in tower blocks; eventually the only prefabs left would be the 145 permanent Mk I AIROHs at Moredun (many of which still

FIGURE 7.5   Aerial view in 1989 of Leith Fort housing scheme designed by Shaw-Stewart, Baikie and Perry as a mixed development of tower blocks, deck-access flats and patio housing.   *RCAHMS*

survive even today). Rogan forced through and accelerated this plan: dwellings under contract soared from 700 in 1961 to 2,700 by 1962; and two years later, before he demitted office, 3,617 houses were under construction.[36]

Following 1960 pilot schemes at Muirhouse and Longstone, the main programme divided into sites

suffering from undermining, and sites free of it – an issue that had not arisen with the prefabs. The undermined sites, in the coalfield belt south of the city, had to be carefully developed, sometimes with lower-than-usual blocks and sometimes with high towers to exploit scattered sites: for example, Southhouse (591 dwellings built in 1962–5 by

FIGURE 7.6   Aerial view of the Muirhouse housing scheme, showing 1950s tenements in the foreground and 1960s tower blocks behind. At the upper left are 1950s 'semis' built as a speculative development by Mactaggart & Mickel. *RCAHMS*

Miller in one- to five-storey blocks), Hyvots Bank (678 dwellings built in 1962–5 by J. Smart in two- to five-storey blocks) and Moredun (1,126 houses built in 1963–7 by MacLeod and Wimpey, with two- to sixteen-storey blocks). North of the city, layouts had greater freedom and could adopt a more continuously massive built form – for

example, the numerous tower blocks of Muirhouse (1961–6) or the dense network of five-storey deck-access blocks of the West Pilton A and B redevelopments (515 and 508 dwellings respectively), built from 1965 (and demolished in 1990).

One of the key elements in Rogan's housing drive was an expansion of the system of package-deal suburban housing pioneered in 1957–8. Some newcomers boldly exploited its opportunities – such as Harry Cruden, who restructured and refinanced his firm in 1957 with a dynamic new management, new chief architect (George Bowie) and a vast design team, orientated towards package-deal housing contracts. Unlike some other major cities such as Birmingham, Edinburgh resisted governmental pressure for mass 'system building' in large-panel prefabricated concrete as a remedy for the renewed building-industry shortages of c. 1960–1. As in Aberdeen, the introverted local industry was effectively able to 'defend its patch', although, under the fierce pressure for output in the new field of tower blocks, some established firms began to wilt a little. Miller experienced problems of adjustment: there were complaints from the SSHA about project management, while many Edinburgh councillors 'objected to all the amount of building they'd done already, and felt they had undue influence on the council'; a 1964 balcony collapse on a five-storey block at 29 Southhouse Broadway (owing to defective joists) hardly helped their position. Some smaller firms fared even worse: for example, William Arnott McLeod's twenty-three-storey Martello Court at Muirhouse – a striking all-round-balconied design by Rowand Anderson, Kininmonth & Paul, awarded in 1962 as a flagship for the local industry, suffered serious difficulties of overspending and time overruns.[37]

There was also a contest among the architects over the huge programme. Private architects were given a slice of the work, subject to the vagaries of contracting and planning policy. For the Niddrie Marischal prefab site, in a sensitive location near Holyrood Park, proposals for a low-rise package-deal layout by Crudens were abandoned, and the young, well-respected firm of Morris & Steedman was engaged. Their 1966 plan divided the development into zones of increasing height, culminating in the 'focal points' of two point blocks. Reflecting the prestige established earlier by Macrae, the City Architect's department controlled the design and contracting of almost all developments, even package deals (except Wimpey's reliable 'no-fines' developments). Following Macrae's

retiral in 1946, he was succeeded by A. J. Forgie (1946–53) and Alexander Steele (1955–72). Steele lacked the driving force to dominate the housing programme, and the initiative passed to one of his staff, Harry Corner, an amiable and efficient negotiator who joined in 1954 and rose to become Depute City Architect (Housing) in the 1960s.[38]

In 1965, Rogan was replaced as housing chairman by a Progressive member: Harry Corner recalled that 'we had a wonderful book of contracts when Pat left the chair!' But his colourful successor, wig-manufacturer G. Adolf Theurer, far from easing back the housing drive, instead redoubled its force, helped by the temporary cross-party consensus on this issue. Theurer was motivated not by socialist egalitarianism but by a passionate civic patriotism, expressed through social regeneration: 'My intention, just like Pat, was to build houses for the people! Some of my fellow-Progressives grumbled bitterly: they didn't want council houses because the low rents would be exploited by the Labour Party; they didn't want to add to national Labour "successes". But I didn't care one bit!'

Disregarding party affiliations, Theurer and Rogan had cultivated a convivial working alliance during the latter's chairmanship.[39] Together, they inspired the climax of Edinburgh's 1960s public-housing drive: the new 'township' of Wester Hailes, a massive, peripheral development of over 5,000 dwellings, built between 1967 and 1975. Its origins lay in 1963, under Rogan's chairmanship, in the strategic realisation that large-scale building could only be sustained by securing large green-belt sites once the prefab stock was exhausted. Following the planning refusal (backed by Labour minister J. Dickson Mabon) of a site acquired by the council at Alnwickhill, adjoining affluent private areas, the less controversial 200-acre site of Wester Hailes was approved. The architect-planners Sir Frank Mears & Partners – heirs to some elements of the Geddesian place-specific tradition – produced a layout tailored to the sloping, hillside site, with a township centre ringed by cellular micro-neighbourhoods, and a road layout with limited vehicle/pedestrian segregation. Some of the areas were dominated by big

FIGURE 7.7   Aerial view in 1991 of Wester Hailes, built from 1967, prior to the demolition of most of the multi-storey block.   *RCAHMS*

ten-storey Crudens slab blocks, but most of Wester Hailes comprised low-rise flats arranged in somewhat picturesquely contoured groupings.[40]

End of the drive

By 1969, however, grand public-housing projects such as Wester Hailes had been overtaken by the march of opinion and policy. The economic crises

of the late 1960s had undermined both the council housing drive and the modestly surging private housing market. In the private sector, house-price inflation began in earnest, with values rising by half in the five years from 1964, to an average figure of £3,336 for a new house. By late 1966, the government's 'credit squeeze' began to bite into the market, with a noticeable slackening in demand for buying houses. In the relatively monopolistic situation of Scottish private housing, Wimpey carved out a period of ascendancy.[41] The full-scale revival of private housing would have to wait until the different conditions of the Tory 1980s and 1990s.

What dominated the scene for now was the growing crisis of social housing. With the sudden arrival at a politically and publicly perceived glut of housing, rising expectations pushed aside the old gratitude for a new home provided by the 'authority'. Many of the newly completed peripheral multi-storey projects, such as Martello Court, were already encountering unexpected management problems. No more big greenfield sites were in prospect after Wester Hailes, while slum clearance was becoming more and more difficult, and beset by 'historic Edinburgh' amenity concerns such as the tough guidelines on high buildings introduced in 1968 by Lord Holford. The main redevelopment of Rogan's own ward – the St Leonard's (Arthur Street) CDA project – was endlessly deferred in the controversies which followed Alexander Steele's first proposal of 1961, envisaging a line of five twenty-five-storey Wimpey tower blocks overlooking Holyrood Park. After repeated whittling-down of the number and height of the towers in the face of protests by the Ministry of Works, amenity societies and the Royal Fine Art Commission for Scotland, Rogan and Theurer were finally told by Mabon in 1966 that seven storeys was to be the maximum, and a dense, medium-rise layout was designed by Corner and Wimpey's staffs and built from 1970.[42]

But by 1970, a process of voluntaristic transformation of Edinburgh social housing was irrevocably under way. Encouraged especially by Sir Robert Matthew and the Edinburgh New Town Conservation Committee, founded in 1970 (see Chapter 9), attention began to shift to the regeneration of the New Town, adopting a 'conservative surgery' approach with social-reformist overtones, focusing on council-aided rehabilitation of the Georgian tenements of the 'tattered edges', such as Stockbridge. The work of philanthropic agencies such as Castle Rock Housing Association or Shelter – organised by professional people, unlike

the new community housing associations of Glasgow – began to rival the council's programmes.[43] After two decades of consensual support for council housing, the early 20th-century Edinburgh aversion to state *dirigisme* in housing was now re-emerging in a very different form, orientated towards a future of combined capitalism and democratic engagement – but that is another story!

Notes

1. Cd 8731, *Report of the Royal Commission on the Housing of the Industrial Population of Scotland Rural and Urban*, 1917 para. 1,938. See also M. Glendinning, 'The Ballantyne Report', in D. Mays (ed.), *The Architecture of Scottish Cities* (East Linton, 1997), pp. 161–70.
2. S. Damer, *A Social History of Glasgow Council Housing 1919–1965*, ESRC Research Project R000231241, 1991, pp. 30, 52.
3. A. O'Carroll, 'The development of owner occupation in Edinburgh', PhD thesis, Heriot-Watt University (1994), p. 210. On Rogan, see M. Glendinning (ed.), *Rebuilding Scotland* (East Linton, 1997), pp. 66–74; D. McCrone, *Understanding Scotland* (London, 1992), p. 157; T. Stephenson, *Industrial Edinburgh* (n.p., 1921).
4. O'Carroll, 'The development of owner occupation', p. 150.
5. *Weekly Scotsman*, 13 May 1939; P. J. Smith, 'Planning as environmental improvement', in A. Sutcliffe (ed.), *The Rise of Modern Urban Planning* (London, 1980), p. 102; O'Carroll, 'The development of owner occupation', p. 366; *Housing Problems in the City of Edinburgh*, Report by the City Chamberlain, March 1925, Edinburgh City Archives (ECA), Q.2/4; A. O'Carroll, 'The influence of local authorities on the growth of owner occupation: Edinburgh and Glasgow 1914–1939', *Planning Perspectives*, 11 (1996): 65.
6. J. Frew, 'Towards a municipal housing blueprint', *Architectural Heritage*, 11 (2000): 43–54.
7. J. Frew, 'Homes fit for heroes: early municipal house-building in Edinburgh', *Architectural Heritage Society of Scotland Journal*, 16 (1989): 26–33; 'Growth of Edinburgh, 1: the Corporation's Housing Schemes', *Weekly Scotsman*, 13 May 1939; 'Gorgie', *The Scotsman*, 19 March 1919, p. 10; Edinburgh Corporation, Minutes of the Town Council (ECMTC), 6 July 1922, p. 591.
8. J. Frew, 'Cottages, tenements and practical idealism', in D. Mays (ed.), *Architecture of Scottish Cities*, p. 179; J. Frew, 'Concrete, cosmopolitanism and

low-cost house design', *Architectural Heritage*, 5 (1995): 29–38.

9. Prestonfield, Saughton Mains, Stenhouse, Craigentinny, Granton, Niddrie Mains, Restalrig: ECMTC, 18 June 1923. Housing and Town Planning Committee, 25 June 1923, 4 June 1923, 29 September 1924.

10. Precognition of Chief Sanitary Inspector on 100–110 Canongate, 1927 (cited in 2002 thesis by Richard Dollamore, Edinburgh University Architecture Department). Edinburgh Town Council, Evidence of sub-committee appointed to consider the progress of the housing programme, 21 January 1937; L. Rosenburg and J. Johnson, *Improvement Schemes in Old Edinburgh 1890–1930*, draft of 14 August 2003.

11. O'Carroll, N. Milnes, 'The development of owner occupation in Edinburgh' (1994); *A Study of Industrial Edinburgh* (1936), pp. 170–4; Edinburgh Corporation Treasurer's Committee Minutes, 1923–33; M. Glendinning and D. Watters (eds), *Home Builders* (Edinburgh, 1999), chapters A3 and B2.

12. Notes from speech by James Miller, 29 March 1973 (McKean Archive, RIAS Library); P. J. Smith, 'Site selection in the Forth Basin', PhD thesis, University of Edinburgh (1964), p. 307; H. M. Bingham, 'Land hoarding in Edinburgh', MSc thesis, Edinburgh College of Art (1974), p. 115.

13. O'Carroll, 'The influence of local authorities' and 'The development of owner occupation'; D. Mickel, 'Statement to Edinburgh Corporation', 3 February 1937; Glendinning and Watters, *Home Builders*, chapter 3.

14. ECMTC, 7 December and 28 December 1932, p. 57; D. Mickel, 'Statement to Edinburgh Corporation', 3 February 1937. ECMTC, 19 December and 28 December 1932, 30 January 1933; Edinburgh Corporation Minutes, Properties Sub-committee (ECMPS), 17 January 1933, 30 January 1933, 20 February 1933. ECMTC, 28 November 1932; O'Carroll, 'The development of owner occupation'; ECMTC, 3 April and 1 May 1933; ECMPS, 24 April 1933; Mactaggart & Mickel Archive, RCAHMS (MMA), letter from Stanley Sutherland to Douglas Mickel, 26 March 1990; *Evening News*, 26 August 1933. ECMPS, 9 November 1933; O'Carroll, 'The development of owner occupation'. Mactaggart & Mickel Board Minutes, 28 December 1933, 7 August 1934; ECMTC, 11 December 1933; ECMPS, 18 December 1933, 17 January 1933, 15 January 1934; ECMTC, 1 June 1936, 3 December 1934, 7 January 1935, 4 February 1935.

15. ECMPS, 15 January 1934, 25 February 1935, 22 April 1935; ECMTC, 28 October 1935, 4 March 1935; MMA,

letter of 11 March 1999 from Connell & Connell, Solicitors. *Scotsman*, 5 January 1935, p. 3, and 23 February 1935, p. 3; *Scotsman*, 17 March 1934, 19 May 1934; *Evening News*, 22 February 1935 and 23 June 1934; *Scotsman*, 19 May 1934, 23 June 1934, 13 October 1934; ECMTC, 25 October 1932, Report by City Architect; ECMPS, 19 February 1934; ECMTC, 15 October 1934; *Evening News*, 7 March 1936, 18 April 1936; Mactaggart & Mickel Board Minutes, 20 January 1936, 14 November 1935, 8 November 1935; *Evening News*, 3 December 1937, 10 December 1937, 18 April 1936, 14 September 1935, 17 April 1937, 28 January 1938; *SMT Magazine*, October and November 1937; *Scotsman*, 18 September 1937; *Daily Record*, 10 September 1938, 8 April 1939.

16. *Scotsman*, 4 February 1935, p. 7; J. Frew, 'Ebenezer MacRae and reformed tenement design', *St Andrews Studies*, ii, 1991, pp. 81, 84; *Report of the Scottish Architectural Advisory Committee on the Incorporation of Architectural Quality and Amenity . . .'*, Edinburgh, 1937; see also later attacks, e.g. in *Evening News*, 28 June 1939 (by Robert Hurd).

17. *Evening Dispatch*, 16 April 1936; *Official Architect*, September 1941, pp. 427–8.

18. N. Morgan, 'Sir James Miller', in A. Slaven and S. Checkland (eds), *Dictionary of Scottish Business Biography*, vol. 2 (Aberdeen, 1990), pp. 163–5. (See also articles on H. Cruden, J. Mactaggart, A. Mickel, W. Tawse and J. Lawrence.)

19. *Evening Dispatch*, 25 January 1944; *Daily Express*, 10 October 1944; *Evening News*, 1 December 1944, 2 December 1944, 18 May 1945; *Daily Express*, 19 May 1945; MMA, letter from Douglas Mickel to Andrew Mickel, 22 October 1945. MMA, Board Minutes, 15 December 1939; MMA, letter from Douglas Mickel to Andrew Mickel, 28 October 1943; MMA, Board Minutes, 4 September 1946, 24 April 1946, 1 August 1946, 8 November 1946; MMA, letter from Douglas Mickel to Andrew Mickel, 5 April 1946; *Glasgow Herald*, 27 August 1947.

20. *Evening Dispatch*, 5 October 1949. Edinburgh Corporation Construction Sub-Committee, 14 October 1947 (revised layout) and 20 January 1948 (shops, names); Housing Committee, 16 December 1947 (BISF), 4 November 1948, and 30 November 1948 (Permanent Aluminium); Construction Sub-Committee, 11 January 1949 (Blackburn), 31 January 1949, and 15 February 1949 (Aluminium, Blackburn); Housing Committee, 24 May 1949, 21 February 1950, 23 May 1950 (cost of Aluminium); Construction Sub-Committee, 21 June 1949 (traditional); Housing

Committee, 22 November 1949 (Blackburn); Scottish Office Building Directorate (SOBD), *A Guide to Non-traditional Housing in Scotland* (Edinburgh, 1987).

21. H. S. Heavenrich, 'Housing in Great Britain', unpublished report for Albert Farwell Bemis Foundation of the Massachusetts Institute of Technology (Cambridge, MA, 1952), p. 78.

22. *Evening News* and *Evening Dispatch*, passim, January 1946.

23. T. Begg, *50 Special Years* (Edinburgh, 1987), p. 119ff.

24 *Edinburgh Evening News*, 22 January 1948 and 15 March 1949; Heavenrich, 'Housing', pp. 119–21; SOBD, *Guide to Non-traditional Housing*, p. 6; Edinburgh Corporation Housing Committee minutes, 5 December 1944 (temporary housing programme); appendix to Housing Committee, 16 October 1945 and Construction Sub-Committee, 9 April 1946 (temporary and permanent programme); Housing Committee, 23 April 1946 (BISF); Construction Sub-Committee, 15 October 1946 (Moredun site, Grant); Sub-Committee on Alternative . . . Construction, 9 May 1947 (Scottish Housing Group, Bunton); Housing Committee, 27 May 1947 (BISF).

25. N. Morgan, 'Harry H. Cruden', in Slaven and Checkland (eds), *Dictionary*, pp. 139–40; SOBD, *Guide to Non-traditional Housing*, p. 9. *The Scotsman*, 26 November 1949. Department of Health for Scotland, Circular 49-1953.

26. MMA, correspondence with Building Research Station, December 1948.

27. *Evening Dispatch*, 22 February 1952; *Evening News*, 8 March 1952; *Glasgow Herald*, 18 April 1952, 18 December 1952; *Scotsman*, 28 February 1952.

28. *Evening Dispatch*, 6 April 1953; *Glasgow Herald*, 13 May 1953; *Bulletin*, 17 April 1954; *Bulletin*, 18 October 1956; *Evening Dispatch*, 26 May 1956; *Scotland's Magazine*, May 1957, pp. 22–6; *Bulletin*, 18 May 1956.

29. Glendinning (ed.), *Rebuilding Scotland*; *Builder*, 12 May 1961, p. 887.

30. Glendinning (ed.), *Rebuilding Scotland*; Housing Committee, 15 December 1959, letter from Central Edinburgh Constituency Labour Party about collapse of part of Beaumont Place, Edinburgh.

31. Clive B. Fenton, 'Postwar housing in west Edinburgh', *Docomomo Newsletter*, 5 (2003); *Concrete Quarterly*, May–June 1951; *Builder*, 20 June 1952; *Scotsman*, 30 June 1951; Construction Sub-Committee, 17 June 1952 and 17 March 1953.

32. Inch debate, *Evening Dispatch*, 24 January 1951; Construction Sub-Committee, 11 June 1957; National Archives of Scotland, file SRO DD6-2154, meeting of

3 July 1958; M. Glendinning and S. Muthesius, *Tower Block* (London, 1994), p. 201.

33. 'All our history': interview with Cllr T. Morgan, 1988. 'Interesting': interview with H. Corner, 1987.

34. Citadel and Central Leith: Housing Committee, 31 July 1962, 7 November 1962, 21 June 1963, 17 November 1964, 11 December 1964.

35. Housing Committee, 28 January 1958; *Builder*, 31 January 1956, p. 214. Interviews with Frank Perry and Adolf Theurer, 1987.

36. Glendinning (ed.), *Rebuilding Scotland* (Rogan) and *Tower Block*, chapter 25 (Gibson). Moredun: City Archives, housing files, 17 January 1964, Depute City Architect to Town Clerk.

37. Insufficient scale: Special Sub-Committee on the Future of the Housing Programme, 17 June 1963. Complaints about project management: interview with H. Buteux, 1987, about Broomhill, Glasgow. Collapse: interview with Morgan; City Archives, 23 November 1964, James Miller Ltd to Corporation. 'Poulson mob': interview with Theurer.

38. Hall, Walls: Housing Committee, 17 July 1963. Niddrie Marischal: City Archives, housing files, letter of 22 November 1961, City Architect to Town Clerk; Housing Committee, 9 December 1966 HC; 9 August 1967, Housing Committee Vacation Committee. 'Golf club', 'paint salesman': interviews with Theurer and Morgan.

39. Interview with Theurer.

40. Housing Committee, 3 December 1963; *Official Architecture and Planning*, May 1964; City Archives housing files, letter of 1 March 1965 from Scottish Development Department to Town Clerk; Sub-Committee on Housing Policy, 15 November 1965; *Official Architecture and Planning*, 1965, p. 1,078; Housing Committee, 8 April 1966, 12 April 1966; interview with H. Corner. City Archives, Dean of Guild files, 20 January 1967 to 22 March 1974.

41. Glendinning and Watters, *Home Builders*, chapters A4, A5; interview with Corner.

42. Martello Court: Housing Committee, 6 April 1965; City Archives housing files, 13 July 1965, letter from S. Brown and 29 July 1965, letter from Assistant Chief Constable. Arthur Street: Housing Committee Annual Visit brochures, 1965, 1970, 1972; *Builder*, 21 April 1961; *Builder*, 2 March 1962; Housing Committee, 23 November 1965. Special Sub-Committee, 1 April 1966; Royal Fine Art Commission for Scotland, *Report* for the years 1964–6.

43. SHELTER Housing Aid Centre, Edinburgh, Progress Report 1973, pp. 9–10.

8 *The changing role of the planner before and after the Second World War and the effect on urban form*

Cliff Hague

Edinburgh played a significant role in the development of planning thought internationally in the first half of the 20th century. However, the impact of planning on Edinburgh during that period was much more muted. Two 'founding fathers' of planning were strongly associated with Scotland's capital – Thomas Adams and Patrick Geddes. They were famed from the Prairies to the Punjab, but they were less influential on the physical development of Edinburgh than the anonymous ranks of speculative builders whose investment led to a doubling of the physical area of the city between 1919 and 1939 (see Chapter 7).

Frank Mears took forward Geddes' ideas of a plan for the city centre – to no avail. The 'golden age' of British planning, that was associated with the passing of the 1947 Town and Country Planning Act, saw another luminary of the planning profession, Patrick Abercrombie, apply his talents to the restructuring of the city; but the local authority had no appetite for grand visions. Then, just a few years after his landmark 1963 report on *Traffic in Towns*, Colin Buchanan became the fourth knighted planner to have his proposals spurned by the city's elected representatives. In the 20th century, Edinburgh's prime contribution to the art and profession of planning was in fact through the export of ideas and influences rather than through inspirational practice within the city itself.

Urban form, planning and the search for a new social compact

As Chapter 4 shows, by the latter part of the 19th century, Edinburgh had become industrial and increasingly suburban. As breweries and factories relocated to less congested sites on the edge of the city, early working-class suburbs sprouted. Chapter 4 shows that the Town Council acted in a promotional manner in support of industrial development. Such endeavours continued into the new century. In 1908, Edinburgh Town Council produced a memorandum about how to attract new industries to the city. They sought to avoid the loss of established enterprises to new locations across the city boundary. The report waxed lyrical about Edinburgh's history, beauty, capital-city status and low rates, and identified the south-west of the city (inside the city boundary) as an area where new industry could be developed.

Patrick Geddes was dismissive of this initiative. He saw the 'haphazard' industrial growth that had taken place, and the 'weltering confusion of the railway lines of competitive companies which have invaded and well-nigh destroyed the regions between Edinburgh and Leith',[1] as a betrayal of the town-planning legacy of the New Town. These 'sordid industrial districts' surrounding the historic core threatened to reduce Edinburgh to 'an ordinary industrial town'.[2] To avoid more of the same, suburbanisation had to be the opportunity to make 'Newer Edinburgh – an industrial city and a garden city in one'.[3] To do this, he argued that industry should be located on the leeward eastern side of the city, close to the Midlothian coalfield (but outside the then city boundary). Geddes' dictum of 'survey, analysis and then plan' would tackle the disorder of industrialism. Planning was a Darwinist science, rolling forward the evolution of the city by reference to its past.

While Geddes' vision was propounded internationally, in Edinburgh conceptions about the nature and purpose of town-planning were contested through class-based politics. The Trades Council and the Edinburgh Labour Party gave evidence to the 1912 Royal Commission on Housing in Scotland. From their perspective, town-planning was a necessary link to the provision of adequate housing for working-class families. They proposed that a department should be set up within the local authority to deal exclusively with housing and town-planning. Its brief would be to undertake 'systematic planning of the whole city, the necessary clearing and opening up of the congested areas, and the suitable provision of housing in the suburbs'.[4] Calls for new working-class suburbs were not new. The Burgh Engineer, John Cooper, in his annual report in 1894 had argued for suburban development to reduce the densities in the inner parts of the town. However, the suburbanisation early in the twentieth century had been overwhelmingly middle-class, and the permissive powers bestowed by the 1909 Act only allowed councils to prepare planning schemes for new suburbs, not for the city as a whole.

In addition, the supply of land for new suburban housing was controlled by landowners. Under the system of feuing land, the landowner and his/her descendants received in perpetuity an annual payment, the 'feu duty', from the owners of property developed on their land. Thus feuing land for development was a long-term investment. This meant imposing legal restrictions on the form of development and use of the land. To protect long-term income, any large landowner would consider the impacts of new development on the value of adjacent land that he/she held. As such, feuing land for working-class housing would have an adverse impact on the value of nearby sites. The market response was to ask for higher feus for land for working-class housing. Builders had to build at high density to create a commercially successful scheme. Charitable trusts were major owners of land in and around the capital. By their nature and constitutions, they had to be prudent and cautious, eyeing long-term stability rather than maximising returns in the short term. Geddes described them as the 'largest ground landlords of Edinburgh' and accused them of creating excessively high densities.[5]

It is not surprising, therefore, to find that Edinburgh's suburbanisation before 1914 was both largely middle-class and on sites beyond the city boundary but served by railways, such as Colinton, Corstorphine and Duddingston, then Liberton and Cramond. Indeed, construction of working-class housing appears to have dried up entirely after 1909. The Merchant Company (one of the educational trusts) attributed this to rising building costs,[6] though the feuing practices of landowners were seen by others as being crucial factors.[7] The Labour movement in the city pressed the case for municipal powers of compulsory purchase and local forms of betterment taxation to break the barriers to land for affordable housing.

The social settlement that followed the First World War provoked new interest in town-planning in Edinburgh. In 1918, the Trades Council, Labour Party and Co-operatives Guilds urged the Council to accept that there was a short-term need for some 10,000 new houses.[8] The Merchant Company counted among its members over 560 leading businessmen, and owned estates valued then at over £1 million, though not all of this was in Edinburgh.[9] It observed that the war had made great changes 'inevitable and imperative': 'War has opened our eyes . . . Our vision has been widened'.[10] The Company set up special committees on the building trades in the city and on the development of the city. The latter, chaired by the architect T. P. Marwick, is especially interesting on the nature and purpose of planning in the capital.

The report recognised the benefits of suburban extension planning, citing the use of competitions by the city of Berlin to produce well-designed layouts. Temporary powers of compulsory purchase and boundary expansions were advocated to allow the local authority to 'acquire all land which they may think it desirable to acquire' at 1913 use values plus severance and 'worsenment' costs but less betterment.[11] Pending such reforms, the Company urged the council to adopt a proactive approach to market acquisition and servicing of sites, giving examples from Bristol and Leeds of councils acting in this positive manner.

The Merchant Company report advocated the need to plan long-term and for growth. The vision was a fifty-year plan for a city of one million people with a radical extension of the then city boundaries. Such a land area would allow for 'extensive schemes of village and garden suburbs to which people would be carried by high-speed tramways, and for new manufactories requiring large areas, as well as for a containing belt of open land to be permanently conserved'.[12] The artisans' housing would be at ten to twelve houses to the acre, factories would be located on land adjacent to roads and railways, there would be areas of public open space, existing amenities would be preserved, and new vistas would be fashioned. The whole design would have a Scottish character and use local building materials. The aspiration was for 'a city that is self-contained and self-sufficing, a city with no soul-starving slums', that would 'foster in every way the health, vigour and contentment of the people'.[13] Planning was about changing the form and identity of the city, to fit it for a future that would be different from the past.

Self-sufficiency was a delusion; the Merchant Company itself was recycling income from its estates across Scotland to sustain its schools in Edinburgh. However, in the extraordinary conditions immediately after the war and the rise of Bolshevism, one of Edinburgh's major landowning institutions formulated a vision of town-planning as strategic, long-term action led by the local authority to deliver urban and industrial growth and social contentment. This form of town-planning would provide the land, infrastructure and long-term certainty within which the private sector would deliver the bulk of the actual development. The report called for a local 'Ministry of Development' that would be managed by successful businessmen, a proto-local economic development agency. Thus the war brought a reassessment of the need for, and form of, town-planning.

The Town Council became active in town-planning during this period, while operating within the constraints of the legislation that restricted planning schemes to new suburban extensions. As early as 1912, a statutory scheme for thirty-six acres in the Bellevue area was sanctioned by Scotland's Board of Health. It was followed a year later by a four-and-a-half-acre scheme at Fountainbridge and a large 896-acre scheme for Craigentinny and Restalrig, in conjunction with Leith, as part of the land was on the Leith side of the boundary between the two local authorities. By 1919, central government had sanctioned another four schemes for Edinburgh's suburban growth, amounting in all to over 3,000 acres. These were at Murrayfield and Ravelston, Murrayfield and Saughton, Gorgie and Abercorn–Duddingston– Niddrie. Sanction was also sought by Edinburgh for a further scheme of almost 1,300 acres at Granton, but this was opposed by Leith.[14]

It seems clear, therefore, that Edinburgh's council was actively looking to use the early planning legislation to create substantial suburban extensions which would implement key elements of the vision propounded in the Merchant Company report. However, by 1928, only the small scheme for Fountainbridge had been approved by the Scottish Board of Health. The Burgh Engineer pointed to the problem: the schemes required an unrealistic degree of detail and 'imposed on landowners detailed lay-out plans for which they had no need and less liking'.[15] Thus landownership remained the key force in determining patterns of development.

Frank Mears, Thomas Adams and the 1932 financial crisis

The Edinburgh Corporation Act of 1926 gave the local authority powers similar to those in the Model Clauses of the 1909 planning legislation that had been produced for England but not replicated for Scotland. The effect was that the council gained the power to require detailed layouts for new developments, thereby allowing the planning schemes themselves to be more indicative and less directive. Thus Edinburgh emerged as a local authority that was quite innovative in seeking ways to promote a flexible form of local planning practice as a means to create an orderly suburban expansion of the city. However, the ambitious visions for planning elaborated in different ways by Geddes and by the Merchant Company in the immediate aftermath of the war were not pursued after the crisis had passed. The reasons seem to have been a mixture of political pragmatism, statutory limitations and limited central-government engagement with planning within Scotland.

In 1924, Frank Mears, Geddes' son-in-law and amanuensis, had pressed the case to the council for replanning the city as a whole. A committee was set up, but no action followed. Mears lamented that 'they are instinctively administrators, not creators . . . they have no time for "wild adventures"'.[16] After a controversial proposal for development at Calton Hill,[17] there were again deliberations in 1929 on the preparation of a plan for the city centre. Mears was frustrated by the formation of a committee 'not even composed of people with special knowledge of town planning'.[18] Despairing of the 'solid officials', Mears opted to produce an independent plan for the city centre.

Mears' plan divided the centre into three east–west zones – the 'Business Mile' (the New Town), the Royal Mile and the 'College Mile'. It would be 'a great concerted scheme to cover perhaps 50 years' that would produce 'a renewed Historic Edinburgh'.[19] It was an attempt to propagate the concept of comprehensive planning as an alternative to 'the haphazard methods of the last century'. Thus to Mears, Geddes' pupil, planning was counterposed to the processes and place identities created by industrial capitalism. Planning stood for order and conscious design that could reproduce, even reinvent, a distinctive place identity that was defined by Scottishness, history and Edinburgh's capital-city status. Nothing expressed the irrationality of *laissez-faire* more starkly than the railways, which carved swathes through the city and provided stations in duplicate. Mears proposed just one 'Union' station at the west of the centre, thereby creating a major opportunity site at Waverley. He proposed redevelopment of this for an exhibition hall, winter garden, market and offices (a proposal dismissed as too visionary when he had floated it a decade earlier).

Mears' plan was a means to affirm through the townscape a civic and/or national identity. For example, the St James Square area was in poor condition and of low status, yet occupied a prominent position above the north-eastern corner of Princes Street. To Mears, it was 'an incomparable site for a great public building of national or civic character'.[20] Mears may not have had the 1960s concrete brutalism of the St James Centre in mind, nor its retail components; but the eventual location there of New St Andrew's House, home to Scottish Office civil servants, was not inconsistent with his thinking.

In aspiring to modernise Edinburgh, Mears departed from Geddesian 'conservative surgery' (see Chapter 6). The leitmotif of his plan was the need to reorganise space to meet the needs of national and civic institutions. For example, an area of working-class housing, small industries and breweries east of Nicolson Street was to be gradually reconstructed to accommodate expansion of the University of Edinburgh. The layout proposed quadrangles and gateways with grand boulevards showcasing university buildings. Conservation of historic buildings was certainly part of Mears' plan, but the needs of low-income groups and small business were subservient to the functional requirements of major institutions and a place narrative of the romantic, historic capital city. However, planned Edinburgh would also be a modern city, with the outmoded road network upgraded to cater for future motor traffic. Mears' plan proposed two main developments, an east–west route through the Cowgate and West Port and a north–south route from the Pleasance across the valley to the east of Waverley Station.

Mears and a group of professional and artistic people and institutions in inter-war Edinburgh developed a discourse in which planning was a means to redesign the city so as to reclaim its historic identity and reaffirm its capital status. The institutions included the Edinburgh Architectural Association, the Royal Incorporation of Architects in Scotland, the Royal Town Planning Institute Scottish Branch, the Outlook Tower, the National Trust for Scotland, the Saltire Society and the Cockburn Association. An exhibition in 1937, prepared by postgraduate planning students in the College of Art, criticised the way that bungalows, an alien species, had been allowed to devour the best agricultural land and woodlands on the urban fringe. The Old Town was 'a hopeless muddle, with industry, slums, and new working-class dwellings jostling and cramping the buildings, some of them new, of great public importance'.[21] Through planning would come 'order and beauty' so that the city might 'regain the pride of civic dignity that was Edinburgh's and is surely worthy of this twentieth-century capital of Scotland'.

Thomas Adams shared some of this discourse, but was more pragmatic and less rooted in febrile Edinburgh professional and cultural life. He was born in Corstorphine in 1871, when it was a village still some distance beyond the edge of the city, but was educated in the city at Daniel Stewart's College. He became the first President of the Town Planning Institute when it formed in 1914. He popularised planning in Canada, and was the founder of the Town Planning Institute of Canada in 1919. He was director of the Regional Plan of New York from 1923 to 1930 and a founding member of the American City Planning Institute. Thus, long before the age of jet travel (Adams died in 1940), he was a prominent practitioner on both sides of the Atlantic.

In 1930, Adams' firm produced the planning scheme for Granton–Cramond that had been commissioned by the Town Council. Recognising the problems highlighted by Macartney in respect of previous planning schemes, Adams advised that the scheme needed to be flexible, broad-brush and agreed with landowners. The aim was 'guidance and direction, rather than control, of growth' so as to achieve public benefits 'without unreasonable cost or injury to private interests'.[22]

Some six months after Mears had produced his plan, Thomas Adams delivered his 'Final Report on Town Planning' to the council. Rather than looking fifty years ahead, it concentrated on the practicable and the short-term. The financial crisis heralded by the Wall Street crash of 1929 had hit Britain in 1930–1. Social expenditure was cut as a condition of international loans as the government sought to maintain the gold standard. Adams and his team responded to this context. Planning meant identifying 'what can be done at least cost to prevent the evil consequences of haphazard growth, and to secure the improvement of traffic

conditions and regulation of land development'.[23] They depicted planning as a means of preventing wasteful expenditures, while securing property values against the uncertainties inherent in an unregulated process of land development.

Adams reviewed his previous draft proposals for the Granton–Cramond Planning Scheme in the light of the financial crisis. He also proposed four further large schemes (Gogar–Corstorphine, 5,900 acres, Colinton, 5,600 acres, Liberton–Gilmerton, 5,600 acres, and Newcraighall, 4,460 acres) so that the city would be swathed by six planning schemes forming a horseshoe shape from the Forth shoreline. However, he recommended that a general development plan for the city should be undertaken, with work on the planning schemes deferred if that was done. This city plan would be non-statutory, as there was no legal basis at that time for such plans. It would be middle-range, not the fifty-year vision advocated by Mears, though it would be based on a civic survey. It would be more comprehensive than any collection of planning schemes, but also more flexible. Adams argued that such a plan would help the council to decide 'what can be done without'[24] so that savings could be achieved in a planned and economical fashion. As well as providing a focus for government and the other institutions involved in the jostle for space in the city centre, the plan would attract industry and steer firms to locations where there would be no deleterious impacts on the city's amenities and tourism.

The Council did not take up Adams' advice. As there was no comprehensive plan, work on planning schemes for new suburban growth continued sporadically. The Craigentinny, Restalrig and Lochend Planning Scheme got approval in 1931, preparation of a scheme for the large area from Fairmilehead to Musselburgh began in 1937, and the following year saw the public inquiry into the Granton–Cramond scheme. Meanwhile, the Housing and Town Planning Committee had been renamed the Streets and Buildings Committee, a symbolic narrowing of the focus of planning between the start and end of the inter-war period. Perhaps the main statutory achievement was the planning scheme for Charlotte Square, which for the first time gave powers to control development in a built-up area.

The Labour movement around the time of the First World War had viewed planning as the means to deliver better lower-density affordable housing for working people and their families. By the late 1930s, the Labour movement's interest in planning *per se* seems to have reduced. While the theme of 'no slums' – which remained an important part of the planning narrative – must have held some appeal, better housing (and access to it) did not depend on planning. From the 1920s onwards, the council had purchased substantial areas of land and was either subsidising private housing for rent or directly providing subsidised housing (see Chapter 7). By 1937, only ten planning schemes had been approved in the whole of Scotland, and it is significant that Sir William Whyte, Secretary to the Scottish Housing and Town Planning Committee, attributed this low level to the local authorities' involvement in providing houses. The Chairman of Edinburgh's Streets and Buildings Committee, Councillor Hay, also blamed the council housing programme for the lack of output in planning.[25]

Thus local structures, institutions and individuals were crucial in constructing and contesting planning and place identity in inter-war Edinburgh. Planning practice was primarily a bureaucratic and technical procedure that did not engage with the strongly expansionist and commercial vision for the city that was set out in the 1919 Merchant Company report. Indeed, the President of the Edinburgh City Business Club complained that the city had not done enough to try to promote and attract industry. He described council policy as 'timid, hesitating and cheese-paring'.[26]

It was the institutional cluster of professional, artistic and antiquarian bodies that championed the idea of planning as a form of governance and a narrative of place identity. The Reverend Percival-Prescott told the Buccleuch Evangelical Church that it was folly to leave town-planning to councillors: give the job to the students of Edinburgh College of Art instead![27] In so far as the civic and the national blurred in the capital city, the ethos that underpinned the arguments of this grouping

can perhaps be described as 'soft nationalist': certainly the nation features more prominently than class as a structuring factor in the underlying analysis. The expectation that civic surveys leading to plans would bring harmony around important national symbols and institutions confirms this view. The built form of the Old Town and the New Town, enduring totems to Scotland's history and Edinburgh's leading role in the Age of Enlightenment, constituted a reproach to contemporary aspirations for a bungalow in a suburb. Planning, through its critique of ascendant urban industrialism, was a narrative of loss that promised also to be the springboard to future restoration of Edinburgh's historic identity in 'civic dignity'.

An idea whose time has come

In 1943, as the Second World War began to point to a democratic future, Edinburgh's council set up a three-man Advisory Committee on City Development – J. L. Clyde, KC (chairman), the former Lord Provost Sir Thomas Whitson, and the Rector of Edinburgh University, Sir Donald Pollock. They were asked to 'report on the general considerations governing the development and redevelopment of the city as the capital of Scotland and the preparation of planning schemes in relation thereto'.[28] They observed that Edinburgh now had 'a rendezvous with destiny'.[29] Their brief required them to have particular regard to 'the character of the city and its place in the national and local administration'. The Lord Provost, Sir William Darling, asked citizens to consider what kind of city they wanted, 'one developed in the industrial plan or on the plan of a great capital city'.[30] Thus the issue of place identity was posed directly, though arguably there was a false dualism at the core of the choice. In the 1940s, great capital cities tended also to be industrial cities. Across Europe, capital cities would soon be drawing up plans for modern cities to betoken a new and better age, so that (as had been the case in 18th-century Edinburgh) town-planning would be a force to drive innovation and modernisation.

There was an intensive phase of public consultation in 1943 in which the pre-war planning lobbyists were prominent, with Mears, for example, prophesying a ring road and a 'real green belt'. However, Hague showed that those who got involved represented a broad social and institutional spectrum.[31] The Chamber of Commerce and Manufacturers called for a positive industrial growth strategy, with new roads, planned edge-of-city industrial estates with houses for workers close by, and slum clearance. However, they also supported a green belt and a strategy to retain Edinburgh's character as a historic and romantic city.

Edinburgh's Advisory Committee diagnosed the problems. There had been 'unregulated expansion in all directions',[32] yet there would be a serious housing shortage when the troops returned home, and it would be necessary to replace overcrowded and slum housing. The essence of the strategy that they recommended was planned and subsidised suburbanisation of industry and housing, combined with preservation of the historic areas, but also modernisation of the road system, including an outer bypass. However, they had their doubts about planners and their followers: 'Fired with enthusiasm for the new science of planning they lay aside all financial considerations, they urge the adoption of the "broad view", they talk of "aiming high", and they recommend the approval of idealistic and often revolutionary proposals, which they fondly hope can be realised fifty or a hundred years hence'.[33] Despite this warning, and against the advice of their Burgh Engineer, the council proceeded to appoint Sir Patrick Abercrombie to turn the Advisory Committee's programme into a comprehensive plan for the city.

The preamble to Abercrombie's Civic Survey and Plan says:

A Plan for Edinburgh must needs be a hazardous undertaking: there can be few cities towards which the inhabitants display a fiercer loyalty or deeper affection . . . Even its blemishes are venerated . . . The planner who dares to propose improvements must go warily . . .

The Plan's proposals included: blasting tunnels through the Old Town and under Calton Hill to carry a new dual carriageway; making Princes Street two-tier by building a new road beneath the existing street level and open to the famous gardens; various other roads cutting through established residential areas; complete clearance of housing from Leith to make the area an industrial zone ('a bit on the drastic side', Abercrombie conceded[34]); comprehensive redevelopment of an area off Princes Street for a new Festival Theatre; and building flats on the playing fields of private schools and in middle-class neighbourhoods to house those displaced by slum clearance. Readers might ponder what further 'improvements' Abercrombie decided to shelve because of the need to 'go warily'.

Abercrombie's plan went some way beyond Geddes' 'conservative surgery' and, in portraying a modernisation of the fabric of the city, was widely interpreted as threatening Edinburgh's identity. 'Sacrilegious', 'scandalous expense', 'desecration' and 'an outrage' were among the words used in the letters column of *The Scotsman*. The chairman of the Planning Committee called the proposals 'revolutionary' and added something about the need for 'long and careful study'.[35] In contrast to the English cities where Abercrombie was applying his planning principles, Edinburgh had suffered very little war damage. He appears to have underestimated how significantly this difference would affect the public response to proposals for redevelopment. The fact that he was not a native of the city did not go unnoticed among critics.

When the Planning Committee discussed the plan, familiar debates about place identity resurfaced. There were those who supported industrial growth, while on the other side a ceiling on population at 500,000 was favoured. The choice was polarised between development of coalfields on the city's periphery and the preservation of Edinburgh as the capital city. The Lord Provost raised the spectre of Glasgow, then a city of a million inhabitants and 'far too big an organisation to control'.[36]

Rejection of what might be termed 'the Glasgow model' was entirely predictable, given Edinburgh's culture and local politics. However, it did leave Edinburgh with a kind of lacuna that then persisted for some four decades until the realities of European competition began to restructure planning and place identity at the end of the 1980s (see Chapter 11). The city had no wish to ape its only recognised competitor, and so there was no urgency to force any new place identity. So it was that the Lord Provost told the Town Planning Officer in 1951: 'I think the [first 1947-style statutory development] plan should cover just the minimum requirements'.[37] Similarly, presenting the 1952 annual report of the Planning Committee, Councillor Bell argued that 'Edinburgh does not need drastic alteration. Nature has provided us with wonderful material and we should not allow our city to be messed about by enthusiastic planners.'[38] Perhaps apathetic planners were tolerated – for, when the first city-wide development plan was finally approved by the Council in 1953, another councillor hailed it as 'the end of a tedious journey in town planning'.[39]

So what had happened to the 'rendezvous with destiny'? Hague argued that in the 1940s planned modernisation of Edinburgh was necessary but politically unacceptable.[40] In addition, there were significant economic hurdles in a period of war-weakened austerity. There was scepticism about the planning evangelists, but also a fusion of place identity and governance in an endeavour to sustain social cohesion during and immediately after the war. This was encapsulated in the idea that containment of Edinburgh by a green belt, limiting its population to 500,000 and avoiding the industrial model, while regulating growth and doing slum clearance, would, as the Advisory Committee put it, 'preserve the essential unity of the city'.[41] The consultation undertaken by the Advisory Committee had no precedent in the planning of the city in the previous decades (though there were 'unofficial' initiatives before the war such as the exhibition organised by the Royal Scottish Society of Painters in Water Colours). Nor was such a process to be repeated until the early 1970s. As in 1918, local institutions and practices sat within an exceptional international context to create an unprecedented, though short-lasting, political commitment to remaking the city. Even in these exceptional times the dominant motif of place remained the historic city – a reassertion of continuity that Abercrombie's plan failed to negotiate.

Not surprisingly, the Development Plan that was approved by the Secretary of State in 1957 was more pragmatic and politically acceptable than Abercrombie's plan had been. Hague compared them in terms of significant proposals.[42] While a city-wide development plan had replaced the more fragmented planning schemes, and (at the insistence of the Department of Health for Scotland) Abercrombie's green belt had been given statutory effect, there was a lot of continuity between the first Development Plan and the pre-war planning strategy. Notwithstanding the green belt, the plan still allowed for a considerable amount of suburban growth (1,452 acres were to be converted from agriculture to urban uses in the first five years and another 1,307 acres in the next quinquennium). By setting a target population of 500,000 for 1973, the development plan allowed for population increase at a level similar to the inter-war period, while offering long-term reassurance that Edinburgh would not slide into becoming another Glasgow. Thus a relatively flexible planning regime was able to combine growth with containment and a modest reassertion of the historical identity of the city.

The most controversial and ingenious of Abercrombie's road proposals, a triple-decker Princes Street, was simply dropped, as were his ambitions to restructure the railways. Residential densities respected tenure and social status, not geographical distance from the centre, as in the Abercrombie plan. Council-housing densities in the redevelopment areas were pushed above the thresholds that the consultant had advised. By the time the public inquiry into objections to the plan commenced in April 1954, there were only a dozen objections that had not been withdrawn, affecting around twenty properties. From the perspective of what had gone before and all that has happened since, this was a remarkably successful exercise in securing acceptance for a development plan.

Driving to the future: conflicts in fashioning the modern city

Thus far, the story of planning in 20th-century Edinburgh has been marked by fluctuations. Periods of crisis (often with some global stimulus) prompted a flurry of ambitious planning ideas, led by planners of international repute. However, the routine years between such interventions were filled by statutory practice that was mainly about regulating private development so as to ensure an orderly process of suburban extension that was primarily residential in character. The basic shape of the city was not changed, as an expanding suburban ring of council flats and private bungalows and 'semis' fringed the 19th-century tenemental city with its historic core. As far as possible, the first Development Plan under the 1947 planning legislation had sought to continue that formula.

For a while, the strategy succeeded. Planning permissions were given for over 9,500 new private houses between 1949 and 1958.[43] Local building companies dominated the market and the supply of land for development (see Chapter 7). Complaints from housebuilders (especially national companies seeking to break into the Edinburgh market) about shortages of suitable sites began in the early 1960s. Despite rising consumer expectations, one Edinburgh household in four occupied accommodation with no fixed bath as late as 1961. By that time, the land banks built up by the council had been substantially used, and only a two-year supply of sites remained.[44] The 1965 Development Plan Review proposed building 33,500 local-authority houses over the twenty-year period covered by the plan, though it could only identify sites for around 24,000 of them. Land for 10,800 private houses was also allocated in the Review (at much lower densities than the local-authority sites), mainly in the south and south-western suburbs at Hunters Tryst, Dreghorn, Woodhall, Baberton and at Southfield and Cammo House. On past trends, this amounted to a supply for around ten years, and the proposition was that future housing would then have to be provided outside the city and beyond the green belt.

The private housebuilders contested this strategy at the public inquiry into the Review. Thus, for the first time in over fifty years, land supply for new edge-of-city housing became a major issue. The choices between containment and spread that had been focused on by the planning lobby in the 1930s, but never resolved in the subsequent

reports and plans, now needed to be faced. However, this debate was largely confined to technical wrangles within the public inquiry, leading to a juggling of densities, zonings and phases. The more fundamental decisions about place identity as a free-standing, contained city, and its consequences of green-belt containment for house prices, access to affordable housing and sustainable travel patterns, still lay in the future.

It was the proposal for major new road-building that sparked unprecedented dissent and challenged the processes of governance associated with development planning in Edinburgh at the time. Car-ownership and use was (and still is) central to the economy of advanced consumer capitalism. While Mears, Adams, Abercrombie, the 1943 Advisory Committee and the first Development Plan had all recognised the need for some restructuring of the road network, the only significantly adverse public reaction had been to Abercrombie's proposals. Only Abercrombie had grappled with the problems posed by the New Town for new road development around the north of the commercial centre.

The conflicts were rehearsed in 1958–9 at Randolph Crescent in the West End of the New Town. The City Engineer planned a roundabout here. It was in the first Development Plan but as an unprogrammed proposal. When central government funds became available, a Development Plan amendment was prepared to bring the roundabout into the first five-year phase of the plan. Implementation would require the filling-in of some basements below the elegant terraces, alteration of street levels and asphalting over the cobbles round the existing semicircular road round the garden, where mature trees would also be threatened. A major protest developed. There was a fear that this was just part of a much wider scheme that was being hatched. The Edinburgh Architectural Association (EAA) argued that the corporation intended to build a whole northern bypass from the planned Forth Road Bridge through Randolph Crescent, Queen Street and London Road and beyond to the A1.[45] Eventually the affair was featured on BBC television's prime current-affairs programme, *Panorama*, at a time when the BBC was one of only two television channels available.

Just about everyone who was anyone in Edinburgh planning and architecture at the time was there at the public inquiry. Sir William Kininmonth spoke of the potential of the roundabout to become a *tour de force* of planning if it were designed as a piazza with a fountain in the middle. In 1960, the Secretary of State ruled that the scheme was premature and that an overall plan was needed for city-centre traffic. A letter published by *The Scotsman* (30 December 1957) argued that Randolph Crescent raised 'much larger questions about the relationship between the Town Council and the general body of citizens. Why is it so difficult for the ordinary citizen to take a practical interest in the affairs of his city: why is it so difficult for him to obtain information on what is going on and what is proposed for the future of his city?'

The 1965 Development Plan Review provided the comprehensive traffic plan that critics of the Randolph Place roundabout had called for. It looked to 2000 when households would have two or three cars. It included an Inner Ring Road. The Eastern Link (programmed for Phase One) would run from St James Square, under Waterloo Place, over the eastern side of Waverley, then tunnel under the Canongate to St Leonard's. Phase Two created a southern link to Tollcross and Haymarket, from where the Western Link would go under Donaldson's Hospital, over the Water of Leith and on to Comely Bank. Once all that was accomplished, the grand finale would be Phase Three, the Northern Link, along the river valley to Canonmills and Broughton. The Inner Ring Road would be a six-lane highway with grade-separated junctions running through seven miles of the city. There were seven other significant new road proposals, Western and Eastern Approach roads, Intermediate and Outer Circular Routes, an Outer Bypass and a Morningside Bypass. Swathes of property were affected, raising fundamental questions about the relationships between citizens and their elected council. The identity of Edinburgh was at stake: 'A renewed historic Edinburgh' trips off the tongue, but 'a historic city adapted to the motor car' has a very different sound.

During 1966, protest groups mushroomed and there were angry public meetings, with the northern and southern legs of the inner ring road the main focus for opposition. Local councillors were challenged, traditional party whips faltered, and the Planning Committee decided that it needed public-relations consultants to help it cope with the public's questions about planning. The eventual public inquiry ended with much of the roads' plan being endorsed. The Reporter's findings of fact observed that there was 'no serious dispute about the need for primary distributor roads or motorways of expressway standard near the centre of the city. The real issue became confined to the form and location of the new primary distributor roads.'[46] However, the Reporter ruled that the corporation had not demonstrated that a complete ring road of motorway standard along the route proposed was the correct solution. He also criticised the communication within the local authority and between it and the public.

Professor Sir Colin Buchanan, the leading planning and transport consultant of his day, was brought in to work alongside Freeman Fox, Wilbur Smith and Associates to produce a solution. From 1969 onwards, this team led an extensive programme of public consultation. Meanwhile, the City Engineer pressed ahead with design work for the Eastern Link that had been approved at the inquiry. It was to have the widest road tunnels in Britain. The idea of open public consultation, where any solution was possible *provided* that it included this link of the inner ring road, left Buchanan in an uncomfortable position. He endorsed the eastern link 'in principle' while expressing unease at the extent to which the designs were constraining the planning for the central area as a whole. As opposition escalated, the consultants tested a 'minimum road investment' option.

The technical work done by the consultants was state-of-the-art. Their second interim report in 1971 made extensive use of computer modelling to test a range of alternatives with robot-like names such as A2, B1 and so on. Cost-benefit analysis allowed for the blending of the best bits of various schemes into the manifestly optimal solution, which was given the brand name 'Scheme X'. It included a tunnel under the West End, a rechristening of the Eastern Link Road to be the Bridges Relief Road with only four traffic lanes, and displacement of all major traffic from Princes Street on to Queen Street. The Inner Ring Road was no more – instead, a 'central area distributor loop' was mainly for local traffic. The other traffic would be catered for by an Intermediate Circular Route (ICR) running mainly through 19th-century suburbs. In solving the problem of the inner ring road, Scheme X created a new one. The map of protest groups now took in areas in the line of the ICR. No doubt with the best intentions, the City Engineer went public with his view that Scheme X should be rejected, and the inner ring road should be built instead.[47] When he published his recommended plan in 1972, Buchanan was quoted as being 'slightly pessimistic' about its implementation (*The Scotsman*, 4 November 1972). He overestimated public affection.

Eventually, the elected representatives could take no more. In the weeks running into a local election, even the most staid councillors can get heady – or desperate. Thus it was that in the spring of 1973 Labour alleged that the right-wing parties had a secret plan to build an inner ring road, to which Labour was unequivocally opposed. The Conservatives dismissed Labour's scaremongering, and played their own trump card – if returned to power, they would reject the Buchanan/Freeman Fox proposals! Their planning spokesman had no need to contain his glee: 'The fact that the Conservatives have rejected the Buchanan Report shows up the Labour Party rumour about the inner ring road to be an election gimmick'. Buchanan's reaction was: 'If this group of people care to chuck out a carefully considered report just like that, without investigating the alternatives they suggest, then that is their responsibility'.[48] They did – and so did Labour the next day.

Thus, by the mid-1970s, Edinburgh had again sidestepped a rendezvous with ambitious plans. Routine would again smother the embers left by threatening visionaries. Planning would fade once more into the back rooms of the local bureaucracy. However, the governance system had been seriously destabilised. Planning had become overtly political, and substantial sections of the voting public expected to have a voice in the process, while politicians knew that officers' recommendations were only one factor to be weighed in reaching a decision. The politics of planning cut across traditional party ideologies. Survival instincts allowed the politicians to negotiate these uncharted waters, but the fundamental tensions that had structured planning in Edinburgh through the previous fifty years were not removed. How can a 'renewed historic Edinburgh' that reproduces social and political unity and economic prosperity be delivered?

Conclusions

Edinburgh changed less than most large UK cities between 1900 and 1975. In part this was because it suffered little war damage, but it also reflected the way that planning operated, especially after 1945. Edinburgh remained a free-standing city not part of a conurbation. Unlike most others, it still had no inner ring road or outer ring road. The shopping hierarchy had hardly changed from the previous century. Edinburgh was still the centripetal city whose suburban spread had been regulated and orderly within (though at times eating into) the green belt.

Planning had sought to reproduce a place identity of a historical city that had once been a romantic national capital, an identity that could be sharply contrasted with that of the industrial Leviathan on the Clyde. The gaze was mainly backward, though at intervals the parameters of continuity had to be reinterpreted and renegotiated. The perspective was mainly parochial, and the most effective players were those who best understood and were able to exploit power relations and the nuances of identity within the city. Throughout, there were two abiding benchmarks. One was the 18th-century New Town, expressive of what elegance and order could be achieved by men of culture and letters with pride in the city as the Scottish capital. Planning's promise of 'order' was also important in this predominantly Presbyterian city – for the other benchmark was Glasgow, whose physical form, industrialism, politics and working-class culture carried the whiff, if not of hedonism, then at least of something temporal and indulgent.

And yet . . . though the focus was narrow and local, all the crises that manifested themselves as crises of planning, all the avoided rendezvous if not with 'destiny' then at least with facing the future, were rooted in global not local change. World wars, financial crises, the rise of consumerism, the post-1968 confrontations with authority and the rise of environmentalism framed the actions in the planning of Edinburgh that this chapter has charted. In the last quarter of the 20th century, Edinburgh would come to encounter a new phase of globalisation and place competition that would force ever more sophisticated arguments over the urban assets that framed its place identity, as will be discussed in Part IV.

Notes

1. P. Geddes, 'The Civic Survey of Edinburgh', in *The Transactions of the Town Planning Conference* (London, 1910), p. 560.
2. Ibid., p. 562.
3. Geddes, 'Civic Survey', p. 563.
4. Edinburgh and District Trades and Labour Council, *47th Annual Report* (1914).
5. Geddes, 'Civic Survey', p. 566.
6. The Company of Merchants of the City of Edinburgh, *Reporty of a Special Committee on the Building Trade in Edinburgh* (Edinburgh, 1918), p. 3.
7. Scottish Land Enquiry Committee, *Scottish Land: The Report of the Scottish Land Enquiry Committee* (London, 1914); Cd 87312, 1917.
8. Edinburgh and District Trades and Labour Council, *51st Annual Report* (1918), p. 16.
9. Company of Merchants of the City of Edinburgh *Report of a Special Committee of the Company on the Development of Edinburgh* (Edinburgh, 1919), p. 6.
10. Ibid., pp. 6, 7.
11. Ibid., p. 35.
12. Company of Merchants of the City of Edinburgh, *Report* (1919), p. 13.
13. Ibid., pp. 13, 14.
14. C. Hague, *The Development of Planning Thought* (London, 1984), p. 168.
15. W. A. Macartney, 'Town planning in Edinburgh', *Journal of the Town Planning Institute*, 15(1) (1928), p. 37.
16. Letter from Mears to Provost Wilson (1930).
17. Hague, *Development*, p. 171.
18. Mears, Letter (1930).
19. F. C. Mears, *The City of Edinburgh: Preliminary suggestions for consideration* (Edinburgh, 1931), p. 4.
20. Ibid., p. 16.
21. Royal Scottish Society of Painters in Water Colours, *Town Planning Exhibition* (Edinburgh, 1937), p. 3.
22. T. Adams, L. Thompson and M. Fry, *Report on the Plan for the Development of the Granton–Cramond Area* (Edinburgh, 1930), p. 3.
23. T. Adams, L. Thompson and M. Fry, *Final Report on Town Planning* (Edinburgh, 1931), p. 6.
24. Ibid., p. 7.
25. *The Scotsman*, 24 February 1937.
26. *Edinburgh Evening News*, 3 November 1937.
27. *Evening Dispatch*, 13 January 1938.
28. City and Royal Burgh of Edinburgh, *The Future of Edinburgh* (Edinburgh, 1943), p. 3.
29. Ibid., p. 10.
30. *The Scotsman*, 23 July 1943.
31. Hague, *Development*, pp. 195–8.
32. City and Royal Burgh of Edinburgh, *Future*, p. 10.
33. Ibid., p. 6.
34. *The Scotsman*, 3 October 1947.
35. Hague, *Development*, pp. 210–11.
36. *The Scotsman*, 1 September 1949.
37. *Edinburgh Evening News*, 5 June 1951.
38. *The Scotsman*, 5 December 1952.
39. *The Scotsman*, 20 March 1953.
40. Hague, *Development*, p. 213.
41. City and Royal Burgh of Edinburgh, *Future*, p. 10.
42. Hague, *Development*, pp. 214–19.
43. Ibid., p. 227.
44. Ibid., p. 226.
45. *The Scotsman*, 5 June 1958.
46. Quoted in Gray, *Streets Ahead* (Edinburgh, 1975), p. 21.
47. *The Scotsman*, 14 December 1971.
48. *Edinburgh Evening News*, 27 April 1973.

PART IV

The City in the Post-industrial and Post-modern Age

Introduction

In parallel with major state investment in housing, particularly from the beginning of the 20th century, new forms of private-sector investment and activity in the built environment have developed and flourished – in housing and also other built forms – as illustrated in Part III. Overall, the built fabric of the city physically expanded rapidly up to the 1960s, with this mainly being through development of new peripheral areas for both residential and industrial use. At the same time, however, major changes in the built fabric took place with the continued decay of central urban areas, this spreading from the Old Town to the New Town. The relative decline in the economy after the Second World War led to a general slowing of new growth after that, with limited state and private-sector investment and a slowing of building in general – which is where Part IV starts.

Part IV takes what could be called a general analytical view of the development of the built environment in Edinburgh from about the 1960s onwards. It does not aim to relate a definitive history of the architectural and/or urban form in this period, but rather has the intention of setting the scene for, and subsequently discussing, the trends in development of the built environment in the city and the underlying forces that affect this, as a means to consider possible future trends and options. Some key issues that become apparent through this period are as follows:

- the move away from the post-war grand designs in planning and the subsequent physical blight, and the opportunity which this subsequently gave the city to 'remake' itself;
- the change of municipal focus from urban management to entrepreneurial action in city development and new relations between the government and private sector, and to some extent between the government and communities;
- the revival of action of civil society in relation to the built environment – mainly in relation to the conservation of buildings and the urban fabric as a whole, as opposed to previous action in relation to public health;
- the eventual revival of investment in central areas, albeit with subsequent continued peripheral growth – the non-residential nature of this latter changing from industrial to commercial;
- the growing relationship between the city and the region in terms of work/residence patterns: whereas previously the city relied on its hinterland for natural resources, it came to rely on a hinterland for its workforce;
- a changing sense of place identity brought about by some of these factors, but also the deliberate marketing of a city image to boost tourism and the city as a good investment location; and
- the return of the Scottish Parliament and a growing role of the city region within the Scottish nation, the UK as a whole, and arguably Europe.

These issues have arguably led to more change in the built environment in Edinburgh in the past decade than took place in the city since the major urban expansions of the first part of the 20th century – and prior to that in the mid-18th- to mid-19th century developments of the New Town. Whereas between the 1960s and the late 1980s one could be fairly sure that, on returning to Edinburgh after a prolonged absence, little would have changed, especially in the central area, this is not now the case. The built environment of the city is now changing rapidly, at both centre and periphery, and the chapters in Part IV hope to identify some of these ongoing changes and the reasons behind them.

Chapter 9, by Jenkins and Holder, provides an overview of the trends in the development of the built environment in the city, looking at urban design, architecture and conservation, and then identifying and discussing some key issues. Chapter 10, by Kerr, examines the political economy behind some of the changes which the built environment is undergoing, with reference to the city in a global 'market place' and major new planned developments. Chapter 11, by Hague and Jenkins, examines the changing image of the city, and the sense of place identity experienced by its citizens, in the 21st century – both how these have changed in the past, and what are possible future development scenarios.

Overall, Part IV is entitled 'The city in the post-industrial and post-modern age', not because we as authors of Chapters 9–11 necessarily agree with the concepts of 'post-industrial' and 'post-modern' as applied to the city, but because these are the intellectual context for much debate about cities and urban built form in this period. Our concern in fact is to challenge these concepts – or at least the facile application of these in the complex actuality of a specific place like Edinburgh – and to suggest that the essentially backward-looking stance that they adopt is not appropriate. This theme is more fully developed in the book's concluding chapter, by the editors. The other main theme running through Part IV is that the study of the political, economic, social and cultural context for the built environment is as essential as any specific study of the changes in the nature and style of the built environment itself – something less well established in the literature on the city.

9 Creation and conservation of the built environment in the later 20th century

PAUL JENKINS AND JULIAN HOLDER

This chapter aims to provide a brief overview of how the built environment has been changing in Edinburgh over the past four decades or so. It looks at new creation in the built environment through an analysis of buildings noted for their architecture, and new urban spaces created through master plans, as well as the growing role of conservation in the built environment. The chapter thus provides a basis for a deeper investigation of some aspects of the trends in the built environment in certain key areas, as well as a central node in a growing city region, which are the focus of Chapters 10 and 11.

Trends in urban design

Perhaps the most important innovation in Edinburgh in terms of development of the built environment was a new approach by the city to urban design in the late 1980s. The main approach previously had been to commission a major city-wide survey and plan (such as the Mears and Abercrombie plans, as discussed in Chapter 8), with all the problems to which this led in terms of state capacity to implement, lack of engagement with the economic sector, and lack of public support – and indeed often strong opposition. The effect had been to blight whole areas of the city while the outcome of the plan deliberations were under way and thereafter due to lack of investment, while strongly controlling the form of expansion through the green-belt policy. Nevertheless, powerful institutional actors had pushed for and obtained approval for major urban developments – such as the greenfield campus site for Heriot-Watt University and the Southside expansion plans for Edinburgh University. However, not

all of these progressed, due to rising public concerns as well as reduced investment capacity. A growing public concern for conservation (see below) had led to a critical approach to the grand plans for the whole city and large areas of comprehensive redevelopment such as in the Southside (Peacock 1974) and to a growing concern for the conservation of the built heritage – initially the New Town, but also later the Old Town.

The private sector was initially happy to invest in refurbishment of the inner city, which had been to a great extent the previous economic base, at least for shopping and office-based activity; but, in time, the need for more dedicated forms of building (e.g. higher standards of services associated with information and computing technology) led to limitations with this approach, as did the sheer demand for space. Commerce also lobbied for out-of-town locations, and was successful in locating a number of these in relation to the new dual-carriageway bypass, built in the 1980s, although national planning guidelines eventually came into effect that began to restrict this form of development, as well as also promoting redevelopment of so-called 'brownfield sites' (generally with previous industrial use) in the city fabric.

In the light of these trends, the main innovation in urban planning for the city was the area-specific master plan[1] as a guide and stimulus for investment, as well as the use of local and national government incentives to kick-start such development. The initial experience with this was to provide for the physical expansion of the financial district from the West End of the New Town into what had been old goods yards and other derelict areas to the west of Lothian Road. The master plan for this was completed in 1989 by Terry Farrell, who later also designed the associated International Conference Centre. The next master plan was completed the following year by Percy Thomas and Kneale & Russell for the Morrison Street goods yards a little further to the west – both these being close by the new, partial rapid-access route into the city from the west – built mainly on disused railway lines (the outer part of the route was reserved but was not developed). Whereas the former master plan was exclusively commercial/recreational (including various office buildings, a hotel and a sports club), the latter also included housing as well as more new hotel provision. The other commercial part of this second plan was not developed, however, and remains a gap site to this day – partly due to subsidence problems.

The third major master plan was for the growing commercial development at the Gyle – the western edge of the city near to the main access routes to Glasgow and the airport. This was also sited nearer to the growing residential occupation of Livingston New Town and other secondary urban areas in the central belt (and north of the Forth estuary, across the road and rail bridges) and close to the large-scale state housing developments of the 1950s and 1960s, and the 1950s industrial parks to the west of the city. As such, it represented a continued move of the city's centre of gravity to the west. The master plan for this area – eventually called Edinburgh Park (see Chapter 10) – was completed by Richard Meier in 1992 and was the trigger for a massive commercial investment, which is still ongoing. This was followed by the Holyrood master plan, completed the same year by John Hope, sited at the eastern end of the Royal Mile, and eventually incorporating the new parliament building as well as a rich mix of other public, recreational, residential, commercial, hotel and educational buildings. This is probably the most complex master plan due to its mixed use and key urban location between the Old Town and Holyrood Park, not to mention the Royal Palace of Holyroodhouse.

In 1995, a new trend in area master plans was developed with a focus on even smaller areas, with the Tollcross master plan together with the Princes

Exchange building by RMJM architects. This again is a mix of commercial offices and residential, on a smaller site that had been blighted since the Abercrombie Plan. Since then, another smaller planned development at Fountainbridge around the canal basin has been started, and the West Calton Hill site (Greenside) finally completed, also catering for in-town recreation and commerce/hotels. Another smaller planned development, this time solely commercial (offices/shops and similar) but incorporating a refurbished bus station, has been completed off St Andrew Square in the New Town, linking this better with the existing St James Centre.

Despite the move to these inner-city developments, the trend for grand peripheral area master-plan development has continued with several large-scale developments. The redevelopment of Leith docks had begun in the early 1990s, and was strongly boosted by the siting of the new Scottish Executive building there in 1995. The subsequent refurbishment of warehouses/lofts and residential new-build has been followed by major new commercial developments linked to the tourist industry – the docking of the decommissioned Royal Yacht Britannia, associated with a major commercial/recreational development called Ocean Terminal. This has been the springboard for the continued redevelopment of parts of the northern seaboard of the city, with the current initial development of three areas of the massive Granton waterfront.

To the south of the city, a similar large-scale public–private initiative has launched the 'Southeast Wedge', kick-started by the resiting of the major Royal Infirmary hospital, but accompanied to its north by major regeneration of the south-east state housing areas, now including a wider mix of housing types and related boosting of the commercial node at the eastern end of the ring road where the A1 road to London reaches the city outskirts. Another large-scale, new city-centre redevelopment is currently in the planning stages for Princes Street Gardens,[2] despite some public opposition. This may be supplanted by an alternative scheme for the redevelopment of parts of Princes Street itself, and a new development is planned for the

Waverley Valley site in a key position vis-à-vis the Old and New Towns.

This area master-plan approach is largely the result of a new entrepreneurial attitude of the City Council in seeking investment and facilitating this, including providing access to cheap land blighted by previous plans, as described in Chapter 10. While this has worked effectively in developing the built environment in some parts of the city, the success of this approach is in danger of being its own downfall, as there may well arise such a diversity of supply, in relation to demand, that there might be insufficient investment to create the momentum necessary for such areas to be fully developed and to become successful in terms of public use. However, much experience has been gained – especially in the smaller inner-city developments – of alternatives to the previous conflict between new-build and conservation/refurbishment of the 1960s and 1970s (see below). The infill and rehabilitation work in and off the High Street/Canongate within the Holyrood master plan is evidence of this.

Perhaps what is needed is more sensitive smaller-scale area master-planning as opposed to the large-scale master plan. This may not be exclusive of the need for continued large-scale developments, however, as demand for housing is strong and the continued spillover of housing in the wider city region has longer-term environmental and economic implications – as well as cultural attitudes to identity. However, as will be argued in Chapter 11, this will entail a wider city-region level of planning than the city-wide master plans of the past have produced.

Even in such larger-scale developments, master plans for smaller areas, within an overall co-ordinated plan, can probably provide better quality and diversity. A newspaper article in June 2004 identified twenty-three areas being regenerated within the city boundaries, many with area-specific master plans.[3] Although some of these are larger developments which aspire to 'New Town' plan status, in fact the New Town was developed as a series of relatively small-scale planned areas over a long period of time – the key to its unique identity being the system of control and limited construction capacity. It can thus be argued that a 'package of plans' approach can replicate general planning controls and guide provision of key infrastructure while permitting diversity, high quality and phasing which perhaps can better relate supply to changing demand and provide for continued high-quality environments.

Trends in new architecture

Since 1960, there have been ongoing changes in the style, type and location of notable buildings in the city.[4] This analysis refers predominantly to the type and location, as the tendency to focus in other reviews on issues of style has led to a debate dominated by stylistic issues at the expense of the other important factors in architectural design, such as function and contribution to the general built environment. The relation of this approach to the debate on architectural style is revisited in this chapter's concluding section.

Referring initially to the trends in production of notable buildings, it is noticeable that there was a considerable lull in completions in the 1960s and more so in the 1970s, with a growth in the 1980s and a surge in completion in the 1990s, which continues in the early years of the current decade. Of the 240 buildings noted, forty or so have been completed in the last few years; and of the 200 or so completed in the 1960–2000 period, more than half were completed in the 1990s and a quarter in the 1980s.

During the 1960s, there were a significant number of educational buildings completed, mostly relating to Edinburgh University, including George Square and the related Bristo Square complex (in addition, the first main phase of the Pollock Halls of Residence had been completed just prior to the 1960s.) During this decade, Heriot-Watt University (Riccarton campus, phase 1), Napier Polytechnic (Colinton Road campus) and Edinburgh College of Art (Architecture Department) buildings were also completed, as were a number of important buildings at city schools (George Watson's, Mary Erskine's and James Gillespie's). This was the largest functional group of notable buildings in the decade, followed by commercial, residential, recreational and public

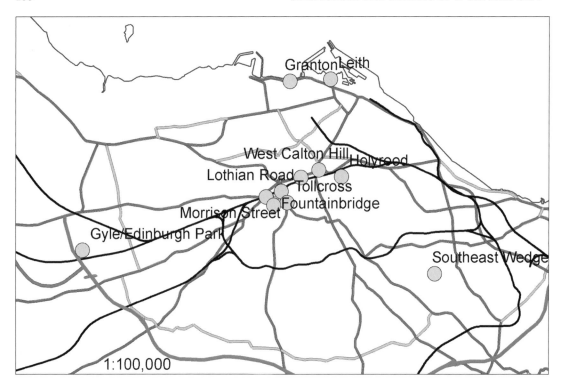

FIGURE 9.1   Map showing key master-planned areas.   *Paul Jenkins (Base map reproduced from Ordnance Survey-based mapping on behalf of The Controller of Her Majesty's Stationery Office © Crown Copyright. Heriot-Watt University / 100041044/2004)*

buildings. Commercial building was concentrated in the New Town (for example, Scottish Widows and Scottish Provident in St Andrew Square and Standard Life in George Street, as well as the much-debated St James Centre development at the eastern edge of the original Craig's New Town), although the Christian Salvesen headquarters showed a new trend towards the northern limits of the New Town in Fettes Avenue in the latter part of the decade.

Residential buildings of note in this period were generally very small developments varying from two modern-style Ravelston Dykes developments to infill/redevelopment projects in the Canongate and Pleasance (which essentially continued the 'conservative surgery' style of earlier – see Chapter 6). However, recreational developments were also of city-wide significance in this period, and included the Commonwealth Pool and Meadowbank Sports Centre, prepared for the

Commonwealth Games of 1970, as well as the new glasshouse in the Botanic Garden with its innovative structure. Public-sector buildings of note were the Nuffield Transplantation Unit at the Western General Hospital, the Crematorium at Mortonhall, and the Lothian Region headquarters at the corner of the Royal Mile and North Bridge. Other than new buildings, there was some notable building conservation and refurbishment – for example, West Register House in Charlotte Square (originally built in 1814), and the 16th-century Stenhouse and 17th-century Dalry houses.

Apart from the overall drop in completions, noted above, the 1970s saw a marked change in the dominant trend in building function, as only one major educational building of note was completed – the College of Art Hunter Building. In contrast to the 1960s, the emphasis in this decade was predominantly on commercial and residential. However, conservation and refurbishment played

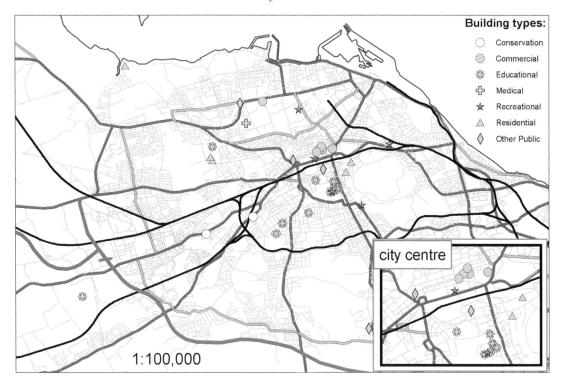

FIGURE 9.2   Map showing notable buildings of the 1960s.   *Paul Jenkins (Base map reproduced from Ordnance Survey-based mapping on behalf of The Controller of Her Majesty's Stationery Office © Crown Copyright. Heriot-Watt University / 100041044/2004)*

a greater part in these developments, with six of the eight notable commercial buildings being refurbishment of New Town buildings – including four in George or Princes Street (three being banks) and a hotel development adjoining Dean Village (the Hilton – partly an old mill). New-build exceptions were Scottish Widows' Dalkeith Road building and the Dunedin Fund Managers' Ravelston Terrace building.

Dean Village was also the site for several housing developments/refurbishments, as was Portsburgh Square – dating from 1900, and one of the first public-housing ventures in the city. Apart from another infill housing development in the Canongate, the other noted residential buildings were in the outlying western suburbs of East Craigs and South Gyle, where the last major state housing investment was concentrated (see Chapter 7). The only public and recreational buildings noted for the period were the new Turnhouse

airport terminal and the refurbishment of the early 19th-century Queen's Hall in the Southside.

This trend of dominance of notable new architecture by the commercial sector was reinforced in the 1980s; however, the proportion of refurbishments fell and the favoured location began to change. In this period, some major refurbishments were still undertaken in the New Town and nearby Dean Village, but more new building was located to the north and west of the New Town in areas such as in Dundas Street and Lothian Road, where a master plan for redevelopment was completed in 1989 (see above). As in the 1960s, new commercial property was predominantly for the growing financial-services industry, with the appearance of the first computer centres for servicing this sector – which required building specifications which were difficult to fit into older forms. Other commercial developments of note were the John Lewis building at the back of the St James Centre, the new Waverley

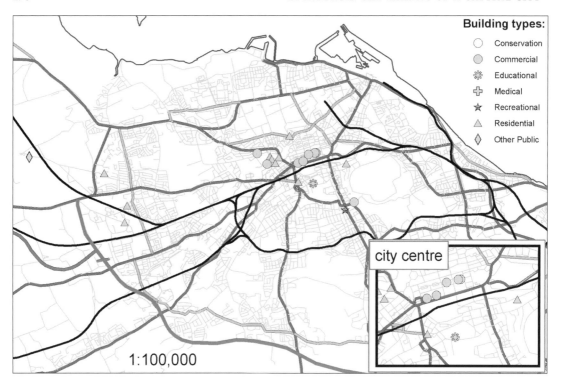

FIGURE 9.3   Map showing notable buildings of the 1970s.   *Paul Jenkins (Base map reproduced from Ordnance Survey-based mapping on behalf of The Controller of Her Majesty's Stationery Office © Crown Copyright. Heriot-Watt University / 100041044/2004)*

Market in the city centre and a new out-of-town shopping centre to the south at Cameron Toll.

A new form of 'refurbishment' of the built environment also appeared with the new-build Scandic Crown Hotel on the Royal Mile, which, although internally modern, was externally designed in a much older period style, and has generated polemical discussion around such stylistic revisionism. Conservation *per se* continued through public buildings, such as the City Art Centre in Market Street, the Royal Society building in George Street and the National Gallery of Modern Art – previously a public school – in Belford Road. Other new public buildings noted included the extension to the National Library, the new St Leonard's police headquarters and Tollcross fire station in the south of the city, as well as new buildings at the Royal Victoria, Royal Infirmary and Murrayfield hospitals. A new series of educational buildings was completed at the

Heriot-Watt University Riccarton campus to the west towards the end of the decade. On the residential front, the trend swung to new-build, with an emphasis on infill developments – Jamaica Street and various sites in the Pleasance/ Southside in particular – most of this being apartments.

The 1990s again saw significant shifts, which built on the initial trends in the 1980s but also included some new trends. The trend to dominance in commercial building continued, with some forty of the 100 noted buildings in this decade. New-build and refurbishment restarted in the New Town itself – again, mostly financial services. Some new commercial developments continued to be located to the north and west of the New Town – again mainly financial services, but also more new hotels – and there was a concentration of these round the extension to the new financial district planned in Lothian Road. New hotels

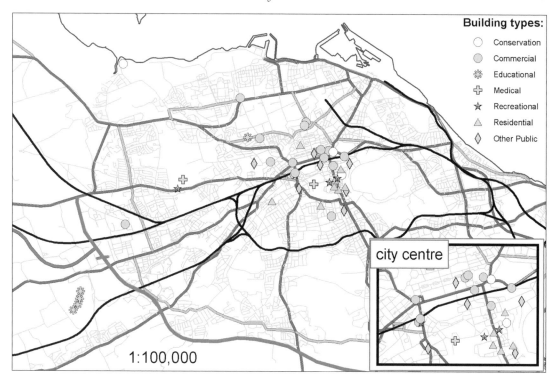

FIGURE 9.4   Map showing notable buildings of the 1980s.   *Paul Jenkins (Base map reproduced from ordnance Survey-based mapping on behalf of The Controller of Her Majesty's Stationery Office © Crown Copyright. Heriot-Watt University / 100041044/2004)*

and refurbishments were also undertaken in the Old Town, especially with the Holyrood master-plan development (see above). However, the major development thrust in this period was the commercial development to the west at the Gyle (Edinburgh Park). Here, sixteen major new buildings were completed before 1999, mostly tailor-built for financial-services institutions, but with some speculative office buildings and other organisational headquarters.

Residential building also increased significantly in the decade, with some twenty-four buildings of note, particularly towards the latter years. This increasingly became the redevelopment of brown-field sites in response to government guidance and support, with innovations such as environmentally sustainable housing at Slateford Green and new-build infill on the previous Morrison Street railway goods yards and at Tollcross – demonstrating the growing role of residential development as

an integral part of master plans. Infill also took place in the Old Town and New Town with innovative modern residential schemes (e.g. the Dublin Street Colonies). The major housing developers in these areas were housing associations, as more (although not all) private-sector housing development continued in peripheral locations.

As the Holyrood master-plan redevelopment began to take off, increasingly new housing, hotels and commercial development (e.g. the new *Scotsman* building) were sited there in the latter part of the decade. Public buildings also experienced resurgence in this period, some being within the Holyrood master plan and others in the western Edinburgh Park development (e.g. the new Scottish Record Office). However, renewed levels of investment were also used to kick-start the Leith redevelopment, with the new Scottish Office being completed there in 1995. A wide range of recreational buildings of note began to be developed in

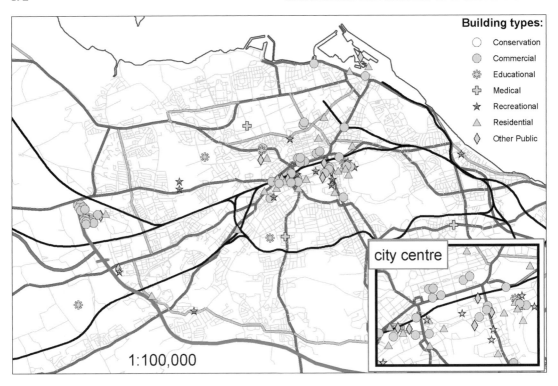

Figure 9.5   Map showing notable buildings of the 1990s.   *Paul Jenkins (Base map reproduced from Ordnance Survey-based mapping on behalf of The Controller of Her Majesty's Stationery Office © Crown Copyright. Heriot-Watt University / 100041044/2004)*

various parts of the city – including major buildings such as the Royal Museum extension, the International Conference Centre near the Lothian Road area, the Festival Theatre in the Southside, Our Dynamic Earth in Holyrood, the Fountain Park recreational centre in Fountainbridge and many more. This represented the demands of a more affluent society and also a trend against 'edge-of-city' developments, which has been important to maintain the city's inner dynamic.

Despite the seeming success of the area-based master-plan approach, these various projects began to compete for investment, which at times has led to only partial development or under-occupancy, especially of new offices and shops. Although this brief review has emphasised major trends in architecture and urban design, it is also important to stress that not all of the notable buildings of course are large-scale; some small-scale architectural innovation has been lauded, such as

the low-cost marketing-office extension to the zoo entrance building and some small house-extension projects. However, the majority of the noted architecture – especially the commercial – has been at significantly high cost, although the public buildings have generally been the most expensive.

The trends established in the 1990s seem to be changing again at this point in the new century. Although the western-edge developments continue to expand and the various master plans become more fully developed, there are new master plans and options for investment under way, as noted above. This has led to a diffusion of location and a much wider impact of new building throughout the city. The nature of the investment also seems to be changing again, however, as new hotels and recreational/shopping centres are more highly in evidence. Although offices continue to be built in a wide variety of locations, the market seems to have become somewhat saturated.

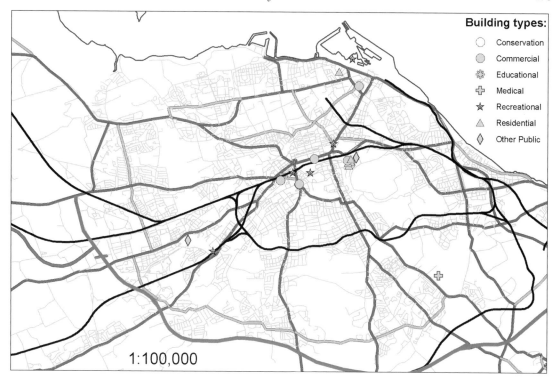

Building types:

○ Conservation
● Commercial
✳ Educational
✛ Medical
★ Recreational
△ Residential
◇ Other Public

1:100,000

FIGURE 9.6   Map showing notable buildings of the new millennium.   *Paul Jenkins (Base map reproduced from Ordnance Survey-based mapping on behalf of The Controller of Her Majesty's Stationery Office © Crown Copyright. Heriot-Watt University / 100041044/2004)*

The Holyrood development continues to advance with the completion of the parliament building, the most expensive building the city has seen in recent years. Although debates on the actual costs and reasons for this (as well as on the location) rumble on, the opening in 2004 has permitted people to see the building close up, which it is hoped will permit a greater focus on the nature of the building itself. New master plans being developed for the Granton Waterfront and the Southeast Wedge also stress new forms of public–private investment in public buildings such as the new Royal Infirmary and its associated medical school and research centre. They are also much more orientated towards residential use than the initial master plans. In addition, major new sites in the city are being opened up (e.g. the previous Royal Infirmary site) and new 'sub-centres' developing, such as the Fountainbridge area – which may reinforce the trend to mixed-use

development with recreational and residential as well as commercial buildings. Increasingly, urban design is related to urban regeneration, and this is mixed-use. A key test of this in future will be the redevelopment of the Cowgate site opened up in the Old Town by the fire in December 2002. How will new-build in this key area with a wide range of functions (the previous functions are to be replicated) be treated? It is to be hoped that innovation is alive and well – although possibly at the expense of conservation, as discussed next.

Trends in conservation

Although conservation – as understood within the context of its international charters – is a relatively recent concept, a regard for old buildings in Edinburgh is not.[5] Two years before the foundation of the Society for the Protection of Ancient Buildings in 1877, the city created its own amenity society in the shape of the Cockburn Association in

FIGURE 9.7   George Square (south side), prior to demolition to make way for the new University Library designed by Spence Glover and Fergusson. Ironically significant elements within both Edinburgh College of Art (where Basil Spence had studied) and some of the staff and former students of the university opposed the demolition.   *RCAHMS*

1875.[6] If its namesake, Lord Cockburn, was an early apologist for conservation – or, more strictly speaking, preservation – then the tradition of 'conservative surgery' established by Patrick Geddes, Sydney Mitchell and others gave the city a unique approach to architectural intervention maintained by Frank Mears, Ian Lindsay and Robert Hurd, and still practised today by architects such as Richard Murphy and Malcolm Fraser.

By the 1960s, Edinburgh enjoyed a justifiable reputation as a conservative city. However, the demolition of the south side of George Square in 1965 to make way for the new university library ushered in a new age of militancy among its citizens. The immediate effect of this unpopular project was to put on hold the full realisation of the

ambitious expansion plans of the university and send worrying signals to the City Council. It also brought into being a new pressure group dedicated to the preservation of the city's Georgian architecture, the Edinburgh (later Scottish) Georgian Society.

As popularly understood in the 1960s, conservation came to mean attempts to preserve historic buildings in the face of not only the university expansion plans but also the designation of Comprehensive Development Areas, such as that proposed for Stockbridge and much of the Southside. Increasingly during the 1960s, the Scottish Georgian Society became the mouthpiece of opposition to such new developments. It also brought into being a significant number of street

FIGURE 9.8 Chessel's Court prior to its restoration by Robert Hurd and Partners, 1958–66. Once restored, it held out a beacon of hope among many of the unnecessary demolitions in the Old Town and South Side. *RCAHMS*

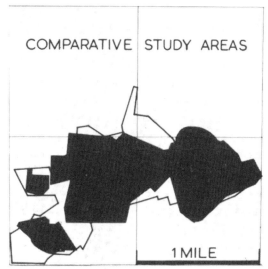

FIGURE 9.9 Maps used by Sir Robert Matthew at 'The Conservation of Georgian Edinburgh' conference in May 1970. The comparison of Edinburgh with Bath, Chester, Chichester and York was cleverly calculated. The four English towns were the subjects of early conservation reports commissioned by the government, yet the endangered area of Edinburgh was bigger than all four put together. *Edinburgh University Press*

associations where residents, opposed to comprehensive development, joined forces with conservationists to argue for sympathetic refurbishment and retention. In addition, the Festival Fringe demonstrated the new uses to which old, and often redundant, buildings could be put. This created a cultural cachet for the city, which it slowly realised was based on its totality of its historic environment. In part, this can also be seen as part of an emerging counter-culture opposed to the throwaway aesthetic of the time. High-profile building redundancies, such as that of St George's Parish Church in Charlotte Square, encouraged the city to consider new uses for old buildings as preservation tactics began to give way to conservation policies based on reuse rather than simple retention.

The most notable conservation-based practices at the time were those of Robert Hurd and Ian Lindsay. In the restoration of Chessel's Court (1958–66), some hope was held out against further losses such as the demolition of St James Square. Ian Lindsay undertook the restoration of Mylne's Court in 1966 to become, ironically, halls of residence for Edinburgh University. What was becoming generally apparent was the sheer scale of the undertaking if Edinburgh's Georgian architecture, principally its New Town, was to be saved. It was

beginning to be appreciated that the importance of the city's Georgian heritage lay not merely in its quality but also in its quantity.

Capitalising on the growing success of the Edinburgh Festival in 1967, the Principal of Edinburgh College of Art, John L. Paterson, together with the Edinburgh Architectural Association, mounted an exhibition to celebrate the 200th anniversary of the New Town entitled 'Two hundred summers in a city'. Helped by such events, gradually public opinion became convinced that Georgian houses were not the slums condemned as 'unfit for human habitation' according to the health legislation, but part of a valuable amenity. However, just as advances on several fronts were being made in defence of Edinburgh's Georgian architecture, so, to use the hyperbole of the conservation movement, the 'threat' to the built heritage transposed into a concern for Victorian architecture.

This threat was most clearly seen in the public outcry over the proposed demolition of the Café

FIGURE 9.10   Design by John L. Paterson for the
exhibition 'Two hundred summers in a city: Edinburgh
1767–1967', which drew public attention to the plight of
the New Town during its bicentenary.   *RCAHMS*

FIGURE 9.11   The New Club, 85 Princes Street, prior to
demolition.   *RCAHMS*

Royal and the successful demolition of the New
Club on Princes Street. Although it was a listed
building, legal protection was not yet on the
statute books, so this had little effect; but the
expected imminent passing of legislation made
the demolition particularly unconscionable. Considering Victorian architecture, Ian Lindsay, by
now the Secretary of State's official advisor on conservation, told those working on listing that 'we
may not like revived baronial but future generations may. Even if they don't, it plays its part in the
history of architecture.'[7]

By the late 1960s, first the Civic Amenities Act of
1967, and then the Town and Country Planning
(Scotland) Act of 1969, gave the local authority
new powers and made both the Scottish Civic
Trust and the Scottish Georgian Society statutory
consultees. Hence, by the end of the 1960s, a raft of
legislation able to oppose the worst excesses of
comprehensive development brought in a sea-
change in attitudes towards poor housing which
enabled comprehensive preservation, and targeted restoration, through the procedure of Listed
Building Consent and Conservation Area Consent.

As the various agents became used to the operation of the new legislation, matters were changing
in the wider world of conservation: as Colin
McWilliam wrote, 'conservation is a bit more than a
new word for preservation'.[8] The landmark international conference on 'The Conservation of Georgian
Edinburgh' in 1970 estimated the cost of the repairs
necessary to maintain the New Town at £15 million.
As a result of the conference, the Edinburgh New
Town Conservation Committee was established
both to offer advice to owners and tenants and to
target grant aid for the repairs identified in the
survey. Its exemplary operation was being copied
within a few years by the establishment of the
Edinburgh Old Town Renewal Trust. This was a
very different organisation, whose origins lay in the
'Forgotten Southside Exhibition' of 1972 and the
resulting Southside Association. The Trust was
more concerned with community renewal than the

FIGURE 9.12 'Hermits and Termits', St Leonard's, Edinburgh, originally the house of the Solicitor of Excise. Restored in 1982 to form architect Benjamin Tindall's house and office, it demonstrated that refurbishment of such neglected properties, in this case formerly left derelict in a coal-yard, was not only possible but also desirable. *Benjamin Tindall Associates*

traditional fabric conservation of the Edinburgh New Town Conservation Committee.

For many, the European Architectural Heritage Year in 1975 represented the triumph of heritage over modernism. It also made 'conservation politically respectable at the vital stage when the new planning authorities were making their appointments'.[9] It was appropriate that 1975 also saw the notion of heritage expand again, as a damaging proposal to the Moderne-style George Cinema in Bath Street, Portobello (1938), was withdrawn after representations from the Scottish Georgian Society.

As this was one of several inter-war buildings under threat, the appropriateness of the Scottish Georgian Society's name began to be questioned, as it was now taking on pre- and post-Georgian buildings. However, this approach also ensured a more flexible attitude to reuse, as conservation widened the range of building types considered, and the modernist drive for housing gave way to wider social and environmental issues. 'During the 1970s the whole scene has changed', reported the Scottish Georgian Society in 1978; 'in short, consultation is replacing confrontation'.[10] According to a recent history, one of the effects of empowering conservationists in this way meant that 'The

1970s were the first and, perhaps, only decade in which the central driving force in Scottish architecture was not new buildings of any kind, but preserved old ones'.[11] Though conservative, conservationists were rarely complacent, John Gifford reminding the Scottish Georgians' membership in 1982 that 'We are not a substitute planning committee but an unashamedly partisan pressure group'.[12] Direct threats to buildings and areas, especially Georgian, were thus reined in as a result of public concern over the loss of communities and the historic environment, targeted political pressure, and the new legislative framework. However, developers sought new opportunities within the grounds of buildings such as Duddingston, Murrayfield and Brunstane Houses through the mechanism of 'enabling development'.

The move from confrontation to consultation is also reflected in a number of high-profile public buildings which also reflect the move from conservation, being inexorably tied into arguments over health and housing, to ones of amenity and re-use. RMJM converted the Scottish Gallery of Modern Art in 1984 and established its own offices in Dean Village. Concern over corporate shop-fronts saw a post-modern response by Simpson & Brown at Trotters, and Ben Tindall Associates at the Fringe Office, two practices taking on the mantle left by Hurd and Lindsay; but a post-modern playfulness was developed on a larger stage at the Dean Gallery by Terry Farrell Associates. For many, the triumph of heritage over modernism was the system-built Scandic Crown Hotel by Ian Begg on the Royal Mile. The inheritor of Robert Hurd's practice, Begg's work ushered in a form of contextualism in the Old Town. A radically different but arguably related approach is demonstrated at 112 Canongate and the Tron, both by Richard Murphy, who delights in tall tenemental forms seeking to reconnect with Edinburgh's historic architecture.

If the central area became generally recognised for its architectural and historic importance, especially with the conferment of World Heritage Site status in 1995, development pressures ensured that conflict returned to conservation, albeit now in suburban areas. Though more carefully taking account of the character of an area through the introduction of master plans, conservationists have sought to place their own conservation plans for particular buildings and areas within such development, as a means of maintaining the argument in favour of heritage within wider concerns. In this, they have been aided considerably by the impact of Heritage Lottery Funding rules.

Though generally containing a more recent, 20th-century building stock, the move to the city margins also witnessed a further shift in concern from the modernism of the inter-war period to the post-war period. In just thirty years, the Scottish Georgian Society had developed from a period pressure group modelled on its English namesake, the Georgian Group, to a more general pressure group. In a repeat of history, a new pressure group emerged in the 1990s to once again defend a particular style. The group was DoCoMoMo Scotland,[13] and the style was modernism.

At its founding conference in 1992, 'Visions Revisited', DoCoMoMo celebrated buildings, such as Edinburgh University Library, which had brought the Scottish Georgians into being in opposition forty years earlier. In 1997, together with the Architectural Heritage Society of Scotland (the rebranded Scottish Georgian Society), it opposed demolition of Edinburgh's so-called 'terror towers', Leith Fort, replacing the comfortable vision of Edinburgh promoted by Sir John Betjeman in 1970 as a 'city to live and walk about in' with the less-than-appealing world of *Trainspotting*. Despite the existence of a 'thirty-year rule', the preservation of the New Brutalism was seen as a step too far.

If, by the 1990s, developer, council and conservation had reached a form of understanding based on thirty years of working under the Acts, a new battle – as confrontational as the 1960s heyday – has been fought over Queensberry House, an important late 17th-century house. The treatment of this Category A listed building was seen by many as a betrayal as great as, if not greater than, the demolition of George Square or the New Club.[14] Forming the Canongate entrance to the new parliament, the house has been the subject of a conjectural restoration which many have seriously questioned. Although overshadowed by the inquiry into the escalating costs of the new parlia-

FIGURE 9.13 Leith Fort redevelopment – the so-called 'terror towers'. Against a background of activism in support of Georgian architecture, Edinburgh mourned the loss of its Victorian and even inter-war heritage, but arguments in favour of retaining such examples of post-war Modernism went largely unheard despite the foundation of DoCoMoMo-Scotland in 1992. *RCAHMS*

ment (in which it became, albeit briefly, a scapegoat), the destruction of a great deal of the original fabric has been seen to question government commitment to conservation. Coming so soon after Scotland created its own conservation charter, Queensberry House may come to be seen as an unfortunate own goal in a very public project.[15]

Key style issues in new provision and conservation

Two main tensions in style have been distinguished in the past in relation to architecture in Scotland: modernism versus tradition and internationalism versus nationalism.[16] To a significant extent, these perceived tensions have been related. Thus, initially, the USA was a major influence in the inter-war period in the form of Beaux Arts modernity, which was based on a stripped-down and modernised form of classicism. The alternative was predominantly a nationalist overlay of more archaic interpreted classicism which continued through to the early 1960s, mainly associated with Lorimer. The rise, from the 1930s, of a new group of modernist architects spearheaded by Basil Spence and Robert Matthew also led to a sharpening of this modernist/traditional divide with an international/national overlay. Initially expressed in a variety of styles, modernism became institutionalised with the growing state influence on design and standards around the time of the Second World War. By the 1950s, however, a more aggressive modernism began to triumph through institutional patronage, which focused on 'function' and 'organic' inspiration, and by the 1960s this stylistic tradition was consolidated, if somewhat toned down. New modern forms were experimented with in the 1950s–60s in private houses (often architects' own houses), showing new influences of North American and northern European architecture, and eventually new stylistic trends in architecture adapted modernism to Scottish themes in form and material (for example, the work of architects Womersley, Morris and Steadman).

One of the aspects of expression of this form of modernism of the 1950s and 1960s in Scotland was the advent of multiple-use mega-structures, such as in some new educational and medical complexes and commercial development (e.g. St James Square in Edinburgh).[17] This was initially based on rational definitions of 'community' as well as analysis of social communication and socio-spatial patterns, but in time the emphasis moved from social engineering to monumentality for its own sake. An uncompleted example of this in Edinburgh was the grand-scale redevelopment of the University of Edinburgh in George Square and the surrounding area in the Southside. This envisaged a multi-level deck redevelopment in a twenty-year four-phase plan – conceived as a 'new New Town'.

Only part of the first stage was implemented, however, including a high tower (Matthews), a theatre and lower-level social-sciences building (RMJM) and a new main library (Spence), due largely to civic pressure as described above.

In counterpoint to the increasingly pervasive modernism and monumentalism, tradition in architectural form was increasingly promoted through the building-conservation movement as outlined above. Conservation began to be stressed from the 1930s, although it had existed prior to this in the tradition of Geddes, Mears and Macrae (see Chapters 6 and 8).[18] A survey of important buildings was undertaken by Ian Lindsay, 1936–8, and this led to the establishment of the Scottish National Buildings Record. Robert Hurd continued the tradition of conservative infill in a number of schemes in the Old Town, including in the Canongate in 1958–66, with Ian Begg as project architect. The role of conservation was not seen in a narrowly 'historic' context, however, as Hurd promoted the repopulation of the Old Town through 'conservative surgery' as an alternative to the 'sanitary isolation' of peripheral state housing estates such as Craigmillar. Arguably the most significant public clash between modern and tradition in conservation was the conflict created by Ian Lindsay when he raised George Square to a Category A listing at the time when the major university redevelopment was most likely to go ahead.[19]

Whereas the 1960s saw the dominance of modernism, the 1970s saw a rejection of the modernist vision of architecture as well as the large-scale social engineering of the previous approach. This was partly expressed in the consolidation of the drive to rehabilitate the New Town and a change from large-scale area redevelopment to area conservation, with a growth in the number of architects specialising in conservation and building refurbishment. In Edinburgh, this predominantly focused on the formal architecture of the city centre, whereas in Glasgow the experience of tenement rehabilitation as a means to revive rather than replace housing stock was a more widespread manifestation of refurbishment. The 'conservative trend' in the built environment also evidenced itself in new building through less monumentality. As noted above, overall the number of completions in this decade was at its lowest ebb for some time, mainly due to the prevailing economic climate with the oil-price-induced recession; and this, undoubtedly, influenced the trend to conserve and refurbish as opposed to new-build, and to smaller-scale new-build.

However, the 1980s saw a marked revival in construction, although initially this was predominantly commercial, with limited public building. Commercial construction, more than other forms, was both the result of a changing economic basis for development and also shared the impact of the international post-modernist movement in design, with its stress on low cost and open function with distinctive façades, particularly in speculative office blocks. This style drew on interpreted classicism in form but was eclectic in detail, often ironically self-referential. Less in evidence in Edinburgh than in Glasgow, it became more prevalent in 1990s developments such as in Lothian Road and Edinburgh Park, where monumentality resurfaced strongly. The previous 'traditional' alternative style evolved in arguably parallel post-modern ways with Scottish baronial revival work, such as Begg's Scandic Crown Hotel (1988–9), and general Mackintosh revival work – which, although mainly expressed in Glasgow, also inspired buildings in Edinburgh such as the Distillers' Headquarters, Causewayside National Library and Tollcross Fire Station. Post-modernism was evidenced not only in buildings but also in urban design, with the growing focus on urban area-regeneration schemes as opposed to the comprehensive redevelopment of the 1960s and the so-called 'directionless' piecemeal development and conservation of the 1970s and 1980s.[20]

Thus, in the late 1980s, under Councillor George Kerevan's influence, the city started a major building drive, including new cultural institutions. However, the area master-plan approach on which this was based (described above) did not preclude isolated dispersed development, although it certainly focused much new provision. In time, the post-modern style became subordinated to architectural innovation in environmental terms – the stress on energy consumption, for instance. A new form of 'vernacular' also began to develop mainly on urban infill sites, spearheaded by Richard Murphy. But, in general, there was a lessening of the perception of tension between the 'traditional' and the 'modern', or the 'national' and the 'international' in architectural style. This has perhaps been most marked with the largest keynote buildings, such as the new National Museum of Scotland building. As such, the current trend is possibly rising to Charles McKean's challenge to develop 'an architecture at once richly Scottish *and* international'.[21]

Thus, in general, referring to style, Edinburgh has been the site of major confrontations of conservation versus large-scale redevelopment, as well as a site where sensitive conservation and smaller-scale redevelopment have been spearheaded in innovative ways. There exists a continuing tension between these influences, which is arguably as important a factor today as the previous stylistic debates of national versus international and tradition versus modernism. The retreat from modernism is permitting a more popular and varied modern architecture, but there is no trend to suggest that such stylistic populism is promoting a return to the popular engagement in the built environment, as expressed in the confrontational politics of the 1960s. The professionalisation of heritage over the last twenty years may have saved more of the historic environment than it would have without this, but it has arguably also lost public support in the process.

Although the dominant stylistic trend may be post-modern and populist, the stylistic debates have of course not vanished, although they have been largely submerged – at least from public consciousness. However, issues of architectural style surface from time to time into public debate when local architects complain of international architects being commissioned for landmark buildings, and where retention of older buildings is integrated with new buildings. A classic example of both issues is in the Scottish Parliament building: how will the nation appreciate its new parliament? The main public attention to date has been on the construction process, cost and siting, as occupation has just been achieved (although completion is still pending) at the time of writing. Whether the public will identify with the resulting building and accept that the desire for an international landmark building has been valid and well provided for, or whether this will continue to be a sort of cultural scapegoat for the public's relative exclusion from engagement with built-environment issues, will be evidenced in the not-so-distant future.

Beyond style: a wider context for evaluating built-environment development

Our concern in this chapter is not to take sides in a debate on style or on conservation/preservation versus new provision – much less 'tradition' versus 'modern', or 'national' versus 'international'. It is to focus on the need for the wider engagement of society in the production of the built environment and thus in such debates, so that these are less elitist and subject to narrow influences, and as a result largely ignored by society or generically criticised. In addition to this social context, we advocate a more realistic assessment of the built environment within its wider economic and political context.

In the introduction to Part IV, the need to perceive the development of the built environment within such a wider context has been stressed. Glendinning and Page (1999) have attempted such a wider interpretation of trends in the built environment, albeit still focusing mainly on stylistic issues. They see a confusion, a proliferation of styles, patterns and forms – anarchic fragmentation and individualism, conflicting, incoherent relationships between people, places and buildings, yet pervasive regimentation – each building creating individual space, and zones becoming introverted through conservation.[22] This, they argue, is largely due to fragmentation of the design process and the dominance of engineers and financiers concerned mainly with standards and profits – what they term the 'new, factual ruling class of the Scottish Built Environment'[23] – with traditional experts' and intellectuals' critical voice and local-authority control functions becoming subordinated. Rather than a possible convergence in the traditional/modern, national/international debates on style, they perceive an 'unordered homogeneity' through atomised commodification of space and buildings, culturally evidenced in post-modernism, as a predicament inherent in a global market society. As such, they focus on the 'insidious' urbanisation of the central belt with mindless, market-driven proliferation of built environments seen as representing a threat to collective identity.

Their book argues that we are on the cusp of a new long wave of innovation, as the past half-century or so has gone through phases of utopian vision – mass provision – intellectual exhaustion and fragmentation – and is now entering reaction, which they perceive as usually a destructive process leading to the definition of new vision. While it is important to see this text mainly as a polemical tract, some of the analysis is useful, mainly as it stresses that architecture by definition broadly expresses the aspirations of the dominant classes – albeit expressed through a complexity of values. As such, their manifesto, while attempting to place itself within broad historical trends, implicitly raises the issue that the analysis of the built environment is often largely unconnected with the political, economic and social – and even wider cultural – contexts that so crucially affect it, as this often focuses on style and form.

Part IV of this book, in which this chapter is located, hopes to redress this approach to some extent, and in so doing not to fire the debate on which style is 'better', 'more appropriate', temporarily or culturally 'relevant', but to relate the changes of the city's built environment to its wider context, especially the social and economic. As such, it hopes to contribute to a deeper understanding of the parameters of change, as a contribution to identifying routes that this might take as the city continues to 'remake' itself in future. Key issues for evaluating the built environment should of course include issues of style, as the socio-cultural evaluation of this has implications for other aspects of evaluation – for instance, how the public views the parliament building *does* matter. However, there is a need to counterbalance the predominant emphasis on style (and geographic origin and period as strong determinants of this form of analysis) to the detriment of the parameters that building design and production/refurbishment work within. Thus other key issues – other than which style is more appropriate, or whether there is any identifiable coherence in style at all in any particular period – should focus on how we evaluate architecture, urban design and built-environment development, including how society engages in this process.

Important questions for the broader built environment in the city in terms of this evaluation are thus as follows:

1. To what extent are 'structural' forces the main parameters for development of the built environment – for example, changing political and economic contexts (such as the current imperative of 'city-marketing', the role of the city in national, macro-regional or global economies), or wider social and cultural values (e.g. the predominant desire for suburban house forms yet the continued valuation of period building)?

2. To what extent are such forces possibly balanced by those expressed mainly by élites – for example, the confrontation or alignment of action by local government and powerful local lobbies, such as the architectural community? Examples include confrontation of large-scale redevelopment in the 1960s (e.g. George Square and the Southside) and alignment in public–private developments (e.g. Edinburgh Park and the new large-scale master plans at Granton and the Southeast Wedge).

3. How can wider groups in society become more fully involved in issues concerning the built environment and thus contribute positively to this, and not be excluded and thus usually see the built environment in predominantly negative terms? Civic engagement has been an important factor in the past (e.g. public-health issues and conservation), but arguably this has tended to the conservative rather than the innovative (e.g. conservation lobbies restricting innovation in suburban areas).

4. If proactive public engagement and/or understanding of innovation in the built environment is important (and increasingly this has been seen to be so elsewhere[24]), what types of mech-

anisms exist for wider interests in the evaluation of the built environment to be stimulated and expressed, and what are the roles of the professions and educational institutions in this?

Space in this chapter does not permit a response to these issues; however, we hope to have provided a basis for opening a debate on these issues through this brief review of trends in new provision and conservation in the built environment of the city in the past four decades or so, which will be returned to in the next few chapters as well as in the Conclusion.

Notes

1. The term 'master plan' here includes different mechanisms to guide urban design: urban design frameworks, master plans *per se*, and specific area development briefs associated with design guidelines, the main point being that the nature of the coverage of these is partial and finer-grained than that of the city-wide master plan, and also it is focused on areas where development is largely guaranteed. This review focuses on areas that have been master-planned and that affect the main urban fabric, with some peripheral master-planned areas (e.g. Straiton commercial park) or special-use master-planned areas (e.g. the National Gallery of Modern Art and Dean Gallery area) excluded.

2. This will incorporate the new Playfair project which links the Royal Scottish Academy and the National Gallery underground, with access to the gardens.

3. These were listed as: Waverley Station; the General Post Office building at the east end of Princes Street; the Waterfront; Leith Docks; Granton; Edinburgh Park; the Royal Bank of Scotland global headquarters to the west, just before the airport; Craigmillar; the biomedical part at the new Royal Infirmary (Little France); the old Edinburgh Royal Infirmary site north of the Meadows; Cameron Toll redevelopment; Tynecastle football ground redevelopment (planned for housing); Fountainbridge and the Edinburgh Quay project; the Scottish Parliament complex; Edinburgh Airport expansion; Haymarket (new tram hub); Princes Street Gardens; the Crichton Street site near George Square (blighted since demolition in the late 1960s); Sighthill Park sports complex; Meadowbank Stadium (to be demolished for housing); the Cowgate fire site; a new 150-acre public park in the Southeast Wedge; and an exten-

sion of the Edinburgh International Conference Centre (*Edinburgh Evening News*, 21 June 2004).

4. This section draws on a database of some 240 buildings noted in some way or other for their architecture in the following books: A. Forrest (ed.), *Scotland's 100 Best New Buildings* (Glasgow, 2000); Miles Glendinning, A. MacKechnie and R. McInnes, *A History of Scottish Architecture* (Edinburgh, 1996); C. McKean, *Edinburgh: An Illustrated Architectural Guide* (Edinburgh, 1992); R. Rodger, *The Transformation of Edinburgh* (Cambridge, 2001). The database appears as Appendix 2 to this book, containing more information on the buildings and the architect.

5. For charters, see Dorothy Bell, *The Historic Scotland Guide to International Conservation Charters* (Edinburgh, 1997).

6. George Bruce, *'Some Practical Good': The Cockburn Association, 1875–1975* (Edinburgh, 1975).

7. Quoted in David Walker, 'Listing in Scotland: origins, survey and resurvey', *Transactions of the Ancient Monuments Society*, 38 (1994): 61.

8. Scottish Georgian Society, *Annual Report* (1969), p. 3.

9. Scottish Georgian Society, *Annual Report* (1975), p. 6.

10. Scottish Georgian Society, *Annual Report* (1978), p. 3.

11. Miles Glendinning et al., *A History of Scottish architecture: From the Renaissance to the Present Day* (Edinburgh, 1996), p. 476.

12. Scottish Georgian Society, *Annual Report* (1982), p. 4.

13. DoCoMoMo (Documentation and Conservation of the Modern Movement) is the international working party for the documentation and conservation of buildings, sites and neighbourhoods of the modern movement. The papers from the founding conference of its Scottish national body were published as Miles Glendinning (ed.), *Rebuilding Scotland: The Postwar Vision 1945–1975* (Edinburgh, 1997).

14. The episode is most passionately stated in James Simpson, 'From a dream to a nightmare', *Edinburgh Evening News*, 11 December 1999. See also David Black, *All the First Minister's Men: Uncovering the Truth behind the Holyrood Scandal* (Edinburgh, 2001).

15. Historic Scotland, *The Stirling Charter: Conserving Scotland's Built Heritage* (Edinburgh, 2000).

16. Glendinning et al., *Scottish Architecture*.

17. The main icon of this phase of architectural development is the town-centre complex in Cumbernauld New Town between Glasgow, Edinburgh and Stirling.

18. Initial significant acts of conservation in the city include the preservation order for Charlotte Square, established by the City Council, and the conservation of Gladstone's Land in the High Street soon afterwards by the newly created National Trust (1931). The Saltire Society was founded in 1936, starting awards for architectural conservation the following year.

19. Glendinning et al., *Scottish Architecture*, p. 425.

20. M. Glendinning and D. Page, *Clone City: Crisis and Renewal in Contemporary Scottish Architecture* (Edinburgh, 1999).

21. Glendinning et al., *Scottish Architecture*, p. 483.

22. Glendinning and Page, *Clone City*.

23. Ibid., p. 3.

24. See for instance P. Jenkins, 'Territorial and place identities', in C. Hague and P. Jenkins (eds), *Place Identity, Participation and Planning* (London, 2004); P. Healey, A. Khakee, A. Motte and B. Needham, *Making Strategic Spatial Plans* (London, 1997).

10 *Preparing for the 21st century: the city in a global environment*

Derek Kerr

Introduction

As pointed out in Chapter 9, during the closing years of the 20th century, Edinburgh experienced one of the most significant transformations of its urban landscape since the building of the New Town. Almost as if it was preparing itself for the new millennium, the ubiquitous tower crane invaded the city's characteristic skyline of spires and domes. Edinburgh's world-famous landmarks still remained, but they now existed within a more dynamic and thrusting city. Following a period of dramatic change, Edinburgh achieved the accolade of being one of the top wealth-creating cities and the second financial centre in the UK. In terms of funds under management, Edinburgh ranked fourth in the European Community, behind London, Paris and Frankfurt, and thirteenth in the world. It became the only city in Scotland to experience both a rising population and almost full employment. House prices soared (second only to London), and Edinburgh's office, retail and cultural landscape underwent rapid transformation. Clearly, this period of transition from one millennium to the next marks an interesting epoch in Edinburgh's history. This chapter focuses on this period and seeks to offer an account of why, during this particular period, it experienced a significant remaking of its built environment.

In approaching this task, the chapter is less concerned with the form of buildings produced (as physical fabric and architectural statement) than with the changing economic and political practices through which they came into being. This is not to say that the built environment, 'as object', can be forgotten about. Part of the complicated politics of the production of space is the already existing built environment that mediates change. This is particularly significant in Edinburgh, where large parts of the city centre are 'protected' by rigorous conservation policies. The chapter starts by outlining an approach to cities that grasps them as parts of broader processes of change. It then considers the ways in which these broader processes have found expression through a remaking of place within contemporary Edinburgh. The chapter finishes by discussing the implications of this understanding for some of the themes structuring the book.

Situating cities

In Chapter 9, Jenkins and Holder question whether it is 'external' or 'internal' forces that are the major determinants of change within the city. While this terminology is understandable, it tends to suggest a notion of a wall surrounding a city, which may or may not be penetrated by external forces knocking at the gate. Another way of thinking is to grasp the city as the coming together of relationships that are more or less stretched out, more or less local, more or less global. For example, businesses within the city may have as many contacts and relationships with businesses and markets in other cities as, if not more so than, they do with proximate businesses or markets. Similarly, local government is not simply local but is part of the national state system. Consequently, events occurring in cities are specific manifestations of broader processes of change.[1] This is evident in the wave of urban rebuilding that affected cities, not just in the UK, but also internationally in the post-1970s period.

The 1970s marked a turning point in global capitalism. The deregulation of the financial markets witnessed the rapid expansion of international credit and the liberation of investment capital, allowing it to search the globe for the most profitable investments and locations. This was accompanied by the further uneven de-industrialisation of the so-called developed nations and a growth in the financial and producer-services sectors within many countries. These changing economic processes found expression through the remaking of cities as some (or parts thereof) were abandoned while others were reinvented. The form of this reinvention was mediated by a changing political context. The increased mobility of investment capital and the growing fiscal crisis in many nation-states led to policies of privatisation, a neo-liberal agenda, and a transformation of central/local-government roles and relations.[2] Henceforth, local government was increasingly encouraged to foster an entrepreneurial development strategy within cities; and, with the private sector apparently playing an increasingly important role, local policymaking was renamed urban governance.[3] New urban landscapes mushroomed, frequently centred on spectacular 'flagship' projects designed by 'signature architects'.[4]

The above suggests that the recent transformation of Edinburgh, at least in its general form if not its specifics, was not peculiar to Edinburgh. However, Edinburgh also has its own specificity, as it is a unique combination (or coming together) of these more or less stretched-out relationships and practices. Part of this uniqueness also stems from the form of Edinburgh's existing built environment and policies surrounding its transformation or protection. This is considered in more detail below.

Changing economic and political relations and the remaking of Edinburgh

By the early 1980s, the wider processes of economic and political restructuring were affecting the relationships that constitute Edinburgh. Economically, the city's service-based economy was less devastated by de-industrialisation than were traditional industrial cities. Nevertheless, Edinburgh's manufacturing base, already small, was being rapidly eroded, and unemployment in certain parts of the city rose to levels not experienced since the 1930s.[5] As an existing centre for finance and services, however, the potential existed for Edinburgh to become an important site within the deregulated international financial and business networks.

Politically, Edinburgh was caught up in the crisis of the state as central government sought to redefine the nature and limits of local government. Within the UK, a shift from local government to local governance was to be achieved through, among other things, incremental policies of deregulation, privatisation and fiscal austerity. This was not a smooth process, particularly in Edinburgh. Lothian Regional Council's controlling Labour group was prominent in challenging the neoliberal onslaught by ignoring government guidelines and expanding service-provision.[6] Local taxes increased dramatically, forcing the Conservative government under Margaret Thatcher to impose penalties for overspending. This affected a number of councils throughout Scotland and partly contributed to the decimation of Conservative support within the country. Edinburgh District Council was not immune to this changing political landscape. Despite the Council having remained under the control of the political right throughout the postwar period, the Labour Party won control over Edinburgh District Council in the local elections of 1984. The ideology of the far left of British politics could now be heard resonating around the City Chambers. For a short period at least, the strategy of the new Labour administration was to address social inequalities, but not through economic development. Policies favouring commercial real-estate development and the financial and business-services sectors were not a key political priority. There was a further barrier to change – the form of the existing built environment.

Throughout much of the post-war period, office-based activity was largely located in the Georgian properties of the (first) New Town, often referred to as the 'golden rectangle'. This encompassed the prime rental areas of Charlotte and St Andrew Squares, and included the West End, extending as far west as Palmerston Place. The New Town, as a World Heritage Site, had effectively been conserved through its use as a business and financial centre. However, by the 1980s and under pressure to 'modernise', this mutually beneficial relationship between New Town and commerce had become strained. Competitive business practices involving the adoption of new technology required larger floor plates and floor-to-ceiling heights than those offered in the New Town. The conservation of the New Town and the requirements of certain types of business occupiers were increasingly in conflict. The market was redefining Edinburgh's 'sustainability', and the flight of capital was a distinct possibility. In a sense, Edinburgh's past was returning to haunt it. In the late 18th century, the New Town was created as a new space, a space of survival, developed to prevent business and finance from fleeing 'Auld Reekie' for more congenial environs (e.g. London). By the end of the 20th century, Edinburgh's survival as an important place for international business and financial services was predicated on the creation of a new space outwith the constraints of the protected New Town. However, creating this new space was limited by existing planning policy.

Planning policy since 1974 had restrained office growth, particularly in the city centre. A less restrictive stance towards office development was required to realise Edinburgh's potential. By the mid-1980s, this was slowly becoming the view not only of private-sector real-estate market-makers but also of the local business community. In 1985, 'big business' published its analysis of Edinburgh's failure to take full advantage of its potential for development.[7] The report's sponsors were more receptive to the emerging discourse of the 'entrepreneurial city' than the city's Labour administration. The Regional Council's 1985 Structure Plan captured this mood-swing. It introduced a more relaxed office policy for central Edinburgh, one that sought to concentrate a measure of new development in the city centre and ensure that the forecast growth in office employment could be achieved. Politically, too, changes were in the air. Labour remained in control in both the Regional and the District Councils; but the 1987

General Election was a watershed, not just locally, but for urban Left councils throughout UK. The Conservatives' third successive victory in taking the reins of national government pulled the rug from under the experiment in municipal socialism.[8] With Margaret Thatcher re-elected, the policies of fiscal austerity and rate-capping continued, and the possibility of being rescued by a Labour government evaporated. Within Edinburgh, the District Council began to build bridges with the private sector and to acknowledge that the city's competitive survival entailed developing a new spatial matrix subservient to the requirements of commerce and finance. A building boom, fronted by commercial development, was the outcome.

Consequently, like many other cities during the late 1980s and 1990s, Edinburgh experienced a substantial change in its built environment. However, the form of this change and the specific ways in which it was achieved were peculiar to Edinburgh. The conservation/change dialectic of the New Town as both World Heritage Site and dwelling place of expanding business and financial communities was managed through spatial displacement and the creation of new places. Chapter 9 provided a listing of the major developments that occurred during this period. The remainder of Chapter 10 provides a brief account of three significant manifestations of change within Edinburgh. These have been chosen because they embrace what Chapter 9 calls the 'area-specific master plan'. They also illustrate the role of the District Council in stimulating change through its role as landowner and by acting, either directly or indirectly, as developer.

The first, the Exchange, deals with the redevelopment of West Central Edinburgh to create a new financial and commercial district. The second, Edinburgh Park, concerns the creation of a new place for commercial land uses on the western edge of the city. Both of these manifestations of change were handmaidens of 'big business'. They were also accompanied by another important development at the foot of the Royal Mile and guided by the Holyrood master plan. This is not considered further in this chapter. The third, the Waterfront, is a recently started urban regeneration project catering for mixed land uses and seeking to displace growth to under-utilised spaces within the north of the city.

The Exchange, West Central Edinburgh

In April 1987, the District Council published the West Central Edinburgh Redevelopment Strategy. This included an objective of securing a new conference centre for Edinburgh and a new office district to cater for an expanding business and financial-services sector. An area between Haymarket and Castle Terrace, known as West Central Edinburgh, was identified as the main location outside, but adjacent to, the New Town capable of providing redevelopment opportunities. Many of these opportunities have been realised, and the entire area has experienced considerable change. At its centre stands the Edinburgh International Conference Centre (EICC) surrounded by a small group of prestige offices, referred to as the Exchange, catering for the financial-services sector. As more and more of the strategy was realised, the boundary of the Exchange became fluid, and the term is now often used to encompass a wider sphere of office developments. These developments have tended to be large prestigious buildings, many forming headquarters for some of the city's major companies including Standard Life, Scottish Widows and Baillie Gifford. Most of the occupiers of the Exchange have come from within central Edinburgh and in particular the New Town area. Despite its significance, the 1987 Strategy was not the trigger for these changes. Rather, it was attempting to formalise changes already under way, in particular the city's long-running conference-centre saga, the growing pressures from the market and business community for a more relaxed attitude to office development, and the legitimisation offered by the 1985 Structure Plan (see above).

Edinburgh's affair with a new purpose-built conference venue started in the 1950s, but it was only towards the end of 1970s that the project climbed the civic agenda. A study revealed that Edinburgh was losing out heavily in the lucrative international conference business. To compete with other UK cities, far less internationally, Edinburgh needed a purpose-built centre. The council-owned site at Lothian Road was identified as an ideal location. However, as the Conservative government was in the process of implementing a neo-liberal agenda that favoured the reduction of public-sector debt, financial support for a public-sector-owned conference centre was refused. In keeping with this ideology, and accepting the decision, the District Council's Conservative administration began selling the Lothian Road site. It sold parts of the site to the American-based Sheraton Hotel Group to develop a five-star hotel and to Miller Developments Ltd to develop a high-quality office building called Capital House. As both developments were located on an otherwise derelict site, the Council created a new civic square, called Festival Square, to enhance their setting. The developments were completed in 1985.

While a number of other proposals for a conference centre were considered in the mid-1980s, they proved unacceptable either to the Council because they were not located on the preferred Lothian Road site, or to the government because of the financial burden to the public sector. But the context was changing. By this time, it was increasingly recognised that the traditional office core was inadequate to the requirements of the financial-services sector. The search was on for new, larger development sites within the city centre and close to the traditional core. Developers and occupiers were, however, reluctant to be the first to move to what was considered an off-pitch location. It was within this context that the Council's 1987 Redevelopment Strategy emerged. It was an attempt to identify and formalise potential sites for office development and to provide confidence in the market.

The Edinburgh Chamber of Commerce and the pressure group Scottish Financial Enterprise supported the strategy. Importantly, both private-sector bodies also supported the development of a conference centre. They claimed that expansion of the financial heart of the capital, necessary for Edinburgh to retain and exploit its position as the UK's second financial centre, hinged to a great extent on a conference centre being built in Lothian

FIGURE 10.1   A view of the Exchange looking north from Lothian Road.   *Derek Kerr*

Road. Following this pressure, the Scottish Office agreed to support a conference centre, but only if it entailed a far greater contribution from the private sector. As the District Council's recently elected Labour administration were now more amenable to working with the private sector, they conceded. The Council agreed to make available its substantial landholding in the Lothian Road/Morrison Street area (total area of 3.8 hectares, 9.5 acres) for a project that would include a conference centre and office developments. The development gain realised from the commercial office development would be used to finance the conference centre. In return, the Secretary of State gave the SDA (Scottish Development Agency; subsequently Lothian and Edinburgh Enterprise Ltd, or LEEL) approval to spend £6.75 million on rendering the site more acceptable to commercial investment.

Edinburgh Development Group (EDG) was selected through competition as developer. EDG's appointed architect, the internationally renowned Terry Farrell, might have had something to do with the selection given the city's recent attraction to 'signature' architects (i.e. at Edinburgh Park; see below). Following initial criticisms, Farrell's revised master plan was accepted in May 1990. For the first time in its chequered history, a conference-centre proposal had been accepted by all parties, including the government. Its associated office developments (subsequently called the Exchange) would also help establish a new office core. But the shock-waves from an emerging UK property-market crisis threatened to undermine the project. EDG's involvement came to an end when one of its constituent partners, with mounting financial problems, went into receivership. Despite this setback, the Council and LEEL decided that the

FIGURE 10.2 A view of inside the Exchange. The crescent connects Lothian Road with the Conference Centre and passes through Conference Square. The crescent is suggestive of that found in the New Town. *Derek Kerr*

project was still viable. They therefore formed a wholly public-sector joint-venture company, Edinburgh International Conference Centre Ltd (EICCL), to implement the project.[9] The Council leased its land to EICCL and provided it with a loan of £25 million to fund construction of the conference centre. In an uncertain property market where office developments were being postponed, the Council was effectively acting as a developer to progress the conference centre. The intention was that the debt would be recouped from the office-development component of the master plan when the property market moved out of recession. In the mid-1990s, CALA-Morrison, the selected joint developers of the site, commenced development. By the end of the decade, Standard Life and the Clydesdale Bank were in occupation and another major financial institution, Scottish Widows, had

acquired and developed a site nearby to provide a new head-office building.

With the Exchange outgrowing its original parameters, a new central office district was emerging southwards and westwards of the traditional office core. The private sector, following the lead set by the Council (via EICCL), was developing and occupying office blocks in locations that would have been considered off-pitch in the mid-1990s. The Bank of Scotland was active in joint-venture developments in the hitherto unfashionable Tollcross and Fountainbridge areas. Nearby, Miller Developments and British Waterways formed a joint-venture company to redevelop Lochrin Basin at the terminus of the Union Canal. The development, called Edinburgh Quay, will contain new waterfront apartments, restaurants, bars and office accommodation. Further west, the Council's development arm EDI

FIGURE 10.3   A view of the approach to the Exchange from Rutland Square.   *Derek Kerr*

had been given control of the Council-owned Morrison Street goods-yard site.[10] It is hoped that the four-acre site will become a landmark entrance to the city centre as well as effectively extending the Exchange financial district to Haymarket.

Edinburgh Park, West Edinburgh

Important to the recent growth of Edinburgh has been the development of its western edge into what has been described as 'the economic dynamo for the city'.[11] It has also been recognised by the Scottish Executive as an area of strategic importance to Scotland's economic growth by becoming the subject of the first area-specific National Planning Policy Guideline. A significant manifestation of the attempt to turn West Edinburgh into an international business location has been the production of Edinburgh Park. The Park is located some five miles from the city centre and two miles

from Edinburgh International Airport and is bounded on the west by the City Bypass. When completed, Edinburgh Park is expected to have a market value in excess of £500 million, offer around 3.5 million square feet (325,000m^2) of office space and be the workplace for over 25,000 employees.

The origins of Edinburgh Park lie in the early 1980s. At this time, the District Council was seeking additional land for possible future development of the western fringe of the city for mixed commercial/industrial use. An opportunity arose when ASDA, then the fourth largest British grocery corporation, informed the Council that it wanted to develop a superstore in West Edinburgh. It had an option to buy land at the Gyle but also needed part of the Council's landholding to create a viable scheme. At the same time, Wimpey Homes had an option to purchase a nearby farm. However, this was not as commercially attractive for housing development as sites nearer the existing city boundary, which were owned by the Council. There was therefore a mismatch between, on the one hand, the aspirations of ASDA, Wimpey Homes and the Council, and on the other the existing landownership/option pattern. The agreed solution was that both ASDA and Wimpey Homes exercise their options to buy and then transfer their freehold interests to the Council. This land, along with some of the Council's existing land, could then be developed for retail, housing and potential business/industrial uses. Under this proposal, the retail element would become a shopping centre rather than simply a superstore. Details of the scheme, known collectively as Maybury Park, were announced in December 1985 and included:

- fifty acres for a new shopping centre, called the Gyle Shopping Centre – Marks & Spencer and ASDA being the main occupiers and joint developers with the ground landlord and owner, the District Council;
- forty acres for around 500 houses, to be owned and developed by Wimpey Homes;
- 123 acres for a high-tech park called the Maybury Business Technology Park, to be owned and developed by the Council.

During the 1980s, business parks were beginning to emerge as a potentially significant real-estate space, and the Council felt that the city could capitalise on this trend. There were also growing signs of a potential shortage of space within the city to cater for business expansion. But achieving this would be difficult. On the one hand, the Council's ability to progress the Maybury Business Technology Park (MBTP) would be virtually impossible given the constraints of local-government finance. On the other hand, the Council wanted to retain control of the development and not sell it to the private sector. As a solution, the Council established its own development company, Enterprise Edinburgh (EE). Although owned by the Council, it would function at 'arm's length' to the Council as a private company and could therefore be used

to bypass government restrictions on spending. Obtaining approval from the Council for establishing the company would have been impossible a few years earlier, but in 1989 the Labour administration was more amenable to the initiative. Once created, the Council endowed EE with the land necessary to develop the MBTP.

Edinburgh was perceived to be in direct competition for business and high-tech industries with a number of other major European cities. If the city was to retain firms already in Edinburgh and bring in new ones, it needed to create an internationally attractive high-quality park environment. To this end, EE followed a growing trend of appointing internationally recognised 'signature' architects. Richard Meier was selected (via competition) to master-plan the MBTP. Through his appointment, EE believed that Meier would turn the Park into a 'designer label' product, thereby raising its international profile and enhancing its profitability. Meier's master plan was revealed in June 1989. Significantly, it was suggested that Meier's plan had more than a hint in the direction of James Craig's plan for the New Town (c. 1767) and that it would realise a 'new New Town': 'the development can be termed as Edinburgh's new New Town; a link between the city's commercial past and its future; a link between the architectural heritage and the Old New Town and the vision of Richard Meier's master plan' (Green 1993: 14).

Given the scale of the project, EE entered into partnership with Miller Developments to form a joint-venture company called New Edinburgh Ltd (NEL). NEL became the developer of the Park in January 1991. By this time, the economy, not just in Scotland but globally, had taken a downturn. Consequently, NEL set about 'improving' certain practical and financial aspects of the project in order to enhance its marketability in a shrinking economy. This included changing the project's name from Maybury Business Technology Park to Edinburgh Park (EP), as the growing evidence suggested that accommodating the service sector would prove more profitable than high-tech industries. No sooner had a revised master plan been accepted than a major site, east of the entry to

FIGURE 10.4   A view of Edinburgh Park, looking north.
The arc of office buildings fronting a new landscaped
loch is suggestive of Richard Meier's homage to
Edinburgh's New Town.   *Derek Kerr*

FIGURE 10.5   Looking north towards Alexander Graham
Bell House, situated at the entrance to Edinburgh Park.
Derek Kerr

the Park, was sold to a major financial institution, Scottish Equitable, who stated no intention of following the plan. However, with the general downturn in the economy, NEL needed both to attract an anchor occupier and raise money to build the Park Centre. The sale satisfied both needs.

The first building on the Park was completed in 1995, and by 2001 a total of fourteen office buildings had been completed and occupied. By then, the Park boasted a number of large national and international institutional landlords and occupiers. Nine of the fourteen occupiers relocated to EP from elsewhere in Edinburgh. However, certain of these also relocated certain functions to the Park from other locations in Scotland in order to consolidate into a single Scottish HQ. The other five organisations were either relocations to Edinburgh or new ventures that chose EP as their start-up location. The attractiveness of West Edinburgh in general and of Edinburgh Park in particular was increased by the decision of the Royal Bank of Scotland to build its global headquarters on a nearby site. Despite its location in the green belt, and concerns over additional traffic-generation in an already congested road network, the prestige and economic advantages of ensuring that the Royal Bank remained in the capital outweighed all objections. The retention of the bank would help ensure the consolidation of Edinburgh as a leading financial centre.

Urban regeneration in North Edinburgh's waterfront

Granton in North Edinburgh played a key role in the city's industrial past, focusing on heavy engineering, chemicals and the oil and gas sectors. This industrial heritage was symbolised by the Granton gas towers that became one of the capital's most prominent features from the north, along with the Castle, Arthur's Seat and Calton Hill. From the 1960s, however, this area, along with the nearby Port of Leith, succumbed to the more widespread processes of de-industrialisation. Lack of job opportunities led to high levels of unemployment and to a reduction of people living in the area. The landscape became one of morbid dereliction. By the turn of the 21st century, however, this landscape was in the early stages of transformation through the implementation of what has been heralded as the largest urban regeneration project in Scotland. The project is to be a major mixed-use, high-density urban development covering some 140 hectares (346 acres). It will eventually include around 340,000m² (3.65 million ft²) of office and business space, up to 27,000m² (290,000 ft²) of light industrial and storage space, two local centres with retail outlets, a new marina and leisure centre, a primary school, a new campus for a further-education college and around 6,500 dwellings. An important feature of the project is that 15 per cent of total residential development must be affordable housing for rent or sale. This project has coalesced with a renaissance in and around the Port of Leith, where slum buildings, disused warehouses and distilleries have been either bulldozed or converted into luxury housing, bistros and business premises. But how did this come about?

Edinburgh's 'reawakening' in the 1980s initially focused on high-end commercial developments such as those epitomised by the Exchange and Edinburgh Park. Granton, with its derelict sites, contaminated land and relatively poor transport communications, was not perceived as a suitable location for this type of development. Leith and the adjacent redundant docklands had, however, been the subject of studies by the SDA and were subsequently identified by the local planning authority as alternative locations to the city centre and Edinburgh Park for major office developments. An important trigger to the regeneration of the Port of Leith was the relocation of the then Scottish Office (now the Scottish Executive) to Victoria Quay. Once this deal was struck, other development opportunities in the vicinity appeared more attractive. However, it was to take until the mid-1990s, as development pressure mounted in the city, for Granton to be identified by both the Council and LEEL as an ideal place for future expansion. The area contained over 50 per cent of all vacant land within the city, and its regeneration would reintegrate Granton and the waterfront into Edinburgh's urban fabric. The image of Edinburgh becoming a waterfront city led to comparisons with cities such as Barcelona, Manchester and Bristol and, in some of the hype, to the notion that Granton could become a 'Riviera on the Forth'.

In 1998, the city and SEEL, with input from Scottish Homes, launched the *Granton Development Framework – A Vision for the Future* which contained the main elements of the regeneration project. The urban designer Llewelyn-Davies turned this vision into a master plan. The final version was published in January 2001 and adopted by the city as an overall development guideline. Implementing the plan, however, would be difficult. Urban regeneration of this scale would not happen if left

to the private sector. In addition, the public-sector initiative was constrained by government controls. Consequently, a joint-venture company, Waterfront Edinburgh Ltd (WEL), was formed in March 2000 as an implementation agency that could access private finance outside the central-government controls. Unlike NEL (developer of Edinburgh Park), WEL was a joint venture between two public-sector bodies – the City of Edinburgh Council and SEEL. SEEL was considered a necessary partner in this urban regeneration, given its remit of delivering economic and social development in East Central Scotland. WEL was supported with an input of landed property (from the city) plus finance from the two parties (a total investment of around £33 million).

Although WEL was charged with implementing the master plan covering 140 hectares, its control of this area was limited. Initially, there were a number of landowners affected by the project, including Texaco, Shell, the Buccleuch Estates, British Gas and Forth Ports. During the second half of the 1990s, the city purchased certain of these interests to ensure an early start to reclamation within the Granton area. However, some owners refused to negotiate at all, while there was a failure to agree terms with others. It took four years of negotiations and the threat of a compulsory purchase order (CPO) before the Duke of Buccleuch, Scotland's biggest private landowner, agreed to sell. The city was unsuccessful with British Gas, another major landowner in the area. In this case, the area of land was such that a CPO against British Gas would be too costly. At the conclusion of the site-assembly process, WEL became only one of three major landowners in the area covered by the master plan. Each of these landowners owns or controls just over 40 hectares (about 100 acres), with the balance in smaller parcels. Moving from east to west, Granton Harbour is owned by Forth Properties, part of Forth Ports plc. In the central part, WEL is the principal landowner; and, to the west, British Gas Properties (subsequently called Lattice Properties and then Second Site Properties) owns the former gas works. Of the 20 or so hectares (approximately 50 acres) remaining, some existing landowners will stay. These include

FIGURE 10.6   An example of gentrified warehouses at Leith Docks.   *Derek Kerr*

FIGURE 10.7   An example of a new housing development at Leith Docks.   *Derek Kerr*

the National Museums of Scotland Research Establishment, to be enlarged and made more available to the public, and Caroline Park House, a Grade-A listed 17th-century house.

Despite its limited power over the entire site, WEL's core strategy is to make the project attractive to national and international investors and developers. Expenditure on environmental improvements, infrastructure and services is the first stage of increasing land values to the levels where the aspirations of the master plan become viable. Symbolically, the project is being marketed by WEL as the 21st-century equivalent of the 18th-century Edinburgh New Town. A measure of international approval has been achieved through the award of a licence for a World Trade Centre (London is the only other city in the UK with a licence). Edinburgh will now join a prestige group of cities – 315 throughout the world in ninety-seven countries – that have reciprocal rights and obligations to share in each other's business initiatives. These have proven worldwide to be powerful engines of regeneration and economic growth. In terms of urban development, WEL has recently concluded a deal for its first major residential development with a joint-venture company, Upper Strand Developments Ltd. They will deliver an urban quarter in sympathy with the master plan devised by Page and Park and consisting of some 500 apartments.[12] The deal is significant, as it nets WEL £60 million which can be used

to repay outstanding debt. A new headquarters building for Scottish Gas has now appeared on the adjoining land owned by Second Site Properties. This building was designed by Norman Foster and arguably becomes the waterfront's first landmark building.

Nearby, at Leith, Forth Ports have continued to regenerate their redundant docks. In 1995, following their success with the Scottish Office accommodation at Victoria Quay, Forth Ports engaged Conran & Partners to design a terminal to enhance the facilities currently on offer to cruise ships visiting Edinburgh (currently around forty per year) and to provide a stylish new shopping experience for both local residents and visitors to the city. They also sought to persuade the Cabinet Office (in London) to allow the development to house the Royal Yacht Britannia when it was taken out of service. The massive £120 million facility, Ocean Terminal, is now complete (opened 2001), and the Royal Yacht is berthed alongside. Ocean Terminal, a joint venture between Forth Ports and the Bank of Scotland, boosts Edinburgh's retail space by 25 per cent. There are more shopping units in the Terminal than there are along Princes Street. In addition, it includes twelve restaurants and a health club, as well as Edinburgh's largest cinema complex.

The Terminal had a mixed start with many of the shop units lying vacant, leading to the comment that the cavernous complex resembled an empty aircraft hangar more than a vibrant shopping complex. It is still striving to lease out all its units. The slump in the property market also forced Forth Ports to shelve their plan for Scotland's first six-star hotel after its potential operator, Scandic, the Swedish hotel group, pulled out. This had a knock-on effect on high-priced apartments to be developed nearby. The developer pulled out of this residential project, citing the replacement of a planned luxury hotel with an office building. The fear was that homebuyers were unlikely to pay premium prices for exclusive flats with an office block or undeveloped dockland next to them. CALA Homes stepped in and proposes to replace the luxury apartment plan with a new design concept offering lower-priced property. Despite these setbacks, Forth Ports have pressed ahead with plans to redevelop Western Harbour and the newly unveiled Edinburgh Harbour.

Discussion

This chapter has considered some of the changes that have occurred in Edinburgh as it moved from one millennium to the next. This period of Edinburgh's existence is significant, if only for the amount of new building work that has taken place in a relatively short period of time. But to what extent can this period of change be used to inform the main themes of this book? This chapter's title, 'Preparing for the 21st century', suggests the notion of some powerful local agency organising itself for a new period in time. However, this notion conceals as much as it reveals.

As suggested above, while Edinburgh has experienced considerable change since the 1980s, this was neither mere happenstance nor simply the product of a local agency preparing itself for the 21st century. As cities are particular expressions of the coming together of more or less stretched-out relationships, they are part of wider processes of change. Economically, these processes included continuing de-industrialisation and the expansion of the financial and business-services sectors. Politically, they included the fiscal crisis of the national state and the movement towards neo-liberal policies. The changing form and content of the relationships constituting cities came into

contradiction with the existing form of cities as manifested in and through their built environments. While these built environments may have been adequate to house relations of different form and content (e.g. heavy industry, earlier forms of business practice), they were no longer adequate. A new form of three-dimensional space was required (e.g. to accommodate information technology) and new locations were sought while others were shunned. Internationally, a wave of city-rebuilding was the outcome.

Considered in this way, Edinburgh's spatial remaking was neither a unique event nor the product of local agents simply deciding that change was required. Rather, it was a necessary prerequisite both to preserve and possibly to enhance Edinburgh's place within a changing form of globalisation. It was a question of survival within a process where the relations of power (e.g. of business and finance) stretched beyond the particularity of the city. For example, the production of the Exchange and Edinburgh Park was justified by the perceived need to compete with other cities in order to preserve jobs and to capture mobile inward investment.

The city is neither self-subsistent nor an autonomous system that can sustain itself through its own actions and following its own agenda. Relations that more or less stretch beyond the city set the agenda of sustainability. If Edinburgh had not been remade in a form attractive to the new requirements of business (i.e. for location and floor space), then its sustainability would have been undermined. Within Edinburgh, local government did play an important role in the process of change, particularly through its role as landowner and developer. But the choices open to local government were limited. The restructuring of the state (particularly in terms of local-government finance) encouraged the city to achieve change through the market (e.g. through partnerships with the private sector, relying on development profits) and for the market. Change was achieved through adopting a market-orientated culture and creating spaces attractive to business. This is clearly illustrated in the case studies outlined above. Considered in this way, Edinburgh's spatial remaking was not simply about the city preparing itself for the 21st century, but more an issue of survival. Furthermore, the ending of one millennium or the starting of the next did not dictate the timing of this remake, as if the city was attempting to deal with a form of the 'millennium bug'. Rather, the timing was dictated by the changing form of global capitalism that happened to coincide with the ending of one millennium.

The issues of conservation and change are also pertinent to the remaking of Edinburgh. Edinburgh's 'conserved' New Town played a significant role in this process. Not only did it encourage the spatial displacement of new development, it was also commandeered as a signifier in the services of an entrepreneurial discourse of 'place-marketing' and as a means to legitimise new space. For example, those new spaces created furthest from the New Town (e.g. Edinburgh Park, Granton Waterfront) have been, metaphorically speaking, returned to the New Town and branded as 'equivalents'. The emblematic power of the New Town to Edinburgh's status and international identity was being drawn upon to propel Edinburgh into a new Europe. This is not so much a case of 'learning from history' as 'repackaging history' in order to sell the present. Edinburgh, of course, is not alone in using history as handmaiden to the present.

Finally, the issue of innovation needs to be questioned. What appears innovative to Edinburgh is not necessarily unique to Edinburgh and could be part of a general trend of change. For example, the Council's intention to develop a business park (that is, Edinburgh Park) was important but not unique and was following a growing international trend. Similarly, the adoption of the area master plan and the use of 'design superstars' to internationally branded developments was again more than local currency at that time. However, the Council's creation of a 'private' company, Enterprise Edinburgh, outside the restrictions of local government to further the Park appeared to be particularly novel at that time. A problem with the term 'innovation' is that it begs the question – from whose point of view? Many of the changes referred to above, innovative or otherwise, have benefited certain sectional interests (e.g. the financial-services sector, professional workers), but

others are dependent on the 'trickle-down' effect. In this sense, 21st-century Edinburgh, so far, is no different from 20th-century Edinburgh.

Notes

1. A. Amin and N. Thrift, *Cities: Reimaging the Urban* (Cambridge, 2002); A. Cochrane, J. Peck and A. Tickell, 'Manchester plays games', *Urban Studies*, 33(8) (1996); M. P. Smith, *Transnational Urbanism: Locating Globalisation* (Oxford, 2001).

2. A. Tickell and J. Peck, 'Accumulation, regulation and the geographies of post-Fordism', *Progress in Human Geography*, 16 (1992).

3. M. Godwin and J. Painter, 'Local governance', *Transactions of the Institute of British Geographies*, 21 (1996); A. Harding, S. Wilks-Heeg and M. Hutchins, 'Business, government and the business of urban governance', *Urban Studies*, 37(5–6) (2000); M. Jones, 'Restructuring the local state', *Political Geography*, 17(8) (1998).

4. D. Crilley, 'Megastructures and urban change', in P. L. Knox (ed.), *The Restless Urban Landscape* (Englewood Cliffs, NJ, 1993); T. Hall and P. Hubbard (eds), *The Entrepreneurial City* (London, 1998).

5. C. Hague and H. Thomas, 'Planning capital cities', in R. MacDonald and H. Thomas (eds), *Nationality and Planning in Scotland and Wales* (Cardiff, 1997); F. Simpson and M. Chapman, 'Comparison of urban governance and planning policy', *Cities*, 16(5) (1999).

6. In April 1975, local government reform created a two-tier structure of Regional and District Councils. The City of Edinburgh now became just one of four, albeit much the largest, Districts in the newly created Lothian Region administered by Lothian Regional Council.

7. Edinburgh Chamber of Commerce and Manufacturers, *Edinburgh's Capital* (Henley-on-Thames and Edinburgh, 1985).

8. S. Lansley, S. Goss and C. Wolmar, *Councils in Conflict* (London, 1989).

9. The Council, now City of Edinburgh Council, owns 100 per cent of the shares in the limited company, while LEEL (now SEEL) holds a 'golden' share and 50 per cent of the seats on the board.

10. EDI was formerly known as Enterprise Edinburgh (EE), initially formed to develop Edinburgh Park.

11. T. Curtis, 'Vision for "economic dynamo" of the future', *Edinburgh Evening News*, 23 August 2002.

12. Each of the three major landowners has engaged its own master-planner to interpret the implications of Llewelyn-Davies' master plan for their landholding.

11 The changing image and identity of the city in the 21st century: 'Athens of the North' or 'North of Athens'

CLIFF HAGUE AND PAUL JENKINS

This book has shown that the built environment of Edinburgh has been constantly changing. Any attempt to capture and contain such changes within abstract concepts is necessarily hazardous. Generalisation obscures details or even risks omission or misunderstanding. Interpretation implies some measure of subjectivity. In addition, to attempt to deconstruct a city as well loved as Edinburgh is to risk the wrath of the multiple custodians of its image and identity. Yet, unless we probe the roots of urban change and the relation of the built environment to the meanings embedded in the idea of 'Edinburgh', we will be left lamenting a lost, idyllic past; indeed, much of the writing about the city has taken precisely that form. It is expressed, for example, in the central and recurring role accorded to the New Town as the metaphor for how Edinburgh was once able to produce elegant and orderly development of international excellence and a source of cultural pride.

However, the conditions of the 21st century require different concepts and analyses from those that fashioned previous understandings of Edinburgh. The intertwined parameters of urban development – technology, economy, society, space and politics – are now significantly different from what they were even as recently as in the 1970s or early 1980s. Consequently, Edinburgh is changing rapidly, and the development decisions that the city faces have become more critical. Before extrapolating these forces into a possible future for the city, some explanation of the basic ideas is required. This will be followed by a brief discussion of some of the images set out – expli-

citly or implicitly – in earlier chapters, as a basis for an assessment of the contemporary city and its context.

Identity and image

It is possible to describe a city in many different ways. Books such as this, architectural guidebooks, sets of economic statistics, picture postcards and lists of key dates in its history are just a few examples. To some degree, such sources will be shared and assimilated by residents, visitors, even total outsiders who have never known the city at first hand. Direct experience of a place is usually mediated by stories and images about that place that we hear from other sources. Rose (1995: 88) observed that 'places are infused with meaning and feeling'. This cocktail of sentiment, observation and received information is filtered by the forces that shape life experience (e.g. age, gender, class, ethnicity) to create place identities. While ultimately identity can be personal and subjective, our argument, which is advanced more fully elsewhere,[1] is that place identity is best understood as relational. By this, we mean that identities are defined in relation to the other – other places, other social groups, other histories.

Image-making is related to, but different from, place identity. Image is consciously created or held in critical suspension – that is, it *is* an image, and there will always be a gap between image and reality. Identity requires less artifice, and is likely to appear to the holder as an authentic way of understanding a place. Of course, there are different, even contesting, narratives of place identity, and this is true of Edinburgh today as in the past. For different groups, and at different times, 'Edinburgh' has meant different things. This book has already told some of those stories – of the city as architecture or landscape, a conserved, historical city that as capital is part of a Scottish heritage, of an industrial Edinburgh, and of a city in transition.

The creation and reproduction of these identities has been socially rooted and culturally defined. To put this idea in the simplest terms, architects tend to see the city as architecture, residents identify it as home, tourists as an attractive famous place. Of course, categories overlap in terms of people – for example, architects are also residents. Our proposition in this chapter is that identity has become increasingly significant but also increasingly problematic. The explanation that we advance is that some of the anchors of identity, notably class and locality (usually related to long-term residence and work in a locale) have been pulled up. The political and economic ascendancy of neo-liberalism in the last quarter of the twentieth century has been a factor in the displacement of class by individualised commodity consumption as the main narrative of identity and as the basis of political life. New scales of labour markets and personal mobility have reduced long-term attachment to a place and direct engagement of the 'local' in creating and reproducing its identity.[2]

These tendencies have implications that we argue can be exemplified in the case of Edinburgh. Firstly, the built environment has always been a significant carrier of stories of place identity. It is part of memory and thus has a long transitional cycle: for instance, the Tron Kirk as the part of the familiar face of the Old Town and Hogmanay, where friends from school or university days were reunited in the jostling celebration of the New Year. However, as commodity spreads into so many facets of everyday life, the centre of Edinburgh becomes a managed, commercial venue, targeting a global youth culture, and competing with London, Berlin, Prague or even places further afield as the 'must-be-there' location for seeing in the New Year. Thus the built environment remains hugely important, but there are new spatialities and scales, new and more diverse users of the

spaces, new relations of control and power, new opportunities and imperatives for business. The historic identity of Edinburgh, where the past is the dominant narrative about place, is thus directly challenged by the society of global commodities, where competition is intense, memory is disposable and transitional cycles are short-term as fashion creates new needs and consigns last year's model to the dustbin.

There are thus a plethora of forces that are again rooted in wider socio-economic change but which result in an ever-increasing number of ways in which Edinburgh is experienced and thus identified. For example, there is the growth of tourism, both quantitatively and qualitatively, in terms of the niche markets (Saga Holidays, stag nights, short breaks, festivals and so on) the boom in higher education and the corresponding student experiences of place, and the spatial extension of labour markets (with more and more people commuting longer distances to work). Places identified with and by communities of residents become less easy to assign without caveats. For example, Leith and Leithers had retained their distinctiveness from the days of the port and the pre-1919 separate local administrative status. However, by the millennium, Leith had at least four distinctive identities – the traditional, ageing, working-class community with its residual facilities (council houses, tenement flats, pubs, churches); the Leith of Irvine Welsh's *Trainspotting*, drug-addicted, with a crumbling social and physical fabric; the Leith of the Asian community, with the Sikh temple and late-night corner shops; and, last but by no means least, the Leith of the loft-living, winebar and gym-visiting young professionals, buying into a very different image of Leith from the area's traditional identity. Thus identity becomes more complex and fragmented as places, and the everyday life that underpins them, are reconfigured and identity itself becomes commodified.

Far from being immune to these market-driven changes, governance and the relation of governance to place have also been deconstructed. The book has charted the changing roles and significance of local government in making and managing Edinburgh. The New Town was made possible by radical action by the Town Council, which was in fact bankrupted by the venture. Public health and housing reform saw the Council take an increasingly significant role as regulator and then direct provider of the built environment. The vision (or lack of vision) of the city's administration has been important in the city's identity and image. However, changes since 1975 have fundamentally altered governance in the city and the relation of the Council to Edinburgh's identity.

The creation of Lothian Regional Council in the local-government reorganisation of 1975 left Edinburgh with a lower-tier council, one of four Districts in the new Region. This was not just an administrative change, as for the first time it gave power over services such as education and strategic planning to a Labour-controlled council (secured by the votes of the electors in the three other districts in the Region). The reversal of these changes by the Conservative government in 1996, creating a unitary local-government structure and restoring powers to an Edinburgh administration, also did not amount to the *status quo ante*. The Edinburgh council early in the twenty-first century is substantially controlled through central government (which has vastly reduced the discretion of local authorities to raise revenue from local forms of taxation). However, that central government is now mainly manifested through the Scottish Parliament, not Westminster. In addition, there are European Union funds to be sought, and engagement with a range of locally powerful stakeholders has become obligatory in city governance. At the same time, voting in elections has become a minority activity in many areas across the city.

The tasks expected of the Council have also changed. In particular, it has come to occupy a much more strategic and focused role in image-making. As noted previously in the book, in the early 1990s it was able to capitalise on its inherited bank of key sites to play a major role as a developer in the city, particularly through its arm's-length company, EDI. However, as the sites became developed, the Council's role was increasingly a reflection of the work it had done in generalising the Festival City image through promoting a range

of festivals throughout the year, culminating in Hogmanay. In other words, the Council has become a major image-builder. In 2004, it took this approach a step further, appointing Sir Terry Farrell, a leading UK architect and urban designer, as the city's first 'Design Champion', with a brief to promote design standards of international quality.

In summary, inevitably the post-modern world of images, in which personal identity is expressed through brands and designer labels – a world of 'I consume therefore I am' – has thoroughly infused the space, built environment and governance of the city. Perhaps the most significant recent expression of this was the siting of the globally important annual MTV Music Awards in the city (in fact in Leith) in late 2004. However, we should not make a fetish of post-modernism or globalisation. The book has shown that Edinburgh's image has always reflected internal as well as external imperatives.

Some key issues

How do we define the city's main image and identity? What do we consider as 'Edinburgh', and who are 'we' anyway? As authors, we argue that the 'we' who should be considered here – and, it is hoped, reflected in the book's readership – is in fact an increasingly diverse group of people who hold a 'stake' in Edinburgh's identity, which needs to be understand by broad categories probably best composed of visitors, workers and residents. For most national and international visitors, the dominant images of the city's identity are probably linked to packaged forms of history, folklore, recreation and culture – Edinburgh being the centre of the international 'Scotch' brand. Other national visitors (British and Scottish) may, however, see the city more as a cultural and educational centre to be visited briefly: here, the dominant images are probably the international festivals, the city as a recreational centre (e.g. sports, restaurants, night clubs), a regional shopping centre and a national-level educational centre, as well as the distinctively Scottish national seat of government, courts and learning. This identity may also be linked to other specialised services (e.g. hospitals and schools) which are accessed from the wider regional or to some extent national level (e.g. key cultural institutions). On the other hand, residents and workers, who increasingly need to be differentiated, as many who work in the city now live outside, fairly obviously identify with the city mainly as a place of work and/or residence but also a place of leisure, commerce and other services which the city provides for many also in the region. This group is affected most directly by the city economy, jobs and the housing market, and includes those who create as well as provide employment – an increasingly non-local group in both cases, as the city attracts employers and employees from an ever wider catchment area, which in itself provides an increasing social and cultural diversity.

The second key issue is what we consider as 'Edinburgh'. This can be related to the above identities, although we would stress that this is not automatic. The long-distance visitors probably do not see much of Edinburgh outside of the central areas: the Old Town and New Town and some other areas where hotels and guest houses or other cultural and recreational facilities are concentrated – perhaps now also including Leith and the new waterfront. Short-distance visitors probably identify most with Princes Street/George Street, the Grassmarket/Cowgate, and a wider set of other recreational and cultural sites (especially during the Festival), with this including Holyrood and the main institutions such as the law courts and universities. The dispersion of shopping around the periphery in the past decade or so has also created new dispersed foci – Ikea at Straiton is probably as important a focal point for many as Princes Street, especially those from the region. For workers/residents and those who provide work and housing, the specific city districts that are identified with are, of course, much wider than those accessed by visitors, including the increasing peripheral areas of employment – which follows the trend of some of the large shopping and recreational areas, although inner-city regeneration is also providing new options. Overall, the spatial relations between residence, work and recreation are becoming much more complex, as many residents and/or

workers have these functions separated and have multiple links.

What does this mean for the city's image and identity? Much of what has been discussed in the book so far has concentrated on relatively small areas of the city – especially the Old and New Towns – although Chapters 7–11 have widened the scope of the coverage considerably. This strong central city image certainly is of direct relevance for the city's identity for long- and short-distance visitors. For the majority of those who live and work in the city, however, we argue that the city region is probably becoming just as important a reference point for identity as the city spills over the green belt in terms of residence, work and some recreational and cultural activities.

The option of ever-widening residential spread in the region, which has been the tendency in recent years, is both creating more transport problems (and associated environmental and accessibility problems) and also the trend for more out-of-town economic development. While this is good for the region, it may dilute the economic basis for regenerating parts of the city – including the New Town, which is losing its current economic function to peripheral locations. The tendency in housing for the majority of residents to opt for detached or semi-detached individual units, which is what the market-providers specialise in, also pushes this low-density spread into the region. There is thus a tension between the opportunity for fairly large-scale regeneration of previous industrial brownfield sites within the city boundaries, and the form of residential provision that will be marketable here. Will this permit the higher density of services-provision which has been a feature of the city's success so far?

Thus some of the key issues which are related to the question of city image and place identity are that images of the city are in fact as diverse as the widespread social and cultural identities which people bring to Edinburgh – visitor, residents and workers – and the dominant images which we hold of the city are changing as social and cultural identities and mixes change, albeit some slower than others. These images and identities are socially and culturally defined, but increasingly manipulated by the media, commerce and government as the quality of a city's image and place identity is increasingly important as an economic factor in an increasingly globally fluid environment. The built environment, however, reflects contemporary place image/identity but also 'captures' it for later generations and thus has a long transitional cycle. The sustainability of these images to date has been a big factor in Edinburgh's 'success' so far; but this is changing. We argue that the nature of place identity is inevitably reflected in engagement with place by those who have a stake in it – that is, there is a crucial relationship between governance, city image and place identity. However, do the stakeholders in Edinburgh's identity identify enough to get involved in issues concerning the built environment? How the increasingly wide range of these stakeholders can engage effectively in this, while the city maintains its competitive international and national image, is the key issue.

Dominant city images in the past and present

To begin to answer some of the above, we need to examine how the competitive environment of Edinburgh has changed and how it is likely to change in future. Although economic analyses of the city have tended to focus on the national (Scotland and/or UK) and have only recently (re)turned to the international, we argue that the city has been affected by international forces throughout its history. One way to approach this briefly is to see how it has been expressed in the three waves of globalisation, of which the current is only the most recent.

The first wave of globalisation as such was that of mercantile expansion.[3] Here, Edinburgh's active role was primarily in the early stages of European mercantile trade, building on post-feudal changes in society and its productive basis. The breakdown of feudalism permitted early investment in new concepts (agricultural, commercial/financial and industrial), and here Scotland's relatively strong contribution to the Enlightenment and invention was born partly from a widespread educational system, the high level of social interaction possible and indeed

encouraged by the physical proximity of the still confined city (the Old Town), and the relative lack of dominant hierarchies – permitting the emergence of key individuals and the fertile social resources for them to develop their ideas.

However, to survive in the new globalising environment of the outwardly mercantile 16th and 17th centuries, larger national units were eventually needed to support the navies that controlled the transport routes, and hence dominance in trade; and so Scotland came to unite with England. This phase in Scottish history is dominated by the creation and then defence of a national Scottish identity, with Edinburgh acting as a national focus in relation to the initially strong European trade – for example, the initial impetus for upgrading the Old Town,[4] but subsequently undermined in its national role by Union. As argued in Chapters 1 and 2, the main rationale for the physical creation of the 'Athens of the North' and the associated imagery was primarily a socio-economic and cultural-identity defence mechanism.

The second wave of globalisation was that of industrial imperialism. As new forms of production led to growing demands for raw materials, the British nation-state consolidated itself as the pre-eminent world industrial power with its dominant access to world markets. Here, the first mercantile wave of global economic expansion from a European base began to be transformed into colonial aspirations to control natural resources and then create wider and captive markets. Edinburgh's role changed in this period to one of providing services, as the Atlantic trade came to dominate previous Scottish-based European trade, better served from Glasgow. The city thus changed its main function, as dominant mercantile and subsequent industrial power moved west; however, a professional control function replaced this as the role of government grew, as did the professions, and hence a level of socio-economic dominance was retained (especially in the civil service, law, finance, education and medicine). The early traditions of the city in providing financial and knowledge services were key to the new role which the city came to play – probably no better exemplified than in the explorations that underpinned colonial imperial expansion and that had links with the city (e.g. explorers and map-printers).

Nevertheless, there is a need to realise that, despite this increasing service-sector focus, there remained also a relatively strong diversity in industrial development, with significant industrial activity for local markets and intensified labour in-migration, albeit not as marked as Glasgow – these including glass, furniture, brewing and a world leader in rubber-processing (see Chapter 4). Here, the city has been characterised as based on 'beer, beauty and Bibles' – referring to its local service industries, early destination for tourism and pub-lishing/educational focus, much enhanced by the writers of note which it produced.[5] While these authors reinforced romantic notions of Scottish national identity (e.g. the work of Robert Louis Stevenson) and thus to some extent the high ground of intellectual aspiration and visual images deriving from the Enlightenment period, the reality of the staid Protestant bourgeois culture of the city was parodied in *The Prime of Miss Jean Brodie*.[6] The abrupt contrast of this with the contin-uing slum conditions of many residents and workers (referred to in Chapter 6) – and the Council's alternative provision in the sprawling housing estates of the first half of the 20th century (as described in Chapter 7) – was, however, also summed up in the derisive label of the city's resi-dents as having a 'fur coat and nae knickers'.[7]

The third, and current, wave of globalisation is characterised by much more mobile forms of capital. The devastation in the two World Wars of the previously dominant colonial powers, and the economic crises of regulated capitalism, led to increasing competition for global resource-exploitation and the shift from direct control to indirect control of economies. This led to the loss of the colonies, but also changes in the nature of global economic dominance from nation-states to transnational corporations. The loss of the gold standard and changing access to labour markets as well as technological advance led to industrial decline in the north and to the rise of service func-tions in importance – producing what has been called the post-industrial or post-modern city. Edinburgh was relatively well positioned to take advantage of these changes, as it had an early stress on its cultural role, with its launch of the Festival City role in the immediate post-war period. While not sitting easily with the dominant image desired by the conservative urban élite (hence Tom Stoppard's characterisation of the city as the 'Reykjavik of the South'), this identity was eventually taken up in city place-marketing (partly spurred on by the success of its rival Glasgow in this).[8]

This new image in the new context of globalisa-tion slowly began to take hold in the city, with the impact in built environment as described in Chapter 9.[9] This was eventually reflected in the change of local politics, identified in Chapter 8, which in its initial swing to the left led to the image epitomised by 'Edingrad'. However, the general neo-liberal economic climate led to political prag-matism, and the city began to compete in the inter-national global market place, as documented in Chapter 10. This entailed promoting a wider con-sensus around a new city image to be marketed – and was focused through a campaign in 1987 to this end entitled 'Count me in' targeted at civic involvement, which led to a council-led seminar on a 'Vision for Edinburgh'. However, in practice, popular involvement was limited, and the even-tual Edinburgh Vision (1990) was a joint public–private statement of city boosterism and eventu-ally the creation of Edinburgh Marketing.[10]

The resurgence of urban-based service functions in economic importance is also linked in Edinburgh's case to the resurgence of (some) state functions as the national capital. Although based on a significant international economic foundation for financial services, this small national capital needs to be seen realistically in the context of the city in a wider, but distant, Europe and as a nodal regional service-provider. As the European 'fortress' is slowly consolidated and macro-regional trading blocks begin to assume forms of global regulation which international governance has failed to provide, the role of the Edinburgh city-region in the European enclave is arguably what will be as important in future as the direct capture of volatile global capital and tourism has been in recent period. What are the future scenarios in this context?

Future scenarios

Edinburgh entered the new millennium as one of the UK's urban success stories. It was experiencing demographic and household growth through in-migration of a youthful workforce. Claimant unemployment was well below the national average. With 15 per cent of Scotland's population, Edinburgh accounted for 20 per cent of the GDP.[11] On top of all this, it had regained something of its capital-city status through the Scottish Parliament. The main problems in fact were problems of growth and success, most notably a shortage of attractive affordable housing[12] and increasing traffic congestion. Given all these favourable circumstances, it is easy to write one scenario in which Edinburgh slips back into the kind of intro-verted smugness that characterised so much of the city's approach to urban development in the mid-20th century. In the 1980s, internal political conflict and the ascendancy of Glasgow in city-marketing had shaken traditional Edinburgh. In particular, the announcement that Glasgow was to be European City of Culture for 1990 was met with undisguised disbelief in the capital. The successes of the 1990s included bettering Glasgow on a couple of occasions – scuppering plans to relocate Scotland's national art gallery to the west, and then thwarting Glasgow's efforts to house the par-liament or even to be its temporary home. In the 'Edingrad' of the mid-1980s, such tussles could well have had different outcomes.

What dynamics of governance and spatial change could propel Edinburgh back into atavis-tic, torpid self-admiration, once more the self-congratulating 'Athens of the North'? How would the city actually develop in such a scenario? There are dynamics within the way that urban develop-ment is now organised that are likely to create divided, inward-looking cities, based on 'closed networks'. Graham and Marvin (2001) argue that the 'unbundling' of infrastructure from the 'modern infrastructural ideal' of universal and standardised provision organised through central state bodies has profound implications for the way in which places are organised and will compete in future. Competition forces firms to invent ways to add value to their product by creating premium services that offer the capacity to bypass the con-gestion and spaces of general user linkages. Gated communities, private or toll roads, digital net-works that bypass low-income areas, and private-school provision (in Edinburgh, one child in four attends these) are examples of how space is appro-priated and controlled in an exclusionary manner. How do current development-policy options relate to this 'closed-network' scenario for the future of Edinburgh?

The two major urban-development issues in the city at the time of writing – affordable housing and transport – have clear implications for this infra-structure and equity issue.[13] An inward-looking and complacent scenario would see Edinburgh residents so beholden to rising property values that they actively oppose affordable housing pro-vision within the city. Remaining areas of social housing, already showing signs of senility, would be demolished and redeveloped for housing at market prices. Such developments would largely be medium to high-density, a success for the compact-city policy, and sold or rented to young upwardly mobile households or to elderly Edinburgh property-owners trading down to fund their old age. Those unable to afford Edinburgh prices, but needing to access employment in the city, would increasingly have to travel across the city boundary. This is in some ways what has been happening for the past decade as the search for living space has pushed many lower-income family households further and further out of the city, initially to places like Penicuik, Loanhead or Lasswade in Midlothian, then to the former mining towns like Tranent to the east, or to the eastern settlements in West Lothian. Subsequently, the extension of commuting across the Forth and from Falkirk and the Borders has become increas-ingly marked. This feeds the growing problems of transport and related congestion. Those driving into Edinburgh at peak hours from the outlying hinterland will be those who will feel the most negative financial and social impacts of the pro-posed congestion charges, whatever the environ-mental benefits to the city itself.

Recent research shows that there is no doubt that

the dispersal of growth across the green belt has exacerbated the problems of car-based journeys to work and traffic congestion, although it is perhaps an inevitable factor requiring better management.[14] Both affordable housing and congestion are closely tied to policy in relation to the green belt. Edinburgh has had a green belt as a key feature of its planning policy since the 1950s, though in practice the area has not been sacrosanct from development in the way that many lay people perceive of its image. The policy has sought to protect the landscape setting of the city, to prevent coalescence with other settlements and encroachment on agricultural land. The identity of Edinburgh today as a contained, free-standing city owes much to this planning policy. However, there is a price attached. Uneasy relations between the City Council and the local authorities that border Edinburgh are likely to be exacerbated as these landward authorities are increasingly expected to provide the land and infrastructure to accommodate Edinburgh's working population, yet they do not benefit so directly from the economic development created by their jobs. Part of the house-price problem in the city (but only part of it) can be attributed to the green-belt restrictions on the supply of land for development.

In summary, in this scenario, Edinburgh remains a contained, free-standing city but becomes an increasingly fragmented city in which movement through the historic centre is on a pay-as-you-go basis, with the main users being tourists and high-income residents – in other words, a city-scale partially 'closed network'. Vitality will increasingly drain to and beyond the edge of the city to locations offering more accessible and cheaper sites from which companies can obtain premium transport links to the airport, avoiding the delays on normal routes. If social tensions rise, then, as well as gated communities, there might be areas to which those seen as posing threats to the rest of Edinburgh are confined, using devices such as electronic tagging to enforce surveillance. Such an Edinburgh would fail. It would have an economic problem and – inevitably – an image problem. Jensen-Butler (1999) sees a polarised income distribution within a city as making it difficult to attract

growth industries and key personnel. It can be reasonably argued that the development of Edinburgh in the period since the late 1980s has recognised that, to be competitive, the city needs to be outward-looking *but also inclusive*. What might this scenario look like?

Paradoxically, a key starting point is a need to deconstruct the existing understanding of Edinburgh as a free-standing city defined by local government boundaries. In functional terms, and certainly in a European spatial context, Edinburgh has long since been a much more extensive entity than that. This recognition underpinned the notion that it was a city-region, an idea expressed administratively by the late but little-lamented Lothian Regional Council (1975–96). The city-region idea has lived on through the Structure Plan and in the political coda to the Cities Review (2003), in which the Scottish Executive gave money to Edinburgh (and the other cities) but required that the spending of it be agreed with other authorities in the city-region. The sentiments were worthy, but the thinking looked distinctly jaded – or constrained by an impending election. The centripetal city-region, whether as elected council or informal co-operation, is not the way forward. It is a 20th-century concept based on the city centre as the point of maximum accessibility and the nation-state as the overarching administrative unit (within which city-regions can be neatly encapsulated). It is no coincidence that the local-government re-organisation in 1975 produced city-regions at the high-water point of Scottish corporatism. The city-region is also a concept that planners feel comfortable with, especially Scottish planners who can trace it back to the Geddesian legacy.

The forward-looking scenario for Edinburgh thus embraces the recognition that the city today is functionally more extensive than its existing administrative boundaries, but eschews the notion of a reinvented city-region system of governance. Instead, it recognises the reality that the key transactions and decisions that will drive the city forward are interscalar, disparate, even chaotic in character, since the degree of public-sector control has been so reduced and the private sphere so increased. During the 1990s, it became increasingly apparent that the comparators for Edinburgh were a list of other medium-sized European cities, and not just Glasgow. A decade on, with the enlargement of the European Union, Edinburgh's position in Europe has become even more peripheral, despite the city's successes. The European Spatial Development Perspective and European policy for territorial cohesion have sought to foster polycentric networks of peripheral cities as a means of increasing and spreading growth beyond the pentagon defined by London, Paris, Munich, Milan and Hamburg, which dominates the development of the European Union. The prospects for creating new 'zones of economic integration' outside this core area have concentrated on the Copenhagen–Malmö 'Øresund' region and on the arc on which the two key nodes are Barcelona and Marseilles.

Locating Edinburgh on this European canvas would reveal that the city alone is simply too small, too peripheral and too disconnected from main European transport networks to be a significant player. However, it would also provide pointers for a scenario based on the key European ideas of competitiveness, cohesion and sustainable development, as set out in the European Spatial Development Perspective. The scenario might be sketched as follows. Through multiple dialogues with other local authorities, the Scottish Parliament, the Regional Assembly for the North-East of England, and the European Commission (to mention the main ones), Edinburgh participates in a spatial development strategy. That strategy sees Edinburgh as a key node on a polycentric network of centres from Glasgow (and points beyond), through the central belt, and with links extending to Newcastle (and beyond) and to Dundee (and beyond), and with strengthened links across to the growing Øresund region. Transport infrastructure improvements pin the network together, but there are also telecommunications networks that are the equal of any in Europe. The strategy includes some measure of complementarity in terms of key services and facilities – co-operation, for example, to stage major sporting or cultural events at different stadia or other venues. Complementarity would also extend to the smaller settlements which are themselves part of local polycentric systems (e.g. West Lothian and North Lanarkshire towns working together, bridging Scotland's historic east–west divide).

This 'open-network' concept is fundamentally different from the 'closed-network' concept and would also imply a development-corridor approach to growth-management – in other words, instead of containment and separation there would be planned extensions of the city along routes that could be served effectively by public transport. This would imply adaptation of the green belt (notably in the west and east) into a system of green wedges. A similar corridor development would be possible along the waterfront from Cramond to Musselburgh. In essence, the scenario would involve spatial policy choices aiming to increasing access and choice within the city and through the city's extended connections. It would tackle the problems of congestion and exclusion by creating a spatial form better suited to absorbing and managing growth. Essentially, it would be based on corridors and linkages as opposed to containment and concentration. In terms of an identity, this scenario would be outward-looking and would refer to the growing importance of a European context. As such, it would stress Edinburgh as the 'North of Athens' – part of a European-wide system of settlements that through their diversity and networking learn from each other and are open to a plethora of creative juxtapositions and cross-currents of people and ideas – in contrast to the retrospective yearning to be seen as a small, contained 'Athens of the North', inevitably doomed to élitism and decline.

Summary and conclusions

Firstly, in the international context, while Edinburgh has managed to capture some global economic functions, these are largely due to the historical base of these (generally financial-services providers) in the city. In European terms, the city is well outside the core regions, and the reality for the North Sea as a European macro-region is one of continued peripherality in European global economic consolidation, despite attempts to the contrary. Economic integration within Europe and the basis which this provides for global economic activity is to a great extent dependent on large population catchments (internal markets) and essential fast transport networks to other key nodes. Despite the European promotion of multi-nodal development, this is more realistically a socially orientated redistributive mechanism rather than a real opportunity to integrate peripheral regions into the global competitive economy. In this, the trend in the city to limited new forms of economic development is worrying: there are already signs of capital flight, with Edinburgh as the east end of 'Silicon Glen' now receding and even phone centres migrating. For now, financial services and the cultural economic base still remain strong; but realistically these will continue to be under constant threat and erosion by changes in the global economic structure and with the advent of other forms of competing global tourism and cultural marketing. In the longer term, the basis of the city as a regional provider of services may well be its dominant function – and here the exclusivity of this role is questionable.

In the regional context, Edinburgh in fact can no longer be considered on a stand-alone basis as its city-region grows to be as important as the bounded city in functional terms. Here, the role and impact of lateral constraint – that is, the green belt – is of prime importance, as is the current trend to the peripheral location of major state investment (if mainly through public–private forms). Essentially, the compact and focused place identity of the city is not possible to retain in the medium to long term. The main approach to Glasgow's socio-economic and physical development in the second half of the 20th century was peripheral and regional in focus but is increasingly becoming urban-regeneration-focused. While Edinburgh has had a much more contained development focus, the effect of this in terms of residential location and workplaces has been much more centralised. The region is now lobbying for more economic development, while the housing market has long since leapfrogged the green belt. Whether the large-scale regeneration projects now under way in Edinburgh can continue to capture sufficient demand or whether this demand is inevitably

regional in dispersion is a moot point. Either way, there have been increasing calls for a clear central-belt development policy which is closer to the European image of the 'open-network' than the 'closed-network' city.

Turning to the internal context, again the effect of enclosure in pricing younger and more mobile populations out into the region carries the danger in the medium/long term of contributing strongly to a change of identity and the resulting impact on city image. If the city is to attract a wide range of dynamic residents/workers, there is a need for creative reinvention of the city's identity to attract this. The change in emphasis to highlight master-planned areas of redevelopment and for new development to be residential as much as services and employment is a step in the right direction; however, the nature of what form of residential environment – and at what prices – will be on offer is as yet not clear. Effectively, there needs to be a massive supply of housing options which can bring down prices and attract back the population groups who are currently forced out; but whether this will be permitted by the status quo in the housing market, or by the regional local authorities who stand to gain or lose in this, is a key question. In all of this, there is a key issue of how the built fabric provided for previous socio-economic needs will be adapted – and the pressures on this. There is a renewed threat to the survival of the New Town with oversupply of office space elsewhere, for instance, yet the costs of transforming this to residential in current market conditions rule this out as highly unlikely.

Here, the role of the conservation lobby is crucial: the question raised in Chapter 9 is what should be preserved and/or conserved. Who decides the relative value of the built environment in this, or new project-development? As touched on in Chapter 9, there is a need to widen social inclusion in the formation of this form of physical as well as socio-economic vision for the city in future. The limited investment in public visioning in Edinburgh to date is a marked lacuna, compared with various other European cities (the UK included; see Hague and Jenkins 2004 for examples). Recently, the city has taken a few initiatives again in this direction. It has appointed the architect-planner Terry Farrell as the honorary City Design Champion, who in his initial comments on this new role has focused on four key themes: maintaining the compact city, making the city more pedestrian-focused, reusing the waterfront and developing a shared vision for the future – residents, workers and visitors. The key city-vision words are 'tolerant and safe, creative and connected', with a focus on the future as much as on the past.

These are more clearly expressed in the City Council's recently published 'future scenarios' report for public feedback, which presents best- and worst-case scenarios for the city in twenty years' time.[15] The worst-case scenario (entitled 'capital punishment') includes a decline driven partly by demographic downturn and reduced economic vitality, especially new-venture development, and inward-looking European isolation. The implied solutions include opening up to inward immigration from Europe and increased economic links with emerging economies worldwide, together with rationalised planning and transportation in the city-region and across the central belt. The best-case scenario (entitled 'capital gains') is based on outward-looking European engagement, also expressed in a vibrant, more widely inclusive city-region – both economically and physically integrated through strategic infrastructure such as high-speed public transport. Here, Edinburgh is no longer seen as the capital of Scotland but as positioning itself as the 'the capital of northern Europe' – truly North of Athens – and competing as a new world city in financial services, health and education industries, culture and recreation, and even international organisation headquarters, with a buoyant immigration policy underpinning its labour base and pushing the greater city population to over one million.

This chapter argues that it is not just *what* the city defines as its key challenges for the future that matters, it is *how* the city approaches these challenges in remaking itself (physically, socially and economically) that is the key. Who decides, and how this takes place, will be intimately linked with cultural issues of how the image and identity of the city are constructed – by the main 'stakeholders'

in the city as much as by the deliberate image-marketeers. We would argue that the city *must* engage with a wider group of these stakeholders to best define this, as otherwise the identity will continue to be élitist – as arguably the conservation and design lobbies have been to date in the built environment.

There is an urgency about this form of visioning and public engagement which is brought about by the rapidly changing economic circumstances, but also by the forthcoming development of large and significant parts of the city's fabric, as noted in Chapter 9. The Waterfront and the Southeast Wedge are important cases, as are the various smaller urban-regeneration schemes, such as the opportunity created by the relocation of the Royal Infirmary. Not only do we argue for a more informed and open debate on options for the future of the city and its key physical rejuvenation, but also there is a need for an effective and wide-ranging discussion on the mechanisms of assessing and promoting innovation in the built environment – especially the relationship between design and the social, economic and technical basis for this.

The current processes for such assessment and/or promotion are often seen as too limited, by the built-environment design professions, and also by the wider population. Planners thus need to understand design better; and architects and other built-environment designers also need to understand planning better. However, both need to engage more effectively with the general public and other 'stakeholders', and not only the key lobbyist groups. Here, there is a key role for education, with more grounded and interdisciplinary education at higher-education level for professionals and other actors in producing/conserving the built-environment, but also at school level in appreciating what built environment design is and how we approach this. This, however, is an area that the concluding chapter will address more fully.

Notes

1. C. Hague and P. Jenkins, *Place Identity, Participation and Planning* (London, 2004).
2. A clear reference to this was made in the Scottish Executive's declarations of the need for economic

migrants, given national population change: see the article by Hague entitled 'We need them but do they need us?' in the *Edinburgh Evening News*, February 26 2004. In fact, the city's population is diversifying, with the proportion of Edinburgh residents born outside of Scotland doubling in the past thirty years – as reported in an article by Hazel Morrison entitled 'Changing face of life in our capital' in the *Edinburgh Evening News*, 10 September 2004.

3. The current concept of globalisation is that generally related to the recent trend for more rapid social and economic integration worldwide permitted by cheaper air travel and information technology – moving funds, people and commodities more easily across the globe. However, we argue here that globalisation as represented in such global movements and levels of integration is not new; only the speed and ease with which this happens is new (and obviously the technologies which permit this). The use of the term here, however, is admittedly still somewhat Eurocentric, as other worldviews would perhaps define different waves of globalisation.

4. An anonymous pamphlet published in 1752, prompted by Lord Provost Drummond, considered: 'If the parliament house, the churches, and a few hospitals be excepted, what other have we to boast of? There is no exchange for our merchants; no safe repository for our public and private records; no place of meeting for our magistrates and town inspection of trade . . . Edinburgh, which ought to have set the first example of industry and improvement, is the last of our trading cities that has shook off the unaccountable supineness which has so long and fatally depressed the spirit of this nation' (quoted in C. Hague, 'Edinburgh: Re-structuring of place and image' (Edinburgh, 1993)).

5. Lord Cockburn was an early champion of the city's urban quality, declaring in 1835: 'The town council approved of a report by a committee suggesting projects for the introduction of manufacture into Edinburgh! . . . But all sane persons can see that the idea of forcing such a thing is absurd, and that, if left to itself, Nature has too much sense to tolerate such an abomination in such a place . . . We must survive in better grounds, on our advantages as the metropolis, our adaptation for education, our literary fame, and especially on the glories of our external position and features, improved by the bluish smoke of human habitation, and undimmed by the black, dirty clouds of manufacture, the absence of which is one of the principal charms of our situation' (quoted in Hague, 'Edinburgh: Re-structuring').

6. Muriel Spark captured some of the ambience of inter-war Edinburgh: 'It is not to be supposed that Miss Brodie was unique . . . There were legions of her kind during the 1930s . . . the vigorous daughters of dead or enfeebled merchants, of ministers of religion, of University professors, doctors, big warehouse owners of the past, or the owners of fisheries who had endowed their daughters with shrewd wit, high-coloured cheeks, constitutions like horses, logical educations, hearty spirits and private means' (quoted in Hague, 'Edinburgh: Re-structuring').

7. Edwin Muir, in his *Scottish Journey* (London, 1935), observed: 'In spite of its proud display, then, Edinburgh cannot hide away its unemployed or its poor. Yet it is a city which must keep up appearances, there are certain rules which it does not like to see broken. It accepts the unemployed groups in the Canongate without visible annoyance; but when about a year ago a procession of the unemployed stopped in the town on their way to London, and slept for the night in Princes Street Gardens there was general indignation . . .'

8. Glasgow's success in place-marketing reached a new high with its being the location for the 1988 Garden Festival, when Mr Happy was painted on the gas towers near the entrance to the city from Edinburgh, indicating that 'Glasgow's Miles Better'. Edinburgh retaliated – after getting over its complacency and shock – by producing car stickers that indicated: 'Edinburgh's Slightly Superior'.

9. In 1986, *The Observer* called Edinburgh 'an evidently majestically capital city built for a purpose which has faded away'.

10. The extent of the social, economic and cultural polarisation is perhaps epitomised in this period by the parallel regeneration of Leith at a time when this was the supposed backdrop for the iconic film of drug-addicted nihilism, *Trainspotting* (1996).

11. See Scottish Executive, *Review of Scotland's Cities: The Analysis* (Edinburgh, 2002).

12. The Bank of Scotland's inaugural first-time house-buyer review listed Edinburgh as the least affordable urban area in Scotland. BBC website, 6 March 2004: http://news.bba.co.uk/1/hi/scotland/35381 69.stm

13. Ed Glaeser, professor of economics at Harvard University, has indicated that he considers action in support of socially isolated and poorer residents, promotion of new housing, transport management and

attracting new investment and skilled workers to be the four main challenges to the city. While the city has a strong track record and potential for the last of these, and the market is gearing up to deal with middle-income housing provision (including lobbying against planning regulation), we focus specifically here on affordable housing and transport-related issues which are less likely to be market-driven in response. E. L. Gleaser, *Four Challenges for Scotland's Cities* (Glasgow, 2004).

14. See Scottish Executive, *Review of Scotland's Cities*.

15. This report came out just before this book went to press and was prepared by group of experts under the direction of a Steering Group and an Advisory Panel, all including a wide range of professionals representing the private and public sectors. In all, some eighty individuals were interviewed, again focusing on private- and public-sector leaders, with some higher-education, religious, media and professional leaders – considered 'the most influential' in the city and country. This report was disseminated as the basis for a conference in spring 2004 on the Edinburgh City Region in the 21st century.

Conclusion: learning from history

BRIAN EDWARDS AND PAUL JENKINS

Although structured in a chronological sequence, this book has sought also to highlight certain thematic strands. The book argues that Edinburgh is a special city, unique in the UK, because of its beauty and the enduring care taken over its husbandry (or what today we would call urban management), and that much can be learnt from analysis of why and how this has taken place. Certain themes were identified at the outset, and the various chapters permit these to be explored in different ways and in a variety of contexts. We return to these themes more explicitly in this Conclusion, as we believe it is through structured analysis that the book can contribute in a collaborative way to answering the key research questions.

The main themes which the authors identified as important can be summarised as a series of questions:

- Has the role of the city as a capital been significant in its development?
- What has been the importance of urban design in the overall development of the city?
- How has the unique blend of space, landscape and topography influenced the city's growth and form?
- How important have the concepts of urban ecology and public action been?
- What has been the relationship between creativity, innovation, conservation, regeneration and sustainability?
- In juxtaposing physical analysis with social, economic, political and cultural analysis, can the relative roles of 'structure' and 'agency' be better understood?
- What can we learn from the wider historical analysis of Edinburgh, especially in terms of governance issues?

This chapter summarises responses to these research questions, drawing on the themes addressed in the various chapters in the book as follows.

Edinburgh, a capital on the world stage

There has been a recurring interest in the importance for Edinburgh of being a capital city even after its formal relegation, after the Act of Union in 1707, to a regional political centre for North Britain. The sense of being a capital city was clearly the motive behind a variety of civic improvements including the construction of new approach roads and bridges, the building of new public institutions and the remaking of the Old Town as well as the making of the New Town and its successive expansions. The continuing unique nature of Scots law, religion, culture and education was an essential element for the continuing strength of a national identity, and the capital played an important role in this. Being a capital has given Edinburgh the chance both to compete on the European stage and to outshine London, its prime UK rival in terms of architectural prestige, and thus to become more easily compared on the stage of world-renowned cities.

In relation to international urban benchmarks, one could argue that the history of Edinburgh has been that of continual embedding of European values at the expense of British ones. This finds its expression in the Renaissance footprint of the Old Town (see Chapters 1 and 2) and the largely French, Dutch and Italian-inspired mansion houses and public buildings which dotted the Royal Mile. Even the New Town outshines anything in Bath or London; and, as Chapter 2 suggests, there are parallels with Lisbon and other European capital cities. It was largely the adoption of often European-inspired Enlightenment values which led Edinburgh in the 18th century to excel in medicine, science, economics and architecture. The New Town and its later public institutions, from art galleries to churches, display the heroic ambition of Greek culture. The Hellenist principles suited well a city intent upon remaking itself as a European capital. And, as a European centre of learning, the symbiotic relationship between the Town Council, the University (of Edinburgh) and legal, religious and educational institutions helped forge an identity in spite of the growing economic muscle of Glasgow and the migration of some of Edinburgh's wealth to London. Irrespective of the shortcomings discussed in Chapter 3, the New Town is the urban embodiment of European enlightenment values.

If being a capital city mattered, Edinburgh has also seen much competitive remaking in its 1,000 years of existence. The early urban foundations of the burghs of Edinburgh and Canongate established the kind of rivalry which then found expression in the competition between the New and Old Towns, and later still between growth in the city centre and expansion at the city edge (where Glasgow is the most common comparison, as noted in Chapter 7). Perhaps it is in the competitive cultural realm that the city has most defined itself – internationally as well as nationally (i.e. Scotland and Britain) – through its post-war development as an early Festival City. The international self-consciousness of being a capital on a world stage has been evidenced in Edinburgh's perpetual internal renaissances and has been the motor for much well-directed urban change. Chapter 11 argues, however, that while internationally recognised, the city must not become complacent in the increasingly competitive global urban networks (explored also in Chapter 10). As such, realistic re-evaluation of the relationship between the city and its region, as well as its role as national capital, need to be seen in the light of its changing function in Europe and internationally.

Embedding design into the culture of the city

The sense that design has always mattered to Edinburgh and has been used to competitively foster its position as a capital city suggests that Edinburgh has taken an unusually active interest in its own self-image. Well before Sir Walter Scott campaigned to save the Old Town from the visual violation of a railway station on its doorstep, the city was active in adapting its image self-consciously. The main agency for this was the Dean of Guild Court, whose powers from 1660 to 1975 gradually extended from street repairs to fire protection, and from building consent to public sanitation. Under the enlightened influence of three centuries of Dean of Guild Courts, streets were made more regular with uniform façades, stone was universally employed for construction, public buildings were given prime sites or cleared of later encumbrances, and building heights were maintained (mainly at four storeys) so that the city's distinctive topography and skyline were preserved. Although public health and safety were key motivations for action, Edinburgh – like Paris under Baron Haussmann – used sanitation to create civic order and beauty. Though some like John Ruskin complained of the visual monotony of over-regulation, Edinburgh matured into a handsome city of fine streets, squares, public monuments and bridges.

Image was also a concern of the powerful property-owning trusts and private landowners, and amenity was valued. Whether it was action by the Heriot's Trustees or the Moray Estates, the city employed a combination of feuing plans (local master plans) and conditions attached to development to create public amenity and private financial gain. These master plans regulated the massing of buildings and their height, use and finish. They also established a planned relationship between architecture and landscape, and between private buildings and public space. For most developers between 1800 and 1920, dressed stone was universally required of the individual builders who constructed houses (or more usually tenements) on the plots, as well as twelve-pane sash windows and raised surrounds at window and door openings. The eaves and cornices were lined up to ensure the long parallel perspectives so typical of Edinburgh. Added to this, under the Burgh Police Act of 1862, development could not be higher than the width of streets, creating cubes of space along the typical Edinburgh street. The proportional consistency between one area of Edinburgh and the next is the result of spatial regulation. The orchestration of streets, parks and squares, so enjoyable today in their maturity, stems from the synchronising of private master plans by an enlightened City Council. Where image mattered most, as in the smarter areas of the New Town or the western suburbs, these elaborate master plans were prepared by some of Scotland's major architects such as Robert Adam, James Gillespie Graham and Rowand Anderson.

Few other European cities could boast such a concern for public amenity and such an abundance of local talent; and, though some of the picturesque effects enjoyed today were perhaps happy accidents, trusts, individuals and the Town Council played an important part in shaping the image of the city enjoyed today. This concern for image and design finds expression today in the sometimes shocking and challenging new architecture dotted around the city. Design has thus played a pivotal role, whether expressed in urban areas (such as the Richard Meier-planned Edinburgh Park), landscape, buildings or interiors. More than any other city in the UK, Edinburgh has used the skills of countless designers to add value to the process of change. One has only to walk through Princes Street Gardens, to visit the William Playfair-designed library in the Old College, to sit in the City Council Chamber, or view Robert Lorimer's Thistle Chapel at St Giles' Cathedral, to witness this power of design and its fundamental role in forming the city's character. As such, there is a need to take stock of the city's indebtedness to its design culture. The added value of design is evident across the city (though there are exceptions), and it has accumulated an inheritance of buildings and landscapes second to none.

Edinburgh continues to be a place of architectural contrasts: beautifully preserved historic quarters and lively, dynamic new ones. It says a great deal for Edinburgh that old and new co-exist – that present-day developers have the courage to commission brave new designers, and that the city fathers have the wisdom to grant development consent. Creativity has been a core value in the making of Edinburgh; and, though sometimes

FIGURE C.1   Edinburgh is both a festive city and, for three weeks of the year, a festival city. Edinburgh Festival has done much to promote the capital on the world stage. *Brian Edwards*

socially conservative, it is rarely so culturally. The vitality of the city and its reputation as a European capital in the widest sense requires the avant-garde to co-exist alongside the best of the past. Putting aside the difficult balance between conservation and physical renewal, there remain the cultural, social and economic benefits which have flowed from an investment in design stretching back for nearly a millennium. Edinburgh is a city of cultural industries and cultural institutions. Art and design play a big part in the chemistry which holds the city together and gives it identity. Buildings and iconic streets like the Royal Mile and Princes Street may have their function, but it is their cultural meaning which is really important. Only recently have these qualities been rediscovered, however, and there is

FIGURE C.2   The design of Edinburgh Park to the west of the city, to designs in 1990 by Richard Meier and Partners, respects the tradition in Edinburgh of tree-lined urban blocks and distinctive public buildings. Most architects have learnt to reach an accommodation with the capital's urban character both at the edge of the city and in the centre. *Jock Pottle/Esto-Richard Meier and Partners*

still a need to embed design more fundamentally in the day-to-day processes of planning and building, which arguably goes beyond the signature master plan or appointment of a design champion to the City Council.

Topography, landscape and memory

Edinburgh is exceptionally lucky in its location. With a combination of hills and deep valleys close at hand, views of distant mountains and the silver-blue Firth of Forth beyond, its landscape provides a wonderful setting for a city. Like Stockholm, one feels the presence of nature and wilderness even in the heart of the city. Characteristically, however, it is the designs of man that have added to the pictu-resque scene, with the irregular outline of the castle set quaintly on the volcanic plug in the centre, and the striking skyline of the Old Town

preserved as a historic prospect to view from Princes Street. Man and nature have long enjoyed a reciprocal relationship in the city, personified by Princes Street Gardens in the centre, Holyrood Park and Calton Hill to the east, the Royal Botanic Garden to the north, the valley of the Water of Leith to the west, and the Meadows to the south. Except in London with its central parks, it is hard to find a better city in Europe where landscape, topography and nature have been dealt with so well by man. Even the bridges which cross the river valleys in the city, and those further afield which span the wide estuary of the Firth of Forth, do so with an impressive sense of occasion. In this, one should not forget the power of engineers to help make the image of Edinburgh.

It is not, however, just the way in which urban growth has respected Edinburgh's spectacular

FIGURE C.3   Terry Farrell and Partners' design of the Edinburgh International Conference Centre (1994) strikes a balance between innovation and conservation, allowing urban renewal to reinforce the city's identity rather than undermine it.   *Terry Farrell and Partners*

setting, it is also the way in which urban and landscape-designers have brought the picturesque assets into view. The monument and memory-littered skyline of Calton Hill terminates the view east along Princes Street and northwards up Leith Walk. The view of the castle is framed by the parallel sides of Castle Street, and the Firth by Forth Street. The High Street itself is a Royal Mile of picturesque vistas: an unfolding sequence of distant and closer views, of green hills and blue sea. It is as if the growth of the city was planned to exploit the assets of nature and landscape on the one hand and to preserve the memory of earlier occupation on the other.

In reality, the vistas were created by architects and politicians who cared for the city. Scott and Robert Louis Stevenson helped create a mood which favoured the conservation of landscape and buildings. A generation later, Patrick Geddes exploited the mood with a collection of new buildings in the Old Town based upon his principle of 'conservative surgery'. The early establishment of a school of landscape design in the city has helped to perpetrate this skilful treatment of urban open space. The city in fact has a rich complement of both private and public open spaces, some highly structured, others picturesque. These have long been seen as urban assets beyond their use value, although the replication of these in the outer areas of the city has been less successful, and there are lessons to be learned here for future provision. Crucial to this is ensuring that new generations of increasingly diverse users have access to and revel in the landscaped spaces which the city provides.

Urban ecology and public action

Patrick Geddes forged an unlikely fusion of social reform, educational enlightenment and physical change which, in its innate conservatism, is the essence of the Edinburgh mood. He restored old buildings, created gardens, built new dwellings in the Old Scottish style, and provided accommodation for students and professors right in the heart of the city. His vision, important again today, was of a marriage of social, political and ecological principles. The Old Town was not just a test-bed for radical ideas at the end of the 19th century, it also established a climate in Edinburgh in favour of conserving the best of the past. It was a legacy which Edinburgh, unlike Glasgow and most UK cities, learnt to cherish in the 20th century. Geddes helped foster an environment in favour of high urban densities, of a relationship between city and region, of mixed-class reoccupation of run-down historic areas, and of building in sympathy with nature. In this, he was helped in the later years by his son-in-law Sir Frank Mears, who, besides teaching at Edinburgh College of Art, became a pioneer of government-led town-planning. In this capacity, he helped shape the suburbs of Edinburgh, creating at Edinburgh Zoo the first zoological gardens where animals were housed in habitats rather than cages. A baton-carrier for Geddes, he influenced a generation of architects and planners who played an important role in the design of Edinburgh before and after the Second World War. Among their number were Robert Hurd and Robert Matthew (of RMJM), who helped establish the New Town Conservation Committee in 1968, and Basil Spence, whose mark is found in the Canongate flats in the Royal Mile and the redevelopment of George Square. What these architects had in common with Geddes was the fusion of old and new, a concern to be modern but also sympathetic to the values of Edinburgh's past.

One of the aspects of Geddes' innovative urban ecological approach was that of public action; and this has been evidenced in the city in various ways, starting with the Victorian voluntary associations which played such an important role in establishing public-welfare issues in relation to the built environment, such as sanitary and building controls. These later lobbied for planning and public-housing provision. The relationship of society to the built environment is always embedded within the governance structures of the period; and, after its Victorian élite patron phase, with its voluntary associations, this became expressed in the more structured corporate organisation of municipal government for a substantial period of the city's history. However, it was the defence of the historic built environment that led to a resurgence of direct civil-society activity in the city in the mid-20th century, as Chapter 9 demonstrates. This peak again declined in the 1970s and 1980s, as public action became institutionalised and professionalised, and then in the 1990s became submerged under the emerging forms of entrepreneurial municipal action. The result has been a gradual erosion not only of public action but also of public interest and evaluation of the city's urban heritage, which has led to greater apathy, with public interest usually only surfacing negatively. The success of the city's built environment, and its urban position internationally, depended on public action in the past, and arguably needs to do so more explicitly in the future as the city faces difficult choices for its development. However, today this unique relation between urban ecology and public action needs to be embedded within the more open governance structures of contemporary democracy and social diversity. Here (as argued in Chapter 11), the city can learn from a number of European cities which have developed innovative programmes to engage the public in defining the future of the city, thus permitting new expressions of Geddes' concepts at the time of his centenary.

A sustained city, or a model of sustainable development?

The survival of Edinburgh as a civilised, culturally rich, socially diverse and visually enriching city tells us something about the modern concept of sustainable development. The city has sustained itself and its natural resources by a combination of good governance, public action, enlightened patronage, respect for nature and a willingness to

FIGURE C.4   Tourism has helped regenerate sites in the inner city, as here in the Grassmarket, where a former university computer building was converted to the Apex Hotel in 1994. Re-use of buildings is a theme increasingly common as the city develops as a World Heritage Site. *Brian Edwards*

FIGURE C.5   Compaction and building height give Edinburgh the qualities of a European city rather than a British one.   *Brian Edwards*

invest in design for the common good. In this, one should not underestimate the importance of the Dean of Guild Court, the influence of the university, the generosity and vision of the educational trusts, the cultural and artistic institutions like the Royal Scottish Academy, and the power of individuals from Mylne and Adam to Scott and Geddes. Sustainable development requires close relations between innovation, conservation and regeneration, and here Edinburgh has struck a better balance than Glasgow which has periodically destroyed itself, St Andrews which has become fossilised, or London which has grown too big for effective sustainable urban management.

Edinburgh remains a compact city, one where the streets are generally safe, where social contact is relatively easy and where densities are high enough to support vibrant streets of well-maintained shops and decent levels of public transport. Edinburgh is also a festival city where, for part of each year, cultural diversity adds to an already vibrant and increasingly diverse social and economic environment. Experiment and creativity are enduring characteristics of the city. Though Edinburgh has its problems of decay, there is a well-preserved and respected centre, a largely coherent urban edge, and corridors of movement which still, at least outside the rush hour, transport people and goods effectively. These qualities of sustainable urban development are a fundamental underlying message of this book, and which – with the experience of nearly 1,000 years – the city needs to reflect on and take forward to the challenges ahead.

The city, however, needs to benchmark itself internationally in measuring its ecological impact – for instance, on issues such as solid waste, environmental quality, traffic and public-transport management, and the best use of brownfield land. Wider issues such as social and economic sustainability are also of crucial concern, and here there is a need to balance international competitiveness with regional collaboration. As argued in Chapter 11, this requires a realisation that the identity of the city already goes well beyond its boundaries, and as a consequence the provision of affordable housing and improved public transport should complement the exploitation of economic development opportunities. Without this realisation, the closed, complacent city of Edinburgh will not be sustainable in the open social and economic context of today's urban world.

Acted on, or acted in?

Various chapters have shown how complex an interaction there is between the factors which act on the city as an entity, but crucially how these also depend on the actors within it. These actors include heroes and champions, not all of whom have been adequately celebrated in the past, but also the faceless members of voluntary associations, municipal employees and private-sector professionals who ensure the day-to-day functioning of the city. We should not disregard the seemingly mundane routine, as over time this has as much influence as the grand plan. Thus we argue that, although Edinburgh has its share of the famous and good who have played essential roles in directing the city's development, it also has embedded practice which has generally supported – and at times guided – this. However, the relation between innovation, which typically forges ahead through strong and charismatic figures with core support groups, and normal practice, which typically rolls along at a measured pace, are often out of synchronisation. Innovation needs to find ways to influence practice, and here the strong basis for the city in professions, educational and research institutions has

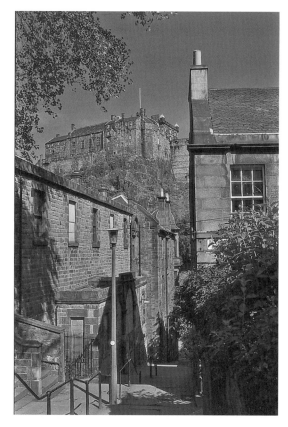

FIGURE C.6   Edinburgh's occupation of the city centre by a diversity of social classes and land uses provides an example of sustainable development for other cities in the UK. However, the city's inability to resolve its traffic and urban waste problems limits claims of sustainability. *Brian Edwards*

provided some wonderful opportunities which need to be continually taken advantage of.

In the past, the relation between 'town' and 'gown' has been important in providing both the catalytic agents and the opportunities for experimentation *in situ*. This has permitted the embedding of innovation in practice, for example through the activities of Adam Smith in the New Town and Patrick Geddes in the Old. This relationship still is in evidence to some extent, but increasingly the main actors for change in the urban environment seem to be in the boardrooms of international or national companies and in the City Chambers. While the former are probably more focused on their shareholders and the balance sheet, the latter often look to success at the next election rather than the long term. The city needs more channels for joint action between its innovative professionals and researchers and its key decision-makers, and also needs to widen the scope of its decision-making to permit more public participation in significant decisions. This is crucial if the city is to retain its sense of identity and, through this, to continue to celebrate and embellish its distinctive physical form. Various chapters illustrate how this has been acted out in the past, and thus it is hoped that the balance between being acted on by economic, social and regulatory forces external to the city, and the action of internal mechanisms for key individuals, institutions and the public to act, can underpin this balance in future.

Whose city is this?

Crucial to this balance is a clear understanding of the diverse place identities and narratives of such a complex entity as the city, and how these are formed. While key decision-makers and the media play an important role, so do those who set intellectual and professional parameters, those who implement day-to-day activities which influence the city over time, and the public which is the repository of the image and identity that are fashioned and refashioned. The city is the result of the efforts of all these actors, and to exclude some from actively participating in the making and remaking of the city can only lead to the submergence and unexpected re-emergence of conflicting identities. A primary example here would be the nature of housing form: while many appreciate the cultural, social, economic and ecological benefits of compact urban living, most aspire to the mass-produced stand-alone suburban house. The image of city living that the compact city can provide has often been devalued without any real evaluation of the alternatives – and these images are manipulated by powerful lobby groups. As Chapters 4 and 11 argue, Edinburgh needs to re-evaluate whose values should be expressed and how these values are formed. A further example is the concept of the 'green belt': we can perhaps agree

on the need for quality green space, but is the concept of containment relevant when the city spills out over the urban edge anyway? Do claimed urban and rural place identities reflect reality or even the needs of an ecological city? Apart from reflection of political and economic leaders, the professional and educational institutions of the city have a clear responsibility to provide ideas and space for discussion of the key values to be embedded in future urban form. The debates are too often simplistic and polarised, and the public has for too long been excluded from constructively engaging in these. This book has been written partly to address this shortcoming.

A creative city

There is something about Edinburgh's relative smallness and the closeness of its internal proximity that enhances its sense of creativity. The intimate size of Edinburgh and its densely packed cultural connectivity means that the city has none of the loss of individuality and humanity which has befallen large conurbations. Smallness can be a virtue when it comes to creativity, and Edinburgh's distinctive urbanity and charm attracts millions of visitors each year to the annual arts festivals. The Edinburgh Festivals are both a symbol of the city's liberal values and creative freedom and an aid in nurturing internal artistic innovation. In this sense, city form and cultural expression are closely related. In his book *Cities in Civilisation*, Peter Hall argues that the key to creative cities is the dialogue between freedom and order. The tension between private innovation, state promotion and public regulation which Hall identifies as a characteristic of creative cities in history (Athens, Florence and Paris) is well represented, as earlier chapters in this book testify, in the making of Edinburgh. Talent has been drawn to the city, and it in turn has generated the wealth to give creativity the kind of expression denied elsewhere. In this sense, the making and remaking of Edinburgh over the past millennium has established an environment which welcomed outside talent as much as it fostered its own indigenous creative bloodstream.

If Edinburgh confirms Hall's premise regarding the conditions which foster creativity, it also supports Mumford's thesis in his book *The Culture of Cities* that bigness is not a virtue when it comes to civilisation. Where Edinburgh was fortunate was in its relationship with Glasgow, which absorbed the bulk of Scotland's population growth in the 19th century while also providing the wealth necessary to support Edinburgh. Industrialisation in the west provided the manufacturing goods which Edinburgh needed at sufficient distance so as not to affect the amenity of the capital. The symbiosis between Edinburgh and Glasgow industrially and intellectually allowed Edinburgh to become the centre of culture in spite of Glasgow's more dynamic economy. There is a lesson here for the future of Edinburgh: culturally creative cities are not normally technologically innovative ones.

As this book seeks to establish, Edinburgh displays the art of living the good life. Transformation of the intellectual, economic and social fabric of the city has generally been towards achieving greater cultural richness and physical sustainability. Over time, the city has become more cosmopolitan and arguably less Scottish. It has assumed the characteristics of a European capital with an extensive web of external links; and, although it remains a centre of power and authority, the city continues to welcome outsiders. Taking a broad view of history, it has not been the intellectual or artistic insiders who have mattered most but those drawn to Edinburgh from outside. Here too, there are lessons for the institutions that guide the city.

The ebb and flow of history has served Edinburgh well. Even the 20th century, which wrought havoc to other UK cities, left Edinburgh relatively unscathed. Although roughly half of this book charts events over the past 100 years, it was the previous 100 which really mattered in forming the city that we have today. At times, wider creative forces have favoured London (as at present) and Glasgow (in the late 19th century), but generally Edinburgh has been the most innovative, artistically and intellectually. One reason for this is the presence of key institutions such as its universities and colleges and other national institutions such as the Royal Scottish Academy, College of Physicians and National Library of Scotland which have promoted experiment, enterprise and higher learning. The triangulation between impassioned individuals, social institutions and government has tended to provide a chemistry which promoted vision rather than the status quo.

Learning by doing

One key theme we have wanted to draw out through this book is that of learning from history. Contrary to the famous dictum, we do learn from history, albeit often in limited ways. This is mainly because history is conceptualised as something 'other' and far away from contemporary reality, and hence the analysis of history often becomes abstract and rarified. However, history is happening now; and, although we find it difficult to assimilate its currents until we develop some structured hindsight, ongoing reflection can influence action and outcomes.

While we obviously cannot see all the patterns that eventually might be used to structure and analyse the recent history of Edinburgh, we also need to apply historical analysis 'on the hoof', bearing in mind that we can adapt our stance as more structured analysis appears. This has been the approach embedded in this book, which has tried to cover a broad sweep from the past through to the present day. In so doing, we have attempted not only to construct an analysis of the past (and also refine previous analyses) but also to apply this approach throughout, including the more immediate period. We believe that we can learn as much from reflection on more recent experience as from historically transmitted knowledge; and, as educators, we accept that we all have relevant experience with which to do this. We do not believe that we need to first 'wipe the slate clean' for a new formative educational environment to emerge, one which draws heavily on self-discovery. Rather, we believe that self-discovery and creativity can be fostered through a critical appreciation of what we know already – even if we do not immediately realise this. Thus the reflective analysis of experience by individuals *and* society is essential if we are to avoid continually repeating the mistakes of the past. How we achieve this 'learning by doing' has a lot to do with open and inclusive debate as a form of enlightenment.

What is the relevance of this reflection for the study of how Edinburgh as a capital has continually made and remade itself? The city has a tradition of fostering self-consciousness and creativity, and this book has tried to illustrate how this has been important for its success. More than any other aspect, it is the transmission of this through society that has guided the city's development – in the actions of its political or economic leaders, its intellectual or cultural élite, professional and regulatory actors, voluntary associations and the general public. Education is one means of transmission, as is publication. Public debate and dissemination are others. Thus, even if this book is able to reach the desired audience of students, teachers, urban developers, professionals, local government and voluntary bodies, what matters most is that it stimulates ideas and debate and through this assists to develop new visions for the city. If we succeed in this, we will have had the opportunity to contribute to the further making and remaking of one of Europe's finest capital cities.

FIGURE C.7 View of Edinburgh Castle from the east end of King's Stables Road. The power of geology in shaping urban form sets Edinburgh apart from most other European cities. *Brian Edwards*

Appendix 1: Housing completions in Edinburgh, 1918–76 (see Chapter 7)

From: A. O'Carroll (1994), 'The development of owner occupation in Edinburgh', PhD thesis, Heriot-Watt University, p. 176.

	Local Authority	Private
1918–26	2,257	2,787
1927–32	4,794	5,794
1933–40	7,712	20,127
TOTAL	14,763	28,708

	LA	SSHA	Temp.	Govt/ha	Priv.
1945	148	13	37		0
1946	135	0	790		44
1947	422	0	1,184		230
1948	913	0	1,813		208
1949	971	0	76		144
1950	717	10			134
1951	749	62			105
1952	1,627	22			165
1953	1,900	84			508
1954	1,142	238			254
1955	1,711	44		312	478
1956	854	162		82	1,262
1957	1,552	120		45	531
1958	788	118		56	889
1959	1,448	0		0	670
1960	1,046	18		0	867
1961	1,649	118		37	915
1962	1,002	0		36	748
1963	1,571	0		0	522
1964	2,318	0		0	887
1965	1,751	0		61	762
1966	1,401	0		52	852
1967	2,968	0		236	641
1968	1,106	0		295	408
1969	1,710	0		20	437
1970	2,749	0		30	371
1971	1,386	0		72	657
1972	1,276	0		68	442
1973	1,201	0		107	657
1974	564	0		26	1,059
1975*	355	102		67	*
1976*	621	184		297	*

Note: Glasgow 1970: 2,587 completions – fewer than Edinburgh.

Municipal housing totals per 1,000 population (source: Tower block).

	Scotland	Edinburgh	Glasgow
1945–50:	85,478 (16.8)	3,306 (7.1)	12,965 (11.9)
1951–5:	153,834 (29.9)	7,129 (15.2)	23,006 (21.2)
1956–60:	129,482 (24.9)	5,688 (12.1)	18,635 (17.7)
1961–5:*	117,727 (22.6)	8,281 (17.5)	16,134 (16.1)
1966–70:	164,596 (31.7)	9,934 (21.4)	18,581 (20.5)
1971–5:	108,202 (20.8)	4,782 (10.7)	12,784 (15.3)

* Dundee 52.5, Lanarks 33.1

Appendix 2: Edinburgh buildings (1960–2000) by date (see Chapter 9)

Date			Location	Building	Architect
1959	Educational	Southside	Dalkeith Rd	Pollock Halls (initial)	Rowand Anderson Kininmonth & Paul
1960–3	Educational	Southside	George Sq	David Hume Tower	RMJM
1963–6	Educational	Southside	George Sq	Appleton Tower	Reiach, Hall & Part
1965–7	Educational	New Town	George Sq	University Library	Spence, Glover & Ferguson
1961	Educational	Southwest	Colinton Rd	Napier Univ	A Hutchison & Part
1961	Educational	Central south	Lauriston Place	ECA Architecture	R Cowan
1961	Commercial	New Town	St Andrew Sq	Scottish Provident, 6	Rowand Anderson Kininmonth & Paul
1961 (1790s)	Residential	West	Cramond	Cottages	Ian Lindsay & Part
1962	Commercial	New Town	St Andrew Sq	Scottish Widows, 9	Spence, Glover & Ferguson
1963	Residential	Central west	Ravelston	65–67 Ravelston Dykes	Morris & Steedman
1963 (1661)	Conservation	Central west	Orwell Place	Dalry House	R Hurd
1964	Educational	Southwest	Colinton Rd	George Watson's Music School	M Laird & Part
1964	Educational	Southside	Lauderdale St	James Gillespie's High School	Rowand Anderson Kininmonth & Paul
1964 (1814)	Public	New Town	Charlotte Sq	West Register House	MPBW Arch
1964, 1970	Commercial	New Town	St James Centre	St James Centre	Burke & Martin, Martin & Part
1964, 75	Commercial	New Town	George St	Standard Life, 3	M Laird & Part
1962–5 (16th c.)	Conservation	Central west	Stenhouse	Stenhouse, conservation centre	Ian Lindsay
1965	Recreational	North	Inverleith	New Glass House	Pearce, MoPBW & Johnson
1966	Residential	Central south	Pleasance	Carnegie Court	Ross Smith & Jamieson
1966 (1824, 59)	Recreational	New Town	Princes St	New Club, 86	Reiach
1966–73	Educational	Southside	Bristo Sq	Student Centre	Morris & Steedman
1966–8	Residential	Old Town	Canongate	79–121 Canongate	Spence, Glover & Ferguson
1967–	Educational	West	Riccarton	Heriot-Watt Univ	Reiach, Hall & Part
1967	Recreational	Southside	Dalkeith Rd	Royal Commonwealth Pool	RMJM
1967	Recreational	Southside	George Sq	Theatre	RMJM
1967	Public	South	Mortonhall	Crematorium	Spence, Glover & Ferguson
1967	Educational	Central west	Ravelston	Mary Erskine School	Rowand Anderson Kininmonth & Paul
1968	Public	Old Town	George IV Bridge	Lothian Region HQ	RMJM
1968	Educational	Southside	George Sq	Adam Ferguson Bldg	RMJM
1968	Recreational	East	London Rd	Meadowbank Sports Centre	City Architects
1968	Public	North	Telford Rd	Fire station	Bamber & Hall
1968	Medical	North	Western General Hos	Nuffield Transplantation Unit	P Wormesley
1969	Commercial	North	Fettes Ave	Christian Salvesen HQ	Morris & Steedman
1969	Residential	Central west	Ravelston	69–85 Ravelston Dykes	Roland Wedgewood Ass
1969	Commercial	New Town	St Andrew Sq	2 New St David's St	Reiach & Hall
1972	Educational	Central south	Lauriston Place	ECA Hunter Bldg	Wheeler & Sproson
1972	Commercial	West	Ravelston Terrace	Dunedin Fund Managers, 25	Roland Wedgewood Ass
1972 (1903)	Commercial	New Town	George St	Nat West Bank, 80	I Burke Ass

Date			Location	Building	Architect
1973 (1675)	Residential	Central north	Dean Village	Baxter's Granary, Bell's Brae 11–13	F R Stevenson
1973 (1805)	Residential	Central north	Dean Village	West Mill	P Cocker & Part
1974 (1790)	Commercial	New Town	George St	127 George St	R Hurd
1974	Residential	North	Dean Village	Hawthornbank House	A Wheeler
1974	Residential	West	South Gyle Gardens	Housing	Edinburgh City Arch
1975	Public	West	Ingliston	Airport Terminal	RMJM
1975	Residential	Central north	Saunders St	Housing	M Laird & Part
1976	Residential	Old Town	Canongate	1–15 Canongate	R Hurd
1976 (1888)	Commercial	New Town	Princes St	Royal Bank	Spence, Glover & Ferguson
1976	Commercial	Southside	Dalkeith Rd	Scottish Widows	Spence, Glover & Ferguson
1977	Residential	Central north	Lynedoch Place	Lynedoch House	Roland Wedgewood Ass
1978 (1807)	Commercial	Central north	Dean Village	Bell's Mills (Hilton Hotel)	Crear & Part
1978 (1823)	Recreational	Southside	Nicolson St	Queens Hall	R Hurd & Part
1978 (1912)	Commercial	New Town	George St	Bank of Scotland, 101–103	R Hurd
1978–80 (1900)	Residential	Old Town	West Port	Portsburgh Sq	T M Gray
1978–81 (1882–4)	Commercial	New Town	Princes St	Debenhams, 109–112	Simpson & Brown
1979	Residential	West	East Craigs	Linkburn	RMJM
1979	Residential	West	South Gyle Mains	Housing	R Hurd & Part
1980	Commercial	North	Dundas St	Royal Bank Computer Centre	M Laird & Part
1980	Residential	New Town	Jamaica St	Housing	P Cocker & Part
1980 (1899)	Public	Old Town	Market Street	City Art Centre	Edin District Arch
1980 (1772)	Commercial	New Town	St Andrew Sq	Buchan House, 21	Covell Matthews
1981	Residential	Southside	Argyll Park	Housing	A Campbell Mars
1981	Recreational	Southside	Bristo Sq	Bristo Sq	Johnson-Marshall & Ass
1981	Medical	Central south	Lauriston Place	Royal Infirmary extension	RMJM
1981	Residential	Southside	Nicolson St/East Crosscauseway	Housing	N Gray & Part
1981	Commercial	North	Orchard Brae	Lloyds Bowmaker	J & F Johnston
1981 (1734)	Conservation	Southside	Pleasance	Hermits & Termits	Benjamin Tindall
1981 (1760?)	Conservation	New Town	Calton Hill	Cockburn Cons Trust, 16–18	R Hurd & Part
1981, 1985	Commercial	South	Lauder Rd	Northwood House	Roland Wedgewood, B Anderson
1982 (1843)	Public	New Town	George St	Royal Society, 22–24	R Hurd & Part
1982 (1899)	Commercial	New Town	St Andrew Sq	Scottish Equitable, 28	M Laird Part
1982	Recreational	Southside	Hill Sq	Symposium Hall	J Parr & Part
1982	Residential	Southside	Nicolson St	Housing, 70–76	Moira & Wann
1983 (15th c.)	Conservation	West	Cramond	Tower	R Hurd & Part
1984 (1825)	Public	West	Belford Rd	Scottish Nat Gallery Modern Art	RMJM
1984 (1881)	Commercial	Central north	Dean Village	Bell's Brae	RMJM
1984 (1954)	Commercial	Central north	Dundas St	TSB Computer Centre	Reiach & Hall
1984	Commercial	South	Cameron Toll	Shopping Centre	M Laird & Part
1984	Commercial	Central west	Lothian Rd	Sheraton Hotel	Crerar & Part
1984	Recreational	Central west	Lothian Rd	Festival Sq	D Lovejoy & Part
1984	Commercial	New Town	Princes St	Waverley Market	Building Design Part
1984	Educational	North	Royal Victoria Hos	North Lothian School of Nursing	Harley Haddow & Part
1985	Commercial	Central west	Lothian Rd	Capital House	Hugh Martin Part
1986	Public	Old Town	High Street	Museum of Childhood	Wheeler & Sproson
1986	Medical	West	Murrayfield	Murrayfield Hospital	Gordon & Latimer
1986	Public	Central west	Tollcross	Fire Station	Lothian Region
1987	Commercial	New Town	Calton Rd	Craigwell Brewery	N Groves-Raines
1987	Recreational	West	Murrayfield	Zoo entrance & shop	Arcadia

Date			Location	Building	Architect
1987	Residential	Central south	Pleasance/ Drummond/ Roxburgh Sts	Housing	Gray Marshall & Ass
1987	Educational	West	Riccarton	Lord Balerno	A Merrylees Ass
1987	Commercial	New Town	St James Centre	John Lewis	Spence, Glover & Ferguson
1987 (1790)	Commercial	New Town	Princes St	2–4 Hope St	Stephen & Maxwell
1987–	Public	Southside	Salisbury Place	National Library ext	A Merrylees Ass
1988	Residential	Southside	Chapel St	Housing	Wann Maclaren
1988	Educational	West	Riccarton	Cameron Smail Library	A Merrylees Ass
1988	Commercial	West	South Gyle	GEC Ferranti	Bamber Gray
1988	Residential	Southwest	Yeaman Place	Housing	Reiach & Hall
1989–	Public	**Central west**	**Lothian Rd**	**The Exchange (masterplan)**	**Terry Farrell**
1989	Commercial	North	Crewe Toll	3M HQ	P Johnson-Marshall & Ass
1989	Commercial	Old Town	High Street	Scandic Crown	Ian Begg
1989	Residential	Southside	Pleasance	St Leonard's St	Fraser Brown
1989	Public	Southside	Pleasance	Police HQ	Lothian Region Arch
1989	Educational	West	Riccarton	Fac Econ & Social Studies	A Merrylees Ass
1989	Educational	West	Riccarton	Esmee Fairbairn Res Centre	A Merrylees Ass
1989	Residential	Southside	West Adam St	Housing	Wheeler & Sproson
1990	Commercial	Central north	Blenheim Pl	Scottish Equitable, 12	Hugh Martin
1990	Commercial	Central north	Dundas St	Life Association	Reiach & Hall
1990	Commercial	Central west	Haymarket Terrace	Apex House	MAP Arch
1990	Medical	South	Morningside Rd	Surgery	Gordon & Latimer
1990	Public	Central west	**Morrison Street masterplan**		**Percy Thomas/Kneale & Russell**
1990	Residential	Southside	Pleasance	Arthur St	City Council
1990	Commercial	Central west	Queensferry Rd	Queensferry House	Cochrane McGregor
1990	Educational	West	Riccarton	James Watt Centre	A Merrylees Ass
1990 (1887)	Residential	Old Town	West Port	62–76 West Port	
1991 (1964,1866)	Commercial	New Town	Princes St	128 Princes St	J & F Johnston
1991	Commercial	New Town	George St	Solicitor's Property Centre, 85	Campbell & Arnott
1991	Residential	Old Town	Castle Terrace	Saltire Court	Campbell & Arnott
1991	Residential	Central north	Dean Village	High Green	Y McAllister
1991	Residential	Central west	Morrison St	Rutland Court	Case Design
1991	Commercial	West	South Gyle	Bank of Scotland Computer centre	Davis Duncan, Reiach & Hall
1991	Commercial	Central north	Tanfield St	Standard Life Computer Centre	M Laird & Part
1991	Residential	Central west	Washington Lane	Housing	PTP Kneale & Russell
1992	Commercial	Southside	Bernard Terrace	Sinclair House	J & F Johnston
1992	Residential	Southside	Buccleuch St	59–69 Buccleuch St	Percy Thomas Part
1992	Commercial	New Town	Calton Rd	Calton Court	R Hunter
1992	Recreational	Central west	Castle Terrace	Traverse Theatre	Groves-Raines
1992	Public	**West**	**Edinburgh Park masterplan**		**Richard Meier**
1992	Public	Old Town	Fishmarket Close	Court House extension	PSA Projects
1992	Public	**Old Town**	**Holyrood North masterplan**		**John C Hope**
1992	Recreational	West	Murrayfield	Penguin pool	Design Group
1992	Public	West	South Gyle	HMSO	RMJM
1992	Commercial	West	South Gyle	Royal Bank Admin Centre	M Laird & Part
1992 (1923)	Commercial	Old Town	South Bridge	Bank Hotel	R Hunter
1993, 1964	Commercial	New Town	St Andrew Sq	Edinburgh House, 3 N	Covell Matthews
1993	Public	Old Town	Mound	Fruitmarket Gallery	Richard Murphy

Date			Location	Building	Architect
1993	Public	West	South Gyle	Scottish Record Office	Building Design Part
1993	Commercial	New Town	St Andrew Sq	Life Assurance	Reiach & Hall
1994	Educational	Southwest	Colinton Rd	Technology Building	Campbell & Arnott
1994	Commercial	West	Edinburgh Park	ICL HQ	Edmund Kirkby
1994	Commercial	West	Edinburgh Park	John Menzies HQ	Bennets Ass
1994	Commercial	New Town	New Town	1 Castle Street	YRM Arch & Plan
1994	Recreational	Southside	Nicolson St	Festival Theatre	Law & Dunbar-Naismith
1995	Commercial	Southwest	Dundee St	Fountain House	Hugh Martin Part
1995	Commercial	West	Edinburgh Park	Lochside Court	Building Design Part
1995	Public	North	Leith	Victoria Quay	RMJM
1995	Public	Central west	Morrison Street	International Conference Centre	Terry Farrell
1995	Residential	Central west	Morrison Street	Morrison Circus	Percy Thomas Part
1995	Residential	Central west	Morrison Street	Morrison Crescent	Percy Thomas Part
1995	Commercial	New Town	New Town	10 George St	Reiach & Hall
1995	Residential	New Town	New Town	17 Royal Terrace Mews	Richard Murphy
1995	Educational	Central west	Ravelston	Sixth Form pavilion	Oberlanders
1995, 1997	Commercial	Central west	Bread Street	Point Hotel	Andrew Doolan
1995/7	Commercial	Central west	Morrison Link	Travel Inn	Andrew Doolan
1995/7	Residential	West	Wester Hailes	Western Ave Housing	Smith Scott Mullen & Ass
1995	Public	**Central south**	**Tollcross East Side masterplan**		**RMJM**
1996	Commercial	West	Edinburgh Park	Scottish Equitable building	Koetter Kim
1996	Commercial	West	Edinburgh Park	The Park Centre	Campbell & Arnott
1996	Public	**Old Town**	**High Street refurbishment**		**Page & Park**
1996	Commercial	Central west	Lothian Rd	Standard Life House	Michael Laird
1996	Residential	West	South Gyle	Midgogarloch Syke Housing	E & F McLachlan
1996	Medical	North	Western General	Maggie's Centre	Richard Murphy
1997	Commercial	West	Edinburgh Park	KSCL	RMJM
1997	Recreational	West	Edinburgh Zoo	Marketing Suite extension	Smith, Scott, Mullan & Ass
1997	Recreational	Old Town	Holyrood	Bakewell Close	Richard Murphy
1997	Residential	Old Town	Holyrood	Wilson Court, 138 Canongate	Campbell & Arnott
1997	Commercial	Central south	Port Hamilton	Scottish Widows HQ	Building Design Partnership
1997	Recreational	Central north	Stockbridge	Pizza Express	Malcolm Fraser
1997	Recreational	West	Wester Hailes	Multiplex cinema	Comprehensive Design Group
1997	Public	West	Wester Hailes	Community Library	Comprehensive Design Group
1997	Public	**West**	**Wester Hailes masterplan**		**Comprehensive Design Group**
1998	Residential	Central north	Broughton Rd	47 Broughton Rd	Percy Thomas Part
1998	Recreational	Southside	Buccleuch St	Mosque and Islamic Centre	Basil al-Bayati
1998	Public	Southside	Chambers St	Museum of Scotland	Benson & Forsyth
1998	Public	Central north	Dean	Dean Gallery	Terry Farrell
1998	Educational	Old Town	Holyrood	Morgan Court	Unglass & Latimer
1998	Residential	Old Town	Holyrood	Hammermen's Entry	Van Heyningen & Haward
1998	Residential	Old Town	Holyrood – Pleasance	St John's Hill Housing	Gray Marshall Ass
1998	Commercial	Old Town	Hunter Sq	Ibis Hotel	Crerar & partners
1998	Residential	North	Leith	Commercial Quay	Cochrane McGregor Group
1998	Residential	North	Leith	Pitt St Housing	Lee Boyd Part
1998	Recreational	Central west	Lothian Rd	Exchange Plaza	Cochrane MacGregor
1998	Residential	New Town	New Town	Dublin Street Colonies	Richard Murphy
1998	Medical	South	Niddrie Mains Rd	Craigmillar Medical Centre	Campbell & Arnott

Date			Location	Building	Architect
1998	Recreational	East	Portobello	Portobello Baths	RMJM
1999	Recreational	Old Town	Castlehill	The Hub	Benjamin Tindall
1999	Recreational	Southwest	Colinton	Parish Church	Page & Park
1999	Commercial	Old Town	Cowgate	Tailors' Hall/Kincaid's Court	Davis Duncan Harrold
1999	Recreational	Southwest	Dundee St	Fountain Park	Hugh Martin Part
1999	Commercial	West	Edinburgh Park	Alexander Graham Bell House	Bennets Ass
1999	Commercial	West	Edinburgh Park	Scottish Equitable Asset Man	Lee Boyd Part
1999	Commercial	West	Edinburgh Park	Cramond House	Reiach Hall
1999	Commercial	West	Edinburgh Park	Diageo/UDV Building	Allan Murray
1999	Commercial	West	Edinburgh Park	G2 Building	Lee Boyd Part
1999	Commercial	West	Edinburgh Park	G3 Building	Page & Park
1999/2000	Commercial	West	Edinburgh Park	F1 & F2 Buildings	Parr Part
1999	Recreational	Old Town	Holyrood	Dynamic Earth	Michael Hopkins & Part
1999	Residential	Old Town	Holyrood	112 Canongate	Richard Murphy
1999	Recreational	Old Town	Holyrood	Scottish Poetry Library	Malcolm Fraser
1999	Residential	Old Town	Holyrood	Gentle's Entry – Slater's Steps	Hackland & Dore/Gilbert Ass
1999	Residential	Old Town	Holyrood	Gentle's Entry – Apartment Hotel	Walter Wood Ass
1999	Commercial	Old Town	Holyrood	MacDonald Hotel	Hendry & Legge
1999	Commercial	Old Town	Holyrood	Scotsman Building	Comprehensive Design Group
1999	Residential	Central south	Lauriston Place	High Riggs housing	Campbell & Arnott
1999	Commercial	North	Leith	St Ninian's Manse/Quayside Mills	Simpson Brown/Jim Johnson
1999	Commercial	North	Newhaven	Restaurant/hotel	Lambie Wright Part
1999	Educational	Central west	Queensferry Rd	Sixth Form pavilion	Oberlanders
1999	Residential	Central west	Slateford Green	Slateford Green Housing	Hackland & Dore
1999	Commercial	West	South Gyle	Younger Building	Michael Laird Part
2000	Public	West	**Edinburgh Park Site A masterplan**		Allan Murray
2000	Commercial	Old Town	Holyrood	Crichton House	Unglass & Latimer
2000	Residential	Old Town	Holyrood	Cooper's Court	E F McLachlan
2000	Medical	South	Little France	Royal Infirmary & Medical School	Keppie Design
2000	Commercial	Central west	Morrison Street	Edinburgh One	Hurd Rolland Part
2000	Public	West	Saughton	Edinburgh Prison Visitor Centre	Gareth Hoskins
2000	Recreational	West	Slateford	Water of Leith Heritage Centre	Malcolm Fraser
2000	Commercial	Central west	Tollcross	Princes Exchange	RMJM
2001	Recreational	Old Town	Grassmarket	DanceBase	Malcolm Fraser
2001	Residential	Old Town	Holyrood	Fishmarket Close	Richard Murphy
2001	Commercial	Old Town	Holyrood	The Tun	Allan Murray
2001	Residential	Old Town	Holyrood	Gentle's Entry – Jackson House	John C Hope
2001	Residential	Old Town	Holyrood	Holyrood Road Apartments	Campbell & Arnott
2001	Commercial	North	Leith	Coalhill	Allan Murray
2001	Recreational	North	Leith	Ocean Terminal	Conran & Part/Keppie Des
2001	Residential	North	Leith	South Fort St Supported Acc	Unglass & Latimer
2001	Recreational	Central north	Leith St	Calton Sq	Allan Murray
2001	Recreational	Central west	Lothian Rd	Sheraton Health Club	Terry Farrell
2002	Public	**North**	**Granton Waterfront masterplan**		**Llewelyn Davies**
2004	Public	Old Town	Holyrood	Scottish Parliament	Miralles, RMJM
2004	Commercial	New Town	New Town	Princes Street Galleries	Comprehensive Design Group

Select bibliography

Abercrombie, P. and D. Plumstead (1949), *A Civic Survey and Plan for Edinburgh*, Edinburgh: Oliver and Boyd.

Adams, I. H. (1978), *The Making of Urban Scotland*, London: Croom Helm.

Adams, T., L. Thompson and M. Fry (1930), *Report on the Plan for the Development of the Granton–Cramond Area*, Report to Edinburgh Corporation, Edinburgh.

Adams, T., L. Thompson and M. Fry (1931), *Final Report on Town Planning*, Report to the City and Royal Burgh of Edinburgh.

Amin, A. and N. Thrift (2002), *Cities: Reimagining the Urban*, Cambridge: Polity Press.

Anon. (1937), *Report of the Scottish Architectural Advisory Committee on the Incorporation of Architectural Quality and Amenity*, Edinburgh: HMSO.

Aston, M. and J. Bond (1987), *The Landscape of Towns*, 2nd edn, Gloucester: Alan Sutton.

Begg, T. (1987), *Fifty Special Years*, Edinburgh: SSHA.

Broadie, A. (2001), *The Scottish Enlightenment*, Edinburgh: Edinburgh University Press.

Burckhardt, J. (1958), *The Civilisation of the Renaissance in Italy*, New York: Harper.

Cd 8731 (1917), *Report of the Royal Commission on the Housing of the Industrial Population of Scotland Rural and Urban*, Edinburgh: HMSO.

City and Royal Burgh of Edinburgh (1943), *The Future of Edinburgh*, The Report of the Advisory Committee on City Development, Edinburgh.

Cochrane, A., J. Peck, and A. Tickell (1996), 'Manchester plays games: exploring the local politics of globalisation', *Urban Studies*, 33(8): 1,319–36.

Colls, R. and R. Rodger (eds) (2004), *Cities of Ideas: Civil Societies and Urban Identities*, Aldershot.

Company of Merchants of the City of Edinburgh, The (1918), *Report of a Special Committee on the Building Trade in Edinburgh*, Edinburgh.

Company of Merchants of the City of Edinburgh, The (1919), *Report of a Special Committee of the Company on the Development of Edinburgh*, Edinburgh.

Cooper, J. (1994), *Report of the Burgh Engineer's Department 1893–94*, Edinburgh: Edinburgh Town Council.

Crilley, D. (1993), 'Megastructures and urban change: aesthetics, ideology and design', in P. L. Knox (ed.), *The Restless Urban Landscape*, Englewood Cliffs, NJ: Prentice Hall, pp. 127–64.

Cruft, K. and A. Fraser (eds) (1995), *James Craig 1744–1795*, Edinburgh: Mercat Press.

Curtis, T. (2002), 'Vision for "economic dynamo" of the future', *Edinburgh Evening News*, 23 August, p. 7.

Dingwall, H. M. (1994), *Late Seventeenth-century Edinburgh: A Demographic Study*, Aldershot: Scolar Press.

Edinburgh and District Trades and Labour Council (1914), *47th Annual Report*, Edinburgh.

Edinburgh and District Trades and Labour Council (1918), *51st Annual Report*, Edinburgh.

Edinburgh Chamber of Commerce and Manufacturers (1985), *Edinburgh's Capital*, Henley-on-Thames and Edinburgh: PEIDA.

Edinburgh Town Council (1908), *Edinburgh as a Site for Factories and Industrial Works*, Municipal Report, Edinburgh.

Fawcett, R. (1994), *Scottish Architecture from the Reformation to the Restoration 1560–1666*, Edinburgh: Edinburgh University Press.

Forrest, A. (ed.) (2000), *Scotland's 100 Best New Buildings*, Glasgow: Carnyx Group.

Frew, J. (1991), 'Ebenezer Macrae and reformed tenement design', *St Andrews Studies*, ii, St Andrews.

Frew, J. (1995), 'Concrete, cosmopolitanism and low-cost house design', *Architectural Heritage*, 5: 29–38.

Geddes, P. (1910), 'The Civic Survey of Edinburgh', in *The Transactions of the Town Planning Conference*, London: Royal Institute of British Architects, pp. 537–74.

Gifford, J., C. McWilliam and D. Walker (1984), *Edinburgh*, Harmondsworth: Penguin Books.

Glaeser, E. L. (2004), *Four Challenges for Scotland's Cities*, Allander Series, Fraser of Allander Institute, University of Strathclyde, available at: http://www.fraser.strath.ac.uk/Allander/Allander%20Papers/Glaeser.pdf

Glendinning, M. (ed.) (1997), *Rebuilding Scotland: The Postwar Vision 1945–1975*, East Linton: Tuckwell Press.

Glendinning, M., A. MacKechnie and R. MacInnes (1996), *A History of Scottish Architecture: From the Renaissance to the Present Day*, Edinburgh: Edinburgh University Press.

Glendinning, M. and S. Muthesius (1994), *Tower Block*, London: Yale University Press.

Glendinning, M. and D. Page (1999), *Clone City: Crisis and Renewal in Contemporary Scottish Architecture*, Edinburgh: RCAHMS and Polygon.

Glendinning, M. and D. Watters (eds) (1999), *Home Builders*, Edinburgh: RCAHMS.

Goodwin, M. and J. Painter (1996), 'Local governance, the crises of Fordism and the changing geographies of regulation', *Transactions of the Institute of British Geographers*, 21: 635–49.

Gordon, G. (ed.) (1985), *Perspectives on the Scottish City*, Aberdeen: Aberdeen University Press.

Gordon, G. and B. Dicks (1983), *Scottish Urban History*, Aberdeen: Aberdeen University Press.

Graham, H. G. (1909), *The Social Life of Scotland in the Eighteenth Century*, London: A. & C. Black.

Graham, S. and S. Marvin (2001), *Splintering Urbanism: Networked Structures, Technological Mobilities and the Urban Condition*, London: Routledge.

Gray, J. G. (1975), *Streets Ahead: A Brief Study of Highway Planning in Edinburgh since 1945*, Edinburgh: Edina Press.

Gray, R. Q. (1976), *The Labour Aristocracy in Victorian Edinburgh*, Oxford: Clarendon.

Green, T. (1993), 'Edinburgh Park: a new "New Town"', in Department of Economic Development & Estates', in *Edinburgh Economic & Employment Review, December*, Edinburgh: The City of Edinburgh District Council, pp. 13–14.

Hague, C. (1984), *The Development of Planning Thought: A Critical Perspective*, London: Hutchinson.

Hague, C. (1993), 'Edinburgh: Re-structuring of place and image', Edinburgh School of Planning and Housing, mimeo.

Hague, C. and P. Jenkins (2004), *Place Identity, Participation and Planning*, London: Routledge RTPI Library Series.

Hague, C. and H. Thomas (1997), 'Planning capital cities: Edinburgh and Cardiff compared', in R. MacDonald and H. Thomas (eds), *Nationality and Planning in Scotland and Wales*, Cardiff: University of Wales Press, pp. 133–58.

Hall, T. and P. Hubbard (eds) (1998), *The Entrepreneurial City: Geographies of Politics, Regime and Representation*, London: Routledge.

Harding, A., S. Wilks-Heeg and M. Hutchins (2000), 'Business, government and the business of urban governance', *Urban Studies*, 37(5–6): 975–94.

Healey, P., A. Khakee, A. Motte and B. Needham (1997), *Making Strategic Spatial Plans: Innovation in Europe*, London: Routledge.

Heavenrich, H. S. (1952), 'Housing in Great Britain', unpublished report for Albert Farwell Bemis Foundation of the Massachusetts Institute of Technology, Cambridge, MA.

Heiton, J. (1861), *The Castes of Edinburgh*, Edinburgh: W. P. Nimmo.

Hitchcock, H.-R. (1958), *Architecture: Nineteenth and Twentieth Centuries*, Harmondsworth: Penguin Books.

Howard, D. (1995), *Scottish Architecture from the Reformation to the Restoration 1371–1560*, Edinburgh: Edinburgh University Press.

Jarman, A. O. H. (ed. and tr.) (1990), *Aneirin: Y Gododdin*, 2nd impression, Llandysul: Gomer Press.

Jenkins, P. (2004), 'Territorial and place identities: new collaborations in strategic planning', in C. Hague and P. Jenkins (eds), *Place Identity, Participation and Planning*, London: Routledge RTPI Library Series.

Jensen-Butler, C. (1999), 'Cities in competition: equity issues', *Urban Studies*, 36(5–6): 865–91.

Jones, M. (1998), 'Restructuring the local state: economic governance or social regulation?', *Political Geography*, 17(8): 959–88.

Lansley, S., S. Goss and C. Wolmar (1989), *Councils in Conflict: The Rise and Fall of the Municipal Left*, London: Macmillan.

Littlejohn, H. D. (1865), *Report on the Sanitary Condition of the City of Edinburgh*, Edinburgh: Colston and Son.

Lowrey, J. (1996), 'Landscape design and Edinburgh New Town', in W. A. Brogden (ed.), *The Neo-classical Town: Scottish Contributions to Urban Design since 1750*, Edinburgh: Rutland Press pp. 66–77.

McAdam, D. (1993), *Edinburgh: A Landscape Fashioned by Geology*, Edinburgh: SNH/British Geological Survey.

Macartney, W. A. (1928), 'Town planning in Edinburgh from the eighteenth to the twentieth century – and its lessons', *Journal of the Town Planning Institute*, 15(1): 29–37.

McDowall, T. and W. McDowall (1849), *New Guide to Edinburgh*, Edinburgh.

McKean, C. (1991), *Edinburgh: Portrait of a City*, London: Century.

McKean, C. (1992), *Edinburgh: An Illustrated Architectural Guide*, Edinburgh: Rutland Press.

Macmillan, D. (1992), 'A single-minded polymath: Patrick Geddes and the spatial form of social thought', *Edinburgh Review*, 88: 78–88.

Mays, D. (ed.) (1997), *The Architecture of Scottish Cities*, East Linton: Tuckwell Press.

Mears, F. C. (1929), *City of Edinburgh 1329–1929*, Edinburgh and London: Oliver & Boyd

Mears, F. C. (1930), Letter from Mears to Provost Whitson, 1930, in Mears Manuscripts, Edinburgh Room, Edinburgh City Library.

Mears, F. C. (1931), *The City of Edinburgh: Preliminary suggestions for consideration by the representative committee in regard to the development and replanning of the central area of the city in relation to public buildings*, Edinburgh.

O'Carroll, A. (1994), 'The development of owner occupation in Edinburgh', PhD thesis, Heriot-Watt University.

Olsen, O. J. (1986), *The City as a Work of Art*, New Haven and London: Yale University Press.

Palliser, D. M. (ed.) (2000), *The Cambridge Urban History of Britain, vol. 1: 600–1540*, Cambridge: Cambridge University Press.

Peacock, H. (1974), *Forgotten Southside: The Problems of Planning Blight in City-centre Planning – a Plea for Action*, Edinburgh University Rector's Working Party Report.

Pipes, R. (1984), *The Colonies of Stockbridge*, Edinburgh: David Flatman.

Porter, R. (2000), *Britain and the Creation of the Modern World*, London.

RCAHMS (1951), *Inventory of the Ancient and Historical Monuments of the City of Edinburgh*, Edinburgh: HMSO.

Rodger, J. (2001), *Edinburgh: A Guide to Recent Architecture*, London: Ellipsis.

Rodger, R. (1999), *Housing the People: The 'Colonies' of Edinburgh 1860–1950*, Edinburgh: RCAHMS.

Rodger, R. (2001), *The Transformation of Edinburgh*, Cambridge: Cambridge University Press.

Rose, G. (1995), 'Place and identity: a sense of place', in D. Massey and P. Jess (eds), *A Place in the World? Places, Cultures and Globalisation*, Oxford University Press/Open University Press.

Royal Scottish Society of Painters in Water Colours (1937), *Town Planning Exhibition: Explanatory and Historical Notes and Catalogue of Exhibits*, Edinburgh.

Scottish Executive (2002), *Review of Scotland's Cities: The Analysis*, Scottish Executive, Edinburgh.

Scottish Georgian Society (1969–78), *Annual Report and Journal*.

Sher, R. B. (1985), *Church and University in the Scottish Enlightenment*, Edinburgh: Edinburgh University Press.

Simpson, F. and M. Chapman (1999), 'Comparison of urban governance and planning policy: East looking West', *Cities*, 16(5): 353–64.

Simpson, M. (1985), *Thomas Adams and the Modern Planning Movement: Britain, Canada and the United States 1900–1940*, London and New York: Mansell.

Sissons, J. B. (1967), *The Evolution of Scotland's Scenery*, Edinburgh: Oliver & Boyd.

Smith, M. P. (2001), *Transnational Urbanism: Locating Globalisation*, Oxford: Blackwell.

Stevenson, R. L. (1878), *Edinburgh Picturesque Notes*, Edinburgh: Grant & Son.

Sutcliffe, A. (ed.) (1974), *Multi-storey Living: The Working-class Experience*, London: Croom Helm.

Tickell, A. and J. Peck (1992), 'Accumulation, regulation and the geographies of post-Fordism', *Progress in Human Geography*, 16: 190–218.

Walker, D. M. (1994), 'Listing in Scotland: origins, survey and resurvey', *Transactions of the Ancient Monuments Society*, 38: 31–96.

Whyte, I. (1990), *Edinburgh and the Borders Heritage*, Edinburgh: David and Charles.

Youngson, A. J. (1966), *The Making of Classical Edinburgh*, Edinburgh: Edinburgh University Press.

Index

Abercrombie, Patrick, 155, 174–5
Abercrombie Plan, 174–5
Adam, John, 44, 45, 46
Adam, Robert, 44, 45, 47, 48
Adams, Thomas, 168, 172
Advocate's Close, 26–7
architectural trends, 187–93
Arthur's Seat, 64, 65
Athens of the North, 20, 35, 59–60, 217–27

Bearford Parks, 37, 45, 67
Bristol, 44, 49
Buchanan, Colin, 177
Burgh Police Act (1862), 98, 113, 232
Burns, Robert, 85–6, 100

Calton Hill, 37, 65, 69
Canongate, 8, 22–8, 105, 138
Castle, 22, 37, 69, 85
Castle Rock, 21
Castle Street, 110–11
Chambers, Robert, 45, 50 105
Chambers, William, 113, 114, 132
character of Edinburgh, 2–3
Charlotte Square, 51, 56, 172, 195
Civic Amenities Act (1967), 196
civic groups, 123–6, 171
civic leaders, xiii
Cockburn, Lord, 54
Cockburn Association, 136, 142, 171, 193–4
College of Edinburgh (University), 29
Colonies, 114–16
compact city, 227, 237
conservation, 11, 193–201, 216, 226, 236
conservative surgery, 135–6, 140–1, 146–7, 160, 194
construction industry, 89–90
contributors, xi, 13
Cowgate, 28
Craig, James, 46, 48, 67
Craig Plan, 38, 46–50, 51, 67–8

creativity, 227, 233, 239–40
cultural factors, 5

David (King), 8
Dean of Guild Court, 32, 98, 113, 232
Dean Village, 189
design (importance of), 2, 6, 227, 232–3
Dundee, 6, 225

Earl of Hertford, 23
Edinburgh Advisory Committee, 174, 175
Edinburgh City Council, 99
Edinburgh College of Art, 13, 171, 173, 195, 236
Edinburgh Co-operative Building Society, 93, 98, 114
Edinburgh Corporation Act (1926), 170
Edinburgh Development Group (EDG), 208
Edinburgh Development Plan, 175–7
Edinburgh Extension Act (1856), 93, 94
Edinburgh New Town Conservation Committee, 165, 196–7
Edinburgh Old Town Renewal Trust, 196
Edinburgh Park, 74, 186, 191, 210–12
Edinburgh Social Union, 134, 138
Edinburgh University, 29, 195, 232
Elgin, 21
Enlightenment, 44–6, 86, 99
Exchange, The, 207–8

Farrell, Terry, 186, 208, 227
Ferguson, Adam, 44, 45
feuing plans, 50, 118–22
Flodden Wall, 22
flooding, 71–4
Fountainbridge, 95
future scenarios, 223–5, 227

Geddes, Patrick, 3–4, 6, 122, 131, 134–5, 136–7, 168–9, 199, 235–6
geology, 64–5

geomorphology, 65
George Heriot's Hospital, 29
George Square, 46, 187, 194, 199
George Street, 48, 49, 50, 67
Gladstone's Land, 31, 32, 106, 139
Glasgow, 6, 9, 20, 121–2, 199, 200, 221, 225, 240
Gordon of Rothiemay Plan, 106
Graham, James Gillespie, 55, 68
Granton, 212–13
Grassmarket, 144–5
Greyfriars Kirk, 24
Gyle, 75, 210

Heriot's Trust, 119–20
High Street, 22–3, 43–4, 47
Holyrood Abbey, 22
Holyrood master-plan, 186, 191, 206
Holyrood Park, 80
Holyroodhouse, 30–1
Hope, John, 186
Housing Act (1890), 137
Housing Act (1919), 142, 150
Housing Act (1923), 150–2
Housing Act (1930), 154
Housing Act (1935), 154
Housing Act (1938), 155
Housing Act (1944), 155
Hume, Robert, 44, 45
Hurd, Robert, 146, 159, 195, 199, 236
Hutton, James, 64–5
hydrology, 69–74

identity, 6, 217–18
image, 217–8, 222, 232–3
improvement, 20, 132–142
Improvement Act (1862), 113, 132
Improvement Act (1867), 99, 132
Improvement Act (1893), 136
Improvement Commissioners, 113
industrial landscape, 91–100
industry, 87–91, 93–100, 222
Inner Ring Road, 177–8
innovation, 5, 11, 216
International Exhibition (1886), 99

James Court, 134–5
John Knox House, 31

key issues, 183, 219–21
key themes, 1–2, 4–5, 231
King's Wall, 22

landscape, 20, 64–9, 234–5
Leith, 159–62, 170, 191, 213, 218
Leith Fort, 198
Lindsey, Ian, 195, 196
Lisbon, 20, 48
Littlejohn, Henry, 113
London, 6, 7, 9, 19, 20, 44, 48
Lothian and Edinburgh Enterprise Ltd (LEEL), 208, 213
Lothian Regional Council, 205–6

Macrae, Ebenezer, 142, 144–7, 153, 163, 199
McTaggart and Nickel, 152–3, 158
McWilliam, Colin, 196
manufacturing, 86–99, 205
Mar Plan, 35–8
Marwick, T. P., 169–70
Matthew, Robert, 165, 199
Meadows, The, 69
Mears, Frank, 143, 146, 163, 171, 199, 236
Meier, Richard, 74, 186, 211
Merchant Company, 169–70, 173
Miller, James, 152–3, 158, 163
Miralles, Enric, 80
model tenements, 114–16
Moray Estate, 54, 68–9
motorway plans, 177
Moubray House, 32, 106, 142
Mylne's Court, 31, 32–3, 108, 195

Netherbow, 22–3
New Edinburgh, 45, 46
New Town, 6, 7, 9, 20, 35, 42–61, 86, 109, 187, 188, 189, 199, 206, 218–19, 220, 232–3
New Town Plan (first), 46–51
New Town Plan (second), 51–2
Nor' Loch, 24, 35, 37, 46, 66

Ocean Terminal, 214–15
Old Town, 7, 8, 9, 19–20, 21–35, 42–6, 50, 56–8, 60, 66–7, 104–8, 131–47, 159, 172, 193, 199, 220
overcrowding, 113–14

Paris, 6, 20
Parliament House, 29, 44
place identity, 2–3
planning, 9, 105, 168–79, 210–5, 224–7
Playfair, William, 59, 69
prefabs, 155–6, 157, 158, 160
population, 9, 105, 108, 113, 117

Princes Street, 186
Princes Street Gardens, 69, 74, 75, 76, 186
printing industry, 88–9
Proposals for Undertaking Certain Works in the City of Edinburgh, 45, 48, 52

Queensferry House, 198

Ramsay Garden, 135, 139
Reid, Robert, 52
Revolutionary Club, 44–5
Riddle's Court, 139, 140
Royal Burgh, 8
Royal Miles, 34, 188
Ruskin, John, 54

St Cuthbert's, 23
St Giles' (Cathedral), 23
St James Centre, 171, 186
St James Square, 50, 171
Scottish Georgian Society, 194–5, 196, 197, 198
Scottish Parliament, 80
Scottish Parliament Building, 80, 200–1
Scottish Special Housing Association (SSHA), 157, 163
sense of place, 5–6
Sibbald, William, 51
slum clearance, 132–4
Smith, Adam, 44, 45
Social and Sanitary Society of Edinburgh, 134
Social Union, 134, 137, 139
Spence, Basil, 159, 199
Stark, William, 55, 68
Steel, James, 119
Stirling, 65
Stockholm, 38

Summerson, John, 12
sustainability, 3, 236–7

tenements, 31–5, 51, 103–24, 145, 152, 153
themes, 1–2, 4–5, 231
Tolbooth, 24–5
topography, 5, 35, 234–5
town and gown, 8
Town Council, 32, 37, 54–5, 131–6, 168, 170–5, 218–19
town planning, 168–79
Trades Council, 169
transport problems, 11, 177–8
Tron Kirk, 25–6, 30

Union (with England), 5, 9, 49, 85, 86
Union Canal, 94
urban design, 185–6
urban expansion, 9–10, 33–8, 93–4

Vatican Borgo, 19
Vienna, 6, 145

Wardrop's Court, 139
Warrender Park Terrace, 120–1
Water of Leith, 71–4, 90–1
water supply, 70–2
Waterfront Edinburgh Ltd, 213–14
Waverley Station, 171
Waverley Valley, 76
West Bow, 57
Wester Hailes, 163–4
working-class housing, 114–17
World Heritage Site, 1, 5, 195, 206

York, 7, 19
Youngson, A. J., 13